SCIENCE IN EVIDENCE

ANDERSON'S

Law School Publications

ADMINISTRATIVE LAW ANTHOLOGY
by Thomas O. Sargentich

ADMINISTRATIVE LAW: CASES AND MATERIALS
by Daniel J. Gifford

ALTERNATIVE DISPUTE RESOLUTION: STRATEGIES FOR LAW AND BUSINESS
by E. Wendy Trachte-Huber and Stephen K. Huber

AN ADMIRALTY LAW ANTHOLOGY
by Robert M. Jarvis

ANALYTIC JURISPRUDENCE ANTHOLOGY
by Anthony D'Amato

AN ANTITRUST ANTHOLOGY
by Andrew I. Gavil

APPELLATE ADVOCACY: PRINCIPLES AND PRACTICE (Second Edition)
Cases and Materials
by Ursula Bentele and Eve Cary

BASIC ACCOUNTING PRINCIPLES FOR LAWYERS:
With Present Value and Expected Value
by C. Steven Bradford and Gary A. Ames

A CAPITAL PUNISHMENT ANTHOLOGY (and Electronic Caselaw Appendix)
by Victor L. Streib

CASES AND PROBLEMS IN CRIMINAL LAW (Third Edition)
by Myron Moskovitz

THE CITATION WORKBOOK
by Maria L. Ciampi, Rivka Widerman, and Vicki Lutz

CIVIL PROCEDURE: CASES, MATERIALS, AND QUESTIONS
by Richard D. Freer and Wendy C. Perdue

COMMERCIAL TRANSACTIONS: PROBLEMS AND MATERIALS
Vol. 1: Secured Transactions Under the UCC
Vol. 2: Sales Under the UCC and the CISG
Vol. 3: Negotiable Instruments Under the UCC and the CIBN
by Louis F. Del Duca, Egon Guttman, Alphonse M. Squillante, Fred H. Miller, and Peter Winship

COMMUNICATIONS LAW: MEDIA, ENTERTAINMENT, AND REGULATION
by Donald E. Lively, Allen S. Hammond, IV, Blake D. Morant, and Russell L. Weaver

A CONSTITUTIONAL LAW ANTHOLOGY
by Michael J. Glennon

CONSTITUTIONAL LAW: CASES, HISTORY, AND DIALOGUES
by Donald E. Lively, Phoebe A. Haddon, Dorothy E. Roberts, and Russell L. Weaver

THE CONSTITUTIONAL LAW OF THE EUROPEAN UNION
by James D. Dinnage and John F. Murphy

THE CONSTITUTIONAL LAW OF THE EUROPEAN UNION:
DOCUMENTARY SUPPLEMENT
by James D. Dinnage and John F. Murphy

CONSTITUTIONAL TORTS
by Sheldon H. Nahmod, Michael L. Wells, and Thomas A. Eaton

CONTRACTS
Contemporary Cases, Comments, and Problems
by Michael L. Closen, Richard M. Perlmutter, and Jeffrey D. Wittenberg

A CONTRACTS ANTHOLOGY (Second Edition)
by Peter Linzer

A CORPORATE LAW ANTHOLOGY
by Franklin A. Gevurtz

Continued

Continued

INTRODUCTION TO THE STUDY OF LAW: CASES AND MATERIALS
by John Makdisi

JUDICIAL EXTERNSHIPS: THE CLINIC INSIDE THE COURTHOUSE
by Rebecca A. Cochran

JUSTICE AND THE LEGAL SYSTEM
A Coursebook
by Anthony D'Amato and Arthur J. Jacobson

THE LAW OF DISABILITY DISCRIMINATION
by Ruth Colker

ADA HANDBOOK
Statutes, Regulations and Related Materials
by Publisher's Staff

THE LAW OF MODERN PAYMENT SYSTEMS AND NOTES
by Fred H. Miller and Alvin C. Harrell

LAWYERS AND FUNDAMENTAL MORAL RESPONSIBILITY
by Daniel R. Coquillette

MICROECONOMIC PREDICATES TO LAW AND ECONOMICS
by Mark Seidenfeld

PATIENTS, PSYCHIATRISTS AND LAWYERS
Law and the Mental Health System (Second Edition)
by Raymond L. Spring, Roy B. Lacoursiere, M.D., and Glen Weissenberger

PRINCIPLES OF EVIDENCE (Third Edition)
by Irving Younger, Michael Goldsmith, and David A. Sonenshein

PROBLEMS AND SIMULATIONS IN EVIDENCE (Second Edition)
by Thomas F. Guernsey

A PRODUCTS LIABILITY ANTHOLOGY
by Anita Bernstein

PROFESSIONAL RESPONSIBILITY ANTHOLOGY
by Thomas B. Metzloff

A PROPERTY ANTHOLOGY
by Richard H. Chused

PUBLIC CHOICE AND PUBLIC LAW: READINGS AND COMMENTARY
by Maxwell L. Stearns

THE REGULATION OF BANKING
Cases and Materials on Depository Institutions and Their Regulators
by Michael P. Malloy

SCIENCE IN EVIDENCE
by David H. Kaye

A SECTION 1983 CIVIL RIGHTS ANTHOLOGY
by Sheldon H. Nahmod

SPORTS LAW: CASES AND MATERIALS (Third Edition)
by Ray L. Yasser, James R. McCurdy, and C. Peter Goplerud

A TORTS ANTHOLOGY
by Lawrence C. Levine, Julie A. Davies, and Edward J. Kionka

TRIAL PRACTICE
by Lawrence A. Dubin and Thomas F. Guernsey

TRIAL PRACTICE AND CASE FILES
by Edward R. Stein and Lawrence A. Dubin

TRIAL PRACTICE AND CASE FILES with *Video* Presentation
by Edward R. Stein and Lawrence A. Dubin

UNINCORPORATED BUSINESS ENTITIES
by Larry E. Ribstein

Continued

FORTHCOMING PUBLICATIONS

A CIVIL PROCEDURE ANTHOLOGY
by David I. Levine, Donald L. Doernberg and Melissa L. Nelken

A CONFLICT OF LAWS ANTHOLOGY
by Gene R. Shreve

CONTRACT LAW AND PRACTICE: CASES AND MATERIALS
by Michael L. Closen, Gerald E. Berendt, Doris Estelle Long,
Marie A. Monahan, Robert J. Nye, and John H. Scheid

EUROPEAN UNION LAW ANTHOLOGY
by Anthony D'Amato and Karen V. Kole

FAMILY LAW ANTHOLOGY
by Frances E. Olsen

LAW AND ECONOMICS: AN ANTHOLOGY
by Kenneth G. Dau-Schmidt and Thomas S. Ulen

MATERIALS ON A NON ADVERSARIAL LEGAL PROCESS
Robert M. Hardaway

OVERVIEW OF AMERICAN LEGAL SYSTEMS
Toni M. Fine

SCIENCE IN EVIDENCE

D.H. Kaye

Regents' Professor
Arizona State University
College of Law

ANDERSON PUBLISHING CO.
CINCINNATI

Science in Evidence, D.H. Kaye

Anderson Publishing Co.
2035 Reading Road / Cincinnati, Ohio 45202
800-582-7295 / e-mail andpubco@aol.com / Fax 513-562-5430

ISBN: 0-87084-480-6

Dedication

This book is dedicated to the scientists and technicians who have worked toward testing the validity and improving the quality of scientific evidence, and to the judges, lawyers, and others who have struggled to use it fully and fairly.

Summary of Contents

Table of Contents

Preface

Scientists are the high priests of modern society. Their mastery of arcane formulae and esoteric machinery commands respect and fear. Unlike their conventional religious counterparts, they traffic in miracles that are subtle and real. They trace the lines of force from invisible fields, deduce the existence of particles that can never be seen, detect the residual glow of the early universe, and decipher the chemistry of life itself.

Like society at large, the legal system exhibits ambivalence toward science. It strives to use scientific knowledge in investigating crimes, accidents, and disasters, but it harnesses the powerful engine of scientific investigation to procedures crafted in the days of the horse-drawn cart. It worries that credulous jurors will defer to the expert opinions of scientists or technicians or succumb to the numerical legerdemain of this priesthood. The result is a complex set of rules and procedures that filter and transform scientific information as it enters the courtroom.

But enter the courtroom it does. As indicated in chapter one, scientific evidence is far more prevalent today than it was one hundred, fifty, twenty-five, or even ten years ago. At least three factors have fueled the virtual explosion of science into evidence. One is the astonishing and accelerating pace of scientific discovery and technology. A century ago, x-rays and blood groups were unknown or just being discovered. Now, CAT scans and DNA are household acronyms. Science has much more to say today. Second, the federal and uniform rules of evidence, adopted in most jurisdictions some twenty years ago, removed various barriers to the admission of expert testimony. Third, the notion that individuals are in control — that they are responsible for the consequences of their actions or for the ills that befall them — has given way to the urge to blame others. In the most extreme cases, vicious murders have been said to have resulted from exposure to television or ingestion of carbohydrates, and birth defects of unknown etiology have been attributed to medicines or spermicides. It has seemed as if somewhere, somehow, some expert could be found to blame almost anything on something else. Thus, lawyers used to enlisting partisan experts in legal causes now draw not merely on medical doctors and coroners, but also on economists, epidemiologists, geneticists, psychologists, statisticians, toxicologists, and many other specialists to dispense opinions favorable to the parties sponsoring them. The "battle of the expert" is nothing new, but as the battles have become more common, visible, and expensive, and as they have covered more terrain, some observers or participants have complained that junk science litters the legal landscape.

As explained in chapter seven, after years of denying petitions for certiorari to address the proper standard for admitting scientific evidence, the Supreme Court wrote an opinion in 1993 instructing trial courts to serve as "gatekeepers," admitting the treasure and refusing the trash. Can they? Judges, practitioners, law professors, and scientists of all stripes were quick to offer their answers. The law governing scientific evidence has moved from the edge of the law of evidence to the center stage that it occupies in this book.

The book collects materials — primarily judicial opinions, legal commentary, and scientific papers — that explore the efforts of lawyers and experts to present science in evidence. The materials are intended to teach law students how the so-called rules of evidence apply to scientific evidence and how these rules change with experience, to explain the science in "scientific evidence," and to identify the conditions that contribute to the introduction of accurate or erroneous scientific findings or opinions in court. The few written rules that are special to scientific evidence are just the tip of the proverbial iceberg. The readings here also try to probe beneath the ocean's surface and to consider the forces that generate the evidence about which lawyers argue and on which courts ultimately rule.

Organized as a traditional casebook, the book also is designed to be of some use outside the circle of law students. References to the scientific and legal literature are included in the hope that lawyers who encounter scientific evidence in their practice may find them helpful in preparing legal arguments or developing lines of inquiry for cross-examination. Nor is the material solely for the benefit of the legal profession. While the book assumes that the reader is familiar with the United States legal system, court procedures, and the general principles of the law of evidence, it does not presume any detailed knowledge of the law of evidence. Therefore, its teachings should be accessible to forensic scientists (and forensic science students) interested in the legal rules governing scientific evidence.

I have found that, with due determination, the materials can be covered in a one semester course. Alternatively, they may be tailored to emphasize certain areas or ideas. Parts I and III supply indispensable perspectives and information, while the remaining chapters pursue particular institutions or scientific areas. Therefore, almost any subject of these remaining chapters could be taken up in almost any order, and the interests of the instructor and the students can determine the choice of topics.

Acknowledgments

This book began as a chapter in Health Care Law, Forensic Science and Public Policy, published in its fourth edition in 1990, by Little Brown and Company. I am greatly indebted to my coauthors of that text, William Curran and Mark Hall, for involving me in the project and for encouraging me to expand, update and modify the chapter.

Many other individuals contributed to the final product — or should I say "interim product," inasmuch as this is a field that remains in flux? The contents have been informed by the reactions and comments of students who have enrolled in related courses or seminars over the years at Arizona State University, Cornell University, the University of Virginia, and the University of Utah. The administration of the College of Law at Arizona State University has been supportive of this work, and many colleagues have patiently suffered through my efforts to develop some of the thoughts expressed here via conversations and expositions at lunch and on other occasions. Ira Ellman and Dennis Karjala have figured prominently in this capacity. David Freedman made detailed comments on chapter 21 (some of which I have chosen, at my peril, to ignore). My secretary, Rosalind Pearlman, also helped in many ways, and Vivian Chang and James Pack provided valuable research assistance.

Part I

ORIENTATION: SCOPE AND DEFINITION OF THE FIELD

Chapter 1
Forensic Science in an Adversarial System

John I. Thornton
Uses and Abuses of Forensic Science*
69 American Bar Association Journal 288, 289-90 (1983)

In the broadest sense, forensic science is any science used in the resolution of legal conflicts. The word "forensic" comes from the Latin *forensus,* meaning "of the forum." The ancient Roman forum was the site of debates concerning governmental issues, but it also was the courthouse, where trials were held. Consequently, forensic science has come to mean the study and practice of applying natural and physical sciences to the just resolution of social and legal issues. What distinguishes it from other sciences is its use by the legal system; what distinguishes a forensic scientist from other scientists is the expectation of routine appearances in a court of law. . . .

Although forensic science historically has been identified closely with the criminal justice system, the forensic scientist now plays an increasingly active role in civil litigation and in regulatory matters. Virtually no limitation exists to the scope of physical evidence that is grist for all forensic scientists. Physical evidence may range in size from the microscopic (for example, a pollen grain) to the macroscopic (for example, a diesel truck). It may be as appalling as the lifeless body of a battered child, as intangible as the fleeting vapors of gasoline following a suspected arson fire, or as obscure as the composition of dyes in the ink of a contested will. . . .

A number of disciplines exist within the rubric of forensic science. Many of these are simply adaptations of existing disciplines — for example, forensic pathology as a specialty of pathology — although at least one subdiscipline — criminalistics — is a novel synthesis of natural and physical sciences. Its origins cannot be attributed to any single parent discipline. The American Academy of Forensic Sciences, the largest professional forensic society in the world, recognizes the following scientific disciplines: forensic pathology, forensic toxicology, forensic anthropology, forensic odontology, forensic psychiatry, questioned documents, forensic engineering, and criminalistics. . . .

---

*Reprinted with permission from the March 1983 *ABA Journal,* The Lawyer's Magazine, published by the American Bar Association.

NOTES

1. *Definitions and lists.* Thornton's list of forensic sciences is not exhaustive of all medicine and science as it appears in the courtroom. For example, orthopedic surgeons probably prepare more medico-legal reports and appear as witnesses in courts and before administrative agencies, such as Workers' Compensation Boards, more frequently than most of the specialists named as forensic scientists. Economists testify in antitrust, personal injury, and employment discrimination cases. Experimental psychologists who study the factors influencing the accuracy of eyewitnesses describe their general findings in criminal cases. Toxicologists and epidemiologists testify in "toxic tort" cases about the causes of diseases and medical conditions. Statisticians act as consultants and witnesses in a broad spectrum of cases.

Nevertheless, the scientists in the disciplines enumerated by the American and British Academies of Forensic Science tend to share certain distinctive professional attitudes and goals. They think of themselves not just as scientists who sometimes have information to contribute in court, but as scientists whose work always is connected with the legal system. They strive to make their disciplines more useful and more relevant to the administration of justice. In Thornton's words, "[a]ll of these disciplines have a unifying theme — the introduction of science into the legal process in an objective and impartial manner . . . ." John I. Thornton, Uses and Abuses of Forensic Science, 69 A.B.A.J. 288, 291 (1983). Thus, one forensic laboratory's director observes that "[w]e see ourselves as different from most of the others in our circle of professional colleagues. That circle is populated by lawyers, police, administrators, an occasional pathologist, and once in a while, the press. For the most part, our nonscience peers do not speak our language and are often apathetic about our concerns." Barry A.J. Fisher, Developing a Forensic Science Laboratory Operating Strategy, 31 J. Forensic Sci. 1177, 1178-79 (1986).

While marked with a distinctive professional identity, the self-designated forensic sciences, as indicated in Fisher's remarks, commonly are part of the law enforcement apparatus. Most practitioners apply their talents in criminal investigation and in aid of police agencies and public prosecutors. This is especially true of criminalists:

> Criminalistics may be described in either a subtractive or an additive manner. In the former sense, it represents what remains other than pathology, odontology, toxicology, and the other forensic subspecialties. In the additive sense, criminalistics is concerned with the analysis, identification, and interpretation of hairs and fibers; bloodstains and seminal stains; firearms evidence; soil, glass and paint classifications; toolmarks; arson accelerants; explosives; serial number restoration; and virtually everything else that does not fit tidily into one of the other disciplines.

John I. Thornton, Uses and Abuses of Forensic Science, 69 A.B.A.J. 288, 290-91 (1983).

This book is concerned broadly with the use of scientific knowledge in adjudication and legislation. Nevertheless, it does not attempt to cover every kind of scientific testimony. Though it is primarily concerned with forensic science, it does not cover any specific area exhaustively. The objective is to convey a flavor of and an appreciation for the way in which law, medicine and science interact in and on the way to the courtroom.

2. *History.* Forensic medicine is by no means a 20th-century innovation. In China, the elements of toxicology were recognized long ago, and the Materia Medica of 3000 B.C. included information on aconite, arsenic and opium. Hsi Yuan Lu (Instructions to Coroners) dealt with practically every topic in forensic medicine. This classic text first appeared in 1250 A.D. and was amended and reprinted up to the 19th century. M.S. Salgado, Forensic Medicine in the Indo-Pacific Region: History and Current Practice of Forensic Medicine, 36 Forensic Sci. Int'l 3, 3 (1988).

Medical testimony in English criminal cases extends back into the Middle Ages, but:

> News of important advances in Italy, Germany, France and other countries crossed the Channel only, it seems, very slowly. Pathology, a sister science, did not even begin to bloom in Britain until the late 1700s . . . . For far too long the average expert medical witness in an English courtroom or inquest chamber was a busy surgeon, obliged to mount the witness box only a few times at most in his career and ill prepared for the experience. Unless he understood a foreign language, Continental lectures, books, and papers were beyond his reach. His medical education scarcely touched on the functions and duties of the expert witness, and the critical importance of useful medical testimony often escaped him—as it did the jurist and indeed the general public. When medical men did appear in court, it was to confirm the fact and more obvious circumstances of death. Very few of these witnesses understood how to search for evidence at the scene of the crime and at the autopsy table, how to record it accurately, and how to present it clearly and without equivocation. But as the eighteenth century drew to a close, concern grew within and without the medical profession that a doctor's training should include at least the fundamentals of forensic medicine . . . . Books and papers began to appear on the subject, a few universities experimented with lectures on the new specialty, and legislation recognizing the importance of the forensic expert and facilitating his work was debated.

Thomas Forbes, Surgeons at the Bailey: English Forensic Medicine to 1878, 3 (1985).

As regards the other subfields of forensic science, however:

> Forensic science is essentially a 20th century innovation. Various attempts were made earlier to use scientific evidence of one sort or anoth-

er, but the results were less than satisfactory. By 1915 only three New England states and the city of New York had replaced their coroner systems with a more progressive medical examiner system. The first operational crime laboratory in the country was not established until 1923 in Los Angeles, followed by the Scientific Crime Detection Laboratory at Northwestern University in 1929, and the Federal Bureau of Investigation laboratory in 1932. Despite what one might infer from Arthur Conan Doyle's writings, England did not create a forensic laboratory until 1935.
. . .

Although one might suppose that the inception of forensic science resulted from progressive attitudes of pathologists, lawyers, police administrators, or scientists, this rarely was the case. Neither physicians nor attorneys led the reform movement that resulted in the establishment of a medical examiner's office for the city of New York. Similarly, public outrage after the 1929 Valentine's Day massacre in Chicago provided the impetus for establishing that city's scientific crime detection laboratory. In fact, many of the nation's crime laboratories owe their existence not to enlightened attitudes of police administrators or other public officials but to adverse publicity or the threat of it. . . .

John I. Thornton, Uses and Abuses of Forensic Science, 69 A.B.A.J. 288, 291 (1983).

3. *References.* General works on forensic science by or with contributions from forensic scientists themselves include Forensic Science (Geoffrey Davies ed., 2d ed. 1985); Peter De Forest et al., Forensic Science: An Introduction to Criminalistics (1983); Scientific and Expert Evidence (Edward Imwinkelreid ed., 2d ed. 1981); 1-3 Forensic Science Handbook (Richard Saferstein ed., 1982, 1987, 1993), Henry J. Walls, Forensic Science (1968), and Forensic Sciences (Cyrus Wecht ed., 1981). Leading texts by attorneys include Paul Giannelli & Edward Imwinkelried, Scientific Evidence (2d ed. 1993), Andre A. Moenssens et al., Scientific Evidence in Civil and Criminal Cases (4th ed. 1995), and 1 McCormick on Evidence §§ 203-211 (John Strong ed., 4th ed. 1992). Books by attorneys that include reviews of scientific research by scientists include Modern Scientific Evidence (David Faigman et al. eds., 1997), and the Reference Manual on Scientific Evidence (Federal Judicial Center ed., 1995). As with most scientific fields, advances and changes are frequent; papers in professional journals typically must be consulted.

Miller v. Pate
386 U.S. 1 (1967)

MR. JUSTICE STEWART delivered the opinion of the Court.

On November 26, 1955, in Canton, Illinois, an eight-year-old girl died as the result of a brutal sexual attack. The petitioner was charged with her murder. Prior to his trial in an Illinois court, his counsel filed a motion for an order permitting a scientific inspection of the physical evidence the prosecution intended to introduce. The motion was resisted by the prosecution and denied by the court. The jury trial ended in a verdict of guilty and a sentence of death. On appeal the judgment was affirmed by the Supreme Court of Illinois. On the basis of leads developed at a subsequent unsuccessful state clemency hearing, the petitioner applied to a federal district court for a writ of habeas corpus. After a hearing, the court granted the writ and ordered the petitioner's release or prompt retrial. The Court of Appeals reversed, and we granted certiorari to consider whether the trial that led to the petitioner's conviction was constitutionally valid. We have concluded that it was not.

There were no eyewitnesses to the brutal crime which the petitioner was charged with perpetrating. A vital component of the case against him was a pair of men's underwear shorts covered with large, dark, reddish-brown stains — People's Exhibit 3 in the trial record. These shorts had been found by a Canton policeman in a place known as the Van Buren Flats three days after the murder. The Van Buren Flats were about a mile from the scene of the crime. It was the prosecution's theory that the petitioner had been wearing these shorts when he committed the murder, and that he had afterwards removed and discarded them at the Van Buren Flats.

During the presentation of the prosecution's case, People's Exhibit 3 was variously described by witnesses in such terms as the "bloody shorts" and "a pair of jockey shorts stained with blood." Early in the trial the victim's mother testified that her daughter "had type 'A' positive blood." Evidence was later introduced to show that the petitioner's blood "was of group 'O'."

Against this background the jury heard the testimony of a chemist for the State Bureau of Crime Identification. The prosecution established his qualifications as an expert, whose "duties include blood identification, grouping and typing both dry and fresh stains," and who had "made approximately one thousand blood typing analyses while at the State Bureau." His crucial testimony was as follows:

> I examined and tested "People's Exhibit 3" to determine the nature of the staining material upon it. The result of the first test was that this material upon the shorts is blood. I made a second examination which disclosed that the blood is of human origin. I made a further examination which disclosed that the blood is of group 'A'.

The petitioner, testifying in his own behalf, denied that he had ever owned or worn the shorts in evidence as People's Exhibit 3. He himself referred to the shorts as having "dried blood on them."

In argument to the jury the prosecutor made the most of People's Exhibit 3:

> Those shorts were found in the Van Buren Flats, with blood. What type blood? Not 'O' blood as the defendant has, but "A" — type "A."

And later in his argument he said to the jury:

> And, if you will recall, it has never been contradicted the blood type of Janice May was blood type "A" positive. Blood type "A". Blood type "A" on these shorts. It wasn't "O" type as the defendant has. It is "A" type, what the little girl had.

Such was the state of the evidence with respect to People's Exhibit 3 as the case went to the jury. And such was the state of the record as the judgment of conviction was reviewed by the Supreme Court of Illinois. The "blood stained shorts" clearly played a vital part in the case for the prosecution. They were an important link in the chain of circumstantial evidence against the petitioner, and, in the context of the revolting crime with which he was charged, their gruesomely emotional impact upon the jury was incalculable.

So matters stood with respect to People's Exhibit 3, until the present habeas corpus proceeding in the Federal District Court. In this proceeding the State was ordered to produce the stained shorts, and they were admitted in evidence. It was established that their appearance was the same as when they had been introduced at the trial as People's Exhibit 3. The petitioner was permitted to have the shorts examined by a chemical microanalyst. What the microanalyst found cast an extraordinary new light on People's Exhibit 3. The reddish-brown stains on the shorts were not blood, but paint.

The witness said that he had tested threads from each of the 10 reddish-brown stained areas on the shorts, and that he had found that all of them were encrusted with mineral pigments ". . . which one commonly uses in the preparation of paints." He found "no traces of human blood." The State did not dispute this testimony, its counsel contenting himself with prevailing upon the witness to concede on cross-examination that he could not swear that there had never been any blood on the shorts.

It was further established that counsel for the prosecution had known at the time of the trial that the shorts were stained with paint. The prosecutor even admitted that the Canton police had prepared a memorandum attempting to explain "how this exhibit contains all the paint on it."

In argument at the close of the habeas corpus hearing counsel for the State contended that "[e]verybody" at the trial had known that the shorts were stained with paint. That contention is totally belied by the record. The microanalyst correctly described the appearance of the shorts when he said, "I assumed I was dealing . . . with a pair of shorts which was heavily stained with blood. . . . [I]t would appear to a layman . . . that what I see before me is a garment heavily stained with blood." The record of the petitioner's trial reflects the prosecution's consistent and repeated misrepresentation that People's Exhibit 3 was, indeed, "a garment heavily stained with blood." The prosecution's whole theory with respect to the exhibit depended upon that misrepresentation. For the theory was that the victim's assailant had discarded the shorts because they were stained with blood. A pair of paint-stained shorts, found in an abandoned building a mile away from the scene of the crime, was virtually valueless as evidence against the petitioner. The prosecution deliberately misrepresented the truth.

More than 30 years ago this Court held that the Fourteenth Amendment cannot tolerate a state criminal conviction obtained by the knowing use of false evidence. There has been no deviation from that established principle. There can be no retreat from that principle here.

The judgment of the Court of Appeals is reversed and the case is remanded for further proceedings consistent with this opinion. It is so ordered.

NOTES

1. *The Court's holding.* What did the Supreme Court hold in *Miller?* What should it have held? That the failure to give the defense access to the shorts before trial violated the defendant's right to due process of law? That the chemist's testimony at the state trial was false and therefore a violation of due process? That the prosecutor presented evidence that he knew was false, thereby violating due process? That the prosecutor withheld evidence that he knew would have exculpated the defendant? An investigation by the bar into the prosecutor's conduct found no material misrepresentation. See Report of the Grievance Committee of the Illinois State Bar Association, May 14, 1968, reprinted as The Vindication of a Prosecutor, 59 J. Crim. L., Criminology & Police Sci. 335 (1968).

2. *The Chemist's Testimony.* Did the chemist who testified at the state trial blunder in performing the blood typing tests and incorrectly conclude that red paint was type A blood? Or did the chemist believe that the red stain was partly blood and partly paint? If he blundered, the ability of the police laboratory to provide valid scientific evidence is thrown into doubt, and it is appropriate to ask what rules of law might enhance laboratory performance. If he withheld information from the court, did he act ethically? The problem of maintaining scientific objectivity in the courtroom is discussed below.

3. *Laboratory proficiency.* For other instances of "questionable forensic science" exposed by defense experts, see Joseph F. Keefe, Forensic Science Services and the Criminal Justice System as Viewed by the Defense, 24 J. Forensic Sci. 673 (1979). Naturally, the quality of laboratories and the technicians and scientists working in them varies. See Nicholas Lappas, Forensic Science Laboratories in the United States: A Survey, 18 J. Forensic Sci. Soc'y 171 (1978). A limited number of proficiency studies, particularly in the area of forensic toxicology, have been undertaken. E.g., M.A. Peat et al., Proficiency Testing in Forensic Toxicology: A Feasibility Study, 28 J. Forensic Sci. 139 (1983); E.C. Dinovo & L.A. Gottschalk, Results of a Nine-Laboratory Survey of Forensic Toxicology Proficiency, 22 Clinical Chemistry 843 (1976); cf. Lawrence Miike & Maria Hewitt, Accuracy and Reliability of Urine Drug Tests, 36 Kan. L. Rev. 641, 656 (1988) ("In a 'blind study' of fifty labs nationwide performing drug tests, there was a 35% false negative rate and a one percent false positive rate"). In the mid-1970s the federal Law Enforcement Assistance Administration sent known samples to many participating police laboratories for identification. The percentage of laboratories with "unacceptable" (inaccurate or incomplete) responses ranged from 1.6% (for a blood stained cloth) to 71.2% (for a semen stained cloth), depending on the nature of the sample. Joseph Peterson et al., Crime Laboratory Proficiency Testing Research Program 251 (U.S. Dep't Justice 1978). For a review of more recent studies, see Joseph L. Peterson & Penelope N. Markham, Crime Laboratory Proficiency Testing Results (pts. 1 & 2), 40 J. Forensic Sci. 994 & 1009 (1995).

The absolute number of mistakes in forensic work, however, is not the relevant benchmark in assessing what forensic science has to offer the legal system. All evidence, from the reports of eyewitnesses to reliance on a person's reputation, is fallible. Is there any reason to think that scientific evidence is any worse than the more familiar modes of proof? Should courts nevertheless screen it more carefully than lay testimony? How? We explore these questions in chapter 6.

Forensic laboratories are exempted from the requirements of the Department of Health and Human Services Comprehensive Clinical Laboratories Improvements Act of 1988. The failure to regulate and license these laboratories is criticized in Randolph N. Jonakait, Forensic Science: The Need for Regulation, 4 Harv. J. L. & Tech. 109 (1991). The issue of quality assurance also is addressed in a report of a commiittee of the National Research Council, which recommends "[e]xternal mechanisms" including "mandatory proficiency testing" for laboratories that perform DNA identification. National Research Council Committee on DNA Technology in Forensic Science, DNA Technology in Forensic Science 109 (1992). See also National Research Council Committee on DNA Forensic Science: An Update, The Evaluation of Forensic DNA Evidence (1996).

4. *The impact of forensic analysis. Miller* highlights the powerful effect that scientific evidence can have — for better or worse — in some cases. But how many? Should more resources be invested in the scientific investigation of crime? Or did the unnamed police administrator have a strong point when he asked "Do you know how many patrol cars that gas chromatography system could buy?" Barry A.J. Fisher, Developing a Forensic Science Laboratory Operating Strategy, 31 J. Forensic Sci. 1177, 1178 (1986). Empirical studies of factors that affect the disposition of cases provide few clear answers. See P.L. Bender et al., Utilization of Forensic Sciences in Police Investigations: A Review of the Literature (U.S. Dep't of Justice 1982); Joseph Peterson et al., Forensic Evidence and the Police: The Effects of Scientific Evidence on Criminal Investigations 210 (U.S. Dep't of Justice 1984) ("The effect of physical evidence on clearance and conviction depends on the type of offense and the jurisdiction involved"); Harry Kalven & Hans Zeisel, The American Jury 139 (1966) (no experts appeared in about three-quarters of criminal trials studied and in only 3% of the trials did both sides employ an expert; prosecutors used experts four times as often as defense attorneys).

Barry A.J. Fisher
Developing a Forensic Science
Laboratory Operating Strategy*
31 Journal of Forensic Sciences 1177, 1178 (1986)

The police investigator sees us as a scientific resource to help prove his case. He is delighted when we can substantiate his theory of how a crime occurred and usually wants more strongly worded opinions than we often like to give. He cringes at the use of what he calls "weasel words" in laboratory reports, for example, "consistent with" and "similar to." He wants absolute statements. The concept of class characteristics is foreign to him, and he would like nothing better than reports stating that, for example, the white cotton fiber found on the victim came from the defendant and no other.

The prosecuting attorney has little appreciation for forensic scientists. After all, how many lawyers successfully made it through physical chemistry for their baccalaureate? For the most part, although there are exceptions, lawyers are intimidated by us. We are indispensable in driving under the influence (DUI) of alcohol cases, required in drug prosecutions, and downright handy in rapes, assaults and murders. Yet many will argue that forensic scientists often confuse the jury as often as they help the case.

Defense attorneys see us as extensions of the police and prosecutors. I once gave a talk to a group of public defenders in Los Angeles. . . . I explained how I saw our role as an independent, scientific evaluator of the physical evidence. The lawyers in that group laughed at me. They saw me and all government employed forensic scientists as being on the side of the prosecution and not at all unbiased.

The courts see us as a bottleneck. If your laboratories are at all similar to mine, I'm certain that at one time or another you have had a backlog in driving under the influence cases or in narcotics cases. And what happens when the labo-

---

* Extracted with permission from the *Journal of Forensic Sciences,* Vol. 31, No. 4, copyright American Society for Testing and Materials, 100 Barr Harbor Drive, West Conshohocken, PA 19428.

ratory begins to fall behind in those cases? The courts are likely to be in an uproar about continuances.

Administrators see us as a bottomless pit into which is continuously poured money — money to buy spectrophotometers, gas chromatographs, mass spectrometers, and other high priced laboratory equipment of that ilk. One administrator once mused to me, "Do you know how many patrol cars that gas chromatography system could buy?"

Finally, the public sees forensic scientists in the most romantic terms. We are a modern incarnation of the legendary Sherlock Holmes. Quincy, the fictional TV forensic pathologist cum criminalist plays a key role in each of our institutions. The public believes that we have unlimited time and resources to expend on each and every case we examine. . . .

Michael J. Saks
Accuracy v. Advocacy:
Expert Testimony Before the Bench*
Technology Review, Aug.-Sept. 1987, at 43, 44-45

[E]xperts [are] vulnerable to the possibly distorting influence of lawyers. Long before the expert and lawyer arrive in court, a bond has formed between them. The influence of the lawyer is considerable. He or she may authorize a limited budget for analyzing the evidence and restrict the information provided to experts about the case. The attorney expects help and cooperation from experts, who know that the lawyer could hire someone else. The question is how far they are willing to be drawn out onto the forensic limb.

One prominent trial judge in Massachusetts likens the process to a seduction. The lawyer attempts to convince the experts to go as far as possible, and the experts try to resist the temptation to acquiesce. It is the lawyer's job to test the limits and the expert's job to set those limits. . . .

In contrast to what attorneys may want, experts' professional colleagues expect them to give a competent and dignified account of the field without going beyond its limits. These expectations are sometimes expressed in a code of ethics. For example, the National Society of Professional Engineers states: "Engineers shall issue public statements only in an objective and truthful manner. Engineers shall be objective and truthful in professional reports, statements, or testimony. They shall include all relevant and pertinent information in such reports, statements, or testimony." . . .

Whatever experts' perceptions of the expectations of their colleagues, the likelihood that any sanctions will be applied against those who overstep their bounds is tiny. This fact was clear in a 1983 study I did with Richard Van Duizend, then an attorney with the National Center for State Courts. We contacted the ethics and discipline committees of professional associations such as the NSPE, the American Academic of Forensic Science, and the American Medical Association. We found that virtually no actions had been taken against members who had misrepresented the field's knowledge or drawn insupportable conclusions on behalf of one party as expert witnesses. Complaints that did surface were typically brought by attorneys complaining that the experts they hired had misrepresented their educational or professional credentials. Professional organizations are in business to ensure their members' well-being more than to police them.

John I. Thornton
Uses and Abuses of Forensic Science*
69 American Bar Association Journal 288, 292 (1983)

[C]onsider the distinction between the introduction of evidence and the introduction of an interpretation of that evidence. The two are by no means synonymous. Not infrequently, the side wishing to introduce its particular interpretation will treat itself to a scientific "smorgasbord," selecting this or that morsel for examination by the forensic scientist. The evidence will be selected or rejected with only those items that conform to the arguments of one side actually being submitted for examination. A distinct possibility exists that the results of the examination by the forensic scientist will be skewed. This is an abuse of science because the scientist is not allowed to consider all alternative interpretations of the evidence. As a result, the ethical standards of the scientist may be challenged by cogent cross-examination.

These situations represent potential sources of mischief. There is nothing necessarily unethical or mendacious about these practices, and they even might not be unfair because opposing counsel is presumed to be equally astute in reviewing the potential evidence to be introduced. Attorneys orchestrate the presentation of physical evidence and bear the responsibility for the conduct of the case in general, and it is understandable that they will wish the evidence to support the best possible case. The danger is that conflicts easily arise between scientist and lawyer — the former attempts to describe the evidence as it actually is, while the latter attempts to describe it in the most favorable light.

---

* Reprinted with permission from the March 1983 ABA Journal, The Lawyer's Magazine, published by the American Bar Association.

NOTES

1. *Independence and objectivity.* Most scientists would insist that "the scientist should have no personal stake in the outcome of a civil or criminal case. The scientist's expertise is in the application of science to a legal controversy and the proper interpretation of scientific findings . . . ." Joseph Peterson, The Team Approach in Forensic Science, in Modern Legal Medicine, Psychiatry and Forensic Science 993-94 (William J. Curran et al. eds., 1980). So too, most subscribe to the ideal of the "introduction of evidence by competent, objective scientists who constantly keep in mind the ethical responsibilities of the profession." John I. Thorton, Uses and Abuses of Forensic Science, 69 A.B.A.J. 288, 291 (1983).

Yet, Saks describes the tendency of experts to identify with the party for whom they testify or to be manipulated by that party. Inasmuch as a witness is expected to answer only those questions put to him, is it reasonable for the National Society of Profession Engineers to admonish its members to "include all relevant and pertinent information in . . . testimony"? If not, will cross-examination or opposing experts flush out the information that might not be elicited on direct examination, as Thornton's mention of "astute" opposing counsel implies? Consider the following incident:

> A convicted murderer who has served eight years of a life sentence today walked free from the Scottish Court of Criminal Appeal in Edinburgh when three judges quashed his conviction. . . . John Preece, aged 49, a former lorry driver, . . . was convicted of murdering Mrs. Helen Will, aged 54, of Mastick, Aberdeen, by a majority verdict at the High Court in Edinburgh in 1973. . . .
>
> Lord Emslie said: "At the time of the trial Dr Clift, highly qualified and experienced, appeared to be an expert witness as to whose quality, detachment and scientific reliability there was no doubt." But the court was now sure that Dr Clift's evidence that the donor of the semen was an "A" secretor was misleading. Dr Clift had kept silent although he had known that the victim, Mrs Will, was also a group "A" secretor like Mr Preece.
>
> The judge added: "This was conduct on the part of an expert witness which demonstrated a complete misunderstanding of the role of scientific witnesses in our courts and a lack of the essential qualities of accuracy and scientific objectivity which are normally to be taken for granted." . . .
>
> Lord Emslie added that Dr Richard Gregory, the Home Office scientist who had corroborated Dr Clift's evidence . . . had been to some extent influenced by his superior — Dr Clift.

Prisoner Cleared of Murder After Serving 8 Years, The Times (London), June 20, 1981, at 1.

An even more egregious example of an expert witness's misconduct surfaced in Lubbock, Texas, when Dr. Ralph Erdmann, a pathologist, included in an autopsy report the weight of the dead man's spleen — even though the spleen previously had been removed in an operation. Dr. Erdmann supposedly performed some 450 autopsies a year for about 40 counties in the Texas Panhandle, but exhumations of some of the corpses revealed bodies without a mark on them. An attorney appointed by a state district court to investigate the matter concluded "If the prosecution theory was that death was caused by a Martian death ray, then that was what Dr. Erdmann reported." Richard L. Fricker, Pathologist's Plea Adds to Turmoil, A.B.A.J., Mar. 1993, at 24. For more, see Geoffrey A. Campbell, Erdmann Faces New Legal Woes, A.B.A.J., Nov. 1995, at 32.

Likewise, in 1994, a serologist was indicted in Texas and West Virginia for falsifying test results in hundreds of cases since 1979. He allegedly reported inconclusive results as conclusive, altered laboratory records, did not report conflicting results, and failed to conduct additional testing to resolve conflicts. His testimony helped sentence defendants who have since been exonerated to long prison terms. Paul C. Giannelli, When the Evidence is a Matter of Life and Death, N.Y. Times, Aug. 21, 1994.

2. *Selection of expert witnesses.* Many attorneys, and much of the public, believe that "an expert can be found to support almost any position." Bert Black, A Unified Theory of Scientific Evidence, 56 Fordham L. Rev. 595, 597-98 (1988). Indeed, the former chief judge of the U.S. District Court for the the Eastern District of New York is persuaded that "[a]n expert can be found to testify to the truth of almost any factual theory, no matter how frivolous, thus validating the case sufficiently to avoid summary judgment and force the case to trial." Jack Weinstein, Improving Expert Testimony, 20 U. Rich. L. Rev. 473, 482 (1986). The availabilty of such testimony from "the expert-for-hire," id., is not necessarily the result of venality. "The scientific community is large and heterogeneous, and a Ph.D. can be found to swear to almost any 'expert' proposition, no matter how false or foolish." Peter Huber, Safety and the Second Best: The Hazards of Public Risk Management in the Court, 85 Colum. L. Rev. 277, 333 (1985).

3. *Relaxing the adversarial role of the forensic expert.* In light of the widely perceived problems noted above, suggestions to reform, if not abandon, the adversary system of adjudication are not lacking. For an empirical study and a sustained critique of the adversarial use of experts, see Samuel Gross, Expert Evidence, 1991 Wis. L. Rev. 1113 (1991). See also Anthony Champagne et al., Expert Witnesses in the Courts: An Empirical Examination, 76 Judicature 5 (1992) (very limited survey finding that lawyers "want articulate, partisan experts with integrity, [who] charge reasonable fees, have an excellent courtroom demeanor, and [are not] tentative in stating conclusions"); John D.J. Havard, Expert Scientific Evidence Under the Adversarial System: A Travesty of Justice? 32 J. Forensic Sci.

Soc'y 225 (1992) (urges movement toward continental system of court experts with written reports and full disclosure); Symposium, Expert Evidence, 16 Law & Hum. Behav. 253 (1992). Professor John Langbein, who maintains that the West German system of adjudication is far superior, is particularly critical of the role of experts in civil trials in the United States. John Langbein, The German Advantage in Civil Procedure, 52 U. Chi. L. Rev. 823, 835-36 (1985). Court appointed experts figure prominently in the Continental, accusatorial systems of criminal justice. For example, court appointed forensic medical experts in some countries usually sit in court during the whole trial, question witnesses, explain their findings and conclusions before being examined by the parties, and may discuss relevant points not raised by the parties. See J. Chr. Giertsen, The Doctor and the Court in Norway, 36 Forensic Sci. Int'l 11, 12-14 (1988). An interim report of a committee reviewing the use of experts in civil cases in England comes close to calling for abandonment of experts retained by the parties. See Peter Fenn et al., Scientific Experts: More Attention Needed, 378 Nature 754 (1995).

Occasionally court appointed experts are employed in this country as well, and there is room to expand their role. See Bert Black et al., Science and the Law in the Wake of *Daubert:* A New Search for Scientific Knowledge, 72 Tex. L. Rev. 715, 795-96 (1994); Panel on Statistical Assessments as Evidence in the Courts, The Evolving Role of Statistical Assessments as Evidence in the Courts 169-72 (Stephen E. Fienberg ed., 1989); Thomas Willging, Court Appointed Experts (U.S. Federal Judicial Center 1986); Jack B. Weinstein, Litigation and Statistics: Obtaining Assistance Without Abuse, Toxics L. Rptr., Dec. 24, 1986, at 812, 819-20; Learned Hand, Historical and Practical Considerations Regarding Expert Testimony, 15 Harv. L. Rev. 40 (1901).

Chapter 2
Communicating Scientific Findings in Court

H.J. Walls, Whither Forensic Science?*
6 Medicine, Science and Law 183 (1966)

[C]ommunication from science to law, which was never easy, is being made more difficult by [a] developing trend towards scientific results being expressed as probabilities — not just as something that might be so, but as something that has a definite numerically expressible chance of being so. The law, of course, wants yes or no, black or white, this or not this. In fact, . . . I have sometimes thought that it looks on "probability" as a dirty word. . . .

[A]ll scientific conclusions are really matters of probability. Sometimes, of course, this is so near 1 (that is, certainty) that it is for all practical purposes indistinguishable from certainty, and the residuum of "reasonable doubt" is vanishingly small. The principle, however, remains valid. For example, nothing is more conclusive than fingerprint evidence, but there is no prescriptive law of nature that prohibits two fingerprints from being identical. There is merely a descriptive one that two never *are* identical. That, of course, is quite easily explained: the number of possible different fingerprint patterns is large that there aren't enough fingers in the whole world over many generations to give a reasonable outside chance of two identical ones turning up.

We have indeed already seen the thin edge of the wedge go in. Courts accept evidence about glass fragments in which all the scientific witness can say is that they are indistinguishable to within certain limits of accuracy, and the odds against — that is, the probability of — that happening by chance are so and so.

There is some very interesting work going on now on the characterisation of human head hair by means of the neutron activation analysis of the trace elements in it. [R]ather bold claims were made some years ago across the Atlantic that in this way a hair could practically be tied to the head from which it came. The present, much more systematic, work has shown that these claims were undoubtedly premature and over-stated, but that considerable differences between hairs from different heads do undoubtedly occur. We are not yet ready to use the results of this work routinely in evidence, but when we are they will be meaningful only if they are given as statistical probabilities. Some quite sophisticated statistical mathematics have been developed in connection with this work, and its use will enable us to give precise estimates of probability instead of, at present, vague statements such as "similar to," "could have come from the same head" and so on. And it would obviously be quite wrong not to be precise instead of vague if the

*This excerpt from the presidential address of Dr. H.J. Walls to the British Academy of Forensic Sciences is reprinted by permission of *Medicine, Science and the Law.*

known facts make that possible.

Indeed there is really no reason why in certain fields that sort of evidence should not now be used more than it is. The distribution of blood groups within the various blood-group systems which we can now determine on dried blood stains is known, at least for the population of this country. . . . Suppose . . . that a specimen of blood is grouped according to four independent systems, and that it belongs to the commonest group in each, and . . . that each of these groups occurs in half the population. Half the population is a large number of people, but when four independent systems are in question, . . . the blood could only have come from half of half of half of half of the population — that is, one-sixteenth. . . . If we could use eight systems, on the same assumption [of independence] we would have come down to one-256th part of the population. And if the groups to which the blood belongs happen to be among the rarer ones, it is quite on the cards that we can say that only one person in several thousand has this combination of groups. As a matter of fact, we do say that sort of thing now when the opportunity to do so arises. But there is no reason why we should not carry it a little farther. It should not be impossible in some cases to make an estimate of the number of persons from whom, on other evidence, the blood *might* have come. Suppose [there] were 100 [such people]. The important question then is: if the bloodstain and the [accused] are of the same rare combination of groups, what is the probability of more than one person in that 100 having it? If . . . one person in 5,000 in the population as a whole shows that particular combination, then . . . the probability of two people out of our 100 showing it is 1/2,500 — that is, the odds against the event are 2,500 to one — and the probability of more than two people out of the 100 having it is quite vanishingly small. And, obviously, the smaller the number of persons from whom the blood might have come, the smaller the corresponding probability. If instead of 100 it was, say, twenty, then the odds against more than one person in that twenty having the same combination of groups are over 60,000 to one. Does that sort of figure constitute proof "beyond all reasonable doubt?"

We as scientists often wonder indeed just what "beyond all reasonable doubt" really means. Can we give it a quantitative connotation? . . . [L]aw and science would at least make a more harmonious marriage if we could put some sort of figure on "beyond reasonable doubt." Does it mean a probability of .99, or .999 or .999999 or something even higher? Should it be a higher probability in a trial for murder than in one for petty larceny? I leave the thought with you.

United States ex rel. DiGiacomo v. Franzen
680 F.2d 515 (7th Cir. 1982)

Per curiam.

In this appeal from the denial of a petition for a writ of habeas corpus, petitioner James G. DiGiacomo claims that he was denied a fair trial when the state was allowed to use mathematical probability to identify him as the perpetrator of a crime. We hold that the admission of the challenged testimony violated no right guaranteed by the Constitution and affirm the district court's judgment denying the petition.

I

In March 1977, James G. DiGiacomo was tried in an Illinois state court on charges of rape, deviate sexual assault, aggravated kidnapping, and battery. The principal witness against DiGiacomo was Patricia Marik, the victim of the assault. Marik testified that DiGiacomo abducted her at knife point from a tavern in Naperville, Illinois, on November 5, 1976, and ordered her to drive him to a cornfield in the country where, after a brief struggle, he forced her to have sexual intercourse with him.

In an effort to bolster Marik's identification of DiGiacomo as her assailant at trial, the state called an expert witness to testify concerning a number of hairs that had been recovered from Marik's automobile after the attack. Sally Dillon, the supervising criminologist at the Illinois Bureau of Identification, testified that she had compared the hairs found in Marik's car with a sample of DiGiacomo's hair and found them to be microscopically similar. She was then asked, over defense counsel's objection, whether she could testify as to the statistical probability of the hair found in Marik's car belonging to someone other than DiGiacomo. Dillon responded that based on a recent study she had read, "the chances of another person belonging to that hair would be one in 4,500."

Several hours after beginning their deliberations, the jury, apparently confused by Dillon's testimony, submitted the following question to the court in writing: "Has it been established by sampling of hair specimens that the defendant was positively proven to have been in the automobile?" After consulting with the parties, the trial judge sent a written response to the jury in which he instructed them that it was their duty to determine the facts from the evidence presented at trial and that he could therefore provide no answer to their question. Neither side objected.

The jury later returned guilty verdicts on each of the charges, and DiGiacomo was sentenced to three concurrent terms of eight to twenty-five years for the kidnapping, rape, and deviate sexual assault, and 364 days, also concurrent, for the battery. . . .

. . . DiGiacomo filed a petition for habeas corpus in the United States District Court for the Northern District of Illinois in which he claimed that the admission of Dillon's testimony regarding the statistical likelihood of the hairs found in Marik's car belonging to him constituted a denial of due process. The district court denied the petition, and this appeal followed.

II

[A] federal court is authorized to issue a writ of habeas corpus in behalf of a person in custody under the judgment of a state court "only on the ground that he is in custody in violation of the Constitution or laws or treaties of the United States." Because the admissibility of evidence in state courts is a matter of state law, evidentiary questions are not subject to federal review . . . unless there is a resultant denial of fundamental fairness or the denial of a specific constitutional right.

In this case, DiGiacomo contends the admission of expert testimony as to the mathematical likelihood of hairs found in Marik's car belonging to him resulted in a denial of fundamental fairness in that it misled the jury into believing that the state had conclusively established that he was in the car. In support of his contention, DiGiacomo cites the Eighth Circuit's decision in United States v. Massey, 594 F.2d 676 (8th Cir. 1979).

In *Massey,* the court held that the trial judge's comments construing expert testimony with respect to comparison of hair samples in terms of mathematical probability of error, coupled with the prosecutor's emphasis upon the mathematical probabilities in his closing argument, constituted plain error . . . and required reversal of the defendant's bank robbery conviction even though no objection had been made at trial. The expert in that case had testified that three of five hairs found in a blue ski mask similar to one worn by one of the perpetrators of the robbery were microscopically similar to the defendant's hair. He was then asked by the trial judge how many people in the country might have similar hair that could not be distinguished. The expert responded that in his own experience there had been only a "couple" cases out of over 2,000 in which he had been unable to distinguish hair from two different individuals. He added, however, that according to a recent study, apparently the same study on which Dillon had based her testimony, there was a one in 4,500 chance of another person having the same hair. In an attempt to clarify the response, the trial judge asked the witness if this meant there was only a one in 4,500 or one in 2,000 chance of his identification being wrong. Although the expert's response was somewhat confusing, the prosecutor later emphasized these numbers throughout his closing argument to the jury, concluding with the statement that by itself "the hair sample would be proof beyond a reasonable doubt because it is so convincing."

In reversing the conviction, the Eighth Circuit held that not only had the Government failed to establish a proper foundation for these mathematical conclusions, but in his closing argument the prosecutor had confused the identification of the hair found in the ski cap with the identification of the perpetrator of the crime. Because of this confusion by the prosecutor and the potential for confusion already inherent in such evidence, the court concluded that plain error had been shown.

DiGiacomo contends that his case is even stronger because the record shows more than a mere possibility that the jury was confused. Here, he contends, it is apparent from the written question the jury submitted to the trial court shortly after beginning its deliberations that the jury was in fact confused by the expert testimony. The jury's confusion, which the trial judge's response wholly failed to remedy, he contends, clearly warrants the granting of federal habeas relief.

We agree that the interjection into the criminal trial process of sophisticated theories of mathematical probability raises a number of serious concerns. As one court has aptly stated, "[m]athematics, a veritable sorcerer in our computerized society, while assisting the trier of fact in the search for truth, must not cast a spell over him." People v. Collins, 68 Cal. 2d 319, 320, 66 Cal. Rptr. 497, 438 P. 2d 33 (1968). While perhaps the most serious danger in admitting evidence of statistical probability in a criminal trial is the possibility that it will be used improperly, the possibility of prejudice also exists even when it is used in accordance with generally accepted principles. In a case involving the admissibility of virtually the same testimony with which we are faced here, the Supreme Court of Minnesota noted:

> Testimony expressing opinions or conclusions in terms of statistical probabilities can make the uncertain seem all but proven, and suggest, by quantification, satisfaction of the requirement that guilt be established "beyond a reasonable doubt." See Tribe, Trial by Mathematics, 84 Harv. L. Rev. 1329. . . .

State v. Carlson, 267 N.W. 2d 170 (Minn. 1978). [T]he court concluded in *Carlson* that an expert's testimony regarding the mathematical probability of certain incriminating hairs belonging to someone other than the defendant was improperly received. The court went on to hold, however, that under the facts of that case the error was harmless.

Even though we share in the concern of these courts that the admission of evidence as to mathematical probability in a criminal trial may mislead and confuse the jury, we do not find on the facts before us that its admission here constituted a denial of due process. Unlike *Massey,* the prosecutor in this case did not suggest in his closing argument that the mathematical odds testified to by the expert witness made her identification of the hair specimen virtually certain. In fact, the prosecutor conceded during argument that "some people have hair like that." Furthermore, the prosecutor in this case did not confuse the issue of whether the hairs found in the car were DiGiacomo's with the issue of whether he in fact committed the crime, although DiGiacomo concedes that in this case the questions are one and the same.

Although it may be true, as the question submitted to the trial court would seem to indicate, that one or more members of the jury were nevertheless confused about the significance of the hair identification testimony, we cannot say that this confusion was caused by any error of constitutional magnitude. Generally, the admission of expert testimony is very much a matter within the broad discretion of the trial judge. The Constitution does not and, indeed, cannot guarantee that only completely reliable evidence will be placed before the jury. Although it does demand that a defendant be given a full and fair opportunity to challenge whatever evidence is admitted, DiGiacomo was afforded that opportunity here. Through his counsel, he was free to challenge Dillon's testimony if it was not true, or clarify it if it was misleading. He was also free to call his own expert if he thought Dillon's testimony was at odds with the established views of the scientific community. DiGiacomo in fact did none of these things. No attempt was made to cross-examine Dillon regarding her testimony that the hairs found in Marik's car belonged to the defendant.

Even now, DiGiacomo does not claim that Dillon was wrong in her conclusion as to the likelihood of the hair found in Marik's car belonging to someone other than him. His contention is only that she should not have been allowed to express that conclusion in terms of mathematical probability. Instead, he contends she should have stated only whether or not the hairs were similar. But to limit her testimony in this way would have robbed the state of the full probative value of its evidence. To say that the defendant's hair is merely similar to hair found in the victim's automobile is significantly different than saying that there's a one in 4,500 chance of it belonging to someone else. If the expert's testimony is the latter, we know of no constitutional principle by which its admission could be held improper. While the better practice may be for the court specifically to instruct the jury on the limitations of mathematical probability whenever such evidence is admitted, we have no authority to impose such a rule upon the Illinois courts. Thus, we are unable to say that DiGiacomo's conviction resulted from a denial of any right guaranteed by the Constitution.

Of course, jury confusion by itself, even when not the product of a constitutional violation, could justify the granting of habeas relief if it resulted in a verdict that no rational trier of fact could have reached on the basis of the evidence presented. But DiGiacomo does not argue that no rational trier of fact could have found him guilty and, even if he did, the record does not support such a claim. Marik's positive identification of him as the man who had assaulted her together with the other evidence introduced by the state was more than sufficient to support a rational jury's verdict of guilty.

The district court's judgment denying the petition is affirmed.

State v. Kim
398 N.W. 2d 544 (Minn. 1987)

WAHL, JUSTICE.

This appeal questions the standard that governs state appeals of pretrial orders in criminal prosecutions as well as the propriety of the trial court ruling in this case. Joon Kyu Kim is charged with accomplishing sexual penetration by use of force or coercion . . . . At a pretrial hearing, the state proffered scientific evidence in the form of blood test results linking Kim to semen found at the scene of the alleged rape and a statistical analysis of the frequency with which Kim's blood type occurred in the local male population. The trial court ruled that the blood test results and expert testimony that the test results were consistent with Kim having been the source of the semen could be admitted at trial, but ruled that the statistical population frequency evidence was to be excluded. . . .

The facts in this case, as derived from police reports, indicate the complainant reported to police that on December 10, 1984, Joon Kyu Kim, her employer, had forcible, nonconsensual sexual intercourse with her. The complainant and her husband were employed as managers of a St. Paul apartment complex owned by Kim. On the evening of December 10, 1984, the complainant told police she was home alone. She and her husband had quarreled earlier in the evening and he had left the apartment. Her husband told police that after he left the apartment, he went to talk with Kim and they discussed, among other things, his marital problems. About 10 p.m., the complainant reported, Kim showed up at her apartment and began to talk about her marital relationship, telling her she wasn't having enough sex with her husband and that he would show her how. She said Kim then grabbed her breast, but she pulled away and told him to leave. Kim grabbed her again, she told police, forced her into the bedroom and onto the bed. She said she felt very afraid. He removed his clothing and her clothing and then climbed on top of her, she stated, sucking on her breasts and penetrating her vagina with his penis until he ejaculated. She said that as he left, Kim gave her a twenty dollar bill and told her next time it would be thirty dollars. He also told her she wouldn't call the police because she "needed the job too much." The complainant contacted the police shortly after Kim left the apartment.

At the time the complainant reported the incident, she turned over to police the sheet from the bed where she alleged she had been raped, a pair of panties she was wearing, a sanitary pad, a towel she had used to clean herself, and the twenty dollar bill she alleged Kim had given her. At the hospital, swab samples were taken of fluid present in the complainant's vagina. The Bureau of Criminal Apprehension Laboratory (BCA) found semen present on the bed sheet and on the vaginal swabs.

Kim was questioned by police the next day and denied having had sexual intercourse, consensual or nonconsensual, with the complainant. He admitted he had gone to her apartment that night, but stated he went there to fire her from her job as caretaker. He claimed her accusation was motivated by this firing. He pleaded not guilty to the criminal sexual conduct charges subsequently filed against him.

The trial court, on the state's motion, ordered samples of Kim's blood, saliva and hair taken for purposes of comparing his blood type with the semen found on the bed sheet and in the complainant's body.[1] Comparison samples of blood were also taken from the complainant and from her husband. The samples were tested at the BCA Lab using blood type testing (ABO system) and electrophoresis testing, a

---

[1] The majority of people, including Kim, secrete their blood type in their body fluids, including semen, saliva, etc.

procedure that identifies distinctive enzymatic genetic markers present in the blood and bodily fluids. The tests were repeated at the Minneapolis War Memorial Blood Bank and the BCA results were replicated. The BCA Lab analyst was prepared to offer testimony that the semen found in the complainant's body and on the bed sheet was consistent with Kim's blood type and PGM reading.[2] Further, the analyst was prepared to testify that 96.4 percent of males in the Twin Cities metropolitan population, but not Kim, could be excluded on the basis of this combination of blood factors as possible sources of the semen found on the bed sheet.

Kim objected to all of the scientific evidence at the pretrial hearing. As to the statistical population frequency evidence, he argued that its prejudicial impact outweighed its probative value. The trial court excluded the statistical population frequency evidence under the rule of State v. Boyd, 331 N.W. 2d 480 (Minn. 1983). This pretrial appeal followed. . . .

[W]e consider first whether the state met its burden of clearly establishing that the trial court's suppression order was erroneous. The court of appeals held that the state did not meet this burden and concluded that the trial court had properly interpreted and applied the rule of our decision in *Boyd* to suppress the statistical population frequency evidence. The defendant in *Boyd* was prosecuted for criminal sexual conduct in the third degree for having sexual intercourse with a 14-year-old girl, who became pregnant and gave birth as a result. We held that expert testimony that there was a 99.911 percent likelihood of paternity, based on population frequency statistics applied to interpret blood test results, must be excluded. "[T]here is a real danger," we stated, "that the jury will use the [statistical population frequency] evidence as a measure of the probability of the defendant's guilt or innocence, and that the evidence will thereby undermine the presumption of innocence, erode the values served by the reasonable doubt standard, and dehumanize our system of justice."

The state argues in this appeal that the statistical evidence it seeks to introduce against Kim can be distinguished from that [sic] we disapproved in *Boyd*. The difference between the evidence in *Boyd* — that 99.911 percent of the population, but not the defendant, could be excluded as donors — and the evidence it has proferred in this case — that 3.6 percent of the population, including the defendant, are possible donors — is the difference between inclusion and exclusion. The state contends that when statistics are stated as an exclusion figure, as in *Boyd,* the risk is greater that the jury will interpret the statistical percentage as a statement of the probability of the defendant's guilt. By contrast, when stated as an inclusion figure, the danger of such quantification is urged to be less.

The court of appeals correctly rejected this purported distinction, stating that *Boyd* "do[es] not focus on the nature of the statistics but rather on the impact of the statistics on the trier of fact." The danger we recognized in *Boyd* is that statis-

---

[2] PGM is an enzyme. It is a genetic marker that may be detected in the blood by use of the electrophoresis testing process.

tics on the frequency with which certain blood type combinations occur in a population will be understood by the jury to be a quantification of the likelihood that the defendant, who shares that unique combination of blood characteristics, is guilty. This danger exists as much in an inclusion as in an exclusion figure because, as the trial court noted, faced with an exclusion percentage, a jury will naturally convert it into an inclusion percentage. Because we cannot meaningfully distinguish the evidence offered in *Boyd* from that in the case now before us, we conclude that *Boyd* controls. We affirm the decision of the court of appeals and hold that the state has not clearly and unequivocally shown that the trial court order suppressing statistical population frequency evidence was erroneous.

The state next argues that if its proffered evidence cannot be distinguished from the evidence we disapproved in *Boyd,* we should modify or overrule *Boyd* but has presented no new or compelling argument. The state argues that the effect of *Boyd* is to exclude from the factfinding process reliable scientific evidence with great probative evidentiary value. The probative value of such evidence is, however, not of controlling significance in the analysis we adopted in *Boyd.* Under the Minnesota Rules of Evidence, relevant evidence may be excluded if its probative value is substantially outweighed by the danger of unfair prejudice. In *Boyd,* we clearly determined that the danger of population frequency statistics used to analyze blood test results unfairly prejudicing a defendant due to its "potentially exaggerated impact on the trier of fact" outweighed any probative value.

Boyd does not foreclose the use of expert interpretations of blood test results.[6] . . . As in *Boyd,* the expert called by the state in this case should not be permitted to express an opinion as to the probability that the semen is Kim's and should not be permitted to get around this by expressing the opinion in terms of the percentage of men in the general population with the same frequency of combinations of blood types. The expert should be permitted to testify, however, as to the basic theory underlying blood testing, to testify that not one of the individual tests excluded Kim as a source of the semen and to give the percentage of people in the general population with each of the individual blood types, and to express an opinion that scientific evidence is consistent with Kim having been the source of the semen. . . .

Affirmed.

KELLEY, JUSTICE (dissenting):
With utmost reluctance, I respectfully dissent. . . . *Carlson* is less than nine years old and *Boyd* is slightly over three. Both decisions were decided by a unanimous court. Normally, desired stability in the law is seldom enhanced by calling into question the correctness of precedents. Especially is that true when the ques-

---

[6] The concern about the prejudicial effect of blood test evidence expressed in *Boyd* does not apply outside of the context of criminal prosecutions. Blood test results and expert explanations thereof are admissible in evidence, for example, in a paternity proceeding.

tioned precedents are of such recent vintage. My reluctance to pen this dissent is prompted not only by that laudatory and necessary stare decisis consideration, but additionally because I joined with the remainder of the court in State v. Boyd. However, no violence is done to that laudatory and venerable doctrine of stare decisis when we re-examine a ruling that appears to be clearly wrong; nor is any valid public purpose promoted by embedding in our body of law an incorrect or outmoded decision. Further study and consideration of the issues in those two cases convinces me that both were wrongly decided.

This court in both State v. Carlson and State v. Boyd, and the majority in the instant case, relied upon an article written by Professor Tribe. In my opinion, the conclusions reached by Professor Tribe . . . in 1971 have since been successfully challenged by other researchers. See, e.g., Stripinis, Probability Theory and Circumstantial Evidence: Implications From a Mathematical Analysis, 22 Jurimetrics J. 59, 75-78 (1981); see also Saks and Kidd, Human Information Processing and Adjudication: Trial by Heuristics, 15 Law & Soc'y 123, 124 (1980-1981). Moreover, the assumptions upon which Tribe based his conclusions, in my opinion, have been fairly rebutted by other writers. See, e.g., Saks and Kidd, supra at 124-26, 145-51.

In a criminal case, we are concerned that no conviction shall be upheld unless guilt has been established beyond a reasonable doubt. In any system of criminal justice, a convicted person will necessarily be convicted on something less than absolute proof. Indeed, because in almost every case some doubt does exist, the law uses the expression "beyond a reasonable doubt" instead of "beyond any doubt." Thus, jurors routinely use probabilities in assessing whether the state has met its evidentiary burden. As demonstrated by Stripinis, "[i]f the probability of the accused being innocent is one in one trillion, then most people [jurors] would agree that he is 'guilty beyond a reasonable doubt.'" Thus, he points out the truism that the determination is a quantifiable solution, and that not all jurors will agree on what quantity of doubt constitutes a "reasonable doubt." The question is whether it is preferable to submit to the jury properly established scientific and mathematical probabilities of the existence of a fact to bear on its decision-making process than to ignore reality by asserting people are convicted only when absolute proof is available when, in fact, absolute proof is rarely, if ever, at hand. Therefore, I conclude with Saks and Kidd that "exclusion of mathematical guides to aid a fact finder, while avoiding some problems, exposes the fact-finding process to the heuristic biases of intuitive decision making."

I suggest that . . . the time may now have come for us to reconsider [*Carlson* and *Boyd*]. Just a few years short of the 21st century, perhaps courts should utilize those kinds of empirical, mathematical, scientific and statistical analyses used by all sorts of professional people including those in science, industry, engineering, administration, education and planning. . . . I agree with the Utah court when it said in rejecting our holding in State v. Carlson, "[We do] not share that philosophy, having a higher opinion of the jury's ability to weigh the credibility of such figures when properly presented and challenged." State v. Clayton, 646 P.2d 723, 727 n.1 (Utah 1982); see also E. Cleary, McCormick on Evidence § 210, at 655 (3d ed. 1984).

In my view the specific facts of this case demonstrate the shortcomings of excluding empirical scientific evidence. The proffered evidence involves the use of population frequency statistics in conjunction with individualization typing-test results. Based upon *Boyd,* the majority sustains the court's ruling permitting introduction of the test results but excluding the population frequency statistics. I concur with one authority in this general area when he noted:

> [I]nterpretation of individualization typing results is intimately tied to population frequency statistics; without being provided the appropriate statistical information, the triers of fact have no rational basis for deciding the significance of a type-for-type match.

George Sensabaugh, Biochemical Markers of Individuality, in Forensic Science Handbook 338, 403 (Richard Safenstein ed., 1982). Courts of other jurisdictions addressing the issue are increasingly recognizing the necessity of providing the fact finder with both the test results and the population frequency statistics. See, e.g., Davis v. State, 476 N.E.2d 127, 135-36 (Ind. Ct. App.1985) (noting that the approach taken by *Carlson* and *Boyd* "has been rejected by an impressive myriad of courts and commentators."); State v. Washington, 229 Kan. 47, 59, 622 P.2d 986, 995 (1981).

I agree. In my view, not to permit this evidence evinces on our part a distrust of both the abilities of the bar to demonstrate any weaknesses in analysis as well as our distrust of the ability of the jury to consider empirical scientific and mathematical statistical evidence with the same discrimination that it has to use, for example, in considering the opinion of a psychiatrist that the accused is insane.

Accordingly, even though with reluctance, I would reverse the trial court and overrule State v. Carlson and State v. Boyd.

NOTES

1. *Hair individualization probabilities.* Dr. Walls' prediction that new "sophisticated statistical mathematics" will yield "precise estimates of probabilities" derived from neutron activation analysis of human hair has yet to be realized. See Rita Cornelis, Truth has Many Facets: The Neutron Activation Analysis Story, 20 J. Forensic Sci. Soc'y 93, 95 (1980); Dennis Karjala, Comment, The Evidentiary Uses of Neutron Activation Analysis, 59 Cal. L. Rev. 997 (1971). The identifications in *DiGiacomo, Massey, Boyd,* and *Carlson,* are based on microscopic comparisons of hair samples. The studies that generated probabilities like the 1/4500 figure are B.D. Gaudette & E.S. Keeping, An Attempt at Determining Probabilities in Human Scalp Hair Comparison, 19 J. Forensic Sci. 599 (1974), and B.D. Gaudette & E.S. Keeping, Probabilities and Human Pubic Hair

Comparison, 21 J. Forensic Sci. 514 (1976). Because the defendants in these cases did not question the methodology of these studies, such opinions accept such numbers as the probability of coincidental misidentification. These estimates, however, are easily challenged. Panel on Statistical Assessments as Evidence in the Courts, The Evolving Role of Statistical Assessments as Evidence in the Courts 64-67 (Stephen E. Fienberg ed., 1989). Thus, probability assessments for hair identification remain controversial. Compare Clive A. Stafford & Patrick D. Goodman, Forensic Hair Analysis: Nineteenth Century Science or Twentieth Century Snake Oil?, 27 Colum. Hum. Rts. L. Rev. 227 (1996), and Larry Miller, Procedural Bias in Forensic Science Examinations of Human Hair, 11 Law & Hum. Behav. 157 (1987), with Edward Imwinkelried, Forensic Hair Analysis: The Case Against the Underemployment of Scientific Evidence, 39 Wash. & Lee L. Rev. 41 (1982). In contrast, the probability of chance matches for many immunogenetic markers is, as Dr. Walls points out, reasonably well known. See infra chapter 8.

2. *Posterior probability and reasonable doubt.* Dr. Walls notes that the probability of finding two or more individuals having an incriminating trait out of 100 persons selected at random from a large population in which one out of every five thousand people has this trait is 1/2500. Cf. David Finney, Probabilities Based on Circumstantial Evidence, 72 J. Am. Stat. Ass'n 316 (1977). He speaks of odds of 2500 to one in favor of guilt because he presupposes that the other non-scientific evidence in the case establishes that there are only 100 individuals who could be guilty. On the mechanics of the calculation that yields the probability of 1/2500, see, e.g., William Fairley & Frederick Mosteller, A Conversation About Collins, 41 U. Chi. L. Rev. 242 (1974); cf. David J. Balding & Peter Donnelly, Inference in Forensic Identification, 157 J. Royal Stat. Soc'y A 21 (1994); R.V. Lenth, On Identification by Probability, 26 J. Forensic Sci. Soc'y 197 (1986).

A more general approach to computing odds on guilt or innocence builds on the mathematics of conditional probabilities. A formula known as Bayes' rule states how new information (like the match in blood types) alters a probability derived from previously available evidence. This theorem involves three quantities — the "prior odds" in favor of some hypothesis H (which we may denote as Odds(H)), the "likelihood ratio" (LR), which states how many times more probable the new evidence E is when H is true than when H is false, and the "posterior odds" (given the new evidence) that H is true. According to Bayes' theorem, the posterior odds are simply the product of the likelihood ratio and the prior odds:

$$\text{Odds}(H|E) = LR \times \text{Odds}(H).$$

See, e.g., C.G.G. Aitken, Statistics and the Evaluation of Evidence for Forensic Scientists (1995); Bernard Robertson & G.A. Vignaux, Interpreting Evidence: Evaluating Forensic Science in the Courtroom 17-18 (1995); David Schum, Evidential Foundations of Probabilistic Reasoning (1994); Michael Finkelstein,

Quantitative Methods in Law (1978).

For example, if there are exactly 100 individuals who might have committed a murder and each one is equally likely to be the murderer, then the prior odds on the hypothesis H that the defendant is the murderer are Odds(H) = 1 to 99. (There is one murderer and 99 innocent people in the suspect population.) If evidence E is introduced to show that the murderer left a bloodstain of a type that occurs in a population like that of the suspects only once in every 5000 people, and if defendant's blood is of this type, then it is 5000 times more likely that the murderer would have the incriminating type than an innocent suspect, so LR = 5000. Therefore, the evidence shifts the odds from the prior level of 1 to 99 to the posterior level of 5000 $\times$ 1 to 99 = 5000 to 99 — just over 50 to 1.

From the standpoint of Bayesian decision theory, evidence that produces a very large posterior odds amounts to proof "beyond a reasonable doubt." Furthermore, the threshold value depends solely on the utilities of the possible outcomes of a correct guilty verdict, a correct acquittal, a false conviction and a false acquittal.[1] See, e.g., D.H. Kaye, Apples and Oranges: Confidence Coefficients

---

[1] Under this view, how large the Odds(H|E) must be to warrant a guilty verdict depends on the "social cost" of errors. Suppose we let H be the hypothesis that the defendant is guilty, we let the posterior probability of this hypothesis (given all the evidence in the case) be some number p, and we say that it is better to acquit 10 guilty people than to convict one innocent person. Bayesian decision theory recommends the verdict that minimizes the "loss function" or "expected cost." The loss function for the two possible verdicts involves both the probability p and the costs of the errors, as indicated in the matrix below:

Truth:	H: D is guilty	not-H: D is Innocent
Probability:	p = P(H|E)	1 − p
Verdict:	Guilty	0 10
	Not guilty	1 0

Matrix of losses for each possible verdict

The expected loss for each verdict is the loss that would result, discounted by the probability of these losses coming to pass under each verdict. A guilty verdict has a probability p of being correct but a loss of 0 if it is correct, and a probability 1 − p of being incorrect but a loss of 10 if it is incorrect. The expected loss for this verdict is therefore

$$0p + 10(1 - p) = 10 - 10p.$$

Similar reasoning shows that the expected loss for a verdict of not guilty is

$$1p + 0(1 - p) = p.$$

To minimize the expected loss, the jury should return a verdict of guilty if

$$10 - 10p < p.$$

Solving for p reveals the minimum that P(G|E) must be to justify conviction is 10/11 = .909. In terms of odds, the odds on guilt must exceed 10 to establish guilt beyond a reasonable doubt. Of course, this result is sensitive to the numerical values for the losses, and the 10 to 1 ratio is merely illustrative. As to what this critical value might be, see, e.g., United States v. Fatico, 458 F. Supp. 388, 410 (E.D.N.Y. 1978); C.M.A. McCauliff, Burdens of Proof: Degrees of Belief, Quanta of Evidence, or Constitutional Guarantees? 35 Vand. L. Rev. 1293, 1325 (1982) (survey of judges). For a brief overview of the issues associated with this perspective on proof, see D.H. Kaye, Introduction: What is Bayesianism? in Inference and Probability in the Law of Evidence: The Limits of Bayesianism 1 (Eric Green & Peter Tillers eds., 1988).

Versus the Burden of Persuasion, 73 Cornell L. Rev. 54 (1987); John Kaplan, Decision Theory and the Factfinding Process, 20 Stan. L. Rev. 1065 (1968).

3. *Virtues and vices of quantification.* Qualitative expressions such as "likely" or "rare" are subject to a broad range of interpretation, even within a single professional group. See Augustine Kong et al., How Medical Professionals Evaluate Expressions of Probability, 315 New Eng. J. Med. 740 (1986); Detlof von Winterfeldt & Ward Edwards, Decision Analysis and Behavioral Research 98-99 (1986); cf. Steven Morse, Crazy Behavior, Morals and Science: An Analysis of Mental Health Law, 51 S. Cal. L. Rev. 527, 591 (1978). Should forensic scientists be encouraged to make quantitative statements of crucial probabilities? To Dr. Walls the answer is clear: "it would obviously be quite wrong not to be precise instead of vague if the known facts make that possible." Do you agree? How should a probability like the 1/4500 figure in *DiGiacomo* be presented in court? Is it, as the expert testified, "the chances of another person belonging to that hair"? The opinions excerpted above reveal that some courts and commentators have serious reservations about "probability evidence." Even so, as the dissent in *Kim* indicates, Minnesota is the only state or federal jurisdiction categorically to exclude apparently well-founded, numerically expressed probabilities and population proportions. And, even in Minnesota, the legislature has attempted to overturn the exclusionary rule,[2] and the Minnesota Supreme has created a "DNA exception" to the rule. State v. Bloom, 516 N.W. 2d 159 (Minn. 1994). The criminal cases and problems associated with testimony as to such numbers are discussed in D.H. Kaye, The Admissibility of "Probability Evidence" in Criminal Trials (pt. 2), 27 Jurimetrics J. 160 (1987). For additional discussions, see, e.g., Daniel Shaviro, Statistical-Probability Evidence and the Appearance of Justice, 103 Harv. L. Rev. 530 (1989); Symposium, Decision and Inference in Litigation, 13 Cardozo L. Rev. 253 (1991). We return to this question in connection with genetic tests for paternity in chapters 9 and 10.

---

[2] See Minn. Stat. § 634.26 (Supp. 1989) ("statistical population frequency evidence" admissible); 1 McCormick on Evidence § 210 (John W. Strong ed., 4th ed. 1992).

Part II

FORENSIC PATHOLOGY AND TOXICOLOGY

Chapter 3
Medicolegal Death Examinations

Marshall Houts
Where Death Delights
82-106 (1967)*

. . . Robert Domer graduated from the the law school of Western Reserve University in 1949, but . . . [f]our years later Domer deserted the law . . . . He formed his own mortgage and loan servicing companies, which at the beginning of 1963 were purported to have assets of $93,000,000. There was considerable water in these figures . . . . In the late afternoon of Saturday, March 30, 1963, the FNMA auditors confronted Domer . . . . "There must be some mistake," he replied with outward calm. "There has to be an explanation. I will have it for you the first thing Monday morning."

Robert Domer then drove thoughtfully home. . . . Alone in his house . . . he dictated a one-hour personal message to his wife. "If I don't know what I am about to do, I'm going to be separated from you anyway because you know very well when the circumstances and facts are made known, this will be only result possible." . . .

. . . [H]e registered in one motel after another [and] was seen and remembered in the bars in several skid rows in Akron, Canton, and Cleveland. . . .

Whoever or whatever directs the destinies of men brought Robert Domer and Howard Riddle together in a cheap Akron bar. On a misty Friday night, April 19th, Riddle approached Domer and asked him to buy him a beer. . . . It was now Monday, April 22. After a meaningless drive to Youngstown, Domer and Riddle returned to the Top-O-The-Mark, where they had been staying . . . . Domer was hungry, so he left to get food to bring back to the room. . . .

When he returned, perhaps two hours later, he saw that "obviously, something was very much wrong." Riddle's motionless body sprawled across the bed, the pillows lying on the floor. There was vomit on the headboard of the bed and on the wall. . . .

"Sometime [the next] afternoon," Domer testified, "I decided to have an accident and leave his body in the car for me." . . . Late in the night of Monday, April 22nd, Robert Domer . . . waited, waited for the train to make its way to the Deerfield crossing. . . . He then doused the body with a can of gasoline. . . .

When Domer heard the train approaching, he struck his match and threw it into the car . . . . The body and car literally blew up in his face, causing second and third degree burns. He realized with horror that he also was on fire . . . then he saw the approaching train was a passenger train instead of a freight train . . . . He was able to run back to the car, release the brakes, cramp the wheels, and let the car roll down off the track. . . .

---

*Reprinted by permission of Mary D. Houts.

The engineer's radio call to the Orrville Control Tower turned the first official wheel that finally stopped in the Canton courtroom. . . . The investigators at the scene were not particularly startled to find a human body, grotesquely contorted and twisted, in the front seat of the car. The face was almost totally destroyed, the arms and legs burned off, the chest wall and abdomen burned away, and the sex organs gone. The intense heat had cracked the bones of the head, which had become friable and brittle. . . . Shortly [after 2 p.m.], Dr. Lester Adelson, Chief Deputy Coroner and Pathologist for Cuyahoga County, began his autopsy. . . .

Back at the Deerfield crossing, investigators found charred portions of a wallet belonging to Robert Domer. They also found his Playboy Club key. Scorched credit cards crumbled in the fingers of the investigators . . . .

This, roughly, was the information available to the investigators and to Dr. Adelson as he began his autopsy on the shrunken seventy-seven pounds of charred bone, skin, muscle and cartilage that was identified as the body of Robert K. Domer. . . . Between twelve and thirteen hours had elapsed since the blazing automobile was first observed by the train crew. The gums of this badly decomposed, brutally charred body were bare. There were no signs of recent extractions. This person's teeth had obviously all been removed some time earlier. Further, there was an odd infarct in the walls of the heart, an area of scar tissue caused by a severe heart attack which had taken place at least weeks or months earlier. The area of scar tissue was sufficiently large so that the person probably would have been hospitalized as a result of the heart attack. . . . Evelyn Domer said her husband had never suffered a heart attack. Furthermore, he had a full set of strong teeth . . . .

An entirely new and different medico-legal problem was injected, one that Dr. Adelson had not faced at the time that he performed his autopsy. The question can be phrased simply: Was Howard Riddle alive at the time the fire in the automobile started? . . . If Howard Riddle was alive, then Robert was a murderer . . . . If, on the other hand, Howard Riddle was dead before the fire began, Robert Domer was not a murderer, and was guilty only of the lesser offense of destroying a dead human body. . . .

The state's medical witnesses faced . . . challenging hurdles . . . to prove that Howard Riddle was alive at the time the fire started. [One was to] show that Riddle took at least one breath after the fire started. . . .

Dr. Adelson had removed thin layers of tissue from the area of Riddle's throat during the autopsy. These were mounted on glass slides so that they could be preserved and studied; and they were built into a large composite photograph which was used at the trial.

The slides of prime interest involved the epithelium covering the vocal cords. . . . Epithelium is the "cemented" structure of cells that lines and covers the internal and external surfaces of the body and its organs.

Dr. Mortiz' testimony at this point refers to these epithelial surfaces: . . .

Q. What conclusion do you come to then with respect to the direction the heat came from that burned off the epithelium?

A. The conclusion I came to was that one or more breaths of very hot air or flame passed over this surface in order to make these heat changes so much more pronounced at that surface than they are a fraction of an inch below it.

Q. Your word "flame" includes burning vapor?

A. It would. . . .

Q. Will you illustrate now on the blackboard, if I can find some chalk, just where the voice box is located?

A. If the circle represents a section right straight through the neck with the spinal column here (indicating) and the voice box here (indicating), with the vocal chords in that kind of a position. . . .

Q. You described in detail the heat changes that you observed on this photograph. Did you observe changes of that quality or characteristic below the voice box?

A. Yes. . . .

This was the state of the medical evidence when Dr. Helpern took the witness stand as the defendant's prime medical witness.

"Now, Dr. Helpern, based upon your study of the autopsy record prepared by Dr. Adelson, based upon these pictures and based further upon reasonable medical certainty, do you have an opinion as to whether the body found in the car at the Deerfield crossing was alive at the time the fire started?" . . .

"I have an opinion."

"What is your opinion."

"In my opinion, the deceased in this case was not alive when the fire started."

"Can you explain the reasons for your opinion?"

"Two important considerations are certainly the findings of no carbon monoxide in the blood and no soot in the deep air passages of the lungs. I would say that over the years I have autopsied or supervised the autopsies of the bodies of at least two thousand persons who have died in fires or conflagrations. I have not encountered a single case of a person who was alive at the time these fires started who did not have carbon monoxide in the blood and soot in the lungs." . . .

"Now, sir, do you have other reasons for expressing the opinion that Howard Riddle was dead at the time the fire started?"

"Yes, the autopsy protocol contain certain findings which compel me to conclude that this person was not only dead at the time the conflagration took place, but had been dead for some time before. I refer to the descriptions of various organs of the body which show that advanced postmortem decomposition had already taken place before the body was incinerated."

"I think, Dr. Helpern, that you should explain to us just what you mean by decomposition and how it takes place." . . .

Judge Rosetti: Do you know that the vocal chords were burned in this man?

A. They could have burned.

Q. Is this what the protocol says?

A. No, sir.

Q. Doesn't that indicate that he breathed some hot gas?

A. No, it means there was a lot of heat around the mouth, and the mouth being a large place, and the nose, being a fairly large place, that material dropped back in there. That is not infrequently seen.

Judge Rosetti: It can also mean that he breathed some hot gas.

A. No, I don't think so. If he breathed in hot gas, he would have had to breathe in soot, he doesn't have any soot in the air passages. He would also have to have carbon. It just doesn't add up any other way. . . .

Mark Hansen
Body of Evidence*
American Bar Association Journal, June 1995, at 60

[A]n Ocean County, N.J., man found unconscious in a parking lot, was taken to a hospital with what the police described as a gunshot wound to the head. After 49 days in a coma, the victim, Robert Webb, died.

The doctors who initially examined the patient were skeptical. Webb had a laceration over the left eye, but there was no evidence of a penetrating wound, and X-rays showed no signs of a bullet. Yet their primary concern was to treat the injury, not to figure out what may have caused it.

Dr. James Kaye, the county medical examiner, assigned the autopsy to a hospital pathologist, who apparently accepted the police account of what had happened at face value. He not only certified the cause of death as a gunshot wound but dutifully described the path of a bullet through the victim's head. Afterward, a suspect, Willie Simpson, was arrested and charged with the crime.

The only trouble was, as shown in a review of the original autopsy report by an outside expert in preparation for Simpson's trial, Webb had not been shot. He died of blunt force trauma, according to the expert, whose findings were consistent with the account of an eyewitness who said the victim had been hit in the head with a brick thrown by somebody other than the defendant. Charges against Simpson were dropped, but no one else has been prosecuted.

---

*Reprinted with permission from the June 1995 *ABA Journal,* The Lawyers Magazine, published by the American Bar Association.

Robert Konzelmann, the assistant public defender who represented Simpson, says he was not surprised by the turn of events in the case against his client. Konzelmann says he once represented a man charged in the stabbing death of another man who was later found to have died from a beating. "The closer you look at some of these autopsy reports, the more you find," he says. . . .

Dr. Werner Spitz, former chief medical examiner for Wayne County, Mich., and a consulting forensic pathologist near Detroit, estimates that up to 70 percent of the nation is poorly served by its system for investigating unnatural deaths. "Is this an enlightened system?" he asks. "No, it's not. It's really no better than what they have in many Third World countries." Death investigators, be they coroners or medical examiners, wield enormous power. In most states, by law, all unnatural deaths — including but not limited to homicides, suicides and accidents — are supposed to be investigated. So, too, in many states, are sudden, unusual, suspicious, unattended or drug-related deaths.

But it is the medical examiner or the coroner who determines the course and scope of any investigation, including whether an autopsy, X-rays or toxicology tests should be done and, if so, who should do them. And it is the medical examiner or the coroner who is ultimately responsible for certifying the cause and manner of death.

Of the nearly 2.2 million deaths reported in the United States in 1992, almost 7 percent, or nearly 143,000 deaths, were classified as unnatural, according to the U.S. Department of Health and Human Services' Division of Vital Statistics.

As a rule of thumb, autopsies are performed in about half of all the deaths that end up being investigated. About 95 percent of the time, the cause and manner of death are readily apparent. It is the remaining 5 percent or so of cases in which the answers are not always so obvious. . . .

To understand the way the system operates, it is important to note that even the use of the word "system" to describe a process that encompasses more than 3,000 individual jurisdictions is a misnomer. There is no uniform method for certifying deaths in this country, and no two states do it exactly alike.

In some states, the process even varies from county to county. Roughly half the nation's population comes under the jurisdiction of coroners, although there are far more places with coroners than there are with medical examiners. The rest of the population falls under the jurisdiction of medical examiners, usually a doctor who is appointed to the job based on merit.

Coroners are usually laypeople who are elected to their jobs. Even today, the qualifications for becoming a coroner, where they exist, typically only address such variables as age, residency and voting status.

Only four states, Kansas, Louisiana, North Dakota and Ohio, require that a coroner be a doctor. In North Dakota, the requirement only applies to counties with more than 8,000 people. Louisiana makes an exception for parishes in which no doctor is willing to serve. In other states, the qualifications are far more lenient. South Carolina, for example, requires only a high school diploma.

In fact, a disproportionate number of coroners are funeral home directors who fell into their line of work because they happened to be in the business of transporting bodies. Sheriff's deputies, school bus drivers and tow truck operators also have served as coroners. So have gas station attendants, tavern owners, jewelry salesmen and accountants.

To be sure, some coroners do exemplary work. And a well-trained coroner who recognizes his or her own limitations can do a better job than a doctor with little or no training in investigating deaths.

"I'm not an expert in anything," says Sue Townsend, the plain-spoken Aiken County, S.C., coroner and president of the South Carolina Coroners Association. "I consider myself a liaison. And when I need somebody [like an entomologist] to tell me how long a body's been in the ground, I know who to call."

Few coroners have had any formal medical training. Many operate on a shoestring budget, which forces them to cut corners whenever and wherever they can. And too many rely for autopsies on hospital pathologists, who are trained to study the ravages of disease, not to reconstruct how somebody died.

"Asking a hospital pathologist to do an autopsy on the victim of a violent death is like asking a dermatologist to perform brain surgery," says [Dr. Michael] Baden [director] of the New York State Police [forensic sciences unit].

Many coroners insist there is nothing wrong with the system that is not already being addressed by a movement within the profession to improve training and qualifications.

And they point out that a majority of states with coroner systems, South Carolina included, recently have upgraded requirements for the office and implemented mandatory on-the-job training.

"It really makes no difference who sits behind the desk as long as you know what to do and you have good people working for you," says Herbert Buzbee, the Peoria County, Ill., coroner and past president of the International Association of Coroners and Medical Examiners.

Since nearly all coroners are elected, they also contend that they are less susceptible to political pressure from other officials and are more accountable to their constituents than medical examiners.

"If a medical examiner screws up, he only has to answer to a chosen few," Buzbee says. "If a coroner screws up, there will be hell to pay in the next election."

Still and all, it would be hard to argue with the proposition that death investigations would best be left in the hands of experts, especially in an age of rapidly advancing technology in the field of forensic science, such as DNA analysis on hair and bones.

That is not to say that medical examiner systems do not come with their own, individualized set of problems.

Only a handful of the states and some of the largest urban areas with medical examiner systems require that death investigations be conducted by board-certified or board-eligible forensic pathologists, specialists with advanced training in analyzing traumatic injuries such as blunt force, poison, and gunshot and stab wounds.

A major problem is the shortage of skilled personnel. Of the nearly 671,000 doctors licensed to practice in the United States, less than 3 percent, or 17,149 doctors, are specialists in pathology, according to the American Medical Association.

Only 435 of them are board-eligible forensic pathologists, of whom 335 are board-certified. Not all forensic pathologists are working full time; at least 12 states do not employ any at all.

One reason there are not enough qualified professionals to go around is the work itself, which can be both dirty and demanding. Medical examiners are on call 24 hours a day. Their caseloads can be crushing. Many of their offices are chronically understaffed and ill-equipped. And they must be comfortable spending a lot of their time in court.

"It takes a special kind of person to do this type of work," says Dr. Patricia McFeeley, New Mexico's assistant chief medical investigator. "[The job] may be a lot of things, but it's never boring."

The relatively poor pay of a medical examiner does not help the situation, either. While a pathologist must spend an additional year in training and pass another set of board exams to become certified in forensic pathology, he or she is likely to make far less money than a hospital pathologist in private practice. Most medical examiners earn less than $100,000 a year, while a hospital pathologist can earn twice as much or more.

As a result, many medical examiners supplement their income by moonlighting. Some earn more in consulting fees than they make from their jobs as full-time medical examiners.

The political aspects of the job can be another big drawback. Medical examiners are subject to a variety of pressures from competing interests. Although most of them are appointed, they work at the pleasure of elected officials, who may have a vested interest in the outcome of an investigation.

And while many medical examiners would deny ever having been pressured to change their findings, the nature of the job is such that they cannot avoid stepping on toes.

"If a decision helps the prosecutor, it hurts the defense. If it helps the insured, it hurts the insurance company," Baden says. "It's very awkward to be a doctor in the public sector."

Also, in the larger scheme of things, the needs of the medical examiner's office typically are regarded as a low priority. After all, its only constituency is the dead. And the dead, as more than one medical examiner is quick to point out, don't vote. . . .

Unfortunately, while the system's shortcomings may be all too obvious, a solution is much more elusive. Some forensic pathologists suggest giving medical examiners civil service status or allying them more closely with medical schools, which have a strong tradition of independence. Some advocate setting up regional forensic science centers that would offer continuing education and the services of an expert as needed; others propose that creation of a private system that would operate on a fee-for-service basis.

But nearly all agree on the need for higher salaries to lure more bright doctors to the field, a uniform set of national standards to govern the profession, better training for employees to minimize the potential for error, and improved funding to ensure that each investigation gets the attention it deserves.

The public should demand no less.

Theodore J. Curphey
Role of the Forensic Pathologist
in the Medicolegal Certification
of Modes of Death*
13 Journal of Forensic Sciences 163 (1968)

In a metropolitan community, figures show that 20 to 25 percent of the total deaths are currently reported [to the medical examiner's office]. Deaths from homicide rarely exceed 5 percent of the total coming to the attention of the medicolegal authorities . . . and by and large receive detailed study by the criminal investigator and the pathologist, the toxicologist, and the district attorney, as well as the medical examiner.

The importance of a complete and accurate investigation of a homicide by the forensic pathologist stands without question and must always carry a high priority in the workload of any active medicolegal office. When one considers, however, that some offices see about 10 percent of their caseloads as suicides, 25 percent as accidents of all kinds, about 60 percent as natural deaths, and up to 5 percent as homicides, the forensic pathologist . . . must find some means of rendering equally good service in the study of all the types of cases he sees. . . .

Unfortunately, this is not the guiding principle in many of our offices, where the medical personnel, as well as the laboratory and clerical organization are geared to serve the high priority case of homicide at the distinct expense of the non-homicide case . . . .

[W]hile sudden death resulting from accident, suicide, or homicide is almost invariably reported to the medical examiner, many delayed deaths of one type or another are certified by the physician and accepted for registration by the Health Department . . . . By so doing, in many instances they unwittingly deny the family their legal access to certain economic indemnities . . . . This is especially true in delayed deaths related to trauma and also in industrial or occupational hazards

* Extracted with permission from the *Journal of Forensic Sciences,* Vol. 31, No. 2, copyright American Society for Testing and Materials, 100 Barr Harbor Drive, West Conshohocken, PA 19428.

where the terminal stage of the disease arises directly from the hazard and is associated, for example, with certain blood dyscrasias such as aplastic anemia, or to pulmonary disease of a chronic inflammatory or neoplastic nature, or to disease of the genitourinary tract, or to hepatorenal involvement.

In such instances the physician certifying the death frequently fails to recognize the probable causal relationship and thus does not report it to the medical examiner, with the result that the economic interests of the family are either seriously impaired or totally denied because of the lack of supporting pathological evidence derived from the autopsy studies, if indeed, the case ever reaches the stage of adjudication. Added to this is vitiation of the vital statistics as to the mortality rate from the particular industrial or occupational hazard in the community, which in turn denies the Health Department the opportunity to institute preventive measures to combat the hazard. . . .

Turning now to the methods of investigation . . . , the current practice is [a multidisplinary] approach in which the skills of the law enforcement officer, the pathologist, and the toxicologist are those most generally involved. . . .

There is, however, a group of cases of growing importance and size . . . where suicide is suspected [and where] the need arises for the behavioral scientist to become involved . . . .

[The pathologist] is frequently all too willing to . . . venture into the area of certification of the mode [rather than the cause of death] when he has little if any knowledge of human behavior vital to being able to evaluate, with any fair degree of accuracy, the mental processes of the victim that were likely to lead to a suicidal death. . . .

Perhaps the consequence of this attitude is best illustrated by a [1965] survey of the reporting of modes of death, specifically from barbituate intoxication, by 19 of the larger medicolegal offices in the nation . . . . [This survey suggests that] only five offices are properly certifying their cases of suicide, two offices their undetermined cases, and three offices their accidental deaths. . . .

NOTES

1. *Dimensions of forensic pathology.* Dr. Curphey's paper depicts the responsibilities of the forensic pathologist and toxicologist working together in a coroner's office or the office of a chief medical examiner. Additional descriptions of the work of forensic pathologists, written especially for attorneys, include 2 Paul C. Giannelli & Edward J. Imwinkelried, Scientific Evidence 41-109 (2d ed. 1993); Cyril Wecht, Forensic Pathology for Trial Lawyers, in Scientific and Expert Evidence 1141 (Edward Imwinkelried ed., 2d ed. 1981); Robert Bucklin, Forensic Pathology, in Scientific and Expert Evidence 1165 (Edward Imwinkelried ed., 2d ed. 1981); John F. Devlin, The Autopsy in Criminal Cases, in Scientific and Expert Testimony 1205 (Edward Imwinkelried ed., 2d ed. 1981). See also Dominic J. Di

Maio et al., Forensic Pathology (1989); Isidor Gordon et al., Forensic Medicine: A Guide to Principles (3d ed. 1988); Bernard Knight, Forensic Pathology (1991); Forensic Medicine: An Illustrated Reference (John K. Mason ed., 1993); Douglas Ubelaker & Henry Scammell, Bones: A Forensic Detective's Casebook (1992); Charles V. Wetli et al., Practical Forensic Pathology (1988).

Murder investigation may be the most glamorous aspect of the work, but, as Curphey emphasizes, it is merely one of many important and challenging types of investigation. See, e.g., David M. Paul, The General Principles of Clinical Forensic Medicine and the Place of Forensic Medicine in a Modern Society, 50 Yale J. Biology & Med. 405 (1977); Symposium on the Adversary System and the Role of the Forensic Scientist: "Scientific Truth" vs. "Legal Truth," 18 J. Forensic Sci. 173 (1973).

2. *Importance of autopsies.* The value of autopsies to accurate determinations of the causes of death has been well documented, e.g., S. Asnaes & F. Paaskeail, Uncertainty of Determining Mode of Death in Medicolegal Material Without Autopsy — A Systematic Autopsy Study, 15 Forensic Sci. Int'l 3 (1980); S. Asnaes & F. Paaske, The Significance of Medicolegal Autopsy in Determining Mode and Cause of Death, 14 Forensic Sci. Int'l 23 (1979), and the need for specialized training in forensic, as opposed to general pathology, has been noted. William Eckert, The Forensic or Medicolegal Autopsy: Friend or Foe? 9 Am. J. Forensic Med. & Pathology 185 (1988). The assassination of President John F. Kennedy is a glaring example of how critical an accurate and complete autopsy report can be to a medicolegal investigation. The forensic pathologists' failure to make a complete report contributed to the lingering controversy and speculation over the exact cause of the president's death. See, e.g., Cyril Wecht, A Critique of the Medical Aspects of the Investigation into the Assassination of President Kennedy, 11 J. Forensic Sci. 300 (1966). For a stark comparison of postmortem protocols that illustrates the importance of the procedure, see Thomas Noguchi, Postmortem Protocols in Official Medical-Legal Investigation — A Study in Contrast (Autopsy Reports in the Assassination Deaths of President John F. Kennedy and Senator Robert F. Kennedy), 1973 Legal Med. Ann. 21.

In addition to their obvious significance to the criminal justice system and the payment of insurance benefits, accurate determinations of death are important to the public health system. David Lilienfeld, Changing Research Methods in Environmental Epidemiology, 3 Stat. Sci. 275, 277 (1988); Mark Rosenberg et al., Operational Criteria for the Determination of Suicide, 33 J. Forensic Sci. 1445, 1446 (1988) ("Although the accuracy of one single [death] certificate may not appear important, collectively the enormous number of death certificates filed becomes the primary data source for mortality statistics in the United States. These data in turn affect the course of health care research, the flow of resources, and, ultimately, public health policy."). But see Carol Conroy & Julie C. Russell, Medical Examiner-Coroner Records: Uses and Limitations in Occupational Injury

Epidemiologic Research, 35 J. Forensic Sci. 932, 933 (1990) ("Although medical examiner-coroner records have not been used extensively by epidemiologists, their usefulness is being increasingly realized."). Non-forensic autopsies also are quite important to the development of medicine and quality control in hospitals. Norman T. Belinger, A Mortal Science, Discovery, Sept. 1994, at 30. Yet, U.S. hospitals perform autopsies on only 10% of their deceased patients, compared to 30 to 50% a quarter century ago. Id. at 31.

   3. *Coroners and medical examiners.* The coronership, established in England in 1194, has undergone considerable change over the centuries. The coroner was an elected official who was not required to be legally or medically qualified. The salary was meager, but if an inquest led to a conviction, the coroner received a portion of the prisoner's goods and chattels. The system did not stimulate thorough investigations of apparently accidental deaths or even suspicious ones that lacked obvious suspects. The result was "corruption and neglect: many homicides were not investigated at all, or at best perfunctorily." Thomas R. Forbes, Surgeons at the Bailey: English Forensic Medicine to 1878, 11 (1985).

   Calls for the replacement of elected coroners with professional medical examiners also have a venerable history. See O. Shultz & E. Morgan, The Coroner and the Medical Examiner (National Research Council 1928); Model Post-Mortem Examination Act, Handbook of the National Conference of commissioners on Uniform State Laws 196-202 (1954). The news article by Mark Hansen indicates, however, that only a minority of U.S. jurisdictions use medical examiners, and even in those jurisdictions the minimum qualifications for the position are not always demanding. According to a survey of the 20 states with medical examiners and the five states with mixed state medical examiner and county coroner-medical examiner systems reported in Joseph A. Prahlow & Patrick E. Lantz, Medical Examiner-Death Investigator Training Requirements in State Medical Examiners Systems, 40 J. Forensic Sci. 55, 57 (1995), "46% of the systems require no formal training, and 33% of those which 'require' continuing education fail to enforce that requirement."

   4. *Civil liability for death examinations.* What steps should be taken to improve death investigations? The previous note raised the question of whether the remaining coroners should be replaced with medical examiners and what qualifications death examiners by any name should have. In addition, we might ask whether officials who perform death investigations should face tort liability for their mistakes. Should there be an action for what amounts to "autopsy malpractice"? See, e.g., Dean v. Chapman, 556 P.2d 257 (Okla. 1976); William Curran, Damage Suits Against Medical Examiners for Authorized Autopsies, 297 New Eng. J. Med. 1220 (1977). And, consider this report:

   > Kenneth Reno knows all too well what can happen when something
   > goes wrong. In 1991, the Detroit-area man spent nearly six months in jail

awaiting trial for a double murder he did not commit.

Reno was watching television with his 21-year-old daughter, Robin, one night when he broke his dentures on a kernel of popcorn. His wife, Carlynne, was in bed, asleep.

He went to the store to get some glue, and when he returned a half-hour later he found his wife dead and his daughter mortally wounded. Each had been stabbed more than a dozen times.

When he asked his daughter who had stabbed her, he says she replied, "Tommy . . . Tom Collins." When he asked her who Collins was, he says she identified him as a friend of the father of her 2-year-old daughter.

Moments later, Reno's daughter died. The next day, Reno was charged with two counts of murder. He was prosecuted mainly on the strength of an autopsy report that stated his daughter's vocal cords had been cut, rendering her incapable of speech.

Despite the autopsy report, Assistant Wayne County Prosecutor Dan Less had doubts about Reno's guilt. Reno did not know the man he says his daughter named as her killer. And it did not make sense for him to make up the story because the whereabouts of the man he had accused could easily be checked.

The autopsy report on Reno's wife provided another clue that something was amiss. It stated that the woman had natural teeth that were still intact, when Less knew the victim had false teeth that had been knocked out during the attack.

So the prosecutor asked four outside experts, including a throat specialist, to review the autopsy report and Robin Reno's larynx, which had been preserved as evidence. All four concluded that her vocal cords had not been cut, making Reno's story all the more credible.

Six months later, Tom Collins, the man Reno's daughter had identified as her assailant, was arrested for a burglary. Eventually, he confessed to the killings and was sentenced to life in prison.

In his confession, Collins implicated the child's paternal grandmother, Linda Lambert, who he says wanted Robin Reno dead so that she could get custody of her granddaughter. Lanbert was subsequently convicted of breaking and entering, an two counts of manslaughter, for which she is now serving a 6 1/2- to 15-year prison sentence.

Reno, who went on to sue the police for false arrest and malicious prosecution, reached a settlement last year for an undisclosed amount of money. He is still appealing the dismissal of his suit against the medical examiner's office, which a judge has ruled is protected by governmental immunity.

"There needs to be some kind of safeguards put in place," Reno says of the system. "It might cost a little more money, but where there's a life involved, it would be worth it."

Mark Hansen, Body of Evidence, A.B.A.J., June 1995, at 60.

5. *Limits of expertise.* The opinions rendered by forensic pathologists on the cause of death can hardly be based *exclusively* on what they see or find on the autopsy table. But when they rely on facts equally accessible to the lay person, does there come a point at which they exceed the area of their expertise? Consider the following opinion rendered by Dr. Milton Helpern, then chief medical examiner for the city of New York, in a notorious case involving a mother, Alice Crimmins, accused of murdering her children:

> "Would you say, Dr. Helpern, that the little boy died a natural death?"
> This was the first time this question had been asked in public. Now, I had no evidence of a direct nature to answer that — the body was a mass of corruption and could give no clues, except to exclude massive violence to bones and tissues like an extensive fracture or gunshot wound.
> But I was a medical examiner, and my job was to assess deaths by a full consideration of what I knew about the whole case history. To focus narrowly on the autopsy table, like a horse with blinkers, would be pedantic and foolish. If you are searching the horizon, you don't look down the end of a fixed telescope. He asked me "Did he die a natural death?" and I knew as the whole of New York and half the United States knew, that little Eddie had been in perfect health the night before he vanished. I knew that he had been found a mile or more from his home, hidden under scrub on a waste lot. I knew his sister had vanished at the same time and had been found strangled. So what possible reason could I — or anyone else in my position — have for evading the issue. The boy had not died a natural death!
> "I would not say that," I told Nicolosi, "and I base my opinion on the classification of the death, the circumstances of the death of the sister, the findings, and so on. It is a conclusion about the manner of death derived from knowledge of the circumstances of the case and of the cause of death of the sister. I would say, in my opinion, that this was not a natural death."

Milton Helpern, Autopsy: The Memoirs of Milton Helpern, the World's Greatest Medical Detective 137 (1977). Was this testimony based on expertise in forensic pathology?[1] Was it an expert opinion that would, in the words of Federal Rule of Evidence 702, "assist the trier of fact to understand the evidence or to determine a fact in issue"? See Daniel Steinbock et al., Expert Testimony on Proximate Cause, 41 Vand. L. Rev. 261 (1988); Bernard Robertson & G.A. Vignaux, Interpreting Evidence: Evaluating Forensic Science in the Courtroom (1995); Willem Wagenaar, The Proper Seat: A Bayesian Discussion of the Position of Expert Witnesses, 12 Law & Hum. Behav. 499 (1988).

---

[1] Dr. Helpern's testimony is criticized in David M. Spain, Post-Mortem 135-55 (1974). Dr. Spain testified as an expert for the defense in the case. For the last of the many opinions involving the trial, appeal, reversal, retrial, and later appeals, see People v. Crimmins, 343 N.E.2d 407 (N.Y. 1975).

6. *"Psychological autopsies."* Dr. Curphey's paper stresses the need for psychological stress and suicide investigation in many cases. See also James Selkin, The Psychological Autopsy in the Courtroom (1987); Edwin Shneidman, Psychological Autopsy, 49 Am. Psychologist, Jan. l994, at 75; Robert Litman, Psycho-Legal Aspects of Suicide, in Modern Legal Medicine, Psychiatry and Forensic Science 841 (William J. Curran et al. eds., 1980); Robert Litman, Psychological-Psychiatric Aspects of Certifying Modes of Death, 13 J. Forensic Sci. 46 (1968); G.E. Murphy et al., On the Improvement of Suicide Determination, 19 J. Forensic Sci. 276 (1974); Charles Vorkoper & Charles Petty, Suicide Investigation, in Modern Legal Medicine, Psychiatry and Forensic Science 171 (William J. Curran et al. eds., 1980).

The "psychological autopsy" technique "involves interviewing family members and reviewing records — generally employment records, school records and psychiatric notes. Its purpose is to determine the probable cause of death or the person's state of mind at the time of the death." Harvey v. Raleigh Police Dep't, 355 S.E. 2d 147, 148 (N.C. Ct. App. 1987). "[B]y reconstructing the decedent's final days behavior and communication in addition to history, personal habits, personality traits and character, [b]ehavioral science investigators develop a psychological profile through interviews with family, friends, co-workers, physicians and others . . . ." David Jobes, The Impact of Psychological Autopsies on Medical Examiners' Determination of Manner of Death, 31 J. Forensic Sci. 177, 178 (1986) (concluding that such investigations provide significant information in cases of equivocal deaths).

On the admissibility of these "psychological autopsies," compare *Harvey* (opinion of expert in "psychiatry, suicidology and police stress" who had conducted "hundreds of psychological autopsies" admissible in workers' compensation proceeding to show that depression attributable to work-related stress caused police officer's suicide) with State v. Butzlaff, 493 N.W.2d 1 (1992) (opinion based on psychological autopsy that deceased acted in self-defense inadmissible); Thompson v. Mayes, 707 S.W.2d 951 (Tex. Civ. App. 1986) (opinion of psychologist who had conducted "psychological autopsy" of suicide victim on whether the deceased had killed his father, who had disappeared two years earlier, properly excluded). On other psychiatric aspects of homicide investigation, see Frank Keil, The Psychiatric Character of the Assailant as Determined by Autopsy Observations of the Victim, 10 J. Forensic Sci. 263 (1965).

7. *References.* General texts that discuss forensic pathology and toxicology include Lester Adelson, The Pathology of Homicide (1974); Modern Legal Medicine, Psychiatry and Forensic Science (W.J. Curran et al. eds. 1980); Forensic Medicine: A Study in Trauma and Environmental Hazards (C.G. Tedeschi et al. eds., 1977); Medicolegal Investigation of Death: Guidelines for the Application of Pathology to Crime Investigation (Werner U. Spitz & Russell S. Fisher eds., 1993). Some of the leading British texts are Glaister's Medical

Jurisprudence and Toxicology (Edgar Rentoul & Hamilton Smith eds., 13th ed. 1973); Gradwohl's Legal Medicine (Francis Camps ed., 3d ed. 1976); B. Knight, Forensic Pathology (1991); Cyril J. Polson et al., The Essentials of Forensic Medicine (4th ed. 1985); Keith Simpson, Forensic Medicine (9th ed. 1985); Taylor's Principles and Practice of Medical Jurisprudence (A. Keith Mant ed., 13th ed. 1984).

Chapter 4
Bringing the Autopsy into the Courtroom

People v. Yoho
517 N.E. 2d 329 (Ill. 1987)

JUSTICE HOPF delivered the opinion of the court:

Defendant, Carroll Yoho, and his brother, Darrell, were charged in Winnebago County with the crime of murder. The brothers were tried jointly before a jury which returned a verdict finding defendant guilty of voluntary manslaughter and not guilty of murder. Darrell Yoho was exonerated of all charges. . . .

In this court, defendant contends . . . that he was denied his right to a fair trial when the trial court allowed an autopsy photograph depicting the decedent's exposed heart within his chest cavity to be submitted to the jury for its deliberation . . . .

In the early hours of November 23, 1985, an altercation occurred between the Yoho brothers and the victim, Ron Gibson, at a tavern . . . . Several witnesses for the prosecution related seeing the altercation between the two Yohos and Ron Gibson. [They testified to the effect that in the parking lot outside the tavern Darrell beat Gibson with a cane and that defendant stabbed him repeatedly in the chest and back, while Gibson, who was unarmed, merely tried to block these blows.]

Dr. Larry Blum, who performed the autopsy on the decedent, also testified for the State. Dr. Blum found knife wounds in the chest, in the bladder above the genitals, on the left side of the back, near the shoulder, in the left upper chest, over the left hip, on the scalp in the left parietal area, and on the penis. In addition to the knife wounds, Blum found multiple abrasions and contusions on Gibson's body as well as blunt trauma wounds. Blum described in detail the stab wound in Gibson's upper chest which punctured his heart. Blum also identified People's exhibit No. 11 as being a photograph of the internal organs of the chest, specifically showing the heart and the stab wound present in the right ventricle of the heart.

[Testimony from defense witnesses indicated that Gibson was a violent person who had provoked and threatened defendant in the tavern, then attacked him in the parking lot.]

Defendant's witness Dr. William Rouse, a general and forensic pathologist, gave an opinion as to the ability of the heart to self-seal itself upon being punctured. He also testified as to the length of time a person could continue activity depending upon the size of the hole made in the person's heart. Rouse described the hole in Gibson's heart as portrayed in People's exhibit No. 11, an autopsy photograph depicting the exposed heart within the chest cavity, to be a middle-sized wound and surmised its size three-fourths of an inch long and about one-eight of an inch wide. Rouse estimated that a person with a wound of that size could continue functioning for a period of time as short as a minute and as long as 7 to 10 minutes. In Rouse's opinion, an individual with a wound of this size would be able to continue fighting if he had already been fighting. The doctor also opined that the wound displayed in the photograph of the heart in People's exhibit No. 11 could continue to pump some blood throughout the victim's system while he continued acting.

The court permitted People's exhibit No. 11 to go to the jury over the specific objection of counsel for the defendant. Defendant contends on appeal that permitting People's exhibit No. 11 to go to the jury for its deliberations was prejudicial and denied defendant a fair trial. At trial defendant did not contest the fact that he stabbed the decedent since his theory of defense was self-defense. Defendant maintains that, when a defendant admits to an offense, gruesome photographs of a victim are rarely admissible since they are not probative of any material fact. See People v. Lefler (1967), 38 Ill. 2d 216, 221-22, 230 N.E. 2d 827 (court erred in permitting autopsy photo showing an infant's chest cavity after the breastbone portion of the ribs, lungs, heart and main blood vessels had been removed and showing the skull and portions of the brain after an area of the skull had been removed to be projected on a 44- x 26-inch screen); People v. Garlick (1977), 46 Ill. App. 3d 216, 224, 4 Ill. Dec. 746, 360 N.E. 2d 1121 (court erred in allowing a gruesome, color photograph of the deceased's massive head wound).

As a physician testified concerning the stab wounds and the undisputed cause of death, defendant argues that the autopsy picture had no probative value and no purpose "other than to horrify the jurors and arouse their emotions against the defendant." [D]efendant contends that the law is adamant that a photograph of a decedent taken after autopsy is not admissible. We do not agree.

It is the function of the trial court to weigh the probative value of evidence and its potential prejudicial effect. Mindful of the prejudice that might be aroused by the introduction of a victim's photograph, courts have been strict in their requirement that a proper purpose be shown for the introduction of such an exhibit. The decision, however, of what shall be taken into the jury room rests within the sound discretion of the trial court and will not be disturbed absent a showing of prejudicial abuse.

Photographic evidence having a natural tendency to establish the facts in controversy is admissible, and it is not an abuse of discretion to allow a jury to consider photographs depicted as disgusting or gruesome. The photograph in question was a color photo roughly 3 1/2 x 5 inches, depicting a close-up view of the heart and its wound within what appears to be the chest cavity. It does not show the body generally, and, but for the presence of the heart and its stab wound, one would not be able to determine what exactly it represented. Thus, People's exhibit No. 11 was not of the gruesome nature as those areas displayed in the blown-up photographs in *Lefler*. Moreover, we are of the opinion that the photograph in the instant case would have materially assisted the jury in understanding both Dr. Blum's and Dr. Rouse's testimony describing the wound to the heart and the result thereof. When taken in conjunction with an evaluation of all the photographs admitted, People's exhibit No. 11 would have materially gone to a fact in controversy, i.e., defendant's claim of self-defense. Hence, the photograph's relevance outweighed any prejudice. Further, based on the record before us and the overwhelming evidence of defendant's guilt in comparison to the nature of this one contested exhibit, we can say beyond a reasonable doubt that the photograph did not contribute to the verdict of guilty and that, therefore, any error in its admission would be harmless. . . .

Affirmed.

NOTES

1. *Pictures of crime scenes and autopsies.* Gruesome photographs of the victims of violent crimes are common grist for the prosecutor's mill. The standard for the admissibility of this type of evidence is codified in Rules 402 and 403 of the federal and uniform rules of evidence, which provide that relevant evidence is admissible unless its prejudicial effect substantially outweighs its probative value. See generally 1 McCormick on Evidence § 185 (John Strong ed., 4th ed. 1992). Pictures taken at the scene of the crime typically are admitted, as in *Yoho,* as long as they have some value in illustrating a pathologist's testimony as to the cause or circumstances of death. E.g., People v. Fierer, 503 N.E. 2d 594 (Ill. Ct. App. 1987) (25 color photographs depicting the defendant's ex-wife as she was found with 27 stab wounds); cf. David M. Spain, Post-Mortem 108 (1974) (six color slides of body of alleged informer executed by Black Panthers excluded as "inflammatory" following testimony from pathologist that "these pictures were of such a poor quality that they could serve no useful purpose in clarifying any of the facts regarding the time of death or cause of the bodily injuries.").

In Kealohapauole v. Shimoda, 800 F.2d 1463 (9th Cir. 1986), the court of appeals held that the due process clause was not offended when a 45-minute black and white videotape of an autopsy of a badly decomposed body found in a sugar cane field in Hawaii was shown in a murder prosecution, and where:

> One of the two pathologists in the case, Dr. Woo, testified that the videotape recording was the best type of available evidence to aid in explaining his testimony to the jury that the cause of the victim's death was a blow to the head with a blunt instrument. Dr. Woo stated that the videotape best illustrated the discoloration and fracture of the victim's skull, which led to Dr. Woo's conclusion that trauma in the skull had occurred as the result of a blow to the head with a blunt instrument. Although the skull was introduced into evidence, the videotape better illustrated the discoloration as

Dr. Woo stated that the stain on the skull had faded significantly since the autopsy. Dr. Woo also testified that the videotape would demonstrate the thoroughness of the pathologist's examination of the victim.

The Court of Appeals, which viewed the tape, described it as:

> in most part clinical in nature and is much clearer than the photographs introduced in evidence in showing the injury to the skull which is relied upon heavily by the pathologists in determining the cause of death. The videotape was taken in what appears to be an autopsy room, not at the scene of the crime. The autopsy procedure does not in itself cause the viewer to associate the process being watched in any way with the defendant, the scene of the crime, or the graphics of the murder. The videotape is unpleasant but not inflammatory. The portion of the videotape showing the pathologist inspecting the skull is of great probative value as it shows more clearly than the photos or the dried skull, the pathology relied upon by the doctors in making their determination of the cause of death.

The court noted also that the accused "refused to stipulate" that the death resulted from blows to the head with a blunt instrument. Would such a stipulation have led to different result? Even if a defendant is willing to stipulate to the cause of death, the government may be allowed to introduce its more graphic and realistic proof of the event. Cf. United States v. Grassi, 602 F.2d 1192 (5th Cir. 1979), vacated and remanded on other grounds, 448 U.S. 902 (1980). As one state supreme court justice explained:

> Defendants — and it is their right to try — want to keep as much grisly evidence from the jury as possible so that they can disassociate themselves from those black moments when their inhumanity surfaced and deliberately caused the death of another person. A sterile courtroom scene, removed as far as possible from the facts of the killing is what they seek. However, the state has a right to try its case and to recreate the crime as it was committed . . . .

Berry v. State, 718 S.W.2d 447, 455 (Ark. 1986) (Hickman, J., dissenting).

The *Kealohapauole* court suggested that a videotaped autopsy may be less troublesome than gruesome pictures of a crime scene, since "[t]he autopsy procedure does not in itself cause the viewer to associate the process being watched in any way with the defendant, the scene of the crime, or the graphics of the murder." Cf. Coleman v. Commonwealth, 307 S.E.2d 864, 873-74 (Va. 1983) ("an autopsy photograph by its very nature is more clinically objective and less bloody than one taken at the scene of a violent crime.").

Generally, however, the courts are more likely to balk at the admission of photographs taken during the autopsy than those of the scene. In State v. Poe, 441 P.2d 512 (Utah 1968), for instance, the defendant was convicted of murder and sentenced to die after the state used a series of color slides of an autopsy. According to the majority, to describe these slides as gruesome "would be a gross understatement. One of them, for example, depicted the deceased's head, showing the base of the skull after the skull cap and brain had been removed by the pathologist. The skin is peeled over the edge of the skull showing the empty brain cavity." The court reasoned that these slides "had no probative value" because "the identity of the deceased, his death and its cause had already been established" by photographs showing the victim as he was found lying in his bed with bullet holes in his head. Opinions in other jurisdictions maintain that autopsic photographs must be "necessary" or "essential" to the state's case. E.g., Berry v. State, 718 S.W.2d 447, 452 (Ark. 1986); People v. Fierer, 503 N.E. 2d 594 (Ill. Ct. App. 1987); State v. Clawson, 270 S.E.2d 659, 672 (W. Va. 1980).

2. *Three problems.* Applying the principles outlined above, how should a trial court rule in the following cases:

(1) Kuntzelman is alleged to have shot and killed Wilson with a .12 gauge shotgun. Eyewitnesses have testified that Wilson died as the result of the gunshot wound inflicted by Kuntzelman. Kuntzelman does not contest the cause of death, and the major issue to be decided by the jury is whether Kuntzelman intended to shoot Wilson or merely fire over his head to scare him.

The prosecution calls as a witness the pathologist who performed the autopsy on Wilson and questions him extensively on the nature of the wound and its relation to Wilson's death. In connection with this testimony, the prosecution offers into evidence six color photographs of Wilson's body and of his organs at various stages of the autopsy. One photograph depicts the open chest cavity and internal organs of Wilson's body, and another depicts Wilson's left lung placed on a slab or table. Kuntzelman objects that these two photographs are inflammatory. See State v. Kuntzelman, 337 N.W. 2d 414 (Neb. 1983); Kuntzelman v. Black, 774 F.2d 291 (8th Cir. 1985).

(2) Bowers is charged with cruelty to a child in violation of a Georgia child abuse statute. She arrived at the home of a neighbor one morning, saying that her two-year-old daughter, Kimberly, might be dead. She said that she had struck Kimberly for wetting her pants, and that the child had fallen into an empty bathtub. The two women immediately took Kimberly to a nearby hospital. Kimberly was dead on arrival. A pathologist performed an autopsy that disclosed bruises on Kimberly's scalp, face, chest, back and right lung, a scar on the inside of the lower lip, a fracture of the left side of her skull, a broken collar bone, a small tear in the liver and a lacerated heart, which he determined to have caused the death. Although Bowers is willing to stipulate that the injury to the heart was the cause of death, the government proffers a color photograph of the child's lacerated heart. Bowers objects. See United States v. Bowers, 660 F.2d 527 (5th Cir. 1981).

(3) Berry is accused of capital felony murder in connection with the brutal beating of her great-aunt, Nancy Sangalli. After plea bargaining, her boyfriend tes-

tifies that he and Berry went to Sangalli's home to knock her unconscious and to steal money to finance an escape from the country. He testifies further that he struck Sangalli from behind with a crowbar taken from Berry's house, but that she did not lose consciousness. When Sangalli tried to escape, he pulled her to the floor and began hitting her. He says that Berry came in as he dragged Sangalli away. The prosecution proffers nine photographs showing the trail of blood where Sangalli was dragged, her body in a pool of blood at the scene, closeup autopsy photographs of her face, a picture of the side of the head with the hair shaved to expose the injuries, and a closeup of her shattered teeth which the medical examiner removed from her mouth. Berry objects to the admission of all these color photographs, pointing out that she never touched the victim and that she does not contest the brutality of the murder, the cause of death or the identity of the killer. Her defense is that she was not aware of her boyfriend's intentions until she entered her aunt's house and that she fled the jurisdiction with him because he threatened to kill her. See Berry v. State, 718 S.W. 2d 447 (Ark. 1986).

Chapter 5
Alcohol Intoxication Tests

Lawrence Taylor
Drunk Driving Defense
8:3 (4th ed. 1994)

. . . The accused's right to jury trial has increasingly been supplanted by "trial by machine" — that is, innocence or guilt is largely determined by a breath analyzing machine. . . .

Many judges . . . will not even permit a drunk driving defendant to enter a plea at his arraignment until the results of the blood or urine analysis are returned from the crime lab. Prosecutors in many, if not most, jurisdictions will use the blood-alcohol reading in a given case as a gauge in plea bargaining. If a reading is below .10 percent, for example, a traffic violation may be offered in lieu of a plea of guilty; if the reading is between .11 percent and .14 percent, a plea to the lesser included offense of reckless driving may be offered; and if the figure is .15 percent or over, the prosecutor will probably insist on a straight plea as charged. Sentencing, too, is affected in many courts by the blood-alcohol level. As an example, one jurisdiction imposes one day in jail for each point above .10 percent . . . .

State v. Brayman
751 P.2d 294 (Wash. 1988)

BRACHTENBACH, JUSTICE.

This case involves the Legislature's 1986 amendments to three statutes involving driving while under the influence of intoxicants (DWI): RCW 46.61.502 (defining DWI), RCW 46.61.504 (defining actual physical control of vehicle while under the influence of intoxicants), and RCW 46.61.506 (setting forth admissible evidence and tests to establish driving or physical control of vehicle while under the influence of intoxicants) (hereinafter referred to as 1986 amendments). The district court found the 1986 amendments unconstitutional. The superior court affirmed. We granted direct review and reverse.

Prior to the 1986 amendments, a person driving a vehicle in this state with "0.10 percent or more by weight of alcohol in his blood as shown by chemical analysis of his breath, blood, or other bodily substance" was guilty of DWI. Effective June 11, 1986,[1] the Legislature redefined the "per se" DWI offense so as

---

[1] The Legislature again amended the DWI statutes in 1987 to reestablish the 0.10 blood alcohol per se standard as an alternative offense in addition to the breath alcohol per se offense enacted in 1986. The 1987 amendments are not at issue in this appeal.

to provide that a person is guilty if he "has 0.10 grams or more of alcohol *per two hundred ten liters of breath,* as shown by analysis of his breath, blood, or other bodily substance . . ." (Italics ours.)

Under the former statutory scheme, breath tests were used to establish the requisite blood-alcohol ratio for the per se DWI offense. Thus, evidence of the relationship between breath alcohol (the test used) and blood alcohol (the statutory element of the per se DWI offense) was relevant to the issue of whether the State had proved the necessary blood alcohol ratio beyond a reasonable doubt.

The 1986 amendments, by redefining the per se DWI offense in terms of breath-alcohol ratio, render evidence of the relationship of breath alcohol to blood alcohol irrelevant because breath alcohol content now forms an element of the per se DWI offense. The State need not prove any blood alcohol level under the 1986 amendments. Instead, the State must prove the necessary breath-alcohol ratio beyond a reasonable doubt.

Each respondent involved here was charged with driving while under the influence of intoxicants pursuant to RCW 46.61.502(1) and (2) (as amended in 1986). Two respondents are females and one is a black male. Each respondent submitted to a breath test and was found to have at least 0.10 grams of alcohol per 210 liters of breath. Each case was assigned to the Seattle District Court for trial. At various pretrial proceedings, respondents challenged the constitutionality of the Legislature's 1986 amendment of RCW 46.61.502(1). . . .

The district court granted respondents' motion to bar prosecution under former RCW 46.61.502(1) and to suppress the breath test results as evidence in prosecutions pursuant to the remaining sections of former RCW 46.61.502. The trial court concluded that the 1986 amendments were unconstitutional. Specifically, the court held that the 1986 amendments violate due process because they (1) include an improper "conclusive presumption" amounting to guilt by machine; (2) foreclose defendants' rights to present witnesses and evidence; and (3) violate principles of fundamental fairness. Moreover, the court ruled that the statutory scheme violates defendants' rights to confrontation and equal protection. The court found that the Legislature's intent in amending the statutes was to eliminate defendants' expert testimony relating to blood-breath ratios and thereby shorten trials and make convictions easier.

. . . The superior court affirmed the district court's rulings.

Scientific Background

Alcohol contained only in the breath does not cause intoxication. It is the impact of alcohol on the central nervous system, particularly on the brain, that causes the physical and psychological changes associated with impairment. Alcohol reaches the central nervous system through the blood. When used to establish blood alcohol levels, breath testing devices use a mathematical constant to approximate the percentage of alcohol in the blood based on the amount of alcohol present in a breath sample. All breath-testing devices currently used in the United States, including the two devices certified for use in Washington — the Smith and Wesson Breathalyzer 900A and the BAC Verifier DataMaster, use a conversion factor of 2100:1. The 2100:1 conversion factor is an assumed blood-breath ratio. The blood-breath ratio represents the relationship between the number of alcohol molecules in the bloodstream to the number present in the breath when both substances are tested simultaneously. Thus, a 2100:1 conversion factor assumes that for each molecule of alcohol in a given volume of breath, there are 2,100 molecules of alcohol in the same volume of blood.

Because blood-breath ratios vary both between individuals, and at different times in the same individual, a breath test based on a 2100:1 blood-breath ratio may not accurately represent a particular individual's blood alcohol level. If the actual blood-breath ratio is lower than 2100:1, a breath test will overestimate blood alcohol, and vice versa. Factors influencing an individual's blood-breath ratio include body temperature, hematocrit level (the ratio between red blood cells and blood plasma), and the time at which alcohol was consumed in relation to the time breath alcohol is measured. Higher than normal body temperatures resulting from fevers, exercise, and menstrual cycle variations in women result in a lower blood-breath ratio than normal. If all other factors are the same in a given individual, a breath test based on that individual's normal blood-breath ratio, given when body temperature is elevated, will overestimate that individual's actual blood alcohol level.

Moreover, because of the way alcohol is transferred from the blood to the lungs, the amount of alcohol in an individual's breath is not constant. Breath testing machines are designed to test the last portion of a person's breath. Typically, there is less alcohol in the first part of the breath than in the last part, which comes from deeper portions of the lungs, the alveolar sacs, where the alcohol is transferred from the blood to the lung air.

I. Due Process

The State challenges the district court's conclusion that the 1986 amendments violate defendants' due process rights by "creating a conclusive presumption that breath alcohol equals blood alcohol, and hence substitutes the judgement of a machine for the judgement of the jury." The superior court affirmed this finding, concluding the statute was "arbitrary in the sense that it is guilt by computer."

A conclusive presumption requires the trier of fact to find the existence of an elemental fact upon proof of a basic fact. A conclusive presumption cannot be used against a defendant in a criminal trial.

The State argues that the 1986 amendments do not create any presumption that breath alcohol equals blood alcohol. Instead, the State contends the 1986 amendments redefine the DWI crime in terms of breath alcohol, rendering blood alcohol irrelevant. The State concludes that the Legislature merely replaced one indicator of driving impairment (blood alcohol) with another (breath alcohol). Respondents argue that blood alcohol is not only an indicator of impairment as is breath alcohol, but actually causes impairment. Thus, by criminalizing breath alcohol, the Legislature attempts to indirectly regulate blood alcohol levels. Respondents conclude that this indirect regulation creates a conclusive presumption by allowing the State to prove a basic fact — breath alcohol — which requires the trier of fact to presume an elemental fact — blood alcohol and thus impairment. . . .

The record establishes that central nervous system alcohol actually causes impairment, and that blood is a transporter of alcohol to the central nervous system tissues. While evidence exists that alcohol in the bloodstream always indicates presence of alcohol in the central nervous system, and thus may cause intoxication in a but/for sense, the evidence establishes that only central nervous system alcohol directly causes intoxication. Even respondents acknowledge that "[s]hort of performing a test of brain tissue in an autopsy, a test of the blood is the most *direct* possible measure of a person's alcohol level." . . .

This court upheld the former blood alcohol per se offense as an alternative method of committing a DWI offense in *State v. Franco,* 96 Wash. 2d 816, 823, 639 P.2d 1320 (1982). Under the prior statutory scheme, a driver with .10 percent by weight of alcohol in his blood was per se DWI if the State proved the elements of the offense beyond a reasonable doubt. This court held that the per se statute did not create any presumption of impairment at that level of blood alcohol, but rather defined one alternative offense of DWI in those terms. Similarly, the 1986 amendments simply redefine the former per se crime in terms of breath alcohol and proof of the offense is essentially the same under the amendments as it was in the statutory scheme upheld in *Franco.* We conclude that the 1986 amendments do not create an impermissible conclusive presumption.

We also disagree with respondents' contention that by redefining the per se DWI offense in terms of breath alcohol, the 1986 amendments take away a defendant's right to present evidence to dispute the reading of the breath testing device. While the 1986 amendments render evidence of blood alcohol irrelevant to the extent it is introduced to disprove the relationship between blood and breath alcohol (the State no longer must prove blood alcohol levels), defendants may still present evidence challenging the accuracy and validity of the breath test reading. Moreover, the State must still prove beyond a reasonable doubt the elements of the per se DWI offense. The 1986 amendments only redefine the element of blood alcohol in terms of breath alcohol.

Defendants have no due process right to the former definition of the DWI per se offense. Breath test evidence alone is not conclusive proof of the per se offense. The State still must establish the foundational requirements of the breath test. WAC 448-12-230 states in part:

To obtain a valid breath test, it must be determined (a) that the subject has had nothing to eat or drink for at least fifteen minutes prior to the admin-

istration of the test, and (b) that the subject does not have any foreign substances, not to include dental work, fixed or removable, in his/her mouth
at the beginning of the fifteen minute observation period.

The prosecution must also prove beyond a reasonable doubt that the machine
was in proper working order and that the 0.10 percent reading was a correct one.

In conducting the test, the operator is to follow the instructions displayed
by the instrument. The temperature of the solution in the simulator must be
34 Centigrade, plus or minus .2 Centigrade, prior to the time the test is
given. The reading from the simulator test must be between .090 and .110
inclusive.

WAC 448-12-230. The officer who gives the test must be certified and the State must
prove his competence to administer the test. See WAC 448-12-230 through 330.

The defense has the same opportunity to attack those results as it always has
had under the prior presumptions and the immediate prior statutory scheme. The
defendant may introduce evidence refuting the accuracy and reliability of the test
reading. The fact finder has the duty to weigh all the evidence to determine,
beyond a reasonable doubt, whether a defendant was driving with 0.10 grams or
more of alcohol per 210 liters of breath.

Alternatively, respondents argue that if the 1986 amendments are interpreted
so as to make the relationship between blood and breath alcohol irrelevant, then
the amendments fail as being in excess of the state's police powers. Both courts
below ruled that the 1986 amendments constituted a valid exercise of the state's
police power.

[T]he State Legislature may prescribe laws to promote the health, peace,
safety, and general welfare of the people of Washington. . . .

A legislative enactment is presumed constitutional and the party challenging it
bears the burden of proving it unconstitutional beyond a reasonable doubt.
Moreover, if a court can reasonably conceive of a state of facts to exist which would
justify the legislation, those facts will be presumed to exist and the statute will be
presumed to have been passed with reference to those facts. Thus, where scientific
opinions conflict on a particular point, the Legislature is free to adopt the opinion it
chooses, and the court will not substitute its judgment for that of the Legislature.

Here, the parties do not dispute that the purpose of the 1986 amendments is
to reduce the drunk-driver hazard on the public highways. Respondents contend,
however, that the chosen means of furthering this goal — breath alcohol content
— is too indirectly related to impairment to justify the statute. Respondents argue
that the State has not established any evidence that directly links breath alcohol to
impairment. Respondents point out their post-hearing objection to the district
court's finding of fact, which states "[m]ost studies done to determine the impact
of alcohol were done using breath tests." Respondents assert that no substantial
evidence supports the court's finding. We disagree.

Witness David Predmore of the Washington State Toxicology Laboratory testified that the correlation between the amount of alcohol in a driver's breath and his ability to drive is "roughly the same as . . . [for] blood alcohol." Moreover, the State points to several studies indicating that breath tests will underestimate blood alcohol levels 80 to 91 percent of the time while overestimating them only 5 to 6 percent of the time. [The court cites two papers in scientific journals and three reports from state laboratories.] The State contends that this evidence alone shows a reasonable and substantial relationship between breath alcohol and impairment based on its relationship to blood alcohol, which was found to be an acceptable means in State v. Franco. The State also asserts that the record contains substantial evidence that breath alcohol is directly related to impairment. There is testimony that the vast majority of impairment studies correlating alcohol consumption with driving abilities have relied on measures of breath alcohol, not blood alcohol. Washington State Patrol Sergeant Rod Gullberg explained that "breath becomes just from a statistical standpoint a better predictor of impairment than does blood simply because of the predominance of the data." The record also contains legislative memoranda indicating that "[m]ost studies of alcohol-related driving impairment have in fact used . . . grams per liter of breath measurement rather than a blood level measurement."

Respondents contend that the State's evidence does not demonstrate any information directly linking breath alcohol readings with impairment. Although respondents point out various factors affecting the relationship between blood alcohol and breath alcohol, contending that although breath alcohol was used to study impairment those studies ultimately correlated the breath levels to blood levels, respondents do not point to any evidence in the record to rebut the State's position. While the record may establish that breath is a less direct measure of blood alcohol levels, it does not establish a lack of a reasonable and substantial relationship between breath alcohol and impairment. We conclude that the 1986 amendments are a valid exercise of police power.

We also conclude that the breath standard used in the 1986 amendments gives fair notice and is not unconstitutionally vague. While the trial court concluded that the word "breath" as used in the 1986 amendments is not unconstitutionally vague, the superior court apparently ruled that the breath standard is too vague to give fair notice and thus violated due process. The superior court ruled, "we have a floating standard and that is a concept that I find very difficult to accept in connection with a criminal statute as the right of people to know what they are defending against."

. . . Respondents contend that no external standards are available from which a driver can predict when his breath level is at or above the prohibited level. Moreover, because of the imperfect correlation between breath and blood alcohol, respondents assert that blood alcohol charts are insufficient to give notice of the prohibited conduct. We disagree.

In State v. Franco, this court held that the former 0.10 percent blood alcohol standard was not unconstitutionally vague. The court found that the standard gave fair warning in that it was reasonable to assume that a driver was impaired at that level of blood alcohol and that charts were available showing the number of drinks necessary to produce the prohibited level.

Likewise, we find it reasonable to assume that drivers are impaired at the statutory breath level and that drivers still have notice under the 1986 amendments that driving while impaired by alcohol is a crime. We note that the breath level offense is one alternative DWI offense; another alternative is to drive while impaired. Overall, the 1986 amendments give fair notice of the forbidden conduct. . . .

II. Equal Protection

The State challenges the trial court's conclusion that the 1986 amendments violate equal protection by discriminating against persons with blood-breath ratios below 2100:1. The State asserts that the 1986 amendments criminalize a particular breath alcohol level without regard to blood alcohol levels. Because no conversion of breath readings into blood readings is required, a person's blood-breath ratio has no impact on guilt. The State argues that the statute distinguishes only between those who have the prohibited amount of alcohol in their breath and those who do not. . . .

Respondents argue that, although facially neutral, the 1986 amendments discriminate in fact against persons who have blood-breath ratios below 2100:1 because although those persons may have a prohibited breath alcohol level, that level does not correlate with a blood alcohol level demonstrating impairment. Respondents assert that this discriminatory impact violates the equal protection rights of several classes of individuals. Respondents contend that because blacks have smaller lung capacities than same-sized white persons, blacks' blood-breath ratios are lower and a breath alcohol test will overestimate their blood alcohol levels. Moreover, persons suffering from certain chronic lung diseases also may have smaller than normal lung capacities also resulting in overestimated blood alcohol levels. Finally, respondents point out that denture wearers, who retain a greater amount of mouth alcohol, can have a breath-alcohol level that overestimates their blood alcohol. . . .

[The court concludes that] the record contains evidence that breath alcohol may not accurately show blood-alcohol in particular individuals, the record does not establish that proscribing a particular level of breath alcohol is wholly irrelevant to achieving the purpose of reducing DWI hazards.

Moreover, the record does not establish that a particular race or class of persons is affected by the classification. . . . While the record indicates that the average black person has a 13 percent smaller lung capacity than the average white person, the record contains no evidence suggesting that breath alcohol readings inaccurately measure impairment among blacks, nor that the average statistic affects particular black individuals. . . . The relationship between the legislative classification and its goal is rational. We conclude that the 1986 amendments do not violate equal protection guaranties.

III. Equal Rights Amendment

Respondents contend that because the 1986 amendments have a disparate impact on women, the amendments violate this state's Equal Rights Amendment. . . .

Article 61 of the Washington Constitution provides: "Equality of rights and responsibility under the law shall not be denied or abridged on account of sex." The protections provided by the ERA go beyond those of the equal protection clause of the federal constitution and the privileges and immunities clause of the state constitution. . . .

Respondents argue that the 1986 amendments, although facially neutral, discriminate against women on the basis of their blood-breath ratios. Respondents' argument is based on the premise that alcohol contained only in the breath has no impact on intoxication. Instead, only when breath alcohol levels reflect blood alcohol levels is breath alcohol an indicator of intoxication because blood is the transporter of alcohol to the central nervous system and central nervous system alcohol causes intoxication. . . .

Respondents contend that although the 1986 amendments purport to criminalize only breath alcohol, the standard adopted in the 1986 amendments implicitly assumes a 2100:1 blood-breath ratio because studies of impairment were made by giving breath tests using that ratio, which were then used to calculate blood alcohol levels. . . .

Respondents also suggest that the 2100:1 ratio used by breath testing machines to convert a breath alcohol reading into a blood alcohol reading was chosen based on studies of mostly male subjects. Because women tend, on an average, to have lower blood-breath ratios than men, respondents reason that the State's use of a male based norm (the 2100:1 blood-breath ratio) in breath testing has the effect of overestimating blood alcohol levels for women.

Respondents thus argue because breath tests overestimate women's blood alcohol on this basis, the breath alcohol standard has a disparate impact on women. The district court found that "[t]heoretically, the average female would have a blood-breath ratio 8-15 percent lower than the average male."

Respondents note also that the blood-breath ratio is affected by lung size. Respondents point out that women have a smaller average lung capacity than do men. A person with smaller lungs will exhale more of their lung capacity into a breath machine than will a person with average lung capacity. (This assumes that the people are the same size except for lung capacity). Thus, a smaller lunged person will exhale more deep lung air than would a person of the same size with average lung size by virtue of emptying more of his or her lungs. The result is that a greater proportion of deep lung air is tested in a person with smaller lungs than a person with average lungs. Because the deep lung air contains more alcohol, the person with smaller lungs will have a higher breath alcohol reading because of lung size.

Respondents also contend that women's blood-breath ratios are lower than the average male's because women tend to have higher average body temperatures. Body temperature is one of the primary components of the blood-breath ratio; the blood-breath ratio is affected 6 percent for each degree in variance from the average human temperature of 37 degrees centigrade. Thus, other factors being equal, a person with a temperature of 38 degrees would have a breath alcohol level 6 percent higher than actual blood alcohol levels. Respondents contend that the variation between average body temperature in men and women means that the presumed blood-breath ratio of 2100:1 overestimates blood alcohol by approximately 4 to 6 percent for women test subjects. Respondents thus argue that because the 1986 amendments implicitly incorporate the 2100:1 blood-breath ratio in the breath alcohol standard, the amendments have a disparate impact on women as a class. . . .

Although the record demonstrates that breath alcohol levels may not accurately represent blood alcohol levels in particular individuals, this evidence alone does not establish that the breath alcohol standard falls more harshly on women as a class. Respondents bear the burden of showing that the Legislature's decision to use a breath alcohol standard to prove impairment falls more harshly on women. Here, no studies have been made of the differences in blood-breath ratios between men and women. At best the record shows that the use of blood-alcohol levels may have a hypothetical disparate impact on women. Here we are concerned with breath alcohol only. The record shows no evidence that breath alcohol levels represent different levels of impairment between men and women as a class. We conclude that, on this record, respondents have failed to satisfy their burden to establish disparate impact, and, thus, respondents have not shown that the 1986 amendments violate the ERA.

IV. Legislative Intent

The State challenges the district court's conclusion that the Legislature's intent in enacting the 1986 amendments "was to eliminate expert testimony by the defense relating to blood breath ratios and thereby shorten trials and make convictions easier." [The court questions whether this was the predominant purpose and holds that even if it were, it] does not support a conclusion that the Legislature intended to discriminate against a certain class of persons.

V. Admissibility of Breath Test Evidence

Because we conclude that the 1986 amendments are constitutional, we reverse the district court's ruling barring the State's use of breath test evidence under former RCW 46.61.504. Moreover, we disagree with respondents' contention that breath test evidence remains inadmissible because defendants cannot obtain independent tests as provided for in RCW 46.61.506(5). Respondents rely on the district court's finding that "as a practical matter, virtually all breath testing devices" are police controlled. Respondents argue that the State thus impermissibly "thwarts" defendant's attempts to exercise their rights to additional tests. In [Blaine v. Suess, 93 Wash. 2d 722, 612 P.2d 789 (1980)], a DWI defendant's conviction was reversed because police officers "thwarted" his attempts to obtain an independent blood test. The defendant indicated he desired an independent blood test after being informed of his right to do so. Police initially indicated that they would transport him to a hospital for testing, but then took him to jail instead. The court concluded that although "law enforcement authorities have no duty to volunteer to arrange for testing, they must not thwart an accused's attempts to make such arrangements."

. . . Here, respondents have shown no evidence of acts by the State that misled or interfered with their attempts to obtain additional tests. Moreover, the record shows that breath testing devices are present in nonstate controlled locations, including detoxification centers, hospitals, and work release facilities. . . . Finally, we note that RCW 46.61.506 specifically states that a defendant's inability to obtain an independent test will not bar admission of a properly administered breath test. The statutory DWI scheme, along with the warnings given to defendants, adequately informs defendants of their rights to independent tests. Breath test evidence is admissible to prove violations of the DWI statutes.

Reversed.

NOTES

Statutes and Proof of Intoxication

1. *The state's interest.* The state interest in deterring driving while under the influence of alcohol is clear. As explained in Robert D. Brewer et al., The Risk of Dying in Alcohol-Related Automobile Crashes Among Habitual Drunk Drivers, 331 New Eng. J. Med. 513, 513 (1994) (footnotes omitted):

> Motor vehicle crashes are the leading cause of death in the United States among people 1 to 34 years of age. Almost half of all traffic fatalities (a total of 17,700 in 1992) are related to alcohol. Furthermore, two out of five people in the United States will be involved in an alcohol-related motor vehicle crash at some time during their lives.
>
> The risk of a fatal crash increases rapidly as the blood alcohol concentration of the driver increases. A driver with a blood alcohol concentration of 100 mg per deciliter (22 mmol per liter) or higher is 7 times more likely to be involved in a fatal motor vehicle crash than a driver who has not consumed alcoholic beverages, and a driver with a blood alcohol concentration of 150 mg per deciliter (33 mmol per liter) or more is about 25 times more likely.

2. *Defining and presuming.* The Washington Supreme Court holds that the law making it an offense to drive with a breath alcohol concentration (BrAC) exceeding .10 g/210L does not create a "conclusive presumption," but "simply redefines" the prior offense of driving with a blood alcohol concentration (BAC) exceeding .10 percent, which itself "defines" an offense of driving while intoxicated. Suppose the legislature defined an offense consisting of two elements: (1) driving a motor vehicle, and (2) having a BrAC of .10 g/210L or more as determined by a roadside measurement of a Smith and Wesson Breathalyzer 900A. Or, suppose the second element were having bloodshot eyes and slurred speech. Must a statute use the word "presume" to embody a presumption? Does the search for "presumptions" aid the analysis of the power of the state to place certain conduct within the grasp of the criminal law? Whether or not one says that such offenses employ "definitions" or that they rest on "presumptions," what constraint does due process impose on this type of legislation? See McCormick on Evidence § 347, at 997 (Edward Cleary ed., 3d ed. 1984) (recent Supreme Court opinions suggest that "[m]andatory presumptions . . . will be rigidly scrutinized in accordance with a test which requires that a rational juror could find the presumed fact beyond a reasonable doubt from the basic facts. . . . [T]he court should be able to use its power to notice legislative facts which might support the inference to be drawn."); cf. 2 McCormick on Evidence § 347, at 490 (John Strong ed., 4th ed. 1992) (some authors have suggested that a mandatory presumption that shifts the burden of persuasion "may not constitutionally exist").

In light of *Brayman,* consider State v. Burling, 400 N.W. 2d 872 (Neb. 1987). Burling was convicted of failing to stop at a stop sign and of driving in violation of a Nebraska statute making it unlawful to drive "under the influence of alcoholic liquor or any drug" or with "ten-hundredths of one per cent or more by weight of alcohol in his or her body fluid as shown by chemical analysis of his or her blood, breath, or urine." Police using an Intoxilyzer Model 4011AS determined that Burling had a blood alcohol level of .164 percent.

A professor of pharmacology testified for Burling that the infrared spectrophotometer measures alcohol in a sample of breath and converts that reading into a blood alcohol concentration, which it reports. The expert testified further that recent research shows that the ratio of breath to blood alcohol, taken by the machine to be 1:2100, actually ranges from 1:1100 to 1:3400, and that forensic toxicologists therefore no longer rely on the 1:2100 ratio.

The Nebraska Supreme Court reasoned that the statute makes breath tests conducted according to a method approved by the state Department of Health admissible to prove BAC, but that the constitutional separation of powers doctrine precludes the legislature from making such evidence conclusive. Cf. United States v. Klein, 80 U.S. (13 Wall.) 128 (1872). Given the undisputed expert testimony that the 1:2100 ratio could overstate BAC by as much as 52.38 percent, it concluded that "in this case, the Intoxilyzer result must be reduced to 52.38 percent of .164 of 1 percent, that is, to .086 of 1 percent." Nevertheless, it affirmed the conviction on the ground that other evidence of intoxication was overwhelming.

Would a statute like the one in *Brayman,* making it unlawful to drive with given breath alcohol concentrations, pass constitutional muster in Nebraska?

State v. Rowell
517 So. 2d 799 (La. 1988)

MARCUS, JUSTICE.

James R. Rowell was charged . . . with operating a motor vehicle while under the influence of alcohol, second offense, with a blood alcohol concentration of 0.10% or more, in violation of La. R.S. 14:98. Defendant filed a motion to suppress the results of the blood alcohol analysis performed on the blood sample drawn from him after his arrest. . . . At the conclusion of trial, the trial judge denied the motion to suppress finding that the Department of Public Safety's regulations on blood alcohol analysis were adequate to insure the accuracy of the test results and found defendant guilty as charged. The court of appeal granted defendant's application for a writ of review and reversed his conviction and sentence . . . . [W]e granted certiorari to review the correctness of that decision.

On May 17, 1986, defendant was involved in an automobile accident during which he collided into the rear of a garbage truck. When the police officers arrived at the scene of the accident, defendant was lying in the grass several feet from his automobile and was bleeding from his nose and face. One of the investigating officers noticed a scent of alcohol on defendant's breath. First aid was administered to defendant and he was taken by ambulance to the hospital. After defendant was advised of his rights, he consented to a blood alcohol analysis. A licensed practical nurse drew two vials of defendant's blood using a B-D Blood Alcohol Kit Number 4990. She then gave the vials to a police officer who sealed them in the kit. Five days later, a forensic chemist employed by Acadiana Criminalistics Laboratory performed a gas chromatographic analysis on defendant's blood samples using an internal standard with a direct injection. The analysis showed defendant's blood alcohol level to be 0.12%, which is above the presumptive level of intoxication.[4]

---

[4] La. R.S. 32:662(A)(1)(c) provides:

A. The chemical test or tests as provided for by this Part shall be subject to the following rules and shall be administered as provided for hereafter:

1. Upon the trial of any criminal action or proceeding arising out of acts alleged to have been committed by any person while driving or in actual physical control of a vehicle while under the influence of alcoholic beverages the amount of alcohol in the person's blood at the time alleged as shown by chemical analysis of the person's blood, urine, breath or other bodily substance shall give rise to the following presumptions:

c. If there was at that time 0.10 per cent or more by weight of alcohol in the person's blood, it shall be presumed that the person was under the influence of alcoholic beverages.

This court has repeatedly recognized the importance of establishing safeguards to guarantee the accuracy of chemical tests used in criminal prosecutions. In order for the state to avail itself of the statutory presumption of a defendant's intoxication arising from a chemical analysis of his blood, it must show that the state has promulgated detailed procedures which will insure the integrity and reliability of the chemical test, including provisions for repair, maintenance, inspection, cleaning, certification, and chemical accuracy. It must also show that the state has strictly complied with the promulgated procedures. . . .

La. R.S. 32:663 authorizes the Department of Public Safety to approve satisfactory techniques or methods to assure the accuracy of breath and blood alcohol analysis. In contrast to the Department's regulations on breath analysis, those on blood analysis are meager. A person seeking a permit to conduct blood analysis must have a Bachelor of Science in chemistry, physics, biology, zoology, medical technology, or a related field and must conduct proficiency testing set up by the state police crime laboratory. Permits are effective for a period of five years. Two methods are approved for blood alcohol analysis: gas chromatography, headspace sampling with internal standard and gas chromatography, direct injection with internal standard. The regulations also provide for certain procedures and controls in conjunction with each batch of samples analyzed. . . .

The regulations concerning the qualifications of a person seeking a permit to conduct blood analysis are insufficient because they do not specify the type of proficiency testing required. Moreover, the regulations do not provide for the repair, maintenance, or inspection of the gas chromatograph. Although the chemist who performed the blood analysis in the instant case testified that he was able to perform some repairs, the regulations do not require a person seeking a permit to have such skills. In view of the chemist's testimony that alcohol can be manufactured in the blood sample if it is not properly preserved, the regulations do not sufficiently provide for the preservation of the blood sample. Finally, the regulations are not sufficient to insure the accuracy of the chemicals used to calibrate the gas chromatograph. . . .

This court has held that the wrongful introduction of a chemical test result, which by law presumes a defendant to be intoxicated, is so prejudicial to the defendant that a resulting conviction cannot stand even if there is other evidence of intoxication. Because this decision does not entail a finding that there was an insufficiency of evidence to convict defendant, but only that the admission of the gas chromatography test results was erroneous, it is proper that defendant be retried * . . . .

---

*Editor's note: In *Burling,* the Nebraska Supreme Court considers the admission of questioned breath test results to be harmless in light of the other, overwhelming evidence of intoxication. In *Rowell,* the Louisiana Supreme Court refuses to apply the harmless error doctrine to blood tests introduced pursuant to inadequate regulations. Can these decisions be harmonized? If not, which is the better approach?

NOTES

1. *Types of DWI statutes.* These cases reveal the evolution of the statutory battle against drunk driving: from laws prohibiting driving while intoxicated, without mention of how intoxication may be proved; to laws against DWI, fortified by a mandatory but rebuttable presumption of intoxication triggered by a minimum blood-alcohol concentration (BAC), usually .10; to "per se" laws against driving with BAC in excess of some specified level; to per se laws against driving with a breath alcohol concentration (BrAC) in excess of such a threshold. Which approach seems most advisable? Many existing statutes follow the model of the Uniform Vehicle Code, which continues to be amended and updated. See National Committee on Uniform Traffic Laws and Ordinances, Uniform Vehicle Code Ann. § 11-902 (1967 & 1984 Supp.). Section 11-902(c) of the 1967 Uniform Law makes chemical analyses "valid" when "performed according to methods approved by the State Department of Health . . . ."

The cases in this section respond to an exhaustive array of sometimes ingenious attacks on this statutory and administrative framework. What do these cases reveal about the following: (a) the constitutionality of making it an offense to drive while having a blood alcohol concentration (BAC) above a given level? (b) the constitutionality of making it an offense to drive while having a breath alcohol concentration (BrAC) above a given level? (c) the constitutionality of presuming intoxication from BrAC readings above a given level? (d) the procedures that police must follow to have BAC or BrAC measurements admitted without expert scientific testimony? When may BAC or BrAC measurements that do not conform with administratively prescribed procedures be admitted?

2. *The domain of the statutory presumptions and procedures.* May a criminal defendant introduce blood or breath test results when the testing does not conform to the statutorily and administratively required procedures? See State v. Trahan, 576 So.2d 1 (La. 1990); State ex rel. Collins v. Seidel, 691 P.2d 678 (Ariz. 1984). May the state avoid the requirements if it is proceeding under a "driving while intoxicated" rather than a "per se" or a "presumption" statute? See *Collins*, supra. May a civil litigant rely on the statutory presumptions to help prove or disprove intoxication? Is compliance with the statutory scheme sufficient to make the measurements admissible? Is it necessary to admissibility? See Divine v. Groshong, 607 P.2d 700 (Kan. 1984); National Committee on Uniform Traffic Laws and Ordinances, Uniform Vehicle Code Ann. § 11-902.1(b) (1984 Supp.). On the impact of civil presumptions generally, see, e.g., McCormick on Evidence § 344 (John Strong ed., 4th ed. 1992).

3. *Proving intoxication with blood tests.* Various chemical techniques are available to measure the concentration of ethyl alcohol in a blood sample. These range from classic separation and reaction techniques to gas chromatography. For details, see 1 Richard Erwin, Defense of Drunk Driving Cases (3d rev. ed., 1994); Yale Caplan, The Determination of Alcohol in Blood and Breath, in Forensic Science Handbook 108-21 (Richard Saferstein ed., 1982). When proper laboratory procedures are observed and the sample is correctly obtained and preserved, the tests give reliable measurements of BAC.

A more serious technical problem lies in discerning the extent of intoxication from a BAC measurement, especially if the blood sample is taken some time after an arrest or accident. Even if BAC were known precisely, substantial variability in tolerances for alcohol, absorption rates, and clearances — both among individuals and within individuals from one situation to another — complicates efforts to deduce the true extent of intoxication at an earlier time.

Many courts and legislators have assumed that a person's BAC is inevitably higher at the time of an accident than it is later, at the time of testing (unless the person has consumed more alcohol after the accident). See, e.g., Ring v. Taylor, 685 P.2d 121 (Ariz. Ct. App. 1984) (linear extrapolation is generally accepted). However, since BAC rises after drinking, then falls, it has been argued that a single measurement is not very revealing when one is interested in BAC at an earlier time. Edward Fitzgerald & David Hume, The Single Chemical Test for Intoxication: A Challenge to Admissibility, 66 Mass. L. Rev. 23 (1981) (urging exclusion of single test results). For further discussions, see M.J. Lewis, Blood Alcohol: The Concentration-Time Curve and Retrospective Estimation of Level, 26 J. Forensic Sci. Soc'y 95 (1986) (outlining a method said to be more accurate than linear extrapolation); Donald H. Nichols, Toward a Coordinated Judicial View of the Accuracy of Breath Testing Devices, 59 N.D. L. Rev. 329, 348 (1983) (advocating measurements at two times); cf. Commonwealth v. Neal, 392 Mass. 1, 464 N.E. 2d 1356, 1369-70 (1984) (two tests not required although they would be "better practice"). But see Paul C. Giannelli & Edward Imwinkelried, Scientific Evidence § 22-4, at 891 (1986) (limited value of two tests). May the state pretermit this issue by defining the offense in terms of the BAC or BrAC at the time of the arrest?

4. *Proving intoxication with breath tests.* Deducing BAC from measurements of the alcohol contained in a sample of a person's breath introduces additional uncertainty in ascertaining the extent of intoxication. As with blood tests, the problem is not so much the accuracy of the instrumentation as maintained and used in laboratory studies. See, e.g., W. Frankvoort et al., The Laboratory Testing of Evidential Breath-Testing (EBT) Machines, 35 Forensic Sci. Int'l 27 (1987); Bruce Goldberger & Yale Caplan, Infrared Quantitative Evidential Blood-Alcohol Analyzers: In Vitro Accuracy and Precision Studies, 31 J. Forensic Sci. 16 (1986). But see Paul Giannelli & Edward Imwinkelried, Scientific Evidence § 22-3, at 876-81 & § 22-6(D), at 899-902 (1986) (collecting cases concerned with possible electromagnetic interference). Rather, the additional difficulty lies in deriving a value for BAC from breath alcohol concentration (BrAC). As discussed in

Brayman, Burling, and *Rowell,* BAC typically is inferred by dividing BrAC by 2100, a figure originally obtained on the theoretical assumption that the air in the sample was in equilibrium with blood in the lungs. If the specimen includes air not expelled from the alveoli (air sacs), the ratio of BAC to the BrAC in the specimen may be higher. For example, Frankvoort et al., supra, at 38, found BrAC in samples obtained after hyperventilation to be 20 to 30 percent below hypoventilated BrAC. Moreover, as several of the opinions in this section acknowledge, the ratio may vary over time in an individual, T.A. Alobaidi et al., Significance of Variations in Blood:Breath Partition Coefficient of Alcohol, 1976 Brit. Med. J. 1479, and it varies among individuals. M.F. Mason & K.M. Dubowski, Breath Alcohol Analysis: Uses, Methods and Some Forensic Problems — Review and Opinion, 21 J. Forensic Sci. 9, 24 (1976); G. Simpson, Accuracy and Precision of Breath-Alcohol Measurements for a Random Subject in the Post-Absorptive State, 33 Clinical Chem. 261 (1987). However, some studies suggest that the discrepancies usually result in underestimates of BAC or that the error is fairly small. E.g., Alfred Biasotti, The Role of the Forensic Scientist in the Application of Chemical Tests for Alcohol in Traffic Law Enforcement, 29 J. Forensic Sci. 1164 (1984); Yale Caplan, The Determination of Alcohol in Blood and Breath, in Forensic Science Handbook 592, 624 (Richard Saferstein ed., 1983); J. Emerson et al., The Measurement of Breath Alcohol, 70 J. Forensic Sci. Soc'y 3 (1980).

   5. *Proving intoxication with other evidence.* Obviously, breath or blood tests are not the only way to prove intoxication. Yet, "[m]any prosecutors, particularly inexperienced ones, will present the testimony of the police officer as almost an after-thought, relying instead on the blood-alcohol evidence to convict. Never mind that the officer can testify that the defendant was falling down and incoherent, the prosecutor will hurry on so that he can display the magic number to the jury." Lawrence Taylor, Drunk Driving Defense 8:4 (4th ed. 1996).
   One non-chemical but scientific technique to test sobriety is the horizontal gaze nystagmus test. See People v. Leahy, 882 P.2d 321 (Cal. 1994); State v. Witte, 836 P.2d 1110 (Kan. 1992); State v. Superior Court, 718 P.2d 171 (Ariz. 1986) (excerpted supra chapter 3). See also Stephanie E. Busloff, Comment, Can Your Eyes Be Used Against You? The Use of the Horizontal Gaze Nystagmus Test in the Courtroom, 84 J. Crim. L. & Criminology 203 (1993); Joseph Meany, Note, Horizontal Gaze Nystagmus: a Closer Look, 36 Jurimetrics J. 383 (1996); Annot., Horizontal Gaze Nystagmus Test: Use in Impaired Driving Prosecution, 60 A.L.R. 4th 1129 (1988).

   6. *Related constitutional questions.* Blood and breath alcohol testing has provoked an impressive array of constitutional questions. See, e.g., Skinner v. Railway Labor Executives' Ass'n, 489 U.S. 602 (1989) (testing of certain railroad employees for blood alcohol concentration of .04 or more while on duty reasonable under the Fourth Amendment even though there was no requirement of a warrant or a reasonable suspicion that any particular employee might be impaired); California v. Trombetta, 467 U.S. 479 (1984) (due process does not require law enforcement agencies to preserve breath samples); Schmerber v. California, 384 U.S. 757 (1966) (compulsory blood test where sample taken in hospital by physician does not violate due process, self-incrimination or search and seizure clause); 2 Paul C. Giannelli & Edward J. Imwinkelried, Scientific Evidence § 22-7 (2d ed. 1993). To facilitate tests for intoxication, most states have implemented implied consent statutes. These statutes provide that as a condition to obtaining a driver's license, the driver consents to the administration of alcohol tests if lawfully stopped on suspicion of drunk driving. In most states, the statutes provide further that if a driver wrongfully refuses to submit to a test, the refusal allows the state to revoke the person's driving privilege. In a few states, the refusal itself is a crime, typically a misdemeanor. Paul C. Giannelli & Edward J. Imwinkelried, Scientific Evidence 853 (1986). The result in *Schmerber* suggests that such "consent" is an unnecessary fiction.

7. *Detecting intoxication from other drugs.* Although police in the United States are routinely trained to recognize and test for alcohol intoxication, tests for other drugs are rarely used in traffic enforcement. Should they be? In a study in Memphis, Tennessee, 150 of 175 people arrested for reckless driving who had no odor of alcohol or who tested negative on breath analysis submitted urine sample for drug testing at the scene of the arrest. Over half were found to be intoxicated with marijuana or cocaine. Of the 94 people judged by police to be moderately or extremely intoxicated, 86% tested positive. Daniel Brookoff et al., Testing Reckless Drivers for Cocaine and Marijuana, 331 New Eng. J. Med. 518 (1994).

Should positive results of urinalysis be admissible? Remember that:

[S]uch tests do not necessarily confirm that drugs were ingested recently. Regular users of very doses of cocaine and marijuana can excrete metabolites for days after their last use, but such persons may also have prolonged impairment due to their chronic intoxication. Correlating blood or urine levels of certain drugs with specific driving problems is not yet possible, and the correlation between impairment and serum levels of drugs may never be established as it has been for alcohol.

Id. at 521 (footnotes omitted).

Part III

JUDICIAL SCRUTINY OF NEW SCIENTIFIC TESTS

Chapter 6
The General Acceptance Standard

Frye v. United States
293 F. 1013 (D.C. Cir. 1923)

VAN ORSDEL, ASSOCIATE JUSTICE.

Appellant . . . was convicted of the crime of murder in the second degree . . . .

A single assignment of error is presented for our consideration. In the course of the trial counsel for defendant offered an expert witness to testify to the result of a deception test made upon defendant. The test is described as the systolic blood pressure deception test. It is asserted that blood pressure is influenced by change in the emotions of the witness, and that the systolic blood pressure rises are brought about by nervous impulses sent to the sympathetic branch of the autonomic nervous system. Scientific experiments, it is claimed, have demonstrated that fear, rage, and pain always produce a rise of systolic blood pressure, and that conscious deception or falsehood, concealment of facts, or guilt of crime, accompanied by fear of detection when the person is under examination, raises the systolic blood pressure in a curve, which corresponds exactly to the struggle going on in the subject's mind, between fear and attempted control of that fear, as the examination touches the vital points in respect of which he is attempting to deceive the examiner.

In other words, the theory seems to be that truth is spontaneous, and comes without conscious effort, while the utterance of a falsehood requires a conscious effort, which is reflected in the blood pressure. The rise thus produced is easily detected and distinguished from the rise produced by mere fear of the examination itself. In the former instance, the pressure rises higher than in the latter, and is more pronounced as the examination proceeds, while in the latter case, if the subject is telling the truth, the pressure registers highest at the beginning of the examination, and gradually diminishes as the examination proceeds.

Prior to the trial defendant was subjected to this deception test, and counsel offered the scientist who conducted the test as an expert to testify to the results obtained. The offer was objected to by counsel for the government, and the court sustained the objection. Counsel for defendant then offered to have the proffered witness conduct a test in the presence of the jury. This also was denied.

Counsel for defendant, in their able presentation of the novel question involved, correctly state in their brief that no cases directly in point have been found. The broad ground, however, upon which they plant their case, is succinctly stated in their brief as follows:

> The rule is that the opinions of experts or skilled witnesses are admissible in evidence in those cases in which the matter of inquiry is such

75

that inexperienced persons are unlikely to prove capable of forming a correct judgment upon it, for the reason that the subject-matter so far partakes of a science, art, or trade as to require a previous habit or experience or study in it, in order to acquire a knowledge of it. When the question involved does not lie within the range of common experience or common knowledge, but requires special experience or special knowledge, then the opinions of witnesses skilled in that particular science, art, or trade to which the question relates are admissible in evidence.

Numerous cases are cited in support of this rule. Just when a scientific principle or discovery crosses the line between the experimental and demonstrable stages is difficult to define. Somewhere in this twilight zone the evidential force of the principle must be recognized, and while courts will go a long way in admitting expert testimony deduced from a well-recognized scientific principle or discovery, the thing from which the deduction is made must be sufficiently established to have gained general acceptance in the particular field in which it belongs.

We think the systolic blood pressure deception test has not yet gained such standing and scientific recognition among physiological and psychological authorities as would justify the courts in admitting expert testimony deduced from the discovery, development, and experiments thus far made.

The judgment is affirmed.

NOTES

1. *The source of the general acceptance standard.* The rule that "the thing from which the deduction is made must be sufficiently established to have gained general acceptance in the particular field in which it belongs" is known as the *Frye* test, or the general acceptance standard. Where does this special requirement for scientific evidence come from? The trial court apparently did not apply this standard, see James E. Starrs, A Still-Life Watercolor: *Frye v. United States,* 27 J. Forensic Sci. 684, 691-92 (1982), and nothing in the appellate court's remarks about expert testimony generally suggests that the information imparted by an expert must have attained general acceptance before it can be placed before a jury. Is the requirement justified by the fact that courts are unable to judge the validity of scientific evidence even with the aid of a qualified expert? See, e.g., United States v. Addison, 498 F.2d 741, 743-44 (D.C. Cir. 1974). That when new techniques or theories first are introduced in court, they are likely to be understood by only one or two experts, so that the opponent of the evidence will have little chance to combat the novel evidence? Id. That jurors tend to be so awed by scientific evidence that such evidence should not be put before them until it has withstood the test of time before its acceptance in the scientific community generally? See John W. Strong, Language and Logic in Expert Testimony: Limiting Expert Testimony by Restrictions of Function, Reliability, and Form, 71 Or. L. Rev. 349,

367 n.81 (1992); Note, The *Frye* Doctrine and Relevancy Approach Controversy: An Empirical Evaluation, 74 Geo. L.J. 1769 (1986).

2. *The acceptance and importance of the general acceptance standard.* On the surface, *Frye* appears to have been remarkably influential. When applied faithfully, it is a more demanding standard than mere relevance (Fed. R. Evid. 401-403), or helpfulness (Fed. R. Evid. 702 ("assist the trier of fact")). Its victims include polygraphy, graphology, hypnotic and drug induced testimony, voice stress analysis, voice spectrograms, ion microprobe mass spectroscopy, infrared sensing of aircraft, retesting of breath samples for alcohol content, psychological profiles of battered women, post traumatic stress disorder as an indicator of rape, astronomical calculations, and certain types of electrophoresis of dried blood stains. See 1 McCormick on Evidence § 203 (John Strong ed., 4th ed., 1992).

Yet, many jurisdictions have disavowed Frye in recent decades. The most noted case is Daubert v. Merrell Dow Pharmaceuticals, Inc., 506 U.S. 738 (1993), which is reprinted in chapter 7. various circuit court opinions, such as United States v. Downing, 753 F.2d 1224 (3d Cir. 1985), canvass the major arguments for and against *Frye* more fully. Even in those jurisdictions that still purport to follow *Frye,* courts repeatedly ignore it or depart from it in hard cases. Most of the scholarly commentary calls for outright rejection of the *Frye* test. See 1 McCormick on Evidence, supra, at § 203.

In any event, courts applying a broader inquiry to scientific evidence — in which the degree of acceptance among scientists is but one of several factors affecting the balance of probative value and prejudicial effect — tend to reach the same results with respect to most forms of scientific evidence as do the courts that formally adhere to *Frye.* See id. at §§ 204-208.

3. *The focus of the general acceptance standard.* What was "the thing" in *Frye* that needed "to have gained general acceptance"? The link between conscious insincerity and changes in blood pressure? The ability of an expert to measure and interpret these changes? Both? More broadly, what must be generally accepted? Scientific theories or principles? The reasoning used by the expert? The expert's methods in the abstract? Their application to the case at bar?

4. *The relevant scientific community.* By whom must "the thing" be accepted? All scientists? All forensic scientists? All scientists who have studied "the thing"?

5. *Proof of general acceptance.* How does one prove general acceptance? By expert testimony about what scientists think? By a review of the scientific literature? By opinions of other courts? The cases in this section, as well as some in succeeding portions of this and other chapters, agonize over such questions.

State v. Superior Court
718 P.2d 171 (Ariz. 1986)

FELDMAN, JUSTICE.

In the early morning hours of March 18, 1985, Frederick Blake was driving a car on State Route 92, south of Sierra Vista. He was stopped by Officer Hohn who had observed the vehicle meandering within its lane, and who therefore suspected Blake of driving under the influence of alcohol. Noting, also, that Blake's appearance and breath indicated intoxication, the officer had Blake perform a battery of six field sobriety tests, including the horizonal gaze nystagmus (HGN) test. Nystagmus is an involuntary jerking of the eyeball. The jerking may be aggravated by central nervous system depressants such as alcohol or barbiturates. Horizonal gaze nystagmus is the inability of the eyes to maintain visual fixation as they are turned to the side.

In the HGN test the driver is asked to cover one eye and focus the other on an object (usually a pen) held by the officer at the driver's eye level. As the officer moves the object gradually out of the driver's field of vision toward his ear, he watches the driver's eyeball to detect involuntary jerking. The test is repeated with the other eye. By observing (1) the inability of each eye to track movement smoothly, (2) pronounced nystagmus at maximum deviation and (3) onset of the nystagmus at an angle less than 45 degrees in relation to the center point, the officer can estimate whether the driver's blood alcohol content (BAC) exceeds the legal limit of .10 percent. . . .

Blake's performance of the first three standard field sobriety tests was "fair" and did not amount to probable cause to arrest Blake for DUI. As a result of the HGN test, however, the officer estimated that Blake had a BAC in excess of .10 percent. Blake's performance on the last two tests strengthened his conclusion. Having also smelled a strong odor of alcohol on Blake's breath and noticed Blake's slurred speech and bloodshot, watery and dilated eyes. Officer Hohn then arrested Blake on a charge of felony DUI . . . . Hohn then transported Blake to the police station where he administered an intoxilyzer test which showed that Blake had a BAC of .163 percent.

Blake made two motions to the trial court: to dismiss the prosecution for lack of probable cause to arrest and to preclude the admission of testimony of the HGN test and its results at trial. At the evidentiary hearing on these two motions the state presented evidence regarding the principles and use of HGN testing from Dr. Marcelline Burns, a research psychologist who studies the effect of alcohol on behavior, Sgt. Richard Studdard of the Los Angeles Police Department, and Sgt. Jeffrey Raynor and Officer Robert Hohn of the Arizona Department of Public Safety.

Dr. Burns, Director the Southern California Research Institute (SCRI or Institute) testified that the Institute had received research contracts from the National Highway Traffic Safety Administration (NHTSA) to develop the best possible field sobriety tests. The result of this research was a three-test battery, which included the walk and turn, the one-leg stand, and the HGN. This battery could be administered without special equipment, required no more than five minutes in most cases, and resulted in 83 percent accuracy in determining BAC above and below .10 percent. Dr. Burns testified that all field sobriety tests help the police officers to estimate BAC. The HGN test is based on the known principle that certain toxic substances, including alcohol, cause nystagmus. The SCRI study found HGN to be the best single index of intoxication, because it is an involuntary response. BAC can even be estimated from the angle of onset of the involuntary jerking: 50 degrees minus the angle of the gaze at the onset of eye oscillation equals the BAC.[1] Dr. Burns testified that the HGN test had been accepted as valid by the highway safety field, including the NHTSA, Finnish researchers, state agencies such as the California Highway Patrol, Arizona Highway Patrol, Washington State Police, and numerous city agencies. Finally, the state offered in evidence an HGN training manual developed by the NHTSA for its nationwide program to train law enforcement officers. Both the manual and training program were based on the Institute's studies.

Sgt. Studdard is currently a supervisor in charge of DUI enforcement for the City of Los Angeles and a consultant to NHTSA on field sobriety testing. Based on his field work administering the HGN test and his participation in double blind studies at the Institute, he testified that the accuracy rate of the HGN test in estimating whether the level of BAC exceeds .10 percent is between 80 and 90 percent. According to Studdard the margin of inaccuracy is caused by the fact that certain drugs, such as barbiturates, cause the same effects as alcohol. We take notice, however, that nystagmus may also indicate a number of neurological conditions, and the presence of any of these would also affect the accuracy of the HGN-based estimate of blood alcohol content. Both Sgt. Studdard and Sgt. Raynor, who currently administers the HGN training program for the State of Arizona, testified that the HGN test is especially useful in detecting violations where a driver with BAC over .10 percent is able to pull himself together sufficiently to pass the traditional field sobriety tests and thus avoid arrest and subsequent chemical testing.

Sgt. Raynor testified that the traditional field sobriety tests are not sensitive enough to detect dangerously impaired drivers with BAC between .10 percent and .14 percent and that the police officers thus must permit them to drive on. Sgt.

---

[1] Thus, nystagmus at 45 degrees corresponds to a blood alcohol content (BAC) of 0.05%; nystagmus at 40 degrees to a BAC of 0.10%; nystagmus at 35 degrees to a BAC of 0.15%; and nystagmus at 30 degrees to a BAC of 0.20%. At BACs above 0.20%, a person's eyes may not be able to follow a moving object. It should be noted however that when officers administer the test they do not necessarily measure the angle of onset; instead they look for three characteristics of high BAC: inability of smooth pursuit, distinct jerkiness at maximum deviation and onset of jerkiness prior to 45 degrees. We do not address the admissibility of quantified BAC estimates based on angle of onset of nystagmus.

Raynor also testified as to the rigor and requirements of the Arizona training and certification program.

At the close of the evidentiary hearing, the trial court concluded that HGN represented a new scientific principle and was therefore subject to the *Frye* standard of admissibility. The court ruled the HGN test did not satisfy *Frye,* was therefore unreliable, and could not form the basis of probable cause. The court granted Blake's motion to dismiss. . . .

[The Supreme Court discussed the application of the Fourth Amendment to roadside stops and sobriety tests, concluding that] roadside sobreity tests that do not involve long delay or unreasonable intrusion . . . may be justified by an officer's reasonable suspicion [and] that Blake's erratic driving, appearance and smell of alcohol were specific articulable facts which gave the officer sufficient grounds to administer roadside sobriety tests, including HGN. . . .

[The court next considered whether there was probable cause to arrest Blake.] Probable cause may not rest on mere suspicion, but neither must it rest on evidence sufficient to convict. . . . Information sufficient to raise a suspicion of criminal behavior by definition need not pass tests of admissibility under our rules of evidence. . . .

We conclude that the testimony presented at the evidentiary hearing regarding the reliability of the HGN test established that in the hands of a trained officer the test is reasonably trustworthy and may be used to help establish probable cause to arrest. . . . Taken together, there was more than sufficient evidence to establish probable cause. Because the trial court ruled that admissibility under *Frye* was a prerequisite for evidence to be used to establish probable cause, we vacate the trial court's order of dismissal of the case and remand the matter for trial. . . .

[It does not follow, however, that] the test results may be admitted in evidence on the question of guilt or innocence. . . .

The HGN test is a different type of test from balancing on one leg or walking a straight line because it rests almost entirely upon an assertion of scientific legitimacy rather than a basis of common knowledge. Different rules therefore apply to determine its admissibility. It is to this question of HGN's admissibility that we now address ourselves.

Rules of evidence are aimed at preventing jury confusion, prejudice and undue consumption of time and trial resources. Scientific evidence is a source of particular judicial caution. Because "science" is often accepted in our society as synonymous with truth, there is a substantial risk that the jury may give undue weight to such evidence. If a technique has an "enormous effect in resolving completely a matter in controversy," it must be demonstrably reliable before it is admissible.

Before expert opinion evidence based on a novel scientific principle can be admitted, the rule of Frye v. United States requires that the theory relied on be in conformity with a generally accepted explanatory theory. The purpose of this requirement is to assure the reliability of the testimony. Because HGN is a new technique based upon scientific principles, its reliability is to be measured against the *Frye* standard. . . . Recognizing that judges and juries are not always in a position to assess the validity of the claims made by an expert witness before making findings of fact, *Frye* guarantees that reliability will be assessed by those in the best position to do so: members of the relevant scientific field who can dispassionately study and test the new theory.

If the scientific principle has gained general acceptance in the particular field in which it belongs, evidence resulting from its application is admissible, "subject to a foundational showing that the expert was qualified, the technique was properly used, and the results were accurately recorded." To determine whether the HGN test satisfies the test of general acceptance we must (1) identify the appropriate scientific community whose acceptance of the nystagmus principles and validity of the HGN test is required, and (2) determine whether there is general acceptance of both the scientific principle and the technique applying the theory. The admissibility of HGN test results under the *Frye* standard is an issue of first impression. Our search has not brought to light any reported American case law ruling on the issue.

The state argues that the relevant scientific community is that of law enforcement and highway safety agencies and behavioral psychologists. Public defender amicus contends that we should disregard these sources and argues that the HGN phenomenon requires assessment by scientists in the fields of neurology, ophthalmology, pharmacology and criminalistics. It claims that narrowing the field deprives the general scientific community of the time needed to evaluate the procedure before it is examined by the legal community. We agree that validation studies must be performed by scientists other than those who have professional and personal interest in the outcome of the evaluation.

We believe, however, that the relevant scientific community that must be shown to have accepted a new scientific procedure is often self-selecting. Scientists who have no interest in a new scientific principle are unlikely to evaluate it, even if a court determines they are part of a relevant scientific community. The HGN test measures a behavioral phenomenon: specifically the effects of alcohol on one aspect of human behavior, the movement of the eye. Thus, it stands to reason that experimental psychologists in the area of behavioral psychology would be interested in verifying the validity of the HGN test and should be included in the relevant scientific community. Similarly, the problem of alcohol's effect on driving ability is a major concern to scientists in the area of highway safety and they, too, should be included.

We disagree with the defendant's implication that those in the field of highway safety or law enforcement are necessarily biased. We believe the National Highway Traffic Safety Administration's interest in funding research to identify the drunk driver is not subject to question in this instance. The NHTSA was addressing a complex problem: every state has either a presumptive or "per se illegal" law that makes reference to BAC (typically .10 percent). Officers whose task it is to remove violators of these laws from the roads may, upon initial suspicion, administer behavioral tests, but until recently the relationship of the tests to specific BAC levels was not well documented. The purpose of NHTSA's program was to develop a test battery to assist officers in discriminating between those drivers who are in violation of these laws and those who are not. Furthermore, it is not to the advantage of law enforcement in the highway safety field to have an unreliable field sobriety test. It is inefficient to arrest and transport a driver for chemical testing, only to find that he is not in violation of the law. We believe that the work of highway safety professionals and behavioral psychologists who study effects of alcohol on behavior is directly affected by the claims and application of the HGN test, so that both these groups must be included in the relevant scientific community.

We are not forced to come to the same conclusion with respect to neurologists, pharmacologists, ophthalmologists and criminalists. Although it is true that the form of nystagmus that concerns us is the result of a neurological malfunction, we agree with Dr. Burns who testified that "the field of neurology does not concern itself specifically with alcohol effects on performance and even more specifically with field sobriety." She did state, however, that a "very small segment of the neurology community" concerns itself with the effects and has produced some literature. No argument has been made why the fields of pharmacology, ophthalmology and criminalistics (beyond those concerned with detecting violators of DUI laws) should be included in the relevant scientific community and no convincing reason occurs to us. We conclude, therefore, that to determine whether the HGN test satisfies the *Frye* requirement of general acceptance the appropriate disciplines include behavioral psychology, highway safety and, to a lesser extent, neurology and criminalistics.

We now turn to the question of whether there has been general acceptance of both the HGN test and its underlying principle. The burden of proving general acceptance is on the proponent of the new technique; it may be proved by expert testimony and scientific and legal literature. We have already summarized the expert testimony presented by the state. In addition, the state submitted both scientific publications and reports of research done for the United States Department of Transportation. These are listed in Appendix A.

At the evidentiary hearing Blake presented no evidence to refute either the substance of the expert opinion testimony or the contention that it had general acceptance. Blake and public defender amicus instead argued that there is a paucity of literature and that the appropriate scientific disciplines have not yet had the opportunity to duplicate and evaluate Dr. Burns' work.

Our own research is listed in Appendix B. The literature demonstrates to our satisfaction that those professionals who have investigated the subject do not dispute the strong correlation between BAC and the different types of nystagmus. Furthermore, those who have investigated the relation between BAC and nystagmus as the eye follows a moving object have uniformly found that the higher the BAC, the earlier the onset of involuntary jerking of the eyeball. Although the publications are not voluminous, they have been before the relevant communities a considerable period of time for any opposing views to have surfaced.

Based on all the evidence we conclude there has been sufficient scrutiny of the HGN test to permit a conclusion as to reliability. The "general acceptance" requirement does not necessitate a showing of universal acceptance of the reliability of the scientific principle and procedure. Neither must the principle and procedure be absolutely accurate or certain.

We believe that the HGN test satisfies the *Frye* standard. The evidence demonstrates that the following propositions have gained general acceptance in the relevant scientific community: (1) HGN occurs in conjunction with alcohol consumption; (2) its onset and distinctness are correlated to BAC; (3) BAC in excess of .10 percent can be estimated with reasonable accuracy from the combination of the eyes' tracking ability, the angle of onset of nystagmus and the degree of nystagmus at maximum deviation; and (4) officers can be trained to observe these phenomena sufficiently to estimate accurately whether BAC is above or below .10 percent. . . .

We find that the horizonal gaze nystagmus test properly administered by a trained police officer is sufficiently reliable to be a factor in establishing probable cause to arrest a driver . . . . We further find that the horizonal gaze nystagmus test satisfies the *Frye* test for reliability and may be admitted in evidence to corroborate or attack, but not to quantify, the chemical analysis of the accused's blood alcohol content. It may not be used to establish the accused's level of blood alcohol in the absence of a chemical analysis showing the proscribed level in the accused's blood, breath or urine. [I]t is admissible, as is other evidence of defendant's behavior, to prove that he was "under the influence." . . .

NOTES

1. *Advisory opinions.* The trial court had dismissed the charges on the ground that the police officer's observations of HGN could not establish probable cause inasmuch as this technique for ascertaining intoxication was not generally accepted in the scientific community. What did the supreme court hold? Was the portion of the opinion deciding that the HGN test satisfies the *Frye* standard part of this holding? If not, why did the court reach this issue?

2. *Reading the scientific literature.* The literature on HGN as an indicator of alcohol cited by the state to show general acceptance of the HGN test in the scientific community consisted of seven articles or reports. The majority, four, never appeared in any scientific journal, but were published by the Department of Transportation, which presumably funded them. Another was a second-hand discussion in a looseleaf treatise for attorneys, 1 Richard Erwin, Defense of Drunk Driving Cases § 815A[3] (3d ed. 1985), asserting that "[a] strong correlation exists

between the BAC and the angle of onset of [gaze] nystagmus." Only two of the seven were refereed papers in respected journals, and neither claimed that measuring the angle of the onset of nystagmus was a reliable indicator of BAC. C. Rashbass, The Relationship Between Saccadic and Smooth Tracking Eye Movements, 159 J. Physiol. 326 (1961) (barbiturate drugs interfere with smooth tracking eye movement); J.M. Wilkinson et al., Alcohol and Human Eye Movement, 97 Brain 785 (1974) (oral dose of ethyl alcohol impaired smooth pursuit eye movement of all human subjects).

The supreme court also undertook its own, unaided study of the scientific literature on HGN and intoxication, which it summarized by listing in an appendix to its opinion the 22 papers it located. The citations there suggest that the court's study went no further than a review of abstracts from computerized databases. Indeed, one paper apparently has never been published, and only the abstract of a conference presentation is mentioned. Some have little to do with the validity or reliability of detecting intoxication by nystagmus. E.g., W.J. Oosterveld et al., Quantitative Effect of Linear Acceleration on Positional Alcohol Nystagmus, 45 Aerospace Med., July 1974, at 695 (G-loading brings about Positional Alcohol Nystagmus even when subject has not ingested alcohol; however when subjects ingested alcohol, no PAN was found when subjects were in supine position, even with G-force at 3). Others appear in unrefereed periodicals that can hardly be considered part of the scientific literature. E.g., Norris, The Correlation of Angle of Onset of Nystagmus With Blood Alcohol Level: Report of a Field Trial, Calif. Ass'n Criminalistics Newsletter, June 1985, at 21, 22; Seelmeyer, Nystagmus, A Valid DUI Test, Law and Order, July 1985, at 29 (horizonal gaze nystagmus test is used in "at least one law enforcement agency in each of the 50 states" and is "a legitimate method of establishing probable cause.").

In State v. Witte, 836 P.2d 1110 (Kan. 1992), the Kansas Supreme Court concluded that scientific literature appearing after State v. Superior Court showed a lack of general scientific acceptance of HGN evidence. However, *Witte* relied on articles written by lawyers, not scientists, and published in legal, not scientific journals and texts. And, its review of the scientific literature seems no deeper than that in *Superior Court*. In People v. Leahy, 882 P.2d 321 (Cal. 1994), the California Supreme Court held that it was error for the trial court to admit HGN evidence without addressing its acceptance in the scientific community. But cf. State v. O'Key, 899 P.2d 663 (Or. 1995) (applying a standard other than general acceptance to "hold that HGN test evidence is admissible in a prosecution for DUI to establish that a person was under the influence of intoxicating liquor, but is not admissible . . . to establish a person's BAC, i.e., that a person was driving while having a BAC of .08 percent or more."). The scientific literature on the value of HGN in detecting drunkenness is reviewed in Joseph R. Meany, Note, Horizontal Gaze Nystagmus: A Closer Look, 36 Jurimetrics J. 383 (1996), which argues that there is little experimental evidence to show that HGN is particularly discriminating when blood alcohol concentrations are neither very high nor very low.

3. *Theories or procedures used exclusively in forensic applications.* State v. Superior Court concerns a test developed specifically for use in law enforcement. Should widespread usage by law enforcement officials or police laboratory technicians demonstrate general acceptance in the requisite community? Was the Arizona court correct in treating "highway safety officials" as part of the scientific community? Arguably, the HGN test for inebriation is a special situation in this regard. Why?

With other types of "forensics-only" evidence, the courts have been more skeptical of the claims of law enforcement technicians or scientists heavily involved in the development and promotion of the methods. E.g., State ex rel. Collins v. Superior Court, 644 P.2d 1266, 1285 (Ariz. 1982); People v. Kelley, 549 P.2d 1240 (Cal. 1976); infra chapter 8 note 1. So-called "voiceprint" evidence, which prompted many courts to abandon or stretch the general acceptance standard beyond recognition, supplies a disturbing example of initial overenthusiasm ultimately revealed by exposure of the technique to criticism from a broader scientific community. See 1 Paul C. Giannelli & Edward J. Imwinkelried, Scientific Evidence § 10-3 (2d ed. 1993); 1 McCormick on Evidence § 207 (John Strong ed., 4th ed. 1991); Andre A. Moenssens et al., Scientific Evidence in Criminal Cases 670 (3d ed. 1986). More recently, critics of "multisystem" electrophoresis of dried blood stains suggested that this method of identifying blood serum enzymes also had been oversold to gullible courts. See infra chapter 8. Generating a certain sense of déja vu, the most recent "forensics-only technique" to take the center stage is named DNA "fingerprinting" by its developers. We treat the legal issues in the forensic use of DNA technology infra at chapters 11-14.

4. *Three problems.* How should the following questions be decided in a *Frye* jurisdiction:

(a) In a homicide prosecution, several witnesses testify that before this case, tests developed specifically for and used for the first time in the case at bar — scientists believed that it was impossible to demonstrate the presence of succinylcholine chloride or its component parts in the body. However, in an effort to resolve the case at bar, a forensic toxicologist developed and performed a test to detect succinic acid, a component of succinylcholine chloride, in the body tissue. He will testify that he found this acid in abnormal amounts in the body of the victim. May he give this testimony? See Coppolino v. State, 223 So.2d 68 (Fla. Dist. Ct. App. 1968), app. dismissed, 234 So.2d 120 (Fla. 1969), cert. denied, 399 U.S. 927 (1970).

(b) The state's expert testifies that "numerous crime laboratories" use thin-layer chromatography to detect monomethylamine nitrate, and one paper attesting to the accuracy of this technique has appeared in a scientific journal. See United States v. Metzger, 778 F.2d 1195, 1204 (6th Cir. 1985); cf. People v. Brown, 790 P.2d 440 (Cal. 1985). What if no scientific reports on the technique are in print?

(c) An impeccably conducted opinion poll of psychophysiologists shows that 61% think that a professionally administered polygraph test is "a useful diagnostic tool" in detecting deception. See Dowd v. Calabrese, 585 F. Supp. 430, 432 (D.D.C. 1984).

Chapter 7
The Scientific Soundness Standard

Daubert v. Merrell Dow Pharmaceuticals, Inc.
506 U.S. 738 (1993)

JUSTICE BLACKMUN delivered the opinion of the Court.

In this case we are called upon to determine the standard for admitting expert scientific testimony in a federal trial.

I

Petitioners Jason Daubert and Eric Schuller are minor children born with serious birth defects. They and their parents sued respondent in California state court, alleging that the birth defects had been caused by the mothers' ingestion of Bendectin, a prescription anti-nausea drug marketed by respondent. Respondent removed the suits to federal court on diversity grounds.

After extensive discovery, respondent moved for summary judgment, contending that Bendectin does not cause birth defects in humans and that petitioners would be unable to come forward with any admissible evidence that it does. In support of its motion, respondent submitted an affidavit of Steven H. Lamm, physician and epidemiologist, who is a well-credentialed expert on the risks from exposure to various chemical substances. Doctor Lamm stated that he had reviewed all the literature on Bendectin and human birth defects — more than 30 published studies involving over 130,000 patients. No study had found Bendectin to be a human teratogen (i.e., a substance capable of causing malformations in fetuses). On the basis of this review, Doctor Lamm concluded that maternal use of Bendectin during the first trimester of pregnancy has not been shown to be a risk factor for human birth defects.

Petitioners did not (and do not) contest this characterization of the published record regarding Bendectin. Instead, they responded to respondent's motion with the testimony of eight experts of their own, each of whom also possessed impressive credentials. These experts had concluded that Bendectin can cause birth defects. Their conclusions were based upon "in vitro" (test tube) and "in vivo" (live) animal studies that found a link between Bendectin and malformations; pharmacological studies of the chemical structure of Bendectin that purported to show similarities between the structure of the drug and that of other substances known to cause birth defects; and the "reanalysis" of previously published epidemiological (human statistical) studies.

The District Court granted respondent's motion for summary judgment. The court stated that scientific evidence is admissible only if the principle upon which it is based is "sufficiently established to have general acceptance in the field to which it belongs." The court concluded that petitioners' evidence did not meet this standard. Given the vast body of epidemiological data concerning Bendectin, the court held, expert opinion which is not based on epidemiological evidence is not admissible to establish causation. Thus, the animal-cell studies, live-animal studies, and chemical-structure analyses on which petitioners had relied could not raise by themselves a reasonably disputable jury issue regarding causation. Petitioners' epidemiological analyses, based as they were on recalculations of data in previously published studies that had found no causal link between the drug and birth defects, were ruled to be inadmissible because they had not been published or subjected to peer review.

The United States Court of Appeals for the Ninth Circuit affirmed. Citing Frye v. United States, 293 F. 1013, 1014 (1923), the court stated that expert opinion based on a scientific technique is inadmissible unless the technique is "generally accepted" as reliable in the relevant scientific community. The court declared that expert opinion based on a methodology that diverges "significantly from the procedures accepted by recognized authorities in the field . . . cannot be shown to be 'generally accepted as a reliable technique.'"

The court emphasized that other Courts of Appeals considering the risks of Bendectin had refused to admit reanalyses of epidemiological studies that had been neither published nor subjected to peer review. Those courts had found unpublished reanalyses "particularly problematic in light of the massive weight of the original published studies supporting [respondent's] position, all of which had undergone full scrutiny from the scientific community." Contending that reanalysis is generally accepted by the scientific community only when it is subjected to verification and scrutiny by others in the field, the Court of Appeals rejected petitioners' reanalyses as "unpublished, not subjected to the normal peer review process and generated solely for use in litigation." The court concluded that petitioners' evidence provided an insufficient foundation to allow admission of expert testimony that Bendectin caused their injuries and, accordingly, that petitioners could not satisfy their burden of proving causation at trial.

We granted certiorari in light of sharp divisions among the courts regarding the proper standard for the admission of expert testimony.

II

A

In the 70 years since its formulation in the *Frye* case, the "general acceptance" test has been the dominant standard for determining the admissibility of novel scientific evidence at trial. Although under increasing attack of late, the rule continues to be followed by a majority of courts, including the Ninth Circuit. . . .

The merits of the *Frye* test have been much debated, and scholarship on its proper scope and application is legion. Petitioners' primary attack, however, is not on the content but on the continuing authority of the rule. They contend that the *Frye* test was superseded by the adoption of the Federal Rules of Evidence. We agree.

We interpret the legislatively-enacted Federal Rules of Evidence as we would any statute. Rule 402 provides the baseline: "All relevant evidence is admissible, except as otherwise provided by the Constitution of the United States, by Act of Congress, by these rules, or by other rules prescribed by the Supreme Court pursuant to statutory authority. Evidence which is not relevant is not admissible." "Relevant evidence" is defined as that which has "any tendency to make the existence of any fact that is of consequence to the determination of the action more probable or less probable than it would be without the evidence." Rule 401. The Rule's basic standard of relevance thus is a liberal one.

Frye, of course, predated the Rules by half a century. In United States v. Abel, 469 U.S. 45 (1984), we considered the pertinence of background common law in interpreting the Rules of Evidence. We noted that the Rules occupy the field, but, quoting Professor Cleary, the Reporter, explained that the common law nevertheless could serve as an aid to their application: "In principle, under the Federal Rules no common law of evidence remains. 'All relevant evidence is admissible, except as otherwise provided....' In reality, of course, the body of common law knowledge continues to exist, though in the somewhat altered form of a source of guidance in the exercise of delegated powers." We found the common-law precept at issue in the *Abel* case entirely consistent with Rule 402's general requirement of admissibility, and considered it unlikely that the drafters had intended to change the rule. In Bourjaily v. United States, 483 U.S. 171 (1987), on the other hand, the Court was unable to find a particular common-law doctrine in the Rules, and so held it superseded.

Here there is a specific Rule that speaks to the contested issue. Rule 702, governing expert testimony, provides: "If scientific, technical, or other specialized knowledge will assist the trier of fact to understand the evidence or to determine a fact in issue, a witness qualified as an expert by knowledge, skill, experience, training, or education, may testify thereto in the form of an opinion or otherwise." Nothing in the text of this Rule establishes "general acceptance" as an absolute prerequisite to admissibility. Nor does respondent present any clear indication that Rule 702 or the Rules as a whole were intended to incorporate a "general acceptance" standard. The drafting history makes no mention of *Frye,* and a rigid "general acceptance" requirement would be at odds with the "liberal thrust" of the Federal Rules and their "general approach of relaxing the traditional barriers to 'opinion' testimony." Beech Aircraft Corp. v. Rainey, 488 U.S. at 169 (citing Rules 701 to 705). Given the Rules' permissive backdrop and their inclusion of a specific rule on expert testimony that does not mention "general acceptance," the assertion that the Rules somehow assimilated Frye is unconvincing. *Frye* made "general acceptance" the exclusive test for admitting expert scientific testimony. That austere standard, absent from and incompatible with the Federal Rules of Evidence, should not be applied in federal trials.

B

That the *Frye* test was displaced by the Rules of Evidence does not mean, however, that the Rules themselves place no limits on the admissibility of purportedly scientific evidence. Nor is the trial judge disabled from screening such evidence. To the contrary, under the Rules the trial judge must ensure that any and all scientific testimony or evidence admitted is not only relevant, but reliable.

The primary locus of this obligation is Rule 702, which clearly contemplates some degree of regulation of the subjects and theories about which an expert may testify. "If scientific, technical, or other specialized knowledge will assist the trier of fact to understand the evidence or to determine a fact in issue" an expert "may testify thereto." The subject of an expert's testimony must be "scientific . . . knowledge."[8] The adjective "scientific" implies a grounding in the methods and procedures of science. Similarly, the word "knowledge" connotes more than subjective belief or unsupported speculation. The term "applies to any body of known facts or to any body of ideas inferred from such facts or accepted as truths on good grounds." Webster's Third New International Dictionary 1252 (1986). Of course, it would be unreasonable to conclude that the subject of scientific testimony must be "known" to a certainty; arguably, there are no certainties in science. But, in order to qualify as "scientific knowledge," an inference or assertion must be derived by the scientific method. Proposed testimony must be supported by appropriate validation — i.e., "good grounds," based on what is known. In short, the requirement that an expert's testimony pertain to "scientific knowledge" establishes a standard of evidentiary reliability.[9]

Rule 702 further requires that the evidence or testimony "assist the trier of fact to understand the evidence or to determine a fact in issue." This condition goes primarily to relevance. "Expert testimony which does not relate to any issue in the case is not relevant and, ergo, non-helpful." 3 Weinstein & Berger ¶ 702[02], p. 702-18. See also United States v. Downing, 753 F.2d 1224, 1242 (CA3 1985) ("An additional consideration under Rule 702 — and another aspect of relevancy — is whether expert testimony proffered in the case is sufficiently tied to the facts

---

[8] Rule 702 also applies to "technical, or other specialized knowledge." Our discussion is limited to the scientific context because that is the nature of the expertise offered here.

[9] We note that scientists typically distinguish between "validity" (does the principle support what it purports to show?) and "reliability" (does application of the principle produce consistent results?). Although "the difference between accuracy, validity, and reliability may be such that each is distinct from the other by no more than a hen's kick," Starrs, Frye v. United States Restructured and Revitalized: A Proposal to Amend Federal Evidence Rule 702, 26 Jurimetrics J. 249, 256 (1986), our reference here is to evidentiary reliability — that is, trustworthiness. Cf., e.g., Advisory Committee's Notes on Fed. Rule Evid. 602 ("'[T]he rule requiring that a witness who testifies to a fact which can be perceived by the senses must have had an opportunity to observe, and must have actually observed the fact' is a 'most pervasive manifestation' of the common law insistence upon 'the most reliable sources of information.'"); Advisory Committee's Notes on Art. VIII of the Rules of Evidence (hearsay exceptions will be recognized only "under circumstances supposed to furnish guarantees of trustworthiness"). In a case involving scientific evidence, evidentiary reliability will be based upon scientific validity.

of the case that it will aid the jury in resolving a factual dispute"). The consideration has been aptly described by Judge Becker as one of "fit." Ibid. "Fit" is not always obvious, and scientific validity for one purpose is not necessarily scientific validity for other, unrelated purposes. The study of the phases of the moon, for example, may provide valid scientific "knowledge" about whether a certain night was dark, and if darkness is a fact in issue, the knowledge will assist the trier of fact. However (absent creditable grounds supporting such a link), evidence that the moon was full on a certain night will not assist the trier of fact in determining whether an individual was unusually likely to have behaved irrationally on that night. Rule 702's "helpfulness" standard requires a valid scientific connection to the pertinent inquiry as a precondition to admissibility.

That these requirements are embodied in Rule 702 is not surprising. Unlike an ordinary witness, see Rule 701, an expert is permitted wide latitude to offer opinions, including those that are not based on first-hand knowledge or observation. See Rules 702 and 703. Presumably, this relaxation of the usual requirement of first-hand knowledge — a rule which represents "a 'most pervasive manifestation' of the common law insistence upon 'the most reliable sources of information'" — is premised on an assumption that the expert's opinion will have a reliable basis in the knowledge and experience of his discipline.

C

Faced with a proffer of expert scientific testimony, then, the trial judge must determine at the outset, pursuant to Rule 104(a),[10] whether the expert is proposing to testify to (1) scientific knowledge that (2) will assist the trier of fact to understand or determine a fact in issue.[11] This entails a preliminary assessment of whether the reasoning or methodology underlying the testimony is scientifically valid and of whether that reasoning or methodology properly can be applied to the facts in issue. We are confident that federal judges possess the capacity to undertake this review. Many factors will bear on the inquiry, and we do not presume to set out a definitive checklist or test. But some general observations are appropriate.

---

[10] Rule 104(a) provides: "Preliminary questions concerning the qualification of a person to be a witness, the existence of a privilege, or the admissibility of evidence shall be determined by the court, subject to the provisions of subdivision (b) [pertaining to conditional admissions]. In making its determination it is not bound by the rules of evidence except those with respect to privileges." These matters should be established by a preponderance of proof. See Bourjaily v. United States, 483 U.S. 171, 175-176 (1987).

[11] Although the Frye decision itself focused exclusively on "novel" scientific techniques, we do not read the requirements of Rule 702 to apply specially or exclusively to unconventional evidence. Of course, well-established propositions are less likely to be challenged than those that are novel, and they are more handily defended. Indeed, theories that are so firmly established as to have attained the status of scientific law, such as the laws of thermodynamics, properly are subject to judicial notice under Fed. Rule Evid. 201.

Ordinarily, a key question to be answered in determining whether a theory or technique is scientific knowledge that will assist the trier of fact will be whether it can be (and has been) tested. "Scientific methodology today is based on generating hypotheses and testing them to see if they can be falsified; indeed, this methodology is what distinguishes science from other fields of human inquiry." Green, at 645. See also C. Hempel, Philosophy of Natural Science 49 (1966) ("[T]he statements constituting a scientific explanation must be capable of empirical test"); K. Popper, Conjectures and Refutations: The Growth of Scientific Knowledge 37 (5th ed. 1989) ("[T]he criterion of the scientific status of a theory is its falsifiability, or refutability, or testability").

Another pertinent consideration is whether the theory or technique has been subjected to peer review and publication. Publication (which is but one element of peer review) is not a sine qua non of admissibility; it does not necessarily correlate with reliability, and in some instances well-grounded but innovative theories will not have been published. Some propositions, moreover, are too particular, too new, or of too limited interest to be published. But submission to the scrutiny of the scientific community is a component of "good science," in part because it increases the likelihood that substantive flaws in methodology will be detected. The fact of publication (or lack thereof) in a peer-reviewed journal thus will be a relevant, though not dispositive, consideration in assessing the scientific validity of a particular technique or methodology on which an opinion is premised.

Additionally, in the case of a particular scientific technique, the court ordinarily should consider the known or potential rate of error, see, e.g., United States v. Smith, 869 F.2d 348, 353-354 (CA7 1989) (surveying studies of the error rate of spectrographic voice identification technique), and the existence and maintenance of standards controlling the technique's operation. See United States v. Williams, 583 F.2d 1194, 1198 (CA2 1978) (noting professional organization's standard governing spectrographic analysis), cert. denied, 439 U.S. 1117 (1979).

Finally, "general acceptance" can yet have a bearing on the inquiry. A "reliability assessment does not require, although it does permit, explicit identification of a relevant scientific community and an express determination of a particular degree of acceptance within that community." United States v. Downing, 753 F.2d, at 1238. Widespread acceptance can be an important factor in ruling particular evidence admissible, and "a known technique that has been able to attract only minimal support within the community," [id.], may properly be viewed with skepticism.

The inquiry envisioned by Rule 702 is, we emphasize, a flexible one.[12] Its overarching subject is the scientific validity — and thus the evidentiary relevance and reliability — of the principles that underlie a proposed submission. The focus,

---

[12] A number of authorities have presented variations on the reliability approach, each with its own slightly different set of factors. . . . To the extent that they focus on the reliability of evidence as ensured by the scientific validity of its underlying principles, all these versions may well have merit, although we express no opinion regarding any of their particular details.

of course, must be solely on principles and methodology, not on the conclusions that they generate.

Throughout, a judge assessing a proffer of expert scientific testimony under Rule 702 should also be mindful of other applicable rules. Rule 703 provides that expert opinions based on otherwise inadmissible hearsay are to be admitted only if the facts or data are "of a type reasonably relied upon by experts in the particular field in forming opinions or inferences upon the subject." Rule 706 allows the court at its discretion to procure the assistance of an expert of its own choosing. Finally, Rule 403 permits the exclusion of relevant evidence "if its probative value is substantially outweighed by the danger of unfair prejudice, confusion of the issues, or misleading the jury. . . ." Judge Weinstein has explained: "Expert evidence can be both powerful and quite misleading because of the difficulty in evaluating it. Because of this risk, the judge in weighing possible prejudice against probative force under Rule 403 of the present rules exercises more control over experts than over lay witnesses."

III

We conclude by briefly addressing what appear to be two underlying concerns of the parties and amici in this case. Respondent expresses apprehension that abandonment of "general acceptance" as the exclusive requirement for admission will result in a "free-for-all" in which befuddled juries are confounded by absurd and irrational pseudoscientific assertions. In this regard respondent seems to us to be overly pessimistic about the capabilities of the jury, and of the adversary system generally. Vigorous cross-examination, presentation of contrary evidence, and careful instruction on the burden of proof are the traditional and appropriate means of attacking shaky but admissible evidence. See Rock v. Arkansas, 483 U.S. 44, 61 (1987). Additionally, in the event the trial court concludes that the scintilla of evidence presented supporting a position is insufficient to allow a reasonable juror to conclude that the position more likely than not is true, the court remains free to direct a judgment, and likewise to grant summary judgment. These conventional devices, rather than wholesale exclusion under an uncompromising "general acceptance" test, are the appropriate safeguards where the basis of scientific testimony meets the standards of Rule 702.

Petitioners and, to a greater extent, their amici exhibit a different concern. They suggest that recognition of a screening role for the judge that allows for the exclusion of "invalid" evidence will sanction a stifling and repressive scientific orthodoxy and will be inimical to the search for truth. It is true that open debate is an essential part of both legal and scientific analyses. Yet there are important differences between the quest for truth in the courtroom and the quest for truth in the laboratory. Scientific conclusions are subject to perpetual revision. Law, on the other hand, must resolve disputes finally and quickly. The scientific project is advanced by broad and wide-ranging consideration of a multitude of hypotheses, for those that are incorrect will eventually be shown to be so, and that in itself is an advance. Conjectures that are probably wrong are of little use, however, in the project of reaching a quick, final, and binding legal judgment — often of great consequence – about a particular set of events in the past. We recognize that in practice, a gatekeeping role for the judge, no matter how flexible, inevitably on occasion will prevent the jury from learning of authentic insights and innovations. That, nevertheless, is the balance that is struck by Rules of Evidence designed not for the exhaustive search for cosmic understanding but for the particularized resolution of legal disputes.

IV

To summarize: "general acceptance" is not a necessary precondition to the admissibility of scientific evidence under the Federal Rules of Evidence, but the Rules of Evidence — especially Rule 702 — do assign to the trial judge the task of ensuring that an expert's testimony both rests on a reliable foundation and is relevant to the task at hand. Pertinent evidence based on scientifically valid principles will satisfy those demands.

The inquiries of the District Court and the Court of Appeals focused almost exclusively on "general acceptance," as gauged by publication and the decisions of other courts. Accordingly, the judgment of the Court of Appeals is vacated and the case is remanded for further proceedings consistent with this opinion.

It is so ordered.

CHIEF JUSTICE REHNQUIST, with whom JUSTICE STEVENS joins, concurring in part and dissenting in part.

The petition for certiorari in this case presents two questions: first, whether the rule of Frye v. United States remains good law after the enactment of the Federal Rules of Evidence; and second, if *Frye* remains valid, whether it requires expert scientific testimony to have been subjected to a peer-review process in order to be admissible. The Court concludes, correctly in my view, that the *Frye* rule did not survive the enactment of the Federal Rules of Evidence, and I therefore join Parts I and II-A of its opinion. The second question presented in the petition for certiorari necessarily is mooted by this holding, but the Court nonetheless proceeds to construe Rules 702 and 703 very much in the abstract, and then offers some "general observations."

"General observations" by this Court customarily carry great weight with lower federal courts, but the ones offered here suffer from the flaw common to most such observations — they are not applied to deciding whether or not particular testimony was or was not admissible, and therefore they tend to be not only general, but vague and abstract. This is particularly unfortunate in a case such as this, where the ultimate legal question depends on an appreciation of one or more bodies of knowledge not judicially noticeable, and subject to different interpretations in the briefs of the parties and their amici. Twenty-two amicus briefs have been filed in the case, and indeed the Court's opinion contains no less than 37 citations to amicus briefs and other secondary sources.

The various briefs filed in this case are markedly different from typical briefs, in that large parts of them do not deal with decided cases or statutory language—the sort of material we customarily interpret. Instead, they deal with definitions of scientific knowledge, scientific method, scientific validity, and peer review — in short, matters far afield from the expertise of judges. This is not to say that such materials are not useful or even necessary in deciding how Rule 703 should be applied; but it is to say that the unusual subject matter should cause us to proceed with great caution in deciding more than we have to, because our reach can so easily exceed our grasp.

But even if it were desirable to make "general observations" not necessary to decide the questions presented, I cannot subscribe to some of the observations made by the Court. In Part II-B, the Court concludes that reliability and relevancy are the touchstones of the admissibility of expert testimony. Federal Rule of Evidence 402 provides, as the Court points out, that "[e]vidence which is not relevant is not admissible." But there is no similar reference in the Rule to "reliability." The Court constructs its argument by parsing the language "[i]f scientific, technical, or other specialized knowledge will assist the trier of fact to understand the evidence or to determine a fact in issue . . . an expert . . . may testify thereto. . . ." Fed. Rule Evid. 702. It stresses that the subject of the expert's testimony must be "scientific ... knowledge," and points out that "scientific" "implies a grounding in the methods and procedures of science," and that the word "knowledge" "connotes more than subjective belief or unsupported speculation." From this it concludes that "scientific knowledge" must be "derived by the scientific method." Proposed testimony, we are told, must be supported by "appropriate validation." Indeed, in footnote 9, the Court decides that "[i]n a case involving scientific evidence, evidentiary reliability will be based upon scientific validity."

Questions arise simply from reading this part of the Court's opinion, and countless more questions will surely arise when hundreds of district judges try to apply its teaching to particular offers of expert testimony. Does all of this dicta apply to an expert seeking to testify on the basis of "technical or other specialized knowledge" — the other types of expert knowledge to which Rule 702 applies — or are the "general observations" limited only to "scientific knowledge"? What is the difference between scientific knowledge and technical knowledge? Does Rule 702 actually contemplate that the phrase "scientific, technical, or other specialized knowledge" be broken down into numerous subspecies of expertise, or did its authors simply pick general descriptive language covering the sort of expert testimony which courts have customarily received? The Court speaks of its confidence that federal judges can make a "preliminary assessment of whether the reasoning or methodology underlying the testimony is scientifically valid and of whether that reasoning or methodology properly can be applied to the facts in issue." The

Court then states that a "key question" to be answered in deciding whether something is "scientific knowledge" "will be whether it can be (and has been) tested." Following this sentence are three quotations from treatises, which speak not only of empirical testing, but one of which states that "the criterion of the scientific status of a theory is its falsifiability, or refutability, or testability."

I defer to no one in my confidence in federal judges; but I am at a loss to know what is meant when it is said that the scientific status of a theory depends on its "falsifiability," and I suspect some of them will be, too.

I do not doubt that Rule 702 confides to the judge some gatekeeping responsibility in deciding questions of the admissibility of proffered expert testimony. But I do not think it imposes on them either the obligation or the authority to become amateur scientists in order to perform that role. I think the Court would be far better advised in this case to decide only the questions presented, and to leave the further development of this important area of the law to future cases.

NOTES

1. *The competititors.* What is the difference between the standards articulated in *Frye* and *Daubert?* Which is more stringent? Which gives the trial judge more discretion? Does evidence that satisfies *Daubert* necessarily satisfy *Frye?* How about the other way around? In the end, does it make much difference which standard is adopted? In the chapters that follow, consider whether there is any correlation between the admissibility of the various types of scientific evidence and the jurisdiction's standard for admitting scientific evidence.

2. *The basis for* Daubert. Does *Daubert* decide that the general acceptance standard is inferior to the standard that it describes? Which is the better standard? Does *Daubert* imply that the general acceptance standard is no longer good law in a state that uses an evidence code that is identical in wording to the federal rules? For powerful criticism of the Court's treatment of Rule 702 and its facile conclusion that the wording of the federal rules displace *Frye,* see Paul C. Giannelli, *Daubert:* Interpreting the Federal Rules of Evidence, 15 Cardozo L. Rev. 1999 (1994). The early responses of state courts to arguments calling for adoption of *Daubert* have been mixed. Compare, e.g., People v. Leahy, 882 P.2d 321 (Cal. 1994), with State v. Alberico, 861 P.2d 192 (N.M. 1994). For a tabulation of the early returns, see Joseph R. Meaney, Note, From *Frye* to *Daubert:* Is a Pattern Unfolding?, 35 Jurimetrics J. 191 (1995).

3. *The scope of the standards.* To what types of expert or scientific testimony do *Frye* and *Daubert* apply. All expert testimony? Only scientific testimony? Only novel scientific testimony? Only testimony from the natural, as opposed to the behavioral, sciences? See Lisa M. Agrimonti, The Limitations of *Daubert* and its Misapplication to Quasi-Experts: A Two-year Case Review of *Daubert v.*

Merrell Dow Pharmaceuticals, Inc., 35 Washburn L.J. 134, 147 (1995); Edward J. Imwinkelried, Evidence Law Visits Jurassic Park: The Far-reaching Implications of the *Daubert* Court's Recognition of the Uncertainty of the Scientific Enterprise, 81 Iowa L. Rev. 55, 69-71 (1995); Edward J. Imwinkelried, The Next Step After *Daubert*: Developing a Similarly Epistemological Approach to Ensuring the Reliability of Nonscientific Expert Testimony, 15 Cardozo L. Rev. 2271 (1994); Linda S. Sinard & William G. Young, *Daubert*'s Gatekeeper: The Role of the District Judge in Admitting Expert Testimony, 68 Tulane L. Rev. 1457 (1994).

    4. *The* Daubert *factors.* Do the factors listed in *Daubert* provide suitable guidance to the trial courts? Should the Court have left the elaboration of the "good grounds" standard to future cases? The concurrence expresses special dissatisfaction with the first factor. The majority wrote that:

> Ordinarily, a key question to be answered in determining whether a theory or technique is scientific knowledge that will assist the trier of fact will be whether it can be (and has been) tested. "Scientific methodology today is based on generating hypotheses and testing them to see if they can be falsified; indeed, this methodology is what distinguishes science from other fields of human inquiry." Green, at 645. See also C. Hempel, Philosophy of Natural Science 49 (1966) ("[T]he statements constituting a scientific explanation must be capable of empirical test"); K. Popper, Conjectures and Refutations: The Growth of Scientific Knowledge 37 (5th ed. 1989) ("[T]he criterion of the scientific status of a theory is its falsifiability, or refutability, or testability").

506 U.S. at 595. To which the Chief Justice responds: "I defer to no one in my confidence in federal judges; but I am at a loss to know what is meant when it is said that the scientific status of a theory depends on its 'falsifiability,' and I suspect some of them will be, too." Id. at 600. To the extent that "falsifiability" is a criterion for distinguishing the empirical from the metaphysical, is it of much use in court? Are there any expert assertions of fact are not, "capable of empirical test[ing]," at least in principle? Consider Popper's explanation of "the technical terms 'falsifiable' . . . and 'falsifiability'":

> [A] statement (a theory, a conjecture) has the status of belonging to the empirical sciences if and only if it is falsifiable.
>   But when is a statement falsifiable? [F]alsifiability in the sense of my demarcation requirement is a purely logical affair. It has to do with the logical structure of statements and of classes of statements. And it has *nothing* to do with the question whether or not certain experimental results would be accepted as falsifications.
>   A statement or theory is, according to my criterion, falsifiable if and only if there exists at least one potential falsifier – at least one possible basic statement that conflicts with it logically. It is important not to demand that the basic statement be *true.* The class of basic statement is

designed so that a basic statement describes a logically possible event of which it is logically possible that it might be observed.

To make these matters less abstract, I shall give four examples here: two of falsifiable statements, and two of unfalsifiable statements.

(1) 'All swans are white'. This theory is falsifiable, since, for example, it contradicts the basic statement (which is, incidentally, false): 'On the 16th of May, 1934, a black swan stood between 10 and 11 o'clock in the morning in front of the statute of Empress Elizabeth in the Volksgarten in Vienna.'

(2) Einstein's principle of proportionality of inert and (passively) heavy mass. This equivalence principle conflicts with many potential falsifiers: events whose observation is logically possible. Yet despite all attempts . . . to realize such a falsification experimentally, the experiments have so far corroborated the principle of equivalence.

(3) 'All human actions are egotistic, motivated by self-interest.' This theory is widely held: it has variants in behaviourism, vulgar-Marxism, religion, and sociology of knowledge. Clearly, this theory with all its variants is not falsifiable: no example of an altruistic action can refute the view that there was an egotistic motive hidden behind it.

(4) Purely existential statements are not falsifiable — as in Rudolf Carnap's famous example: 'There is a colour ('Trumpet-red') which incites terror in those who look at it.' Another example is: 'There is a ceremony whose exact performance forces the devil to appear.' Such statements are not falsifiable. (They are, in principle, verifiable: it is logically possible to find a ceremony whose performance leads to the appearance of a human-like form with horns and hooves. And if a repetition of the ceremony fails to achieve the same result, that would be no falsification, for perhaps an unnoticed yet essential aspect of the correct ceremony was omitted.)

Karl R. Popper, Realism and the Aim of Science xix-xx (W.W. Bartley ed., 1983).

Should the emphasis be placed on the parenthetical "has been" rather than the hypothetical "can be" tested? See Clifton T. Hutchinson & Danny S. Ashby, *Daubert v. Merrell Dow Pharmaceutical, Inc.*: Redefining the Bases for Admissibility of Expert Scientific Testimony, 15 Cardozo L. Rev. 1875, 1887-95 (1994). Is the survival of a theory as against efforts to falsify it the measure of its verification? Popper relied on falsification not merely to delineate the realm of the metaphysical, but especially to define the degree to which a scientific fact or theory had been corroborated. The degree of corroboration, he insisted, could not be captured in any system of inductive probabilities that tried to count confirming observations or the like, but must be understood in terms of a process akin to natural selection, by which theories that survived the most severe tests, emerge as highly "corroborated." Karl Popper, The Logic of Scientific Discovery §§ 81-84 (1959). Many philosophers of science do not accept his specific views on the appropriate measure of confirmation or corroboration. Cf. Ronald J. Allen,

Expertise and the *Daubert* Decision, 84 J. Crim. L. & Criminology 1157, 1169-73 (1994) (criticizing "Popperian falsifiability" as a description of how scientists think and as an explanation of what makes a theory scientifically acceptable); Sean O'Connor, The Supreme Court's Philosophy of Science: Will the Real Karl Popper Please Stand Up?, 35 Jurimetrics J. 263 (1995) (noting that "'Popperianism' has not been a dominant trend in philosophy of science for some time," but defending the program from Allen's criticisms).

5. *Methodology or conclusion?* Exactly what must be decided on the remand in *Daubert?* What, in other words, is the "methodology" in question? See David L. Faigman et al., Check Your Crystal Ball at the Courthouse Door, Please: Exploring the Past, Understanding the Present, and Worrying About the Future of Scientific Evidence, 15 Cardozo L. Rev. 1799, 1831-33 (1994). Indeed, what aspect of the methodology used by plaintiffs' experts was not generally accepted in the scientific community? Compare Kenneth J. Chesebro, Taking *Daubert's* "Focus" Seriously: The Methodology-Conclusion Distinction, 15 Cardozo L. Rev. 1745, 1749 (1994). Does the difficulty in identifying "the thing" to be accepted under *Frye* also plague the thing to be validated under *Daubert?* Consider the following two affidavits submitted in connection with the motion for summary judgment in *Daubert:*

STATEMENT OF STEVEN H. LAMM, M.D., DFTPH

I am a physician and epidemiologist who specializes in assessing the magnitude of risk from exposures to various chemical and biological substances. I am currently the President of Consultants in Epidemiology and Occupational Health, Inc. at 2428 Wisconsin Avenue, N.W., Washington, D.C. 20007. In this capacity, I evaluate the risks of various cancers and birth defects from specific exposures. I have attached hereto my curriculum vitae, which includes a bibliography of various medical articles that I have authored or co-authored.

I first became involved in the Bendectin litigation when asked by the Guardian *ad litem* for class B plaintiffs, Samuel H. Porter, esq. in the multidistrict litigation in Cincinnati, In Re Richardson-Merrell, Inc. "Bendectin" Product Liability Litigation II, MDL No. 486, to prepare a report for Judge Carl Rubin who had certified a class action in that litigation.

I was sought by the Guardian *ad litem* to prepare a report for Judge Rubin to assist him in identifying the characteristics of the class. Preparation of this report necessitated assessment of the magnitude of risk of birth defects from maternal ingestion of Bendectin. In order to do this, I reviewed the literature submitted to the court by plaintiffs' and defendant's experts. In this preparation of my preliminary report (October 15, 1984), I reviewed the world's literature on Bendectin and human birth defects, including all those articles relied upon by either the experts for the plaintiffs or the defendants. These studies included reports on over 130,000 newborn infants. In toto, they showed no difference in the risk of birth defects between those infants whose mothers had taken Bendectin during the first trimester of pregnancy and those infants whose mothers had not.

I next reviewed in a similar manner the literature on Bendectin and limb reduction birth defects. I found no association between Bendectin and the occurrence of limb reduction birth defects.

In addition to reviewing the published scientific literature, I reviewed the overall experience that American women concurrently had with birth defects and with Bendectin usage during the years 1970 to 1984. I found no relationship between the annual frequency of Bendectin usage and the annual occurrences of specific birth defects. As no birth defects showed a drop in frequency when there was a drop in the frequency of Bendectin use, I concluded that there was no evidence from this data that Bendectin usage had anything to do with birth defect rates.

Since the time of that report, I have continued to monitor the literature and data on birth defect rates and on Bendectin usage. My current conclusions are no different from my conclusion of 1984, which is that although approximately 3-4% of all human births exhibit some congenital malformations, the frequency is no greater for the infants of mothers who took Bendectin during the first trimester of pregnancy than for the infants of mothers who did not take Bendectin during the first trimester of pregnancy. Based on my review of the scientific literature, I conclude that maternal use of Bendectin during the first trimester of pregnancy is not a risk factor for human birth defects in general, for limb reduction defects specifically, or for any other particular human birth defect.

I declare under penalty of perjury that the foregoing is true and correct.

/s/ _____
STEVEN H. LAMM, M.D., DTPH

Washington, D.C.

Subscribed and sworn to before me this 1 day of August 1989. [Notarization omitted.]

STATEMENT OF SHANNA NELEN SWAN, Ph.D.

1. My name is Shanna Helen Swan.

2. I am an epidemiologist and biostatistician. I have a Ph.D. in statistics. I practice in the field of reproductive epidemiology full time for the State of California. A copy of my curriculum vitae is attached hereto.

I was graduated from the City College of New York with my major in mathematics. I received a masters in biostatistics from Columbia University and then received a Ph.D. in statistics from the University of California at Berkeley. I have taught at the University of California. My teaching has involved in the areas of statistics, biostatistics, epidemiology, and mathematics. Mathematics is the foundation for each of biostatistics and epidemiology. It is necessary that one have an understanding of statistics in order to teach epidemiology and to understand the meaning of epidemiology findings. I hold a [lecturer] position in epidemiology in the School of Public Health at the University [of] California at Berk[e]ley.

My current title is Chief of Reproductive and Epidemiological Program of the Epidemiological Study Section of the California Department of Health and Services. My duties include the study of causes of adverse reproductive outcomes.

I have served as consultant to the World Health Organization, to the Food and Drug Administration, and to the National Institutes of Health. I belong to numerous professional societies that deal with epidemiology and statistics including the American College of Epidemiology, the American Statistical Association, the Society for Epidemiological Research, the Institute of Mathematics Statistics, the Biometrics Society and the American Public Health Association. I am a member of the Phi Beta Kappa Society. I have served as a reviewer for the epidemiological, statistical and medical publications including the American Journal of Epidemiology, American Journal of Public Health, The American Statistical Association, the Journal of the American Medical Association and others. I have served on study sections for the National Institutes of Health. I have published approximately 25 to 30 times in the field of epidemiology, biostatistics and statistics including an abstract with respect of Bendectin. I have co-authored numerous government documents from the state of California including those pertaining to pregnancy and pregnancy outcomes.

3. In my position with the State of California I am called upon to help determine causes of adverse pregnancy outcomes including birth defects where we utilize primary and secondary data. The types of data that I utilize and will be discussing below is all of the type of data that is generally and reasonably relied upon by epidemiologists to help determine whether o[r] not there is a statistical association between a drug, such as Bendectin, and a class of birth defects such as limb reduction.

4. I have reviewed, to the best of my knowledge, all the epidemiological literature pertaining to Bendectin.

5. Because of my position, experience, education, and training I am aware that in vitro studies, animal studies and the pharmacology of drugs are all important along with epidemiology studies in determining whether or not there is a cause and effect relationship between drug and a birth defects. Decisions concerning whether or not there is such a cause and effect relationship between a drug and birth defects are not made solely on epidemiological data when one is concerned about teratogenicity issues. One would not rely solely on epidemiological studies that failed to show a statistical association at the 95% confidence level between a substance and a defect to determine that the substance does not cause the defect.

6. In order to understand epidemiology studies one must understand that the results can be positive, negative, or inconclusive. An inconclusive study is one that does reach traditional levels of statistical significance but does not have the statistical power to rule out appreciable relative risks. In other words, the

data could be consistent both with no effect and with an effect that one was worried about such as a doubling of risks. A positive study at a traditional level of statistical significance, e.g. 5% would enable one to conclude with 95% certainty that there is statistical association between a cause and effect or between a drug and a birth defect. In analyzing the validity of an epidemiological study one must analyze not only the chance of the error of a false positive, e.g. 5%, but also the "power" of the study, the chance of detecting an association if it exists. A confidence interval indicates that the true association level is somewhere in the range between the lower limit and the higher limit of probability. The less sure one wants to be about the finding, the narrower is this range. For example, for a 90% confidence level, the range would be narrower than for a 95% level and even narrower for an 85% confidence level and so on. It is erroneous to conclude that merely because a confidence interval includes the number 1.0 that one can conclude from such data that there is no statistical association or no causation. One must look at all the studies and evaluate their quality and power using one's education, training, and experience and generally accepted methodology to come to an opinion as to whether or not the data shows an association.

7. It is not usual epidemiological practice for the author of a study to "conclude" that the data does or does not "prove" a cause and effect relationship. That is neither the nature nor the purpose of such a study or studies. The purpose of such data collection is to add another body of data to other scientific data such as pharmacological data, animal studies data, and in vitro data to enable one to reach an opinion concerning the effect of the agent.

8. For example, in reviewing the various epidemiological studies on Bendectin, the most powerful study, i.e. "Jick", only has approximately a 17.6% chance of finding a doubling of the rate of defects. The other studies are even less apt to find even a doubling. Even if one were to put all the studies together that involve the limbs, there would still be less than a 50% chance of finding a doubling of increased limb defects and only a minuscule chance of finding 50% increase or a 20% increase. In analyzing the various epidemiology studies, one quickly can see that the studies either have insufficient numbers, inappropriate control groups, inappropriate pooling of malformations, misclassification of exposure, or confounders.

9. It is not accepted epidemiological practice to rely solely on epidemiological studies that provide relative risks with confidence intervals which include 1.0 and conclude that Bendectin does not cause birth defects. Such studies may in fact provide data consistent with a greatly increased risk.

10. Having reviewed the epidemiological studies including, but not limited to Heinonen, Jick, Aselton, Morelock, Cordero, Eskenazi, McCredie, and based upon generally accepted epidemiological techniques and utilizing my education, training and experience it is my opinion that one cannot conclude that there is in fact no statistical association between Bendectin and limb reduction defects. More specifically one cannot draw a conclusion from those studies that Bendectin does not cause limb reduction defects.

11. Because limb defects are a rare occurrence, occurring less than one per one thousand live births, many thousands of births would be necessary in a

controlled study to reveal even a 100% increase. The chances of finding a smaller increase such as a 10% or 20% would therefore be minuscule. That is one reason why an epidemiologist would not rely only on epidemiology studies in the face of other scientific data to suggest that a drug, such as Bendectin, does not cause birth defects. On the contrary, the prudent epidemiologist would be concerned about the public safety and when there is data consistent with increased risks, as with Bendectin, conclude that it is more probable than not that Bendectin is associated with birth defects.

12. Rather, considering the foregoing studies, within a reasonable degree of certainty, based upon my education, training and experience, it is my opinion that considering all available data that is provided in animal, in vitro and epidemiological studies, including the relative risks, the confidence limits and also the power of the studies, that it is more likely than not that Bendectin is, in fact, associated with limb reduction defects. In reaching that opinion, I have used the methodology that is generally and reasonably relied upon by epidemiologists to analyze, study and interpret data that has been collected, published and unpublished in trying to draw opinions concerning whether or not there is a cause and effect relationship between a drug and a birth defect.

13. I have previously given testimony in cases involving Bendectin and subsequently learned that the defendant in these cases has taken bits and pieces of my testimony out of context. However, so there be no question, it is my opinion within a reasonable degree of certainty, based on all of the available data, the Bendectin is associated with birth defects, including limb defects.

/s/ _____

Shanna Helen Swan

Sworn to and subscribed in my presence on this 27th day of September 1989. [Notarization omitted.]

6. *Terminology.* As *Daubert* notes, courts and attorneys typically use the word "reliability" to denote that which can be relied upon without undue risk of error. In experimental science and statistics, however, "reliability" has a more restricted meaning. It refers to the reproducability or consistency of results. A measuring instrument, say a scale, is perfectly reliable if it always gives the same reading when the same weight is placed on it.

The term "validity," on the other hand, relates to the ability of the instrument to measure that which it is supposed to measure. A scale that used only the volume of an object to determine its weight would not be valid because even a perfectly reliable volume-measuring scale would be inaccurate as applied to objects of different densities. Thus, reliability in the technical sense of consistency does not assure accurate or correct answers. The instrument must implement (reliably) a true (valid) theory.

In these terms, the probative value of evidence derived from a scientific theory depends on (1) the validity of the theory, (2) the validity and potential reliability of the technique for applying that theory, and (3) the proper application of the technique on a particular occasion. As the cases reproduced here reveal, the validity of the theory and the technique for applying it may be established through judicial notice or the presentation of evidence, including expert testimony. In appropriate circumstances, legislative recognition or a stipulation between the parties also may demonstrate validity, but the proper application of a scientific technique on a particular occasion must be shown by case-specific information. It cannot be the subject of judicial notice. E.g., Wamser v. State, 672 P.2d 163, 164 (Alaska Ct. App. 1983).

7. *Weight.* The battle between the adherents to the general acceptance standard and its detractors will continue in many jurisdictions. See supra note 2. Whatever its ultimate outcome, the degree of acceptance of a principle, theory, or methodology will remain important. In addition to having some bearing — determinative or otherwise — on admissibility, it also affects the weight that the judge or jury may be disposed to place on the evidence. Parties opposing the forensic application of methods that are controversial within the scientific community or that have not had sufficient time to be accepted as valid and potentially reliable by many scientists may well argue that these results should be viewed with considerable caution.

8. *Beyond Rule 702.* Although *Daubert* relies primarily on Federal Rule of Evidence Rule 702, the Court cautions that other rules apply:

> Throughout, a judge assessing a proffer of expert scientific testimony under Rule 702 should also be mindful of other applicable rules. Rule 703 provides that expert opinions based on otherwise inadmissible hearsay are to be admitted only if the facts or data are "of a type reasonably relied upon by experts in the particular field in forming opinions or inferences upon the subject." Rule 706 allows the court at its discretion to procure the assistance of an expert of its own choosing. Finally, Rule 403 permits the exclusion of relevant evidence "if its probative value is substantially outweighed by the danger of unfair prejudice, confusion of the issues, or misleading the jury. . . ."

506 U.S. at 595.

When does the requirement of "reasonable reliance" apply? Only when the expert relies on hearsay peculiar to the case, such as the medical examiner who relies on the report of a toxicologist in determining the cause of death? Or more broadly, as when the expert relies on general scientific principles or findings, such as the proposition that Bendectin is (or is not) a teratogen? See, e.g., Faust F. Rossi, Expert Witnesses (1991); Michael C. McCarthy, Note, "Helpful" or "Reasonably Reliable"? Analyzing the Expert Witness's Methodology Under Federal Rules of Evidence 702 and 703, 77 Cornell L. Rev. 350 (1992). Even if

Rule 703 is construed to reach beyond case-specific, adjudicative facts, should the court use its own conception of what is reasonable, or must it defer to the practice of experts? See Rossi, supra. The district court in *Daubert* relied on rule 703 in granting summary judgment:

> [E]xpert opinion which is not based on epidemiologic evidence is not admissible to establish causation because it lacks the sufficient foundation necessary under FRE 703. . . . The plaintiffs' experts must be competent to testify that some epidemiologic study or recalculation shows a statistically significant relationship between the ingestion of Bendectin and birth defects and that this study forms the basis of their opinion.

727 F. Supp. 570, 575 (S.D. Cal. 1989).

How should Rule 403 be applied? Plainly, the Court envisions the possibility that testimony based on valid scientific knowledge will nevertheless be excludable? What factors might produce this result? See David L. Faigman et al., Check Your Crystal Ball at the Courthouse Door, Please: Exploring the Past, Understanding the Present, and Worrying About the Future of Scientific Evidence, 15 Cardozo L. Rev. 1799, 1833-34 (1994).

Part IV

GENETIC MARKERS
FOR IDENTIFICATION

Chapter 8
Serology

People v. Young
391 N.W. 2d 270 (Mich. 1986)

LEVIN, Justice. . . .

I

Defendant Jeffrey Allen Young was convicted of first-degree murder . . . . The Court of Appeals affirmed. . . . On the earlier submission of Young's appeal to this Court, we held that . . . "the results of the blood analyses were [not] admissible at trial without a prior showing that the technique of serological electrophoresis enjoys general scientific acceptance among impartial and disinterested experts. . . ."

We declined to respond to the question "whether the results of blood analyses are admissible to *include* an accused within the class of possible perpetrators" . . . until "development of a record by the trial court at the hearing which we order to determine if serological electrophoretic analysis has achieved general scientific acceptance for reliability, by disinterested and impartial experts." . . .

We retained jurisdiction. The hearing on the admissibility of the bloodstain evidence was held in the circuit court, and the record was transmitted to us. [T]he cause was reargued.

II

Evaluating the scientific community's acceptance of the reliability of electrophoresis of dried evidentiary bloodstains presents some unusual problems. The number of scientists not working for a police agency who are familiar with electrophoresis of evidentiary bloodstains is small. If these scientists alone were considered, the community would be too small for a fair sampling of scientific opinion. There is, however, a larger number of nonforensic scientists using electrophoresis who are capable of evaluating the reliability of electrophoresis of evidentiary bloodstains if presented with the information they need to fill the gaps in their own knowledge and experience. The two groups combined constitute a group of scientists large enough to make a fair determination of whether electrophoresis of evidentiary bloodstains is generally accepted by experts in the scientific community.

The prosecution has the burden of establishing this community's general acceptance of the reliability of electrophoresis of evidentiary bloodstains. In the instant case, there is disagreement within the community on three separate issues: the length of time that genetic markers, particularly erythrocyte acid phosphatase (EAP), can be accurately read in dried blood, the reliability of the thin-gel multisystem analysis, and the effects of crime-scene contaminants. The prosecution did not fulfill its burden respecting the last two issues raised by the defense.

The only prosecution witness having substantial experience with electrophoresis of evidentiary bloodstains relied on his own unpublished observations and an unpublished reliability study by the developer of the multisystem to conclude that the thin-gel multisystem analysis was reliable. A defense witness questioned both the reliability of the technique and the study. The other prosecution witnesses were unfamiliar with the thin-gel multisystem, and their conclusion about the reliability of the method was based on the absence of any study showing that it did not work. No independently conducted reliability study supported that conclusion. Another defense witness said that the scientific community would not agree on the reliability of that conclusion without better supporting evidence.

Nor have comprehensive control tests been run with respect to the effects of crime scene contaminants. Prosecution witnesses testified, on the basis of their experience with bloodstains drawn under laboratory conditions, that they can identify bacterial contamination, at least if it is of the type normally encountered. They also claimed that bacterial contamination has not affected the reliability of the electrophoresis tests they have conducted. This is, however, the type of self-verification considered inconclusive in the scientific community. The record does not indicate that any work has been done on the effects of soil and chemical contamination on the reliability of electrophoresis.

We conclude that the scientific community's general acceptance of the reliability of electrophoresis of evidentiary bloodstains has not been established in the instant case. Reliability remains in dispute and unresolved because of the questions unanswered. The questions are not likely to be answered and the reliability of electrophoresis of evidentiary bloodstains established until independently conducted validation studies on the thin-gel multisystem analysis are undertaken and comprehensive control tests evaluating the effects of different contaminants are run, and the results have been subjected to the scrutiny of the scientific community. The evidence produced by electrophoresis should, therefore, not have been admitted. . . .

If it were clear that the erroneous admission of the electrophoresis evidence did not prejudice Young, the error would be harmless. We are, however, of the opinion that but for the electrophoresis evidence the jury may have had a reasonable doubt, and that evidence might have made the difference. We therefore remand for a new trial on the charge of second-degree murder.

NOTES

Applying the General Acceptance Test

1. *Requiring "impartiality" and "independent" verification.* Compare *Young* with *Superior Court,* supra chapter 6. Given the Michigan Supreme Court's requirements of "disinterested and impartial" witnesses and "independent verification," is the HGN test for intoxication generally accepted in the relevant scientific community? In a portion of the opinion not reproduced here, the *Young* court observed that:

> An argument could be made that neither Grunbaum nor Sensabaugh are disinterested and impartial, and should therefore be excluded despite their expertise. Grunbaum was the leader of the team of scientists that sought to develop a bloodstain analysis system for use in crime laboratories. He brought in Brian Wraxall and Stolorow to work on the project. After expressing dissatisfaction with the multisystem being developed, he withdrew from the project and suggested that it be discontinued. The project continued and when the results were published, he claimed they included misrepresentations. An independent review group found no grounds for Grunbaum's charges, but the sponsors of the project decided not to publish its results. Arguably, Grunbaum is still seeking to vindicate his original position. Sensabaugh also is not clearly disinterested. He has been a collaborator with Brian Wraxall and a paid consultant with the Oakland Crime Laboratory. He has also contributed to a prosecution response to an amicus curiae brief in a case pending before the California Supreme Court.
>
> Nevertheless, a certain degree of "interest" must be tolerated if scientists familiar with the theory and practice of a new technique are to testify at all. The standard developed by this Court is whether the expert's "livelihood was not intimately connected with the new technique." The livelihood of Stolorow and James Kearney, the prosecution witness who directs the FBI serology laboratory, is intimately connected with the new technique. The livelihood of Grunbaum and Sensabaugh is not so intimately connected.

The "disinterested" requirement has been defended as preventing a court from defining a "field . . . so narrowly that it encompasses only advocates and no real critics." Bert Black et al., Science and the Law in the Wake of *Daubert*: A New Search for Scientific Knowledge, 72 Tex. L. Rev. 715, 729 (1994).

2. *The thing that must be generally accepted.* Reread Frye v. United States, supra chapter 6. Does the general acceptance standard go to anything more than the theoretical underpinnings of electrophoresis — the physics of proteins in an electric field? How much more? Often, the specificity of "the thing" that must be generally accepted seems to foreordain the outcome of the *Frye* test. The Massachusetts Supreme Judicial Court, in the case presented immediately below, described electrophoresis and its application to forensic individualization, as follows:

> Electrophoresis is the movement of charged particles through a buffered conducting medium by application of a direct current. The term isozyme is used to describe enzymically active blood proteins which can be identified by their relative mobilities in an electric field. After separation of the proteins into marker bands by application of a current, specific chemicals are applied to make the proteins visible. . . . The relative distance of the bands from a common origin is compared with known standards, and evaluated by established guidelines. The results are then compared to population studies which show the known frequency of each factor in a given population. This produces a statistic which is representative of the percentage of the population that has that group and those factors in common. "The more genetic markers identified, the smaller the population of persons who might possess a particular combination of factors." Thus, the electrophoresis procedure permits an investigator to type a blood sample with greater precision than is possible with the familiar ABO system, and results of the test may serve to establish a "strong association between the bloodstain and its possible donor or the exclusion of the criminally accused as a donor of the bloodstain."

Commonwealth v. Gomes
526 N.E. 2d 1270 (Mass. 1988)

Lynch, Justice.

Antonio Gomes was indicted for the murders in the first degree of Basilisa Melendez, Joanna Aponte Rodriguez, and Kenneth Aponte Rodriguez, and for breaking and entering a dwelling house in the nighttime with intent to commit a felony and making an armed assault therein. The defendant filed a motion in limine to exclude evidence of blood enzyme testing. The motion was denied after hearing, but the defendant was granted the opportunity to present further evidence on the motion. The defendant was convicted and sentenced to three consecutive life sentences on the murder charges, and to a further concurrent life term on the breaking and entering charge. We affirm.

We summarize the relevant facts as the jury could have found them. [In] 1979, Eduardo Aponte Rodriguez (Aponte) [lived with] his common law wife, Basilisa, and . . . their three children . . . at 12 Jacobs Street, Boston . . . .

[When Aponte came home on the evening of December 5, 1979] Aponte put his key into the lock but the door would not open; the door or doorlock had been broken. Part of the door fell forward and Aponte pushed the door open.

Aponte saw his wife's body lying on the floor, and exclaimed, "Oh, my God, Bassi, what have they done to you?" He told Cardoza [his landlord, who had come with him to collect the rent] to call the police. He then went out on the porch and, holding onto one of the columns, screamed, "Oh, God, please help me, please help me, God." While he was calling out for help, Aponte saw three adults emerge from nearby 24 Jacobs Street, the building where the defendant lived. They looked at him, got into an automobile parked in front of 24 Jacobs Street, and drove away.

Boston police officers . . . arrived on the scene at 6:36 P.M. [T]hey observed the bodies of Aponte's wife and two of the children. The third child, an infant, lay in a crib in another room, unharmed. Aponte's wife was covered with blood, her face and head severely battered. She had been stabbed. She was naked from the breastline down. The children had also been stabbed. One had been thrown up against the wall; the other lay tangled up with a wooden chair. One of the children had been "almost decapitated" and her throat had been cut. . . .

[A] detective . . . observed a brown paper bag in the front bedroom of the house. On the bag were some reddish stains, later determined to be blood. Inside were Christmas gifts that Aponte had bought two or three days earlier, some children's clothes. . . .

. . . Boston police criminalist Stanley Bogdan . . . collected specimens of a number of reddish stains throughout the apartment. After chemical analysis he concluded that the specimens were blood stains of human origin. He tested each specimen to determine its blood type within the ABO blood grouping system.

The mother and children all had type O blood, as did Aponte and the landlord. Aponte's friend Harry had type B. Bogdan found certain specimens to be type O. ABO tests were inconclusive as to a number of other items, including stains collected from a chair in the doorway. However, Bogdan was able to determine that the stains from the chair were consistent with a mixture of two blood types: O and A. This was consistent with two people — one with type O blood, the other with type A — bleeding at the same time in the same immediate area. Chemical analysis revealed type A blood in the following items: reddish stains from the back of a bedspread, reddish spots from the front bedroom floor, stains from the bed, stains from the edge of the front bedroom door, stains from a hanging string of beads, and stains from the paper bag found in the front bedroom. Further tests revealed that the type A bloodstain on the paper bag was Rh positive. Bogdan sent the specimen from the paper bag to FBI agent William McInnis for additional blood grouping tests, described in detail in the body of this opinion.

The defendant's activities on the night of the murders are described as follows. At 7:00 P.M. that night the defendant was admitted to the emergency room at Boston City Hospital complaining of a stab wound to his right forearm and a bruise on his right hand. He told the treating physician that he had sustained these injuries while punching an assailant. He said that he had been stabbed. The doctor testified that the wound was of the type that would have bled.

Boston police officers . . . responded to Boston City Hospital upon report of a stabbing. They did not know about the incident at 12 Jacobs Street. [Defendant reacted to their arrival with some concern.]

. . . He did not give clear answers to the police questions and fumbled with his words. When questioned as to the particulars of how his injury had occurred, the defendant "seemed to agree with whatever was suggested to him." He was anxious to leave . . . .

The police [were unable to corroborate his story of how he came to be stabbed]. The next day, . . . police detective[s] went to the defendant's house . . . . On this occasion the defendant's account of his activities on the night of the murder differed from the account he had given at the hospital. . . . The defendant himself then raised the subject of the three murders at 12 Jacobs Street. He began to yell, "If you want my ideas on this thing next door, I'll tell you right now that those Puerto Ricans are all f---ing each other and they're doing their relatives and everything else."

[The next day] the same officers returned to speak further with the defendant. During the course of this conversation the defendant showed the officers the cut on his arm and said, "See, it's only a little scratch. . . . [About that] report I made to the police, it never happened." The defendant said he had cut himself. Then, fifty seconds to a minute later, he said, "I didn't cut myself. I had a fight with my girl and she stabbed me." . . . The defendant again brought up the subject of the murders, saying "I hate those f---ing people anyway. [N]ow get the f--- out of my house."

[In] 1982, Boston police detective Mark Madden obtained a warrant for a sample of the defendant's blood for chemical analysis. The defendant went with the police to the hospital where the blood sample was drawn. Test results for the defendant's blood and conclusive blood-grouping results obtained two years earlier from the blood-stained paper bag were identical.

[Two months later, when] the defendant was arrested [he gave the police yet another explanation of how he had cut his arm. He also said that before going to the hospital, he heard a six o'clock news broadcast about the murders at 12 Jacobs Street. Police investigation showed that there was no such broadcast.]

After questioning the defendant was detained in a cell at . . . police headquarters. The next [evening], [an police officer] found the defendant hanging by the neck on a cord fastened to the wall of his cell, unconscious but still alive. The officer took him down and resuscitated him.

Several days later the defendant, still in his cell, engaged in a shouting argument with some recently arrested juveniles seated outside his cell. When [the officer] intervened, the defendant said to him, "Tell them what I did. Tell them why I'm here. They don't want to mess with me."

At trial the defendant offered alibi testimony from his mother and his girl friend.

1. *Admission of evidence of electrophoretic testing.* The defendant claims that the judge erroneously admitted evidence of a genetic marker analysis performed upon bloodstains on the paper bag found at the crime scene because the Commonwealth failed to establish that the procedure employed to analyse the stain — electrophoresis — is generally accepted within the relevant scientific community. There was no error. . . .

The particular electrophoretic method at issue here is known as "multisystem" electrophoresis, so-called because it entails separating a number of enzymes simultaneously on the same sample. Such a method has the advantages of saving time and requiring less bloodstain material. [Some of its developers, Wraxall and Storolow, also have] suggested that the multisystem approach provides "a substantial improvement of the resolution of the isozyme bands of [certain enzymes] compared to their respective single-system methods of conventional electrophoresis."

Both multisystem and conventional electrophoresis methods were employed in this case by FBI serologist William McInnis. McInnis received from the Boston police crime laboratory the paper bag recovered from the crime scene, on which he determined there were two bloodstains. McInnis applied the electrophoresis technique to the stains, testing for seven enzyme and protein systems, abbreviated as follows: PGM, EsD, GLO-1, EAP, ADA, AK, and Hp. With the exception of the Hp system, McInnis tested for all the systems using the multisystem approach. McInnis also performed the more traditional antigen antibody tests on the stains, testing Rh and Mn factors. As a result of these tests, in combination with testing earlier performed by the Boston crime laboratory, it was determined that one stain exhibited identifiable types in six systems of genetic markers: ABO (type A); Rh (type D positive); Mn (type M negative); EAP (type B); ADA (type 1); Hp (type 1). Of the United States population, McInnis testified, 0.6% of whites and 1.2% of blacks would present this particular combination of genetic markers. As noted previously, a sample of the defendant's blood was taken and McInnis performed thereon ABO testing, Rh, and Mn typing, and electrophoretic analysis for the seven enzyme and protein systems. The test results corresponded identically to the results obtained from the stain on the paper bag.[1]

The defendant claims that electrophoresis may not be considered to be generally accepted in the scientific community because: the reliability of the multisystem approach is not agreed upon; there is disagreement as to the length of time that

---

[1] Boston police department criminalist Stanley Bogdan had performed ABO and Rh testing on the sample, and determined it to be type A, Rh positive. McInnis's testing was inconclusive as to all genetic markers on one of the stains. As to the other stain, McInnis tested in the Mn system for the M factor only and none was present; since all his controls reacted properly, McInnis termed this a negative reading. However, the jury heard testimony that failure to detect the M factor does not conclusively mean M is not present; the failure may be caused by degradation in the stain. Furthermore, in addition to the seven systems noted above, McInnis employed electrophoresis to test for four additional systems—PGM, EsD, GLO-1 and AK. In these systems, he obtained inconclusive results. . . .

certain genetic markers can be read in dried blood; and there are questions as to the effect on the same of crime scene contaminants. We reject these claims. . . .

The Commonwealth's expert, Mark Stolorow, testified that electrophoresis, including the multisystem, is generally accepted in the forensic science community. Stolorow is serology coordinator for the Illinois Department of Law Enforcement and holds a Master of Science degree in forensic chemistry. He has testified as an expert in forensic serology over one hundred times in six States, for both prosecution and defense. As serology coordinator, he is responsible for training new serologists, proficiency testing of staff serologists in seven crime laboratories, updating staff serologists on new developments in the field of blood analysis, and evaluation and research of new equipment in the field. His achievements and experience in the field of electrophoresis are extensive.

In 1972, Stolorow participated in an electrophoresis course taught by Brian Culliford of Scotland Yard, then recognized as one of the foremost experts in the field. In 1977, Stolorow participated in a research project at the laboratory of Dr. Benjamin Grunbaum at the University of California at Berkeley. The project goal was to improve the capability of crime laboratories in electrophoretic analysis of dried bloodstains. Stolorow spent approximately six months on the project, "participating in the developmental phase . . . inventing the method that ultimately resulted from that research." Initially, Grunbaum, Stolorow, and Brian Wraxall collaborated in the development of the multisystem. While Stolorow acknowledged that studies have been published pointing out problems in the use of electrophoresis, he indicated that such studies are intended to alert those using the technique to potential pitfalls, not to call into question the technique's underlying reliability. He knew of no scientific publication that had ever refuted the reliability of electrophoresis.[8] He concluded that electrophoretic testing of dried evidentiary bloodstains "certainly has gained general acceptance in the forensic science community."

The defendant offered the testimony of Diane Juricek, Ph.D., a researcher in genetics. Dr. Juricek had performed electrophoretic testing on fresh materials, but not on dried evidentiary blood stains. She testified that electrophoresis is unreliable when applied to dried evidentiary blood because such blood not only degrades with age, but also may be subject to crime scene contaminants and adverse environmental conditions which, she claimed, may result in erroneous readings. Dr. Juricek also testified that the multisystem was unreliable because it compromises among optimum testing conditions in order to test several enzymes simultaneously. According to Dr. Juricek, the unreliability of the multisystem is illustrated by the lack of scientific publications affirming its reliability. Finally, she criticized the actual testing procedures in this case.

---

[8] The absence of published refutations attests to the techniques reliability. . . .

Also testifying as an expert for the defense was Dr. Benjamin Grunbaum, a biochemist. Grunbaum testified that electrophoresis is reliable for testing fresh blood and dried bloodstains of known origin prepared under laboratory conditions. However, Grunbaum contended that the reliability of multisystem electrophoresis for testing evidentiary bloodstains from a crime scene has never been independently verified.

A review of relevant scientific literature and court decisions reveals that, despite Grunbaum's and Juricek's criticisms, when applied properly by trained analysts cognizant of the scientific literature as to the warning signs of erroneous readings, conventional and multisystem electrophoresis are generally accepted within the scientific community. As was noted in People v. Reilly, 196 Cal. App. 3d 1127, 1148, 242 Cal. Rptr. 496 (1987), "Dr. Grunbaum stands virtually alone in his opposition to electrophoretic typing of dried bloodstain evidence." The *Reilly* court surveyed opinion of a number of experts. One of them, Dr. Edward Blake, testified that electrophoresis is generally accepted in the scientific community when performed properly, and that "[h]e was unaware of any dissension on the point until he read Dr. Grunbaum's amicus brief in [another case] and knows of no one who shares Grunbaum's views. Nor [was] he aware of any publications that indicate lack of reliability."[9] Another expert, Dr. George Sensabaugh, testified in *Reilly* that Doctors Grunbaum and Juricek were the only scientists he knew of who questioned the reliability of electrophoresis. He, too, knew of no publications questioning the technique's reliability. Indeed, Sensabaugh earlier had published a refutation of Juricek's assertions of unreliability . . . concluding that Juricek's analysis evidenced "a naive and often erroneous characterization of genetic typing analysis . . . [and a] . . . disregard of pertinent literature [and] distortion of context of cited works."

As to the effects of adverse environmental factors and aging on the sample, the *Reilly* court noted that Dr. Grunbaum's "criticism [as to the effects of these factors] was repeatedly qualified by noting that well trained, competent analysts who use proper procedures and are aware of the published literature warning of typing problems can account for those possibilities." . . . Thus, the above authorities indicate that, so long as the analyst is trained to recognize the signposts of adverse environmental factors, the reliability of the test is not compromised.

With the exception of . . . People v. Young, 424 Mich. 470, 391 N.W. 2d 270 (1986), all courts considering the issue have held evidence of electrophoretic testing admissible. Of these, four jurisdictions have specifically held that the multisystem method is generally accepted in the relevant scientific community. We conclude, therefore, that both multisystem and conventional electrophoretic testing of

---

[9] Blake also disagreed with the conclusions of an associate law professor, Randolph Jonakait, who has used some of his (Blake's) publications as support for a law review article criticizing the reliability of the technique as applied to bloodstain analysis. See Jonakait, Will Blood Tell? Genetic Markers in Criminal Cases, 31 Emory L.J. 833 (1982).

dried evidentiary bloodstains are generally accepted as reliable in the relevant scientific community.

However, the defendant contends, even if the procedure is generally accepted in the scientific community, evidence of the test results nonetheless should not have been admitted because the test was not properly performed and FBI agent McInnis was not properly qualified as an expert. Testimony indicated that agent McInnis was an experienced analyst, trained in the electrophoretic technique and that he carefully conducted the genetic marker typing and used appropriate standards and controls. He was aware of typing problems described in the relevant scientific literature. Mark Storolow testified that the technique used by the FBI in this case was reliable. On this evidence there was "sufficient basis for finding, as a preliminary question of fact, that this witness was qualified to testify as an expert" and that the procedures employed were performed properly and reliably. Therefore, the defendant's various attacks alleging infirmities in the performance of the testing or the skill or knowledge of the witness go only to the weight of the evidence, not to its admissibility. The evidence of electrophoretic testing was properly admitted; thereafter, any attacks on the evidence were for the jury to weigh. . . .

2. *Statistical evidence.* The defendant claims that it was error for the judge to admit McInnis' expert testimony that, in the United States, 1.2% of blacks present the particular combination of genetic markers found in the bloodstain . . . The judge could find . . . that the statistical evidence presented was based on established, empirical data rather than speculation and that the evidence was more probative than prejudicial. Therefore, the evidence was properly admitted.

3. *Failure to photograph the electrophoretogram.* . . . The defendant claims that the failure of the Commonwealth to photograph the electrophoretogram denied him his due process right to a fair trial. He concedes, however, that the Commonwealth provided him with FBI laboratory notes and reports. . . .[12]

> In this Commonwealth, when potentially exculpatory evidence is lost or destroyed, a balancing test is employed to determine the appropriateness and extent of remedial action. The courts must weigh the culpability of the Commonwealth, the materiality of the evidence and the potential prejudice to the defendant. . . . Where evidence is lost or destroyed, it may be difficult to determine the precise nature of the evidence. While the defendant need not prove that the evidence would have been exculpatory, he must establish "a 'reasonable possibility, based on concrete evidence rather than a fertile imagination,' that access to the [material] would have produced evidence favorable to his cause."

---

[12] The defendant assumes that the Commonwealth's failure to photograph the test results is the equivalent of losing or destroying the evidence. Although this assumption is open to question, we analyze the issue as though it is correct.

Applying the balancing test above, we note that the Commonwealth was culpable in some degree for failing to photograph the material. However, that culpability is mitigated to a great extent by the fact that the defendant has been provided with laboratory notes and reports of the test results from the FBI laboratory. Neither is this a case where the Commonwealth ignored or rejected a defense request to preserve evidence by special means. Rather, the Commonwealth had completed its testing over two years before the defendant's arrest, so "there was no lawyer to whom notice could have been given concerning the testing."

Furthermore, the defendant has failed to show how his case was prejudiced by the lack of photographs. The defendant had available agent McInnis's laboratory report and notes, from which defense counsel conducted an extensive cross-examination. Moreover, that photographs of the test results might have been useful to the defense, does not rise to a showing of "a 'reasonable possibility, based on concrete evidence . . .' that access to [a photograph] would have produced evidence favorable to his cause."

Indeed, as one commentator has remarked: "Photography of electrophoretograms of ideal samples may be reliable for the purposes of leisurely scientific appraisal, however, I know of no such proven testing of samples of varying activities as does occur in forensic samples. A single photograph of such a separation could not adequately cover the range of such activity with the sensitivity of the human eye. Photography does not necessarily represent the true picture and can lead to artifacts." Therefore, we conclude that the failure of the Commonwealth to provide a photograph of the electrophoretogram did not deprive the defendant of a fair trial. . . .

Judgments affirmed.

NOTE

The General Acceptance of Thin-gel, Multisystem
Electrophoresis of Aged or Contaminated Blood

For a concise overview of the migration of protein electrophoresis from the genetics research laboratory to the crime laboratory, stressing the limited efforts at validation in forensic applications, see Peter Neufeld & Colman, When Science Takes the Witness Stand, Sci. Am., May 1990, at 46, 49-50. Why did the *Gomes* court differ with the *Young* court? Was the evidence on the general acceptance of thin-gel, multisystem electrophoresis of aged or contaminated blood stains different? Did the courts apply the general acceptance test differently? In what way or ways?

Does the *Gomes* opinion address and satisfy all the concerns raised in *Young*? Should the *Gomes* court have relied on judicial opinions conflicting with *Young* to ascertain the views of the pertinent scientific community? What are the implications of the fact that the multisystem, thin-gel findings in *Gomes* were replicated by a more conventional form of electrophoresis? In addressing these questions, consider the following portions of the opinion in *Young:*

People v. Young
391 N.W.2d 270 (Mich. 1986)

At the evidentiary hearing to determine the reliability of electrophoresis of evidentiary bloodstains, the prosecution presented seven witnesses, and the defense presented two witnesses. The prosecution and defense each presented one forensic scientist having substantial experience with electrophoresis of evidentiary bloodstains. Three of the prosecution's witnesses and the other defense witness were geneticists, familiar with electrophoresis, but unfamiliar with electrophoresis of evidentiary bloodstains. The other three prosecution witnesses were technicians, two of whom were full-time employees of law enforcement agencies. Before analyzing their conclusions it is first necessary to determine whether some or all of them are "disinterested and impartial experts in the particular field."

Because a theoretical understanding is essential, the relevant scientific community is scientists not technicians. Practical experience with the process, however, is also necessary. Ideally the community would be scientists with direct empirical experience with the procedure in question.

Two of the witnesses fit this description. Dr. George Sensabaugh is an associate professor of public health at the University of California at Berkeley and a specialist in forensic science. He has also conducted electrophoresis studies of dried bloodstains. Dr. Benjamin Grunbaum is a retired biochemist from the University of California with a specialty in criminalistics, the science of identification of physical evidence in criminal cases. He has been recognized to be "a leader in the development of electrophoresis to test body-fluid enzymes for purposes of forensic identification."

Grunbaum and Sensabaugh appear to be a part of a small community of scientists doing work on electrophoresis of evidentiary bloodstains.[21] The number of scientists within this community willing to testify seems even smaller. Grunbaum, Sensabaugh, and Mark Stolorow, the police detective who did the electrophoresis in the instant case, figure prominently in the few reported cases involving electrophoresis of evidentiary bloodstains. Those cases might be described as reflecting and reporting a debate between Stolorow and Grunbaum. . . .

The precise issue in the instant case is whether electrophoresis of evidentiary

---

[21] Grunbaum invited Brian Wraxall and Mark Stolorow to join him at the University of California at Berkeley to develop the multisystem. Sensabaugh has collaborated with Wraxall. As the defense commented in its brief in this Court, Grunbaum and Sensabaugh "appear to be the only such (independent) scientists in the country with regard to evidentiary bloodstain electrophoresis."

bloodstains passes the general acceptance test. General acceptance of electrophoresis in other areas is not necessarily relevant. The defendant concedes that serological electrophoresis of fresh blood in paternity testing and genetics research is considered generally reliable. Electrophoresis of evidentiary bloodstains presents, however, a number of complications, particularly the electrophoresis conducted in the instant case.

The complications are the bloodstain is not fresh, it is tested by thin-gel multisystem analysis, and most importantly, it has possibly been exposed to unknown contaminants.

A

Electrophoresis for paternity testing and genetics research is generally done on fresh blood. Electrophoresis of evidentiary stains is for the most part done on dried blood. . . . The important difference is that the blood is not fresh, and blood begins to degrade as soon as it leaves the body. The "crucial question is whether the marker detected in aged blood is a reliable indication of that found in fresh blood from the same person." The dispute centers on the results of the EAP test. . . .

Despite these disagreements, if the only question about the reliability of electrophoresis of evidentiary bloodstains was the survivability of degraded samples, it would be questionable whether electrophoresis evidence should be excluded where the bloodstain is less than three weeks old. The most detailed independent study discussed by the scientists suggests degraded EAP markers can be accurately read up to thirteen weeks. Before this study was written, other scientists believed EAP markers could be accurately read up to two to three weeks, which was the length of time involved in the instant case. The main support for the defense's critique of the studies are test results from too small a sample to carry much weight in the scientific community.

B

The second point of contention is the reliability of the thin-gel multisystem used in the instant case, which simultaneously analyzes three genetic markers, PGM, EsD, and GLO, on a single, thin-layer starch gel. Although other combination systems exist, the multisystem was designed by police scientists for police work; it allows the maximum amount of information to be drawn from electrophoresis of a small stain. . . .

The defense argues that the thin-gel multisystem is unreliable with respect to dried blood because the blood sample is too marginal to begin with to be accurately read after further diffusion. Once the electrophoretic separation has been conducted, a filter paper containing a chemical reagent is placed over the gel. The filter paper is meant to stain the EsD molecules, but it also soaks up PGM molecules. Grunbaum says this "compromises" the PGM test because "the PGM molecules have diffused sideways, some have disappeared . . . [and] the intensity of the PGM bands are not the same as if they were stained first, before the EsD." Grunbaum said he could "deduce from the photographs [taken of the test] that a leaching out of the PGM has occurred and you can see it very well" in the instant case. The defense argues that the multisystem "aggravates" the problem inherent in analyzing degraded samples.

The defense further argues that no independent study verifying the reliability of the thin-gel multisystem has ever been published. No prosecution witness contradicted this argument. The developer of the thin-gel multisystem, Brian Wraxall, did conduct his own blind trials,[46] but self-verification is not a sufficiently reliable procedure.

The prosecutor's response was to present witnesses who have done electrophoresis with other combination tests. Dr. Rachael Fisher and Dr. Harvey Mohrenweiser have used combination systems involving a thick-slab starch gel. Grunbaum distinguished the thick- from the thin-gel combination system. "They [those using the thick gel] slice their gel in such a way that they had several layers, like a layer cake, and they had fresh surfaces, and they stained only one for a given system. So this was not a compromising system." Testimony by at least one of the prosecution witnesses suggested there was some overlap on [the PGM and EOP] systems he used. He did not think the overlap compromised the system . . . . There was no further testimony by either side to resolve the dispute about the effect of the overlapping tests.

The prosecution also asked the scientists using the other combination tests why they believed the thin-gel multisystem was reliable. Their collective response could be summarized in the following comment by Dr. Rachael Fisher, "I have no reason to suppose it wouldn't work." They testified that they had seen no study demonstrating that the multisystem was unreliable. This line of reasoning would be adequate if the burden of establishing general acceptance of *unreliability* were placed on the defense. The burden of establishing general acceptance of *reliability* is, however, on the prosecution.

In sum, there are substantial unanswered questions respecting the reliability of Wraxall's thin-gel multisystem. Conflicting expert testimony indicates that until independent verification tests have been conducted regarding the thin-gel multisystem, general agreement in the scientific community on the reliability of that multisystem is unlikely. A specific question left unresolved is whether the filter used in the test of the EsD molecules compromises the analysis of the PGM molecules.

---

[46] This study is what Sensabaugh was referring to when he said blind trials conducted between four laboratories established the reliability of the multisystem.

C

The reliability of blood degraded by dirt, gasoline, urine, sweat, and other possible crime scene contaminants is also at issue in the instant case. Electrophoresis for paternity testing and genetics research is not beset with these problems. The only scientists that have done electrophoresis of blood exposed to these contaminants are those with forensic experience.

Both witnesses for the defense, Grunbaum and Dr. Diane Juricek, testified that it is not possible to determine the reliability of electrophoresis of evidentiary bloodstains until the effects of crime scene contaminants are understood. Juricek said that for electrophoresis of evidentiary bloodstains to be accepted as reliable, scientists would have to study the effects of "common gasoline contaminants which appear on sidewalks, DDT, which can, you know, from spraying grass . . . appear. . . . There is [sic] also bacterial contamination possibilities. There are molds that could have an effect." Although Juricek would not say for certain whether the contaminants would affect the electrophoresis, she said there was a "very strong theoretical possibility" that they would. Grunbaum testified "[t]here is just no way of knowing the degree of . . . the humidity, . . . heat . . . bacterial . . . [and], chemical contamination, and . . . this is a range that goes on beyond anybody's imagination."

Both witnesses testified that the reliability of electrophoresis of evidentiary bloodstains would not be established in the scientific community until controlled studies were conducted taking into account the possible contaminants present at a crime scene. Juricek said "[y]ou would have to check all of these different factors . . . singularly and then in combination. . . ." The studies would then have to be published and "verified independently."

It appears from the record and a survey of the scientific literature that such comprehensive control studies have not been conducted.

The prosecution relies instead on inferences drawn from tests performed on dried bloodstains prepared under ideal contamination-free conditions. The only publication referred to by name was the Denault study . . . . Reliance on this study is curious given Denault's own caveat.

> [E]mphasis must be placed on the limitations of this study. It is intended as a starting point for future research. . . . Moreover, the tests were conducted on clean specimens free of impurities. It is realized that in actual practice serological evidence preserved under known and constant conditions is rare, and the specimens may be contaminated with impurities such as perspiration, urine, soil, and bacteria. These factors limit the application of the results of the study.

When questioned about the proviso, the prosecution's only expert with significant experience with evidentiary bloodstains commented, the cleanliness of the stains is not "as significant a problem as they think it is." The prosecution emphasizes that no study has shown unreliability.

Prosecution witnesses testified about their experience with contaminants. Sensabaugh, relying on his own unpublished laboratory study, said that bacterial contamination would signal itself. He said the person interpreting the test would see "new bands appearing in odd positions. . . ." Fisher also testified that bacterial contamination would result in a "different activity, different position." She suggested the contamination "will flag you. . . ."

Juricek has written, however, that bacterial contamination does not necessarily create easily excludable bizarre bands. "Many bacteria have been found to have Type 2 PGM, for example. Thus, Type 1 blood when contaminated by bacteria that have Type 2 PGM would be identified as Type 2-1 despite the use of starch gels and proper controls." The result of the PGM test in the instant case was Type 2-1. Fisher was more willing to recognize uncertainty with respect to unknown contaminants. When asked about soil, Fisher answered, "If it is contaminated with soil, I have no idea. It depends on what is in the soil." . . . Although she followed up with the comment that "I can't conceive of anybody [having problems], unless one is going to go around sprinkling the place with rare chemicals," the testimony of another prosecution witness, Dr. Harvey Mohrenweiser, suggests that it is only fair to conclude that examiners will "catch flags" they are used to seeing. . . . The only stains he had examined were those produced in laboratories. Because these stains were not collected under sterile conditions, there could be "some bacterial contamination." Mohrenweiser and the other prosecution witnesses did not respond to the questions raised by the defense about the effect on electrophoresis of other likely crime scene contaminants such as chemicals and soil.

In sum, scientists do not agree what effect common crime scene contaminants may have on electrophoresis. They do not agree because comprehensive control tests have not been undertaken. The scientists testifying at trial had no experience with soil or chemical contamination and could only guess what effect such contaminants might engender. Although the scientists had some experience with the type of bacterial contamination found in laboratories, the bloodstains here were made during or following the commission of a crime and not under laboratory conditions. . . .

The scientific tradition expects independent verification of new procedures. When other scientists analyze and repeat the tests, they counteract the dangers of biased reporting. It is scientists not responsible for the original research that confirm its validity. Although electrophoresis has been generally accepted as reliable in the scientific community for many years, Wraxall's multisystem test is a new technique. No independently conducted verification studies have been undertaken. . . .

The dangers of allowing implementation of an inadequately tested device are well-known. The paraffin test and the Dalkon Shield are two familiar examples. . . .

NOTES

1. *Other individualizing tests of bodily fluids and specimens.* The evidence in *Young* and *Gomes* included serologic tests for red blood cell antigens.

Electrophoresis of the isoenzymes found in blood and other bodily fluids is but one of many methods for identifying various components of these fluids. See, e.g., United States v. Gwaltney, 790 F.2d 1378 (9th Cir. 1986). These components are synthesized within a person's cells according to instructions in the cell's genetic material (DNA). Thus, the molecules identified via electrophoresis, serologic reactions, or other methods may be thought of as genetic markers. A thorough and comprehensive discussion of the many markers, genetic systems, and methods of detection can be found in R.E. Gaensslen, Sourcebook in Forensic Serology, Immunology, and Biochemistry (U.S. Dep't of Justice 1983). "DNA typing," which looks to variations in the DNA itself, rather than its protein products, is discussed in chapters 11-14.

2. *The admissibility of population statistics.* Despite earlier dicta from the Massachusetts Supreme Judicial Court "disfavoring" explicit probabilities or statistics, *Gomes* holds the population statistics on the prevalence of the incriminating isoenzymes admissible. In a footnote omitted from the opinion reproduced above, the court observed that the defense witness, Dr. Juricek, questioned the accuracy of these estimates, but held that this attack affected the weight rather than the admissibility of those numbers. Should *Frye* apply to particular tables of population frequencies and numbers deduced from these tables, or only to the method of gathering the statistics? For additional materials on "probability evidence," see supra chapter 2. Some technical discussions focusing on probabilities involving genetic markers in blood are Steven Selvin & Benjamin W. Grunbaum, Genetic Marker Determination in Evidence Bloodstains: The Effect of Classification Errors on Probability of Non-Discrimination and Probability of Concordance, 27 J. Forensic Sci. Soc'y 57 (1987); G. Gettinby, An Empirical Approach to Estimating the Probability of Innocently Acquiring Bloodstains of Different ABO Groups on Clothing, 24 J. Forensic Sci. Soc'y 221 (1984).

3. *The government's duty to preserve scientific evidence.* The *Gomes* court holds that the Commonwealth's failure to photograph the pattern on the gel after electrophoresis did not deprive the defendant of due process of law. Why? What uses might the defense have made of such a photograph? Dr. Grunbaum testified in *Young* that he could "deduce from the photographs that a leaching out of the PGM has occurred."

When, if ever, does due process require the government to preserve trace evidence for scientific analysis by the defense? When the government knows or strongly suspects that the evidence would exonerate the defendant? Cf. Brady v. Maryland, 373 U.S. 83 (1963) (due process requires prosecution to disclose, on request, exculpatory evidence). When a reasonable investigator would want the evidence analyzed? When the government should have analyzed the evidence, but did not? See Arizona v. Youngblood, 488 U.S. 51 (1988) (semen stain); California v. Trombetta, 467 U.S. 479 (1984) (breath sample); 1 Paul C. Giannelli & Edward

J. Imwinkelried, Scientific Evidence §3-7 (2d ed. 1993); Comment, The Prosecution's Duty to Preserve Evidence Before Trial, 72 Cal. L. Rev. 1019 (1984).

Chapter 9
Parentage Testing: Civil Cases

Plemel v. Walter
735 P.2d 1209 (Or. 1987)

LENT, JUSTICE.

In this filiation proceeding the jury, by a 9-3 vote, found that Brent Walter was the father of Dena Plemel's child. Plemel's expert witness testified that blood tests of Plemel, Walter and the child did not exclude the possibility that Walter was the father. Walter did not challenge the validity of the tests or the failure of the tests to exclude him but did object, on grounds of irrelevance and prejudice, to testimony by the expert regarding the probability that he was the father. The trial court permitted the testimony, and the Court of Appeals affirmed. Because we hold that the testimony was inadmissible in the form that it was presented, we reverse and remand for a new trial.

I

Plemel's child was born on June 9, 1983. [S]he initiated filiation proceedings against Walter, alleging that he was the father of the child. Subsequently, the state intervened as a petitioner. Walter denied paternity.

Plemel testified that she and Walter had intercourse on one occasion, September 11, 1982. Walter admitted having intercourse with Plemel but testified that it had occurred on the night of August 13-14, 1982. Both Plemel and Walter introduced the testimony of witnesses to corroborate their respective versions of when they had been together. A nurse practitioner who had examined Plemel testified that conception of the child would have been impossible in mid-August; she estimated that conception occurred between September 9 and September 16.

Plemel also called as a witness Dr. E.W. Lovrien, the director of the Oregon Health Sciences University Phenotype Laboratory. The laboratory had conducted blood tests of Plemel, Walter and the child. Lovrien testified that: (1) the tests did not exclude the possibility that Walter was the father; (2) the probability that the tests would have excluded a "falsely accused father" was 97.5 percent; (3) Walter's "paternity index" was 178; (4) Walter's "chance of paternity" was 99.4 percent; (5) Walter's "chance of nonpaternity" was 0.6 percent; and (6) it was "extremely likely" that Walter was the father. The last three statements were essentially equivalent to, and derived from, the paternity index. The "chance of paternity" was the "paternity index" stated as a percentage chance (i.e., odds of 178 to 1 are equal to a 99.4 percent chance); the "chance of nonpaternity" was the "chance of paternity" stated negatively; the expression "extremely likely" was taken from a table developed by a joint committee of the American Medical Association and the American Bar Association [in 1976] to express the significance of any given "chance of paternity."

Walter, by way of a motion *in limine* and an objection, sought to exclude that portion of Lovrien's testimony related to the paternity index and its equivalents. He argued that the testimony was irrelevant because the "probability of excluding a falsely accused father" provided the jury with all of the information that could be obtained from the blood tests. The argument was premised on his contention that in order to derive the paternity index, Lovrien had made an arbitrary assumption about the strength of the other evidence presented in the case. Walter also argued that the testimony was prejudicial in that the jury would be too confused by it to understand its proper significance. The trial court, without stating its reasons, denied Walter's motion in limine and overruled his objection. The Court of Appeals affirmed, holding that the testimony regarding the paternity index helped the jury to interpret the blood test results and that Lovrien's testimony minimized any potential for jury confusion by clearly explaining the limited significance of the statistics he presented.

Because courts have so frequently misinterpreted the meaning and significance of paternity test results, we believe that some background is appropriate before we analyze Walter's arguments.

Lovrien referred to the group of blood tests performed in this case as an "extended red cell enzyme" test. This group of tests reveals the presence of various antigens, red cell enzymes and plasma proteins in the blood. By knowing which of these substances are in the blood of the mother, child and putative father, a geneticist can state whether it is possible for the putative father to be the true father.

Each person has a large number of inherited traits, such as eye color and facial features. Different versions of a particular trait are known as phenotypes. For the inherited trait of eye color, for example, blue eyes are one phenotype, brown eyes are another. The antigens, enzymes and proteins in a person's blood are also inherited traits. One set, or "system," of antigens are the ABO antigens, which have been widely used in the classification of blood. Because no individual possesses every antigen in the ABO system, the ABO antigens that an individual does possess determine that individual's "blood type," or phenotype, for the ABO system. The ABO system can be divided into six phenotypes: O, A_1, A_2, B, A_1B or A_2B. If a person has the phenotype A_1, this means that a blood test revealed the presence of the A_1 antigen. Similarly, if a person has the phenotype A_1B, the blood test revealed the presence of both the A_1 antigen and the B antigen. If the person's phenotype is O, the blood test was unable to detect the presence of any of the antigens for the ABO system.

The specific set of phenotypes that a person possesses is determined by that person's genes. Genes occur in pairs that contain one gene from each parent. A specific gene pair or a specific group of gene pairs control a particular body trait, and an individual's phenotype for that trait will reflect the nature of the genes that make up the controlling pair or pairs. If a person has the phenotype A_1B, that person's ABO gene pair consists of an A_1 gene and a B gene. If the phenotype is A_1, the pair consists of an A_1 gene and either another A_1 gene or an O gene. This is because the O gene does not produce a detectable antigen. If the phenotype is O, both genes are O.

Information about a person's phenotypes, then, can be used to derive information concerning that person's corresponding gene pairs. Moreover, because each parent contributes one gene to a pair, knowledge of a person's phenotypes can also be used to derive information about that person's parents' or children's phenotypes.

For example, Plemel's phenotype for the ABO system was found to be A_1. Thus, she had an A_1 gene and either another A_1 gene or an O gene. The child's phenotype was found to be A_1B, requiring that the child have an A_1 gene and a B gene. Because the child received one gene from Plemel and one from its father, and because Plemel did not have a B gene, the child had to have received the A_1 gene from Plemel and the B gene from its father. The child's father's phenotype would therefore have to be one of the "B phenotypes": B, A_1B or A_2B. If Walter's phenotype for this system were O, A_1 or A_2, he could not have been the father. Because Walter's phenotype was found to be A_2B, a phenotype consistent with paternity, the test for this system could not exclude him as a potential father.

In addition to the ABO system, Lovrien's laboratory determined Walter's, Plemel's and the child's phenotypes for 18 other blood systems. Lovrien testified that for each of these systems, Walter's phenotypes were consistent with the accusation of paternity. The "extended red cell enzyme" test did not exclude the possibility that Walter was the father of Plemel's child.

If the frequency with which phenotypes occur in the population of potential fathers is known, more can be said than that the paternity test has failed to exclude the putative father. It is also possible to derive statistics about the ability of the paternity test to exonerate men falsely accused of paternity and the relative likelihood that the putative father is the true father.

Probability of Excluding a Falsely Accused Father. This statistic, sometimes termed the "prior probability of exclusion" or, simply, the "probability of exclusion," measures the ability of a paternity test to exclude men falsely accused of paternity. The statistic is calculated as follows: For each mother-child combination of phenotypes, certain phenotypes will be inconsistent with paternity. For example, if the mother is A_1 and the child is B, the father cannot be A_1. The frequency with which such combinations occur in the population is the probability of excluding a falsely accused father. If there are no such combinations in the population, e.g., if everyone is A_1, then the probability of excluding a falsely accused father is zero. A test with this probability would be useless.

As more blood systems are tested, the probability of excluding a falsely accused father can become quite high. The test in this case used 19 systems and had a probability of excluding a falsely accused father of 97.5 percent. Expressed in another way, in 39 instances out of 40 in which a man is falsely accused of being the father of a child, the tests conducted in this case would prove that the man did not father the child.

This statistic frequently is confused with the percentage of men in the population whose phenotypes are inconsistent with paternity, a percentage that is also often called the "probability of exclusion." The parties in this case, as well as the Court of Appeals, appear to have fallen into this confusion. Although the "extended red cell enzyme" test had a probability of excluding a falsely accused father of 97.5 percent, this does not imply that the proportion of the male population capable of fathering Plemel's child is 2.5 percent. The probability of excluding a falsely accused father is a measure of the ability of the paternity test to exclude falsely accused fathers without reference to the phenotypes of any particular mother-child combination; the probability will be 97.5 percent for everyone tested. The results from the ABO system in this case provide a good illustration of the distinction. Lovrien testified that the ABO system alone will exclude falsely accused fathers in about 17 percent of cases. The father of Plemel's child, however, must have a B gene, which, according to Lovrien, occurs in only about 5 percent of the population. Thus, although the ABO system has a probability of excluding a falsely accused father of 17 percent, 95 percent of the male population has been excluded by the ABO system in this case.[4]

No statistic on the percentage of the relevant population capable of fathering Plemel's child was presented by Lovrien.

Paternity Index. This statistic, also known as the "likelihood ratio," the "chance of paternity" and the "likelihood of paternity," measures the putative father's likelihood of producing the child's phenotypes against the likelihood of a randomly selected man doing so. Despite the alternative labels, it is not the probability that the accused is the father.

Within the group of men genetically capable of fathering a particular child, some will be genetically more likely to have done so than others. For example, we noted above that Walter's phenotype for the ABO system was A_2B and that the child's father had to have one of the "B phenotypes." Walter could transmit to his child either his A_2 or his B gene. The chance that he would transmit the B gene would be 50 percent. A man who had a B phenotype and two B genes (as opposed to a man with a B phenotype and one B gene and one O gene), however, would have a 100 percent chance of transmitting a B gene. Other things being equal, this man would be more likely to be the father of Plemel's child than would Walter.

The paternity index, which is a ratio that compares the putative father's likelihood of producing the child's phenotypes with the likelihood of a randomly

---

[4] If the testing excluded a total of 99 percent of the population as the potential father, it might be tempting to conclude that the probability that the putative father was the true father was also 99 percent. It is easy to see, though, that this is not the case. If the relevant population were 1,000,000, and if 99 percent were excluded by the testing, then 990,000 would have been excluded, leaving 10,000 as potential fathers. On the basis of the blood tests alone, then, the probability of the putative father's paternity would not be 99 percent, but 1/10,000, or 0.01 percent.

selected man doing so, is not the likelihood of producing the child in question, but the relative likelihood of producing a child with the same phenotypes. The numerator of the ratio is the probability that a man with the phenotypes of the putative father and a woman with the mother's phenotypes would produce an offspring with the child's phenotypes. The denominator is the probability that a randomly selected man and a woman with the mother's phenotypes would produce an offspring with the child's phenotypes.

For example, as we noted above, the father of Plemel's child had to transmit a B gene to the child. We also noted that the chance that someone with Walter's phenotypes would do so was 0.5. This is the numerator of Walter's paternity index for the ABO system. The chance that a randomly selected man would produce an offspring with the child's phenotypes is simply the frequency with which the B gene occurs in the relevant male population, as compared to other genes. In the white male population this frequency is approximately 0.0658. (The percentage of white males with B genes will be somewhat less because some men will possess two B genes rather than only one.) This number is the denominator of the paternity index. Dividing the numerator by the denominator yields approximately 7.6, which is Walter's paternity index for the ABO system. Multiplying together his paternity indexes for all 19 serologic systems tested yields his overall paternity index, 178.

From the example above, it can be seen that the denominator of the paternity index will be the same for every putative father. This is because the denominator is the gene frequency in the population. The numerator, however, will vary from putative father to putative father because their phenotypes will vary. In the ABO system, some men will have two B genes, some, such as Walter, will have one B gene, and some will have no B gene. For each combination of genes, there will be a different probability of producing the child's phenotypes. Because the numerator varies from putative father to putative father, the paternity index will also vary. Thus, even though all men not excluded by a paternity test are capable of fathering the child, they will have different paternity indexes and thus different relative likelihoods of having fathered the child.

Because Walter's paternity index was 178, Walter was 178 times more likely than a randomly selected man to have fathered a child with the phenotypes of Plemel's child. Converting this into a percentage resulted in a "chance of paternity" of 99.4 percent and a "chance of nonpaternity" of 0.6 percent. The AMA-ABA "verbal predicate" used to describe a "chance of paternity" of 99.4 percent is "extremely likely." Again, this does not mean that it is "extremely likely" that Walter is the father of Plemel's child, only that, compared to a randomly selected man, it is "extremely likely" that Walter is the father of Plemel's child.

Probability of Paternity. In order to convert the paternity index and its equivalents into a probability of paternity, i.e., the actual likelihood that this putative father is the father of the child at issue, some estimate of the strength of the other evidence in the case must be made. If Walter were sterile, he would still have a paternity index of 178 and a "chance of paternity" of 99.4 percent, but obviously his probability of paternity would be zero. Similarly, barring divine intervention, if Walter were the only person to have had intercourse with the mother, his paternity index would be 178 and his "chance of paternity" would be 99.4 percent, but his probability of paternity would be 100 percent. Of course, most cases will fall between these extremes.

The usual method for calculating the probability of paternity is Bayes' formula. This formula demonstrates the effect of a new item of evidence on a previously established probability. In this instance, the new item of evidence is the blood test result (i.e., the paternity index), and the previously established, or prior, probability is the probability of paternity based on the other evidence in the case. The calculation is simplified if the probabilities are expressed as odds. The odds of paternity using Bayes' formula are simply the product of the prior odds and the paternity index. For example, if the other evidence in this case had established that Walter was sterile, his prior odds of paternity would have been zero. His odds of paternity, then, would have been zero times his paternity index of 178, which equals zero. On the other hand, if the other evidence in the case had led one to believe that the odds that Walter was the father were one to one, his odds of paternity would have been one times 178, which equals 178 or a probability of paternity of 99.4 percent. It can be seen, then, that the paternity index will equal the probability of paternity only when the other evidence in the case establishes prior odds of paternity of exactly one. This is because the paternity index's comparison of the putative father with a randomly selected man is mathematically equivalent to the assumption that the prior odds of paternity are one to one, or that the prior probability is 50 percent.

Lovrien did not derive a statistic for probability of paternity, although, as we note below, his testimony frequently referred to the paternity index and its equivalents in language suggestive of a probability of paternity. If the paternity index or its equivalents are presented as the probability of paternity, this amounts to an unstated assumption of a prior probability of 50 percent.

II

Whether the paternity index and its equivalents were admissible is controlled in the first instance by ORS 109.258, which in relevant part provides:

> If . . . the blood tests show the possibility of the alleged father's paternity, admission of this evidence is within the discretion of the court, depending upon the infrequency of the genetic marker.

The words "this evidence" refer to "the possibility of the alleged father's paternity," but it is not clear whether this phrase is limited to the bare possibility of paternity or includes a statement of the degree of possibility.

ORS 109.258 is virtually identical to section 4 of the Uniform Act on Blood Tests to Determine Paternity (UABT), which was enacted in Oregon in 1953.

When the UABT was proposed in 1952, courts admitted only evidence of exclusion; blood test results consistent with paternity were inadmissible. One objective of the UABT was to make results consistent with paternity admissible. The commentary to the UABT states:

> [I]f the [blood] test showed that the alleged father could be the father of the child and if the blood type discovered disclosed that the type of blood and the combination in the child was of a rare type and that it would be infrequent to find such a combination of blood, . . . such evidence ought to be admissible as evidence of proof of paternity.

We infer that "such evidence" refers to the infrequency of the blood type. This interpretation is consistent with the statutory language, which directs the court to exercise its discretion to admit blood test evidence in accordance with the "infrequency of the genetic marker." No mention is made of calculations of relative or absolute probabilities of paternity. For these reasons, we conclude that whether a putative father's paternity index, probability of paternity and similar statistical calculations are admissible is a matter to be determined by generally applicable laws of evidence.

The admissibility of expert testimony is governed by three general constraints. First, expert testimony must be relevant. Relevant testimony is testimony "having any tendency to make the existence of any fact that is of consequence to the determination of the action more probable or less probable than it would be without the evidence." OEC 401. Second, expert testimony is subject to OEC 702: "If scientific, technical or other specialized knowledge will assist the trier of fact to understand the evidence or to determine a fact in issue, a witness qualified as an expert may testify thereto in the form of an opinion or otherwise." Finally, expert testimony must not be unduly prejudicial, confusing or time-consuming . . . . OEC 403. . . .

Walter contends that Lovrien's testimony regarding the paternity index and its equivalents was not probative because it provided the trier of fact with no information beyond that provided by the "probability of excluding a falsely accused father." This contention is not correct and is based on a misunderstanding of these statistics.

As we noted above, the "probability of excluding a falsely accused father" measures only the power of the test to exclude any falsely accused father; it does not describe the percentage of the relevant male population that could be the father in a particular case. It also does not reveal the relative likelihoods of paternity among the men not excluded by the blood test. This relative likelihood is conveyed by the paternity index, and for this reason the paternity index has probative value beyond that provided by an exclusion statistic. For example, even if the blood test reveals that the putative father is a member of a small percentage of the population capable of fathering the child, his paternity index, and hence his relative likelihood of paternity, may also be very small.

In addition, the presentation of paternity test results in terms of probabilities or likelihoods of paternity rather than population percentages may enable the trier of fact to understand better the significance of the test results . . . . First, a population percentage may be too easily confused with the probability of paternity. From the statistic that 97.5 percent of the population is incapable of being the father, the trier of fact may wrongly jump to the conclusion that there is a 97.5 percent probability that the putative father is the true father.[8] Second, even if it is explained to the trier of fact that the population percentage is not the probability of paternity, the trier of fact may be left wondering what the probability of paternity is and what significance the population percentage has for it.

We conclude that the paternity index and its equivalents are probative. This conclusion, however, does not end our inquiry. We must still assess whether, as asserted by Walter, the probative value is substantially outweighed by any prejudice and confusion engendered by its presentation. The fundamental problem in the presentation of blood test results is conveying to the trier of fact the need to integrate the blood test results with the other evidence presented in the case. Although there have been many recent advances in paternity testing, leading to very high probabilities of excluding falsely accused fathers, paternity testing alone cannot yet prove paternity. Other evidence must narrow the number of potential fathers so that the test results become meaningful. The presentation to the trier of fact of the putative father's "paternity index," "chance of paternity" or "probability of paternity" creates several difficulties for conveying to the trier of fact the need to integrate these statistics with the other evidence in the case.

First, the expert is unqualified to state that any single figure is the accused's "probability of paternity." As noted above, such a statement requires an estimation of the strength of the other evidence presented in the case (i.e., an estimation of the "prior probability of paternity"), an estimation that the expert is in no better position to make than the trier of fact.[9] If the expert were to make such an estima

---

[8] This confusion probably could be dispelled easily by the putative father's attorney. The attorney need only note that, if the relevant population were 100,000, exclusion of 97.5 percent would still leave 2500 potential fathers. Absent other evidence, the probability of paternity would not be 97.5 percent, but 1 in 2500, or 0.04 percent.

[9] The standard assumption in calculating the probability of paternity is that the prior probability of paternity is 50 percent. With this assumption the probability of paternity is equal to the paternity index. Studies in Poland and New York City have suggested that this assumption favors the putative father, because in an estimated 60 to 70 percent of paternity cases the mother's accusation of paternity is correct. Of course, the purpose of paternity litigation is to determine whether the mother's accusation is correct, and for that reason it would be both unfair and improper to apply the assumption in any particular case.

We also note that the Court of Appeals' justification of the assumption of a 50 percent prior probability of paternity is erroneous for another reason. The court stated that the "paternity index shows * * * that [the] assumption was, if anything, unduly favorable to father." The paternity index has absolutely no bearing on the prior probability of paternity; the prior probability is independent of the blood test results.

tion, it could not satisfy [the] requirement of assistance to the trier of fact.[10]

Second, the paternity index and its equivalents frequently are confused with the probability of paternity. This case is an example. Lovrien did not calculate a "probability of paternity," but his testimony regarding Walter's paternity index and its equivalents could easily have been confused with a probability of paternity. Lovrien correctly described the paternity index as the chance that the child received its "genes from this man [Walter] compared with just an average man." Lovrien also testified, however, that the index meant that the odds were "178 times to 1 that he [Walter] is the right father," that a paternity index of 178 meant that "the chance that Brent Walter is the father is extremely likely," that Walter's "chance of paternity" was 99.4 percent, and that the "chance he is not the father based upon these [test results] is 0.6 percent." We doubt that any of the jurors would have made a distinction between the likelihood that Walter, rather than a randomly selected man, was the father (which is what the paternity index and its equivalents measure) and the probability that Walter was in fact the father.

Finally, the paternity index's comparison of the putative father with a randomly selected man is only indirectly relevant to the issue the trier of fact must decide. "The [trier of fact's] function is not to compare a defendant with a person selected randomly but to weigh the probability of defendant's [responsibility] against the probability that anyone else is responsible." The comparison with a random man is obviously probative, but there is a danger that the trier of fact will accord it too much weight when it comes to decide whether the putative father is the true father. For example, if an individual purchases 178 of a total of 100,000 raffle tickets, and if the average person purchases one ticket, that individual will be 178 times more likely to win the raffle than a randomly selected person. The individual's chances of winning the raffle prize, however, are still minuscule because the proper comparison is not with the number of tickets purchased by a randomly selected person, but with the total tickets purchased by everyone. Similarly, Walter is 178 times more likely to be the father of Plemel's child than a randomly selected man, but this figure standing alone is not particularly meaningful. It is important for the trier of fact to understand that the paternity index must not be taken as practically conclusive evidence of paternity but should be considered in conjunction with other evidence presented in the case.

Where the determination whether the probative value of evidence is substantially outweighed by the dangers set forth in OEC 403 must be made on a case-by-case basis, we ordinarily defer to the determination of the trial court. We

---

[10] We emphasize that the estimation is objectionable under OEC 702. Such an estimation would not necessarily violate OEC 703 or OEC 705. Under OEC 703, other evidence presented in the case could be made known to the expert, and the expert could then form an opinion as to the proper prior probability of paternity to use in calculating the probability of paternity. Under OEC 705, the expert could testify to the probability of paternity without initially disclosing the basis for the calculation. Such disclosure, however, must be made at the direction of the court or on cross-examination.

conclude that this is not such a case. The probative value of the statistics derived from blood test results and the dangers in their presentation to the trier of fact will be substantially the same in every case. This court, as an appellate court, should determine the admissibility of this evidence.

Evidence of the putative father's paternity index and its equivalents is highly probative but also presents a substantial danger of misleading the trier of fact. For that reason, we conclude that this evidence should be admissible, but only subject to certain conditions. The purpose of these conditions is to convey to the trier of fact the significance of this evidence and the need to weigh it with the other evidence presented in the case. First, the paternity index is admissible so long as the expert explains that the index is not the probability that the defendant is the father, but measures only the chance that the defendant is the father compared to the chance that a randomly selected man is the father. The expert should also not be allowed to use misleading formulations of the paternity index such as "the chance of paternity" and "the chance of nonpaternity" without making this qualification. If the expert's testimony does not satisfy this condition, the objecting party is entitled to have this testimony stricken and the jury instructed to disregard it.

Second, the expert, whether testifying in person or by affidavit [as permitted under an Oregon statute], should never be allowed to present over objection a single figure as "the" probability of paternity. If the expert does so, the objecting party is entitled to have that testimony stricken and the jury instructed to disregard it. The reason for this limitation is that the probability of paternity cannot be stated mathematically without making certain assumptions concerning the strength of the other evidence presented in the case. Similarly, the expert should not be allowed to make statements such as "it is extremely likely" or "it is practically proven" that the defendant is the father.

Finally, as a corollary to the above conditions, if the expert testifies to the defendant's paternity index or a substantially equivalent statistic, the expert must, if requested, calculate the probability that the defendant is the father by using more than a single assumption about the strength of the other evidence in the case. The expert may also so testify without request or without testifying as to the paternity index. This condition is not at odds with the second condition because this condition requires the expert to use various assumptions about the strength of the other evidence in the case rather than making a single assumption and presenting the probability calculated from that assumption as "the" probability of paternity. In this way the strength of the blood test results can be demonstrated without overstating the information that can be derived from them. If the expert uses various assumptions and makes these assumptions known, the factfinder's attention will be directed to the other evidence in the case, and it will not be misled into adopting the expert's assumption as the correct weight to be assigned to the other evidence. The expert should present calculations based on assumed prior probabilities of 0, 10, 20, 30, 40, 50, 60, 70, 80, 90 and 100 percent. If the expert is requested to do so and fails to make these calculations, the trier of fact should be instructed to ignore the paternity index and its equivalents. Other statistics, such as the probability of excluding a falsely accused father and the proportion of the relevant population excluded by the blood tests, would still be admissible.

III

With respect to the disposition of this case, we conclude that it is necessary to remand for a new trial. Lovrien testified that Walter's paternity index of 178 meant that he was 178 times more likely to be the father of Plemel's child than "an average man." While that testimony was accurate, other statements made by him, as we noted above, could have led the jury to infer that the paternity index was the probability that Walter was the father. Lovrien also testified that the paternity index was based on the assumption that "the most logical person" had been identified and accused of being the father and that if there was a zero prior probability that Walter was the father, the paternity index would be meaningless. From these statements the jury could have inferred that the significance of the paternity index would depend to some extent on the other evidence presented in the case, but this relationship was not made clear by Lovrien. Perhaps particularly confusing to the jury was the following statement made by Lovrien near the close of his testimony:

> [A]ssuming that the right man has been accused or investigated, then the laboratory is used as a means of investigating, if he denies fatherhood, then you want a good laboratory test to say well if he is not the father, let's show that he is not. And that is what we did. We used a good laboratory test here. And if he is not the father, he should have been excluded, but he wasn't.

On the record before us, we cannot say that the result would have been the same if Lovrien's testimony had been presented under the conditions set forth above.

The decision of the Court of Appeals is reversed. The judgment of the trial court is reversed, and the case is remanded to the trial court for a new trial.

NOTES

1. *Admissibility of biostatistical proof of paternity.* What special limitations, if any, should be imposed on genetic proof of paternity? The requirement of a display of prior and posterior probabilities of paternity was proposed in Ira M. Ellman & David Kaye, Probabilities and Proof: Can HLA and Blood Group Testing Prove Paternity? 54 NYU L. Rev. 1131 (1979), and the *Plemel* case is discussed in D.H. Kaye, *Plemel* as a Primer on Proving Paternity, 24 Willamette L.J. 867 (1988). In Commonwealth v. Beausoleil, 490 N.E. 2d 788 (Mass. 1986), the Supreme Judicial Court, in what amounted to an advisory opinion, rejected the requirement of a display of prior and posterior probabilities as unduly complicated. Instead, that court issued four prophylactic rules for paternity probability evidence. These rules are criticized in D.H. Kaye, The Probability of an Ultimate Issue: The Strange Cases of Paternity Testing, 74 Iowa L. Rev. 75 (1989), and in 1 McCormick on Evidence § 211 (J. Strong ed., 4th ed. 1992).

2. *The biostatistical methods.* The various probabilities bandied about in parentage cases can be confusing when first encountered. Accounts in legal journals and treatises, not to mention opinions, are sometimes garbled. For more precise expositions of the biostatistical analysis, see, e.g., Mikel Aickin & D.H. Kaye, Some Mathematical and Legal Considerations in Using Serological Tests to Prove Paternity, in Inclusion Probabilities in Parentage Testing 155 (Richard H. Walker ed., 1983); Donald Berry & Seymour Geisser, Inference in Cases of Disputed Paternity, in Statistics and the Law 353 (Morris DeGroot et al. eds., 1986).

An unusual feature of paternity litigation is that the proportion of true claims brought by plaintiffs can be estimated from the rate of inclusions in genetic tests. For example, if a laboratory finds that 70% of the men referred for testing last year were included by tests that would include only 1% of falsely accused men, then nearly all the included men were true fathers. As noted in *Plemel,* laboratories have found that the base rate, or prevalence, of true claims of paternity is of this magnitude. See M.R. Mickey et al., Empirical Validation of the Essen-Möller Probability of Paternity, 39 Am. J. Human Genetics 123 (1986). The *Plemel* court writes in note 9 that such prior experience may not be used in assessing the probability that the man at bar is a biological father. Why not? Should the factfinder be informed of the base rate for valid claims? See Daniel Shaviro, Statistical-Probability Evidence and the Appearance of Justice, 103 Harv. L. Rev. 530 (1989); Jonathan J. Koehler, Probabilities in the Courtroom: An Evaluation of the Objectives and Policies, in Handbook of Psychology and the Law (D.K. Kagehiro & W.S. Laufer eds., 1992); Michael Saks & Robert Kidd, Human Information Processing and Adjudication: Trial by Heuristics, 15 Law & Soc'y Rev. 123 (1980-81).

3. *The prevalence and variety of statutes. Plemel* describes some of the Uniform Laws on the admissibility of genetic marker identification in parentage litigation. In recent years, most jurisdictions have amended their statutes, moving from the "exclusionary" statutes exemplified in *Beausoleil* to "inclusionary" ones. D.H. Kaye & Ronald Kanwischer, Admissibility of Genetic Testing in Paternity Litigation: A Survey of State Statutes, 22 Family L.Q. 109 (1988). Seeking to enhance the impact of the genetic proof still more, a minority of jurisdictions use the "probability of paternity" or the paternity index to trigger a presumption of paternity. This legislation is analyzed and criticized in D.H. Kaye, Presumptions, Probability and Paternity, 30 Jurimetrics J. 323 (1990).

4. *Advances in technology.* The *Plemel* court states that "[a]lthough there have been many recent advances in paternity testing, leading to very high proba-

bilities of excluding falsely accused fathers, paternity testing alone cannot yet prove paternity." 735 P.2d at 1217. In the decade since this opinion, even more dramatic advances have been made. See, e.g., D.H. Kaye, DNA Paternity Probabilities, 24 Fam. L.Q. 279 (1990). Instead of paternity indices of 178, experts now report indices in the millions. Have we reached the point where genetic testing alone can prove paternity? If not, what would it take?

The cases usually insist that something more than a high paternity index is still essential. E.g., Zearfoss v. Frattaroli, 646 A.2d 1238, 1243 (Pa. Super. Ct. 1994) (error to grant summary for mother when "probability of paternity" exceeded 99.99%). But cf. Department of Human Serv. v. Moore, 632 So.2d 929 (Miss. 1994) (error to instruct jury that tests with a 99.99% "probability of paternity" and a paternity index of 22,473,773 merely established "biological possibility" and that they must "independently" find that sexual intercourse occurred); Commissioner of Social Serv. v. Hector S., 628 N.Y.S.2d 270 (App. Div. 1995) (tests of red cell antigens, enzymes and serum proteins, leukocyte antigens, and DNA gave a 99.99% "probability of paternity" and a paternity index of 11,734,738, but also excluded defendant as the father of the fraternal twin; medical testimony established that it is possible for two men to father fraternal twins, and the appellate division held that the trial court erred in failing to find paternity because the "staggering" genetic marker test results were "sufficiently persuasive despite petitioner's cloudy and somewhat contradictory testimony as to her sexual activity and menstrual history." The court remarked, "[w]e prefer the more modern trend toward admissibility and greater weight given to these genetic marker test results, rather than considering them as just another factor equal to the cloudy testimonial recollections of the parties.").

Chapter 10
Parentage Testing: Criminal Cases

Genetic evidence of parentage is not limited to paternity litigation. It is used in cases involving citizenship, slander, job terminations, and estates or insurance. Neither is it limited to civil cases, for proof of paternity can be telling evidence in some cases of sexual assaults and other crimes. But biostatistical evidence of paternity has met more effective resistance in criminal cases than in the civil arena. In Minnesota, the "probability of paternity" is admissible to identify a father in civil actions, but not in criminal prosecutions,[1] and several other state supreme courts have held it to be reversible error to admit testimony as to the "probability of paternity" under certain conditions in criminal cases. In State v. Spann, 617 A.2d 247 (N.J. 1993), Joseph Spann, a corrections officer at a county jail, was convicted of having intercourse with a woman detainee. The state introduced evidence to show that Spann was the father of a child conceived while the woman was imprisoned. Based on blood and tissue tests, the expert concluded that "[t]he likelihood of this woman and this man producing this child with all of the genetic makeup versus this woman with a random male out of the black population . . . [results in] a probability of paternity [of] 96.55 percent," making it "very likely" that he was the father. In summation, the prosecutor told the jury that "guilt . . . is proved to a mathematical certainty . . . by carefully applying an objective scientific technique to the hard facts of this case." The expert never explained how she arrived the 96.55% figure. Except for the elliptical statement that "everything is equal . . . he may or may not be the father of the child," she did not reveal on direct examination that she assumed a prior probability of 50%. On cross-examination, she acknowledged the assumption, and defended it as "neutral." According to this expert, the "purely objective" nature of the analysis was "one of the beauties of the test": it "makes no assumption other than everything is equal," and "the jury simply has objective information." In response, defense counsel established that even if it were conclusively proven that defendant had been out of the country at the time when conception could have occurred, this expert still would have concluded that the probability defendant was the father was 96.55%.

The intermediate appellate court ruled that the probability of paternity was inadmissible to prove intercourse because the calculation itself assumed that intercourse had taken place. The Supreme Court rejected this reasoning. Although the expert "practically [conceded] the point and both counsel [agreed] that intercourse was assumed in the calculation," the Supreme Court noted that

> Those [prior] odds, for instance, are wholly consistent with a fact pattern that one and only one man had access to and intercourse with the victim and that one of two, and only two, men, including defendant, could possi-

---

[1] See State v. Kim, excerpted supra, chapter 2. Is this distinction tenable? Should testimony about posterior probabilities be excluded in criminal cases?

bly have been that one man, neither one more likely than the other to be the father. The fifty-fifty odds calculated into the probability of paternity percentage do not at all assume that defendant had intercourse with the victim; indeed, defendant might have been the one with no access to the victim. Those odds say only that the chances are fifty-fifty that he is the father. Obviously, they assume a substantial possibility, 50%, that he had intercourse with the victim, but not that he positively did.

Nevertheless, the court agreed that the admission of the probability of paternity opinion "as presented in this case" was error:

> Although the jury learned, in cross-examination of the expert, of the expert's assumption of a 50% prior probability that defendant was the father, the clear impression given by the expert was that it was somehow a "scientific" assumption, an accepted part of a scientific calculation, "objective," "neutral," "fair." It is no such thing — although it is often, indeed apparently almost regularly, used by forensic experts testifying in paternity matters. While counsel could have demonstrated this inherent lack of neutrality through fuller cross-examination, we think that his objections to the introduction of the probability of paternity percentage on that ground were well founded, fairly clearly stated, and should have been sustained.

And, the court went on to offer the following dictum:

> More than that, we conclude that even if not objected to sufficiently by counsel, the expert's opinion on probability of paternity did not satisfy the most fundamental requirement of expert testimony: its ability to aid the jury in its deliberations. Moreover, as presented, the testimony "create[d] [a] substantial danger of . . . misleading the jury." In this criminal case, the jury had no idea what to do with the probability of paternity percentage if its own estimate of probabilities (the prior probability of paternity as estimated by the jury apart from blood and tissue tests) was different from .5. There was neither guidance from the expert nor specific instructions from the trial court regarding this crucial aspect of the probability of paternity opinion.

To solve this problem, the New Jersey Supreme Court suggested that a procedure comparable to that adopted by the Oregon Supreme Court in *Plemel* be used because "[s]uch an approach ensures that the jury's attention will be focused on the other evidence in the case and that it will not be misled by the expert's assumption of a prior probability of .5."

In a "comment" that was "not intended to be binding," the *Spann* court further observed that "in addition to the probability of exclusion, the related paternity index — if that has been calculated — is admissible at trial." Finally, the court tempered its earlier endorsement of *Plemel* in the criminal context with a lengthy discussion of the "general acceptance" of using Bayes' rule in trials and its "jurisprudential" acceptability. It directed the trial court to hold a hearing on the admissibility of this type of testimony in light of these concerns.

State v. Spann
617 A.2d 247 (N.J. 1993)

PER CURIAM . . .

The disagreement on the subject is such as to prevent us from reaching any conclusion about "general acceptance." * What is needed is what the trial court will have: examination and cross-examination on that issue. It boils down to this: you have a mathematical formula that invariably works in converting a mathematical statistical probability into a new probability by using in that formula new information about the matter, here the likelihood ratio based on the blood-tissue tests. The question is whether the formula produces reliable results when it is applied to a jury's conclusion about the prior probability — for instance when a jury, let us say in this case, concludes that even without the blood-tissue tests it believes defendant is guilty, that he is the father, and it quantifies that belief by saying that it is 60% probable that he is the father. Ordinarily, a 60% probability means that out of ten chances, the event in question will occur six times, but not the four other times. But what does a 60% probability mean in this case other than the strength of the jury's belief in guilt? . . .

The fundamental objections to the use of Bayes' Theorem to establish probability of paternity are both mathematical and jurisprudential. The mathematical objections are suggested above: they raise doubts about the validity of applying a

---

* Editor's note: The court explained that

> The controversy, rather than the "general acceptance," concerning the use of the probability of paternity opinion and Bayes' Theorem or formula — indeed the evidentiary use of Bayes' Theorem at all — is best reflected in the scholarly articles on this issue. Indeed, even the experts have difficulty with it. One, for instance, referred to the Bayes' Theorem in 1987 as the "reigning" view, D.H. Kaye, Apples and Oranges: Confidence Coefficients and the Burden of Persuasion, 73 Cornell L. Rev. 54 (1987), but five years earlier had described it as "not used as widely as the classical theories." D.H. Kaye, The Numbers Game: Statistical Inference in Discrimination Cases, 80 Mich. L. Rev. 833, 853 (1982). This same authority, Professor Kaye, although apparently supportive of the use of the formula to establish probability of paternity in 1979, 54 N.Y.U. L. Rev. at 1149, expressly suggested its exclusion in criminal cases in 1987, D.H. Kaye, The Admissibility of Probability Evidence in Criminal Trials, 27 Jurimetrics J. 160, 172 (1987).

This paragraph makes the issue seem more confusing than it is. The 1982 article correctly states that most statisticians analyze data without using Bayesian procedures. The 1987 article refers to a scholarly debate over the meaning of the burden of persuasion. It suggests that this burden can be understood in terms of a posterior probability (based on all the evidence in the case) that must exceed some threshhold that varies with the nature of the case — the threshhold being 50% in civil cases and much closer to 100% in criminal cases. See supra chapter 2. Plainly, there is no conflict between the fact that most statisticians do not assign subjective probabilities to statistical hypotheses and the view that the legal burden of persuasion is satisfied when the subjective probability of the plaintiff's story is large enough. And, whether it is inconsistent to recommend the use of Bayes' rule to display the probative value of the genetic evidence in civil but not criminal cases is just the topic of this section.

formula designed for statistical probabilities to an assessment of proofs by the jury that, although it can be expressed as a probability, is in fact simply a statement of the strength, or weakness, of the jury's belief in a fact, forced into the mold of a statement of probability. The "prior probability" that is the basis for the Bayes' Theorem calculation is truly no prior probability at all so far as the jury is concerned. Jurors simply believe, at whatever stage of the proceedings they have to make the assessment, that defendant is guilty or not, and have varying degrees of confidence in that belief. If forced to — and they will be, if Bayes' Theorem is admitted — they can express that degree of confidence as a "prior probability," the defendant's probability of guilt is 80%, 50% or 10%. The question remains whether Bayes' Theorem, when applied to such a non-statistical probability estimate, is likely to yield reliable results. That is one of the issues the trial court will deal with . . . .

The jurisprudential objection is different. It says that even if reliable, this factfinding method should not be used by juries except in the most unusual situations, or where the law explicitly requires a calculation of probabilities. In criminal cases, those objections go beyond the possibility of confusing or overwhelming the jury with mathematical complexities. They go to the heart of the jury's function — the finding of guilt beyond a reasonable doubt.

These jurisprudential (and other) concerns are set forth in Laurence H. Tribe, Trial by Mathematics: Precision and Ritual in the Legal Process, 84 Harv. L. Rev. 1329 (1971). Writing concededly in reaction to a perceived risk at the time that mathematics was about to take over the jury's factfinding role, Professor Tribe persuasively argued that probabilistic analysis should but rarely be allowed to aid factfinding in criminal trials — and Bayes' Theorem was very much in mind. Although expressly rejecting a per se exclusion of such evidence, his position comes very close to that. Some of his arguments, expressed as well by others, must be dealt with.

One argument notes the possibility that the jury will use the associative evidence — the probability of exclusion — twice. First, having heard defendant has the blood-tissue type that the guilty suspect must have and that only one in one hundred have it, the jury will include that fact in its initial assessment of guilt, i.e., in its determination of the prior probability. When Bayes' Theorem is then applied to that prior probability to reach a conclusion of probability of paternity, the calculation will necessarily again factor in the probability of exclusion, because it is part of the Bayes' Theorem probability of paternity calculation, impermissibly using the exclusionary percentage twice.

Second, because Bayes' Theorem will be introduced in the State's case and because its use depends on the jury's prior-probability finding, the jury inevitably will be impelled to focus, during the State's case, before all of the evidence is in, on the probability of defendant's guilt. Professor Tribe notes the inconsistency of that result with the presumption of innocence, the jury, of course, required to regard defendant as innocent until found guilty beyond a reasonable doubt. Simply put, the argument is that the use of that calculation during the State's case impermissibly violates the jury's obligation to keep an open mind until all of the evidence is in and deliberations start.

Third, the jury is implicitly asked to find defendant guilty beyond a reasonable doubt even though the probability of paternity itself has a quantifiable element of uncertainty and doubt. Stated otherwise, even if the probability of paternity is 95%, does our system of criminal justice encourage a jury to find guilt beyond a reasonable doubt when there is a 5% chance that defendant is innocent?

Finally, the argument notes the counter-intuitive impact of Bayes' Theorem and the probability of paternity that can result. The ability of the calculation to convert a very low jury estimate based on the facts into an extremely high one after the formula is applied is one such counter-intuitive result. The formula's ability to declare both the defendant and a suspect (with the same blood type) as each having a 95% probability of being the father is another. With such counter-intuitive results persuasively supported by expert testimony, the fear is the jurors will lose sense of the need to use their intuition, common sense, and sense of community values. Tribe likens the process to a return to trial by battle.

Although some of these issues, both mathematical and jurisprudential, may ultimately become issues of law for this Court, we prefer to commit their resolution initially to the trial court where they will be subjected to adversarial testing. We are inclined to believe that appropriate jury instructions can cure all of them, or at least diminish their risk to the point that the advantages of the expert's calculation outweigh these risks, assuming the opinion is otherwise admissible.

Given the guidance of the trial court and the argument of competent counsel, we think juries will be able to cope with the complexities and pitfalls of this kind of probabilistic evidence. Although the dispute on this subject presumably continues, we are not dealing here with some abstruse application of mathematics: the probability of paternity opinion is regularly and routinely used in civil cases and apparently favored if not mandated by both our Legislature and the federal government. The probability of paternity opinion is also routinely used by laboratories that perform this blood-tissue testing. . . .

If the State in a criminal case offers expert proof of the probability of paternity, the trial court should hold a . . . hearing. That hearing should focus on whether the relevant scientific community generally accepts the probability of paternity opinion as a reliable indicator of paternity. The trial court should also inquire concerning the appropriateness of the admissibility of probability of paternity opinions in criminal cases. . . .

If the trial court allows this testimony — the opinion of probability of paternity — other matters, including conditions on its admissibility, should be considered. The expert should be qualified not only as a geneticist but also as a mathematician (which the expert in this case was not); or, alternatively, a mathematician should testify as well as the geneticist concerning the formula. The expert should explain the formula and indicate what it means, but should never be allowed to state that "in my opinion the probability of paternity . . ." is a particular percentage. No verbal predicate should be stated in any way, not even a reference to the verbal predicates approved by the Joint AMA—ABA Guidelines (e.g., "very likely,"

"likely"). A range of possible prior probabilities should be presented to the jury, along with the probability of paternity applicable to each, resulting from the formula. The jury should be made aware of the formula's ability, given high exclusionary percentages, to convert low prior probabilities into extremely high probability of paternity opinions. The jury should also be informed, where appropriate, of other counter-intuitive results the formula might produce. And, as in all other cases, the jury should be told that it need not accept the expert's testimony, that it may reject it either in whole or in part, that it is simply offered to help it in the evaluation of the impact of the blood-tissue evidence and the exclusionary percentage. Finally, the jury must be instructed that the ultimate question — whether defendant, beyond a reasonable doubt, had intercourse with the victim, or, its equivalent in this case, whether defendant, beyond a reasonable doubt, is the father — is for the jury and only the jury to determine; that issue must be determined as stated "beyond a reasonable doubt"; and that no mathematical formulation can relieve it of the obligation to make that determination. The formula, the probability of paternity, all of these things, along with all of the other evidence, are there to aid the jury in its ultimate fact-finding obligation. That obligation, however, does not change. . . .

In conclusion, we agree with the Appellate Division's reversal of the conviction: the probability of paternity opinion was improperly admitted as presented in this case. On remand the trial court will decide that issue, if the offer is again made, considering the matters mentioned in this opinion. . . .

State v. Skipper
637 A.2d 1101 (Conn. 1994)

CALLAHAN, ASSOCIATE JUSTICE.

The dispositive issue in this appeal is the admissibility of the probability of paternity statistic calculated from DNA evidence. The defendant was [convicted of multiple counts of various crimes involving sexual conduct with a minor but acquitted of simple assault.] The trial court sentenced the defendant to a term of imprisonment of twenty-four years, execution suspended after twelve years, followed by five years probation. Thereafter, the defendant appealed to the Appellate Court. We transferred his appeal to this court . . . . We reverse the judgment of the trial court.

The jury could reasonably have found the following facts. The defendant began to make sexual overtures to the victim, who was the daughter of a neighbor and a friend of his own daughter, sometime in 1982, when the victim was approximately eight years old and in the third grade. In response to the victim's protests, the defendant told her that he would leave her alone if she allowed him to take topless photographs of her. When the victim complied, however, the defendant persisted in his contact with her, threatening to show the photographs to her friends if she refused to see him. By the time the victim was in the fourth grade, the defendant had begun to molest her physically. At some point, while she was still in the fourth or fifth grade, the defendant began to have sexual intercourse with the victim. Even after she moved out of his neighborhood, the defendant continued on a regular basis to have sexual relations with the victim in his van at various locations.

When the victim was in the tenth grade, she told the defendant that she wanted him to leave her alone and that she no longer cared what he did with photographs he had taken. At that time, the victim's parents were in the process of attempting to adopt a little girl. When the victim persisted in her refusal to see him, the defendant intimated to her that the adoption would not go through if the authorities were notified of their relationship.

The sexual relationship between the defendant and the victim continued until March, 1989. At that time, the defendant, in an attempt to end a platonic friendship between the victim and a classmate named Marvin, told her to advise Marvin that she was pregnant and provided her with a falsified home pregnancy test that ostensibly displayed a positive result. Marvin promptly informed the victim's parents. When confronted by her mother, the victim broke down and told her of the nature of her relationship with the defendant.

On March 9, 1989, the victim gave a statement to the police. The next day, the victim's mother took her for a medical examination that revealed that the victim was in fact pregnant. On March 22, 1989, the victim had an abortion. . . .

The defendant claims that the trial court improperly admitted testimony of the probability of paternity percentage based on DNA testing. We agree and, on this basis, reverse the judgment of the trial court and remand the case for a new trial.

Kevin McElfresh, the state's expert witness and the director of Identity Testing Laboratories of Lifecodes Corporation (Lifecodes), testified at trial regarding the defendant's paternity index. The paternity index is an odds ratio, based on DNA tests,[6] measuring the likelihood that the defendant would produce a child with the same phenotypes as the fetus in question as compared to an unrelated random male. The paternity index in this case was 3496, indicating that only one out of 3497 randomly selected males would have the phenotypes compatible with the fetus in question.[9]

---

[6] In the present case, Lifecodes performed DNA tests on blood samples from the defendant and the victim and on a tissue sample from the aborted fetus. Lifecodes is a private biotechnology company involved in DNA base identification, testing, research and development, and training in the use of DNA technology for identity tests.

[9] Although the defendant asserts in his brief that there are 340 other individuals in Bridgeport who could have been the biological father based on the paternity index, we are unable to determine from the record how he arrived at that number. Our mathematical calculations, arrived at by dividing the number of African-American males, according to the 1990 census, in Connecticut and the United States by the paternity index, indicate that there are approximately twenty African-American males between sixteen and fifty years old in Connecticut, and 2138 in the United States, who could have been the biological father of the victim's fetus. The probability of paternity percentage cannot, however, tell us which of these males is the father.

Editor's note: The court's characterization of the paternity index as an "odds ratio" and its interpretation of this quantity as the rate at which the tests would include men as genetically possible fathers are incorrect. Do you see why? (Reconsider the description of the paternity index in *Plemel*.)

McElfresh further testified that the paternity index could be converted into a statistic indicating the percentage of the defendant's probability of paternity. In the present case, he testified that he had made that conversion and that the percentage of probability that it was the defendant who had fathered the fetus was 99.97 percent. The usual method for calculating the probability of paternity, and the method that McElfresh used in the present case, is Bayes' Theorem. . . . In the context of determining paternity, Bayes' Theorem postulates the multiplication of the paternity index, i.e., the new statistical evidence, by an assumed prior percentage of probability of paternity in order to obtain a new percentage of probability of paternity. In order to assume a prior probability of paternity, however, it is also necessary to assume a prior probability of intercourse.

In Bayes' Theorem, the prior probability of paternity is not cast as any particular figure. Generally, experts who testify in paternity proceedings choose a number to represent the prior probability. Most experts, as did McElfresh here, set the prior probability at 50 percent, expressed as odds of one, i.e., fifty-fifty, reasoning that 50 percent is a neutral starting point because it assumes that it is just as likely that the defendant is not the father as it is that he is the father.

Our criminal justice system is built upon the premise that the prosecution must prove "'every fact necessary to constitute the crime with which [the defendant] is charged' beyond a reasonable doubt." State v. Salz, 226 Conn. 20, 28, 627 A.2d 862 (1993), quoting In re Winship, 397 U.S. 358, 364 (1970). The right to have one's guilt proven beyond a reasonable doubt is of constitutional dimension. In a sexual assault prosecution, sexual intercourse is an element that must be proven by the state beyond a reasonable doubt. The utilization of Bayes' Theorem by the prosecution, however, permitted the introduction of evidence predicated on an assumption that there was a fifty-fifty chance that sexual intercourse had occurred in order to prove that sexual intercourse had in fact occurred.* The fifty-fifty assumption that sexual intercourse had occurred was not predicated on the evidence in the case but was simply an assumption made by the expert. . . .

The assumption that there is a substantial possibility that the defendant had intercourse with the victim, however, raises serious concerns in sexual assault cases. It is antithetical to our criminal justice system to presume anything but innocence at the outset of a trial. It is not until the defendant has been convicted that the presumption of innocence disappears. Herrera v. Collins, 113 S.Ct. 853, 860 (1993). "The defendant's presumption of innocence until proven guilty is an 'axiomatic and elementary' principle whose 'enforcement lies at the foundation of the administration of our criminal law.'" State v. Allen, 205 Conn. 370, 376, 533 A.2d 559 (1987), quoting Coffin v. United States, 156 U.S. 432, 453 (1895). The presumption allocates the burden of proof in a criminal trial to the state. Bell v.

---

* Editor's note: Rather than expressing the probability of *intercourse,* a prior probability of *paternity* provides a lower bound. If the probability that a given man is a father is 1/2, then it cannot be any less probable that he had intercourse with the mother, but it can be more probable that he did.

Wolfish, 441 U.S. 520, 533 (1979). "[T]o implement that presumption, 'courts must be alert to factors that may undermine the fairness of the factfinding process. In the administration of criminal justice, courts must carefully guard against dilution of the principle that guilt is to be established by probative evidence and beyond a reasonable doubt. In re Winship, [surpa, 397 U.S. at 364].'"

Without first assuming a prior probability of paternity, i.e., guilt, Bayes' Theorem cannot be applied, and the probability of paternity cannot be computed in sexual assault cases. Because Bayes' Theorem requires the assumption of a prior probability of paternity, i.e., guilt, its use is inconsistent with the presumption of innocence in a criminal case such as this, in which Bayes' Theorem was used to establish the probability of paternity, i.e., that the defendant was the father of the product of conception of an alleged sexual assault. Whether a prior probability of 50 percent is automatically used or whether the jury is instructed to adopt its own prior probability,[18] when the probability of paternity statistic is introduced,

---

[18] It has been suggested that jurors be shown a chart illustrating a range of prior probabilities and the resulting probabilities of paternity. Permitting the jury to derive its own prior probability to arrive at a corresponding probability of paternity, however, still implicates the presumption of innocence. See, e.g., L. Tribe, "Trial by Mathematics: Precision and Ritual in the Legal Process," 84 Harv. L. Rev. 1329, 1368-75 (1971). "It may be supposed that no juror would be permitted to announce publicly in mid-trial that the defendant was already burdened with, say, a sixty percent probability of guilt — but even without such a public statement it would be exceedingly difficult for the accused, for the prosecution, and ultimately for the community, to avoid the explicit recognition that, having been forced to focus on the question, the rational juror could hardly avoid reaching some such answer. And, once that recognition had become a general one, our society's traditional affirmation of the 'presumption of innocence' could lose much of its value." Id., 1370. Moreover, allowing the jury to adopt a prior probability and, hence, arrive at a probability of guilt, raises concerns in criminal cases regarding the burden of proof of guilt beyond a reasonable doubt. In adopting a prior probability of guilt and viewing the corresponding probability of paternity on a chart, the jury is left "with a number that purports to represent [its] assessment of the probability that the defendant is guilty as charged. Needless to say, that number will never quite equal 1.0, so the result will be to produce a quantity . . . which openly signifies a measurable . . . margin of doubt. . . ." Id., 1372; see also R. Jonakait, "When Blood Is Their Argument: Probabilities in Criminal Cases, Genetic Markers, and, Once Again, Bayes' Theorem," 1983 U. Ill. L. Rev. 369, 415-20 (1983). "[A]ny conceptualization of reasonable doubt in probabilistic form is inconsistent with the functional role the concept is designed to play." C. Nesson, "Reasonable Doubt and Permissive Inferences: The Value of Complexity," 92 Harv. L. Rev. 1187, 1225 (1979); see also State v. DelVecchio, 191 Conn. 412, 417-18, 464 A.2d 813 (1983) (jury instruction using a football field simile and instructing the jury that "it . . . is up to you to decide" where reasonable doubt lies between the fifty yard line and one hundred yard line diluted the constitutional standard of proof beyond a reasonable doubt). Allowing jurors to reach their own prior probability also presents practical problems. See L. Tribe, 84 Harv. L. Rev., supra, pp. 1359-66. We cannot say that merely introducing a chart illustrating a range of prior probabilities for educational purposes without requiring the jury to adopt a specific figure would alleviate our concerns. "[W]hether the benefits of using this method of statistical inference solely to educate the jury by displaying the probative force of the evidentiary findings would be worth the costs in terms of time-consumption and possible confusion is a close . . . question." 1 C. McCormick, Evidence (4th ed. 1992) § 210, p. 959; D. Kaye, "The Admissibility of 'Probability Evidence' in Criminal Trials — Part II," 27 Jurimetrics J. 160, 171 (1987); but see State v. Spann, 130 N.J. 484, 518, 617 A.2d 247 (1993) ("[w]e . . . believe that appropriate jury instructions can cure all of [the problems with letting the jury derive its own prior probability], or at least diminish their risk to the point that the advantages of the expert's calculation outweigh these risks, assuming the opinion is otherwise admissible"). For an exhaustive explanation of the practical problems associated with a chart approach, see L. Tribe, 84 Harv. L. Rev., supra, pp. 1358-68, and R. Jonakait, 1983 U. Ill. L. Rev., supra, pp. 403-405.

an assumption is required to be made by the jury before it has heard all of the evidence — that there is a quantifiable probability that the defendant committed the crime. In fact, if the presumption of innocence were factored into Bayes' Theorem, the probability of paternity statistic would be useless. If we assume that the presumption of innocence standard would require the prior probability of guilt to be zero, the probability of paternity in a criminal case would always be zero because Bayes' Theorem requires the paternity index to be multiplied by a positive prior probability in order to have any utility. "In other words, Bayes' Theorem can only work if the presumption of innocence disappears from consideration."

We conclude that the trial court should not have admitted the expert testimony stating a probability of paternity statistic. Moreover, we cannot say with any degree of confidence that a probability of paternity statistic of 99.97 percent, as testified to by the state's expert, would not have influenced the jury's decision to convict the defendant of both sexual assault and risk of injury. Because the admissibility of the probability of paternity statistic involves a constitutional issue, and because we cannot say that the admission of that statistic here was harmless beyond a reasonable doubt, a new trial is required. . . .

NOTE

What do the courts in *Spann* and *Skipper* hold? Do these cases preclude all uses of Bayes' theorem in criminal cases? Should the "chart approach" be permitted (or required) in civil cases (à la *Plemel*), but excluded in criminal ones? What would justify such a distinction? The requirement of "proof beyond a reasonable doubt" and the "presumption of innocence" in criminal cases? How do these two protections differ? Is *Skipper* correct in equating the presumption of innocence to a prior probability of zero? Does testimony explaining the impact of the genetic tests on a wide range of prior probabilities necessarily vitiate the "presumption of innocence"? Consider the following Internet electronic mail messages distributed to subscribers to a "Bayesian evidence" discussion list:[7]

From: Bernard Robertson
Date: July 19, 1994
Subject: State v. Skipper

The presumption of innocence does not require assessing a prior probability of zero for the following reasons:

a. [A] prior probability of zero is simply a formal way of saying "I have an unshakeable belief, which cannot be affected by any evidence, that chummy did not do it." Any juror who announced this would presumably be disqualified.

b. [T]he presumption of innocence is simply a restatement of the burden and

---

[7] These messages, along with others, are published in Ronald J. Allen et al., Probability and Proof in State v. Skipper: An Internet Exchange, 35 Jurimetrics J. 277 (1995).

standard of proof. The Supreme Court of Connecticut has here fallen for a persistent fallacy that should have been laid to rest by now. See 9 Wigmore ¶ 2511.

From: David Kaye and David Balding
Date: August 8, 1994
Subject: Skipper

The court seems to rely on two constitutional principles for holding that the use of an undisclosed prior probability of one-half is error. First, it relies on the "right to have one's guilt proven beyond a reasonable doubt." The use of a prior of one-half offends this principle, as far as we can tell, because it gives the prosecution a head-start in proving its case. If one conceives of the DNA evidence coming after other evidence in the case, then the "prior" probability reflects that evidence and may be lower than one-half. If one conceives of the DNA evidence as the first datum, then some prior probability has to be assumed. We discuss this in connection with the "presumption of innocence" below, where we suggest that the prior should be closer to zero than to one-half. The point here is that the burden of persuasion concerns the probability required for a conviction and does not preclude the updating of probabilities via Bayes' theorem. In notes 15 and 18, the court disavows the idea that a juror should adopt explicit probabilities of intercourse, but it is difficult to see how this result follows from the burden of persuasion. The court quotes Tribe for the view that any posterior probability less than one indicates "measurable doubt" and therefore should not be acknowledged. Why the requirement of proof beyond a reasonable doubt bars some measurable doubt is left unstated.

The second basis for the holding has to do with the "presumption of innocence." The court writes that the presumption requires the use of a prior probability of zero, which always would yield a posterior probability of zero. This is not a criticism of Bayes' theorem, either as an analytical device or as an explicit tool at trial, but an obvious misconception. As Bernard Robertson points out, a prior probability of zero is not a presumption of innocence, but rather an unalterable (and impermissible) conclusion of innocence. In a Bayesian framework, the presumption can be interpreted in two ways. Bernard gives one view, which is that the presumption is just another way of saying that the prosecution must adduce enough evidence to dispel all reasonable doubt. Roughly speaking, another view is that the presumption means that before evidence is presented, the defendant should be thought no more likely than anyone else to be guilty. This translates into a small, but non-zero prior probability. Since a prior probability of one-half (at the outset) violates this conception of the presumption of innocence, the court's conclusion is consistent with a Bayesian analysis.

Chapter 11
DNA Typing: The Salad Days[1]

People v. Wesley
533 N.Y.S. 2d 643 (Sup. Ct. 1988)
aff'd, 633 N.E.2d 451 (N.Y. 1994)

HARRIS, J.

[T]he People move for an Order to extract blood from [defendants] for the purpose of comparing the "DNA" therein with "DNA" contained in biological evidence reasonably believed to be relevant . . . . In People v. Cameron Bailey, the defendant is charged with rape in the 1st degree; the evidence believed to be relevant is an aborted fetus. In People v. George Wesley, the defendant is charged with burglary in the 2nd degree and suspected of murder in the 2nd degree. Bloodstained clothing was retrieved from the defendant; the People propose to compare the "DNA" contained in said bloodstains with "DNA" extracted from the deceased victim and for control purposes with "DNA" to be extracted from a known blood sample of defendant Wesley.

The process sought to be used by the People is colloquially and most frequently referred to in forensic science as "DNA Fingerprinting" . . . . DNA Fingerprinting is at the "cutting edge" of forensic science, just as molecular biology and genetic engineering are at the "cutting edge" of revolutionary applications in medicine and control of such genetic or genetic-influenced diseases as diabetes, diverse forms of cancer, muscular dystrophy, Down's Syndrome, and Acquired Immune Deficiency Syndrome (AIDS). . . .

[I]f DNA Fingerprinting proves acceptable in criminal courts, [it] will revolutionize the administration of criminal justice. Where applicable, it would reduce to insignificance the standard alibi defense. [E]yewitness testimony . . . has been claimed to be responsible for more miscarriages of justice than any other type of evidence, [and] DNA Fingerprinting would tend to reduce the importance of eyewitness testimony. And in the area of clogged calendars and the conservation of judicial resources, DNA Fingerprinting, if accepted, will revolutionize the disposition of criminal cases. In short, if DNA Fingerprinting works and receives evidentiary acceptance, it can constitute the single greatest advance in the "search for truth" and the goal of convicting the guilty and acquitting the innocent since the advent of cross-examination. . . .

---

[1] See William Shakespeare, Anthony and Cleopatra act 1, sc. 5 (Cleopatra: "My salad days, when I was green in judgment, cold in blood.").

1 McCormick on Evidence
§ 205, at 896-900
(John W. Strong ed., 4th ed. 1992)
(illustrations added)

In contrast to the widespread acceptance of red blood cell grouping, blood serum protein and enzyme analysis, and HLA typing, the evidentiary status of forensic applications of recombinant-DNA technology is in flux. A proper evidentiary analysis must attend to the fact that there is no single method of DNA typing. As with conventional immunogenetic testing, the probative value of the laboratory findings depends both on the procedure employed and the genetic characteristics that are discerned. We shall describe some of these procedures and the theory that lies behind them . . . .

DNA is a long molecule with two strands that spiral around one another, forming a double helix. Within the double helix are molecules, called nucleotide bases, that link one strand to the other, like the steps of a spiral staircase. There are four of these bases, which can be referred to by their initials, A, T, G and C. The A on one strand pairs with T on the other, and the G bonds to C. The lengthy sequence of AT and GC "stairs" within the DNA contained in human cells includes all the genes and control sequences (for turning certain genes on and off). The genes are stretches of base pairs whose order determines the composition of proteins and related products synthesized by various cells. Oddly enough, however, much of the DNA has no known function.

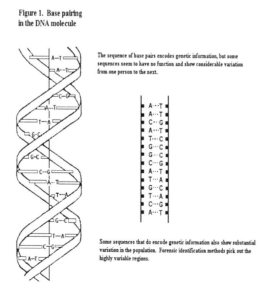

Figure 1. Base pairing in the DNA molecule

The sequence of base pairs encodes genetic information, but some sequences seem to have no function and show considerable variation from one person to the next.

Some sequences that do encode genetic information also show substantial variation in the population. Forensic identification methods pick out the highly variable regions.

Examining cell surface antigens (such as the ABO and HLA systems) or blood serum enzymes or proteins gives some information about the DNA sequences that code for these particular substances; if the markers differ, then the underlying DNA must differ. In contrast, DNA analysis is not limited to identifying variations within these coding sequences. With appropriate "DNA probes," one can detect differences in the base pair sequences anywhere in the DNA. A probe is a short piece of a single strand of DNA with a radioactive or other readily identifiable compound attached, like a sticker or tag on a suitcase. If the bases in the target DNA are in an order matching those in the probe, the probe will bind to the target DNA.

Because 99.9% of the DNA sequence in any two people is identical, the technical challenge is to detect the relatively rare stretches of DNA, sometimes called alleles, that vary among individuals. Two procedures to do this are in use. In one, the DNA is "amplified" by heating and cooling it with an enzyme called DNA polymerase. Even if the sample contains only one or two copies of the allele, the polymerase induces a chain reaction that increases the number to about 10 million. The amplified DNA is "spotted" onto a membrane, and a probe added. If the sequence complementary to the probe is there, it will be tagged. If a radioactive element is used for the tag, for example, the spot will become radioactive and a dark dot will appear if the membrane is placed on X-ray film. The analyst simply looks to see whether the dot, and hence the allele, is present. The test resembles serologic tests in giving a categorical answer: either the allele is present or it is not.

The great advantage of the polymerase chain reaction over conventional immunogenetic and other DNA typing techniques is that it requires very little biological material. As with serologic tests, however, a single allele may be common in the population, and hence not especially revealing. Of course, a series of probes may narrow the percentage of the population that could have been the source of the sample, but the procedure cannot identify any one individual as the only possible source.

The more frequently used procedure for identifying DNA variation ("polymorphisms") involves "digesting" DNA into fragments with enzymes ("restriction enzymes") from bacteria, separating the restriction fragments according to length by gel electrophoresis, blotting the array of fragments onto a nylon membrane, tagging the fragments with a probe, then placing X-ray film to the membrane to give an image with dark bands at the locations of the tagged fragments. The pattern of bands is the DNA "print" or "profile."

How many people have a given DNA profile (and hence, how valuable the profile is for identification) depends on where the restriction enzyme cuts the DNA (the restriction sites) and on the probe that picks out some of the resulting fragments. Suppose that some people have two restriction sites 32,000 bases apart, while others have an extra site located 12,000 bases inside the 32,000 base region. If the probe recognizes a sequence that occurs only on the shorter side of the extra restriction site, people with the extra site will have a profile consisting of one band for the 12,000 base fragment. People without the extra site also will have one band, but it will correspond to a fragment 32,000 bases long. Because the shorter

12,000 base band will migrate farther down the gel during electrophoresis, by placing DNA from two samples in parallel lanes on the same gel, an observer can tell whether one sample produces the smaller fragment while the other does not. The extra site thus gives rise to a restriction fragment length polymorphism (RFLP) detectable with a particular enzyme-probe combination. However, there may be many people with each of the two possible bands, and this one simple site RFLP may not be very revealing.

Figure 2. Schematic portrayal of some major steps in single locus RFLP profiling. In step 1, all the "raw" DNA in the cells in the sample are extracted, including many copies of the two duplex strands of the DNA from the two homologous chromosomes per cell that the single-locus test probe will characterize. In step 2, the many duplex DNA strands are treated chemically or heated to separate the strands. In step 3, restriction enzymes "digest" the long, single strands into shorter fragments by cutting the strands at restriction sites. In step 4, the many single-stranded DNA fragments are separated by length on an electrophoretic gel, then transferred to a nylon membrane for ease in handling. In step 5, "probes" designed to bind to a specific base-pair sequence are added to the restriction fragments, marking those pairs with the target sequence. In step 6, the fragments to which the probes have become bound are photographed on an autoradiogram; the many other fragments, which do not contain the sequence to which the probe is sensitive, are not seen.

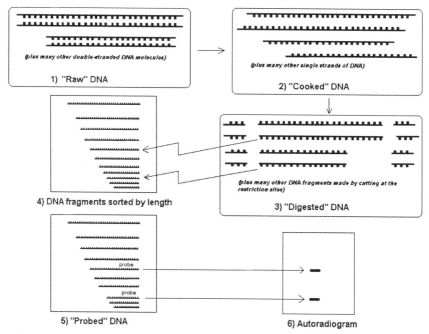

Other enzyme-probe combinations generate many more possible length measurements within a population. Suppose that the 32,000 base pair sequence differs among individuals, not by a change in a single base pair at a given locus, creating or deleting an interior restriction site, but instead by the insertion of a short sequence starting at this locus and repeating itself many times. The more tandem repeats there are inside the restriction fragment, the longer it will be. A probe that detects the core repetitive sequence starting at this single site will detect these variable length fragments. A person with a single copy of the core sequence will have a band at the 32,000 point, someone with one hundred repeats of a core sequence 10 base pairs long will have a band at the 33,000 point, and so on. Because the number of repeating units at a "variable number tandem repeat locus" (VNTR locus) can vary greatly within a population, the probes that detect this type of repetitive DNA are generally much more informative than probes for simple site polymorphisms. . . .

Initial journalistic and judicial praise for applications of RFLPs in homicide, rape, paternity, and other cases has been effusive. . . . In this first wave of cases, expert testimony for the prosecution rarely was countered, and courts readily admitted RFLP findings.

Figure 3. Single locus VNTR profiles at one locus for 12 individuals. Source: FBI, 1988 (as reproduced in Office of Technology Assessment, Genetic Witness: Forensic Uses of DNA Tests 47 (1990))

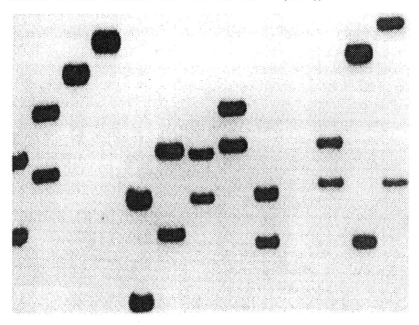

Andrews v. State
533 So. 2d 841 (Fla. Dist. Ct. App. 1988)

ORFINGER, J.

The issue in this case concerns the admissibility of "genetic fingerprint" evidence . . . . The trial court admitted the evidence, and the jury convicted defendant of aggravated battery, sexual battery and armed burglary of a dwelling. . . . We conclude that the evidence was properly admitted . . . .

In the early morning hours of February 21, 1987, the victim was awakened when someone jumped on top of her and held what felt like a straight edge razor to her neck. The intruder, who the victim could only identify at trial as a strong, black male, held his hand over her mouth, told her to keep quiet and threatened to kill her if she saw his face. The victim struggled with the intruder and for her efforts was cut on her face, neck, legs and feet.

The intruder then forced vaginal intercourse with the victim, following which he stole her purse containing about $40, and then left the house. A physical examination made after the attack was reported to the police revealed the presence of semen in the victim's vagina. A crime lab analyst testified that both the victim and appellant were blood type O but that appellant, like a majority of the population, is a secretor (secretes his blood type in his saliva and other body fluids) while the victim was not. Blood type O was found in the vaginal swabs taken from the victim, though the analyst conceded that while this result could have come from the semen found in the victim's vagina, it also could have come from the victim's blood picked up by the swab. The analyst concluded that appellant was included in the population (which he stated constituted 65% of the male population) that could be the source of the semen.

A crime scene technician testified that on the morning following the crime one of the windows of the victim's house was open, and the screen was missing. The victim had testified that this window had been broken previously and was held together with wire from a coat hanger. A screen was found on the ground and fingerprints were lifted from it. A fingerprint expert testified that two of the prints lifted from the screen matched appellant's right index and middle finger.

Over objection, the state presented DNA print identification evidence linking appellant to the crime. The DNA test compared the appellant's DNA structure as found in his blood with the DNA structure of the victim's blood and the DNA found in the vaginal swab, taken from the victim shortly after the attack. The test was conducted by Lifecodes Corp., a corporation specializing in DNA identity testing. Dr. Baird of Lifecodes testified to a match between the DNA in appellant's blood and the DNA from the vaginal swab, stating that the percentage of the population which would have the DNA bands indicated by the samples would be 0.0000012%. In other words, the chance that the DNA strands found in appellant's blood would be duplicated in some other person's cells was 1 in 839,914,540.

We have found no other appellate decision addressing the admissibility of

DNA identification evidence in criminal cases. Although appellant primarily attacks the methods used by Lifecodes as opposed to the admissibility of DNA evidence in general, the novelty of the question requires, in our opinion, that we address both issues. . . .

We begin by confessing some uncertainty as to the standard applicable in this state governing admissibility into evidence of a new scientific technique. [The opinion reviews the Florida cases on the admissibility of scientific evidence. It concludes that a normal relevancy approach] seems preferable to the "general acceptance" approach of *Frye* which is predicated on a "nose counting," and may result in the exclusion of reliable evidence [and that] in this case the evidence would meet the *Frye* standard as well as the relevancy test. . . .

Several witnesses testified for the State concerning the test. Dr. David E. Housman, the holder of a bachelor's degree and a Ph.D in biology, of the Massachusetts Institute of Technology, is a professor of molecular genetics, which deals with the structure and function of the DNA molecule and has taught at several universities since 1973. He has engaged in DNA analysis for some eleven years. He has published approximately 120 papers on molecular genetics, most of which deal with DNA, and has served on advisory boards involving genetics for the National Institute of Health, the Heredity Disease Foundation, and the Tourette's Syndrome Foundation. Housman visited Lifecodes, Inc., the company which performed the instant test and examined the procedures of the company though he did not witness the instant test.

Allen Guisti is a forensic scientist employed by Lifecodes, Inc. and performed the DNA print identification tests here. He holds a Bachelor of Science degree from Yale University and has published several papers on genetics, one of which involved his own research on DNA analysis. He has performed the identification test about 200 times.

Dr. Michael Baird is the manager of forensic testing at Lifecodes. He received a doctorate in genetics from the University of Chicago in 1978. He worked as a research associate at both the University of Michigan and Columbia University in the field of blood diseases at the DNA level and joined Lifecodes at its inception in 1982. He has been the manager of forensic testing for the past year and one-half. He teaches graduate courses in DNA technology at New York Medical College and has published a number of articles on DNA testing.

[The court describes the principles and techniques of RFLP testing.] The test here was performed by Lifecodes, Inc., a licensed clinical laboratory in the State of New York. The testimony revealed that Lifecodes was founded in 1982 as a research and development laboratory, specializing in DNA paternity and identity testing and began developing DNA probes. The company currently performs forensic and paternity testing as well as testing in diagnosing genetic-type diseases. The DNA test is essentially the same for all of these purposes, with the difference being in the probe that is used.

There was extensive testimony as to the precise methods used by Lifecodes in performing the instant test. Dr. Guisti testified about each step in the process and Dr. Housman, who reviewed Dr. Guisti's results testified that in his opinion the test was accurately and properly performed. There was also testimony that various controls were used in the testing process. For example, Dr. Baird testified that every reagent and enzyme purchased by Lifecodes is tested on known DNA samples. Similar tests are performed on the gel used in the electrophoresis process. Appellant contends that this test is unreliable, because the new gel is only tested to be certain that it works the way the old gel worked and that if the old gel worked improperly, that error would be carried over to the new batch. We find no merit in this contention. In addition to the foregoing tests, control samples containing known fragment sizes are loaded in the test to monitor the electrophoresis and assure an accurate result. The evidence reveals that if the gel is not properly prepared or if it is bad, the test will ordinarily not work rather than leading to an incorrect result. Indeed, if there were any voltage fluctuations or problem with the solutions ordinarily no result is received as opposed to an erroneous result. Use of control samples is also a check as they would also be affected by any error.

The scientific testimony indicates acceptance of the testing procedures. The probative value of the evidence is for the jury. The radiographs of the victim's and appellant's blood and the vaginal smear were exhibited to the jury, the comparison was explained, and the radiographs were admitted into evidence. Dr. Baird concluded that to a reasonable degree of scientific certainty, appellant's DNA was present in the vaginal smear taken from the victim. The State's expert witnesses were skillfully and thoroughly cross-examined, but no expert witness testified for the defense. . . .

In applying the relevancy test, it seems clear that the DNA print results would be helpful to the jury. Each of the State's witnesses was accepted by the trial court as an eminently qualified expert in the field of molecular genetics.[9] The crucial question here is whether the probative value of the testimony and test is substantially outweighed by its potential prejudicial effect. [U]nder the relevancy approach where a form of scientific expertise has no established "track record" in litigation, courts may look to other factors which bear on the reliability of the evidence. One of these is the novelty of the technique, i.e., its relationship to more established modes of scientific analysis. DNA testing has been utilized for approximately ten years and is indicated by the evidence to be a reliable, well established procedure, performed in a number of laboratories around the world. Further, it has been used in the diagnosis, treatment and study of genetically inherited diseases. This extensive nonjudicial use of the test is evidence tending to show the reliability of the technique.

---

[9] Appellant argues that these witnesses, particularly Dr. Baird, possess a built-in bias because their reputations and careers are built on DNA comparison work. Several courts have questioned whether a leading proponent of a particular technique could fairly and impartially testify concerning admission of the tests. Neither Frye nor our evidence code require impartiality. Further, the point would not appear substantial here given that unlike voiceprints, DNA comparison work has a number of uses in fields other than forensic medicine such as diagnosis and treatment of disease.

Another factor is the existence of specialized literature dealing with the technique. The record reveals that a great many scientific works exist regarding DNA identification. According to Dr. Baird, Lifecodes maintains a file on all scientific journal articles and publications with regard to DNA testing and he was unaware of any that argue against the test's reliability.

A further component of reliability is the frequency with which a technique leads to erroneous results. . . . The testimony here was that if there was something wrong with the process, it would ordinarily lead to no result being obtained rather than an erroneous result. Further control samples are employed throughout the process which permits errors, if any, to be discovered. These factors are further indicia of reliability.

The frequency by which given DNA bands appear in the population is calculated by using an established statistical data base, employing a statistical formula known as the Hardy-Weinberg equilibria. This principle is used for determining other genetic characteristics such as blood type or Rh factors, dates back to the 1920's and has been generally accepted in the scientific community as being accurate for this calculation. Appellant contends that the data base of 710 samples is too small to be statistically significant. The only evidence in the case supports the statistical value of the randomly selected samples. The testimony reveals that as the data base expands, the probability numbers do not change statistically, and that The American Association of Blood Banks, in its book entitled Probability of Inclusion in Paternity Testing (1982) concludes that a data base of two to five hundred samples was found to provide adequate statistical results.

Admittedly, the scientific evidence here, unlike that presented with fingerprint, footprint or bite mark evidence, is highly technical, incapable of observation and requires the jury to either accept or reject the scientist's conclusion that it can be done. While this factor requires courts to proceed with special caution, it does not of itself render the evidence unreliable.

The trial court did not abuse its discretion in ruling the test results admissible in this case. In contrast to evidence derived from hypnosis, truth serum and polygraph, evidence derived from DNA print identification appears based on proven scientific principles. Indeed, there was testimony that such evidence has been used to exonerate those suspected of criminal activity.

Given the evidence in this case that the test was administered in conformity with accepted scientific procedures so as to ensure to the greatest degree possible a reliable result, appellant has failed to show error on this point. . . .

Finding no error, the convictions and sentences are affirmed.

NOTES

1. *General acceptance of RFLPs: the initial perception. Andrews* is the first reported appellate decision on RFLP (pronounced "riflip") testing. An extensive and impressive hearing on the scientific status of the procedure and Lifecodes' laboratory protocol is summarized in People v. Wesley. In neither *Andrews* nor *Wesley* did the defense seriously contest the general acceptance and validity of the applicable principles and techniques of molecular biology and genetics. The use of suitable restriction enzymes followed by separation by gel electrophoresis and radioactive tagging of the fragments is a well established and fruitful research tool in molecular biology, genetics, and medicine. See, e.g., Anthony J.F. Griffiths et al., An Introduction to Genetic Analysis (5th ed. 1993); Victor A. Bernstam, Handbook of Gene Level Diagnostics in Clinical Practice (1992); Maxine Singer & Paul Berg, Genes and Genomes: A Changing Perspective (1991).

However, the companies seeking to exploit this technology in criminal and disputed paternity cases often use probes that have no other medical or scientific application. Should a court in a *Frye* jurisdiction insist that each probe (and the estimated frequency of the incriminating pattern of RFLPs detected by that probe) be "generally accepted" by geneticists? Does it matter if geneticists and molecular biologists do not normally work with forensic sources of the DNA — dried blood, semen or hair? Exactly what, under *Frye,* must be generally accepted? For the view that the results in *Wesley* and *Andrews* represent a "lenient" application of the general acceptance test, see William C. Thompson & Simon Ford, DNA Typing: Acceptance and Weight of the New Genetic Identification Tests, 75 Va. L. Rev. 601 (1989).

2. *The risk of error.* *Andrews* observes that there are "ordinarily" no false positive DNA identifications. Testimony about false positives in some cases has been more extravagant. E.g., People v. Wesley, 533 N.Y.S.2d 643, 652 (N.Y. Co. Sup. Ct. 1988) ("it is impossible under the scientific principles, technology and procedures of DNA Fingerprinting (outside of an identical twin), to get a 'false positive' — i.e., to identify the wrong individual as the contributor of the DNA being tested"), aff'd, 183 A.D. 2d 75, 589 N.Y.S. 2d 197 (1992). For commentary disputing this claim, see Dan L. Burk, DNA Fingerprinting: Possibilities and Pitfalls of a New Technique, 29 Jurimetrics J. 455 (1988); Eric Lander, DNA Fingerprinting on Trial, 339 Nature 501 (1989); Laurel Beeler & William R. Wiebe, Note, DNA Identification Tests and the Courts, 63 Wash. L. Rev. 903 (1988); authorities cited, William C. Thompson, Lessons from the "DNA War," 84 J. Crim. L. & Criminology 22, 92 n.310 (1993).

To quantify the risk of error, some observers have called for externally administered, blind, realistic proficiency tests of individual laboratories. E.g., Committee on DNA Technology in Forensic Science, National Research Council, DNA Technology in Forensic Science (1992); 1 McCormick on Evidence § 205 (John Strong 4th ed., 1992); Michael J. Saks & Jonathan J. Koehler, What DNA "Fingerprinting" Can Teach the Law about the Rest of Forensic Science, 13 Cardozo L. Rev. 361 (1991). To date, however, little such testing has been undertaken. Should proficiency testing be treated as a prequisite to admissibility? Is it essential to establishing scientific soundness or general acceptance? Compare R.C. Lewontin, Letter, 372 Nature 398 (1994) ("In the absence of blind proficiency testing, quality-control protocols and unannounced periodic checks designed and supervised by disinterested parties, the test results from federal, state and local crime laboratories, and private contract laboratories must be regarded as unreliable."), and Barry C. Scheck, DNA and *Daubert,* 15 Cardozo L. Rev. 1959 (1994) (arguing that DNA tests should be inadmissible without routine, external, blind proficiency tests), with Edward J. Imwinkelried, Coming to Grips with Scientific Research in *Daubert's* "Brave New World": The Courts' Need to Appreciate the Evidentiary Differences Between Validity and Proficiency Studies, 61 Brook. L. Rev. 1247 (1995).

In the absence of definite proof that false positives are as rare as the frequency of matching DNA profiles in the general population, some commentators have argued that the frequency estimates should be excluded as unduly misleading and that the jury should hear only a statistic that merges the probability that a suspect's DNA would be reported to match the crime-scene DNA (due to laboratory error) with the probability that a randomly selected person would have the same DNA profile as the crime-scene DNA.[3] E.g., Jonathan J. Koehler et al., The Random Match Probability in DNA Evidence: Irrelevant and Prejudicial? 35 Jurimetrics J. 201 (1995); Thompson, supra, at 91-92; cf. Paul J. Hagerman, DNA Typing in the Forensic Arena, 47 Am. J. Hum. Genetics 876 (1990) (letter arguing that probability of a false match should be presented as the laboratory rate of false positives in external, blinded testing rather than the estimated population frequency of the incriminating pattern); Richard Lempert, Some Caveats Concerning DNA as Criminal Identification Evidence: With Thanks to the Reverend Bayes, 13 Cardozo L. Rev. 303, 325 (1991) ("jurors ordinarily should receive only the laboratory's false positive error rate as an estimate of the likelihood that the evidence DNA did not come from the defendant").

A committee of the National Academy of Sciences, however, questions whether accurate estimates of the false positive error rate can be derived from proficiency testing. See also B. Devlin et al., Comments on the Statistical Aspects of the NRC's Report on DNA Typing, 39 J. Forensic Sci. 28 (1994). The committee writes:

> • The question to be decided is not the general error rate for a laboratory or laboratories over time, but rather whether the laboratory doing DNA testing in this particular case made a critical error. The risk of error in any

---

[3] To see how this would work, suppose that the chance of a false positive match (E, for error) is 1,000, and the chance of a random true match is 1/100,000. The chance that a match would be declared (M) if the suspect were not the source of the' crime-scene DNA (O, for other source) would be

$$P(M \mid O) = P(M \text{ \& } E \mid O) + P(M \text{ \& not-}E \mid O) = 0.00100 + 0.00001 \approx 0.00101.$$

When the chance of a reported match due to an error is much greater than the chance of a coincidental true match, as in this example, the former probability swamps the latter.

particular case depends on many variables (such as the number of samples, redundancy in testing, and analyst proficiency), and there is no simple equation to translate these variables into the probability that a reported match is spurious.

- To estimate accurately, from proficiency test results, the overall rate at
  which a laboratory declares nonmatching samples to match . . . would
  require a laboratory to undergo an unrealistically large number of proficiency trials. . . .

- The pooling of proficiency-test results across laboratories has been sug-
  ested as a means of estimating an "industry-wide" error rate, [b]ut that
  could penalize the better laboratories . . . .

- Estimating rates at which nonmatching samples are declared to match
  from historical performance on proficiency tests is almost certain to yield
  wrong values. When errors are discovered, they are investigated thoroughly so that corrections can be made. A laboratory is not likely to make
  the same error again. . . .

Committee on DNA Forensic Science: An Update, National Research
Council, The Evaluation of Forensic DNA Evidence 3-10 (1996) (pre-publication
copy). Given these difficulties in quantifying the risk of a false positive error, the
committee recommends that "[w]henever feasible, forensic samples should be
divided into two or more parts at the earliest practicable stage and the unused parts
retained to permit additional tests" performed independently at a different laboratory. Id. at 3-12. See also Richard Lempert, Some Caveats Concerning DNA as
Criminal Identification Evidence: With Thanks to the Reverend Bayes, 13
Cardozo L. Rev. 303, 327 (1991) ("whenever possible, DNA should be sent to
two, or better yet, three laboratories for independent analysis"); James Wooley &
Rockne P. Harmon, The Forensic DNA Brouhaha: Science or Debate? 51 Am. J.
Hum. Genetics 1164 (1992); Barry C. Scheck, DNA and *Daubert,* 15 Cardozo L.
Rev. 1959, 1969-70 (1994).

Which is the better policy — excluding testimony about random match probabilities because false match probabilities are larger, or allowing testimony about
both quantities?[4] What additional information would be helpful in answering this
question? If the committee's view that it is all but impossible to estimate the false
positive risk from proficiency tests is correct, should the error rates on such tests
even be admissible? See Armstead v. State, 673 A.2d 221 (Md. 1996).

---

[4] The committee concludes that:

> The risk of error is properly considered case by case, taking into account
> the record of the laboratory performing the tests, the extent of redundan-
> cy, and the overall quality of the results. However, there is no need to
> debate differing estimates of false-match error rates when the question of
> a possible match can be put to direct test.

Id. at 3-11.

3. *RFLPs in Paternity Testing.* The first reported paternity case to evaluate DNA typing is In re "Baby Girl S," 532 N.Y.S. 2d 634 (N.Y. Co. Surrog. Ct. 1988). Here, the court relies on restriction analysis, along with much other evidence, to find — in the face of the once conclusive presumption that a child born in wedlock is legitimate — that the man claiming paternity, and not the estranged husband, is the father. It holds the RFLP evidence admissible under a statute making blood tests admissible in parentage disputes. Furthermore, the court brushes aside an expert's reservations about including these results in the paternity index and, hence, the "probability of paternity."

Other courts needing to resolve questions of paternity have embraced DNA analysis with similar gusto. See, e.g., Dep't of Social Serv. v. Thomas, 660 So.2d 163 (La. Ct. App. 1995) ("Although alone insufficient to prove paternity, scientific testing provides persuasive and objective evidence that can well help establish proof by a preponderance," and the trial court's failure to find paternity given a paternity index of 16,500 was "manifest error."); Commissioner of Social Serv. v. Hector S., 628 N.Y.S.2d 270 (App. Div. 1995) ("the trial court erred in failing to find paternity because 'staggering' genetic marker test results [based on DNA and other markers yielding a paternity index of 11,734,738] were sufficiently persuasive despite petitioner's cloudy and somewhat contradictory testimony as to her sexual activity and menstrual history."); King v. Tanner, 539 N.Y.S. 2d 617 (Sup. Ct. 1989) (granting summary judgment for defendant alleged to have slandered married man by asserting that he fathered her child); Alexander v. Alexander, 537 N.E. 2d 1310 (Ohio Probate Ct.1988) (permitting disinterment for "a DNA test" by an illegitimate child claiming an inheritance). But cf. State v. Skipper, supra, chapter 10 (reversing criminal conviction for presenting a DNA-based "probability of paternity" without disclosing that the figure presupposed a prior probability of one-half).

With paternity indexes in the millions arising from the addition of VNTR polymorphisms to the information available from other genetic markers, one might think that the debate noted in chapter 9 over the presentation of the "probability of paternity" is becoming academic because the probabilities will be overwhelming. For papers indicating that some of the probabilities introduced in courts may be overstated or oversimplified, however, see David Gjertson et al., Assessing Calculation of Paternity Using DNA Sequences, 43 Am. J. Hum. Genetics 860 (1988); Jeffrey Morris et al., Biostatistical Evaluation of Evidence from Continuous Allele Frequency Distribution DNA Probes in Reference to Disputed Paternity and Disputed Identity, 34 J. Forensic Sci. 1311 (1989); cf. Franson v. Micelli, 645 N.E. 2d 404 (Ill. Ct. App. 1994) (VNTR tests yielding paternity index of 29,217,637 were inadmissible under Frye because of the "population structure" debate analyzed infra chapters 13 and 14), vacated on other grounds, 172 Ill.2d 352, 355 (1996).

Chapter 12
DNA Typing: A Time to Question

D.H. Kaye
DNA Evidence: Probability,
Population Genetics, and the Courts
7 Harvard Journal of Law and Technology 101 (1994)
(notes omitted)

In the wake of [the] early enthusiasm for DNA evidence, doubts emerged. Diligent attorneys and enterprising defendants enlisted well-credentialed experts to scrutinize the work of commercial and crime laboratories. The resulting plethora of questions about laboratory procedures and analyses convinced many courts, including the Supreme Courts of Georgia, Massachusetts and Minnesota, to exclude at least some aspects of DNA evidence. Nevertheless, in the majority of cases, the courts continued to hold DNA matches and probabilities admissible even in the face of conflicting expert testimony. . . .

United States v. Yee
134 F.R.D. 161 (N.D. Ohio 1991)
aff'd sub nom. United States v. Bonds
12 F.3d 540 (6th Cir. 1993)

JAMES G. CARR, United States Magistrate Judge.

This is a criminal case in which pretrial matters have . . . been referred to the undersigned for initial hearing and determination. . . .

[T]he results at issue in this case show that samples of blood taken from the defendant Johnny Ray Bonds contain DNA fragments that match with DNA fragments from blood found at the scene of a homicide. The government's counsel also represents . . . that the probability that such a pattern of matches would be found in the United States Caucasian population is 1/35,000. . . .

Despite the complexity of much of the evidence, the issues about which the experts testified can be fairly easily described. The first of these issues relates to the F.B.I. protocol and procedures for determining that DNA fragments, generally referred to in the testimony as bands or alleles, from the known and unknown sources match. In order for its DNA evidence to be admissible, the government must show that there is general acceptance in the scientific community with regard to the F.B.I.'s ability reliably to declare matches over several loci.

The principal thrust of the defense challenge regarding that issue involved challenges to the design of the standards for declaring a match, quality of basic scientific work required to ensure that a laboratory can perform its work in a reliable and reproducible manner, adequacy of the F.B.I.'s research into the effects of environmental insults and other outside forces on the DNA fragments that it was testing, failure to implement a program of proficiency testing of its examiners, and ability to perform basic scientific procedures in an acceptable manner.

. . .

The second issue related to the ability of the F.B.I. to make a reliable and scientifically acceptable estimate of the probability that a match once observed, would be encountered within the American Caucasian population. . . .*

1. Determining a Match

With regard to the general acceptance and reliability of the F.B.I.'s application of DNA identification technology to forensics, Dr. Conneally** testified that it was acceptable to apply the theories and methods of DNA testing to the forensic arena. He asserted that it was acceptable for different laboratories to apply different methods and techniques and stated that using a quasi-continuous allele system with VNTRs was an acceptable practice in forensics.

When asked whether there was an unacceptable level of subjectivity involved in the forensic application of DNA technology, especially with respect to the declaration of a match, Dr. Conneally responded that he believed there was not. In his view, the RFLP technique could be applied in a reliable manner in the forensic setting using the F.B.I. probes: "I have read about them [the probes] in the literature, and I believe you can [use them in forensics], yes." Dr. Conneally stated that he had never heard of an instance of a "false positive," where a person was wrongly identified in a DNA test.

After opining that the RFLP technique applied to VNTRs was a reliable technique that was generally accepted in the relevant scientific community, Dr. Daiger*** concurred with the statement that the technique was basically the same technique employed by the forensic scientist. Furthermore he stated, "in my opinion the forensic applications of DNA laboratory procedures and DNA concepts are simply a specific application of a very broad general category of techniques and concepts which are used throughout the scientific community." Dr. Daiger also stated that he believed that this opinion was shared by the relevant scientific community.

Dr. Daiger testified that he was quite familiar with the F.B.I. laboratory and

---

*Editor's note: The discussion of this issue is omitted.

**Editor's note: Dr. Patrick Conneally is Distinguished Professor of Medical Genetics and Neurology at the Indiana University School of Medicine.

***Editor's note: Dr. Stephen P. Daiger is Professor, Graduate School of Biomedical Sciences at the University of Texas Health Science Center.

with the written protocols and controls used there. When asked whether, as a result of its procedures, that the F.B.I.'s method could result in a DNA pattern that appeared to be a true pattern but was actually a different pattern from the correct pattern Dr. Daiger said:

> I don't see a credible biological or laboratory scenario, short of say sabotage, that would lead to a false positive in the laboratory. Essentially, all of the kinds of damage, degradation, laboratory mishaps that relate to samples would lead to either an [inconclusive result] or in fact a false [exclusion]. When again asked about the possibility of a false positive he stated, "I think it's virtually nil."

> . . .

With respect to the criteria used at the F.B.I. for declaring a match, Dr. Daiger stated that he believed that they were "cautious in their interpretation." In his view, the nature of the subjective judgment involved in DNA forensic analysis was perfectly acceptable to him. After testifying about his familiarity with the tests and procedures utilized by the F.B.I. to establish its match criteria Dr. Daiger stated, "the empirically derived match criteria developed by the F.B.I. has indeed been generated in an appropriate and scientifically conservative manner." Regarding the environmental insult studies performed by the F.B.I. Dr. Daiger testified:

> I think the conclusion is essentially for all of the environmental insults that have been described, one of three things can happen. Either it has no effect on the outcome of the analysis, or it leads to essentially the difference [destruction] of the DNA in its entirety. Or under some circumstances it leads to a pattern on the gel which is so obviously distorted and inappropriate that it leads to an [inconclusive].

Dr. Daiger stated that he had never seen an example of a false positive. He responded negatively when asked whether there was anything about a quasi-continuous allele system that would suggest that it was unreliable.

When asked on cross-examination about the match window chosen by the F.B.I., Dr. Daiger stated that the window was selected to be "extremely generous" and "conservative" to the defendant. In response to a question posed to him by the court, Dr. Daiger said that the +/– 2.5% match window used by the F.B.I. was conservative with respect to potential for prejudice to the defendant.

On cross-examination Dr. Daiger pointed out that even if an F.B.I. examiner would conclude from a visual inspection that bands matched, if the subsequent computer assisted quantitative method indicated that the bands did not fall within the F.B.I.'s matching window, the Bureau would not declare a match but would declare it uncertain. Dr. Daiger stated that the number of articles published in scientific journals that address the application of DNA in a forensic setting is on the order of two dozen.

Dr. Caskey* testified, when asked to compare the RFLP process in medical diagnostics with the process in forensics, that:

> The procedures that are used in arriving at the answer, the result, are identical. There's no variation that exists in the fundamental process. However in the case of forensics, what one is doing is developing a generic test system which has a high [out] put and great simplicity and high reproducibility . . . . Dr. Caskey indicated that he was not troubled by the fact that different forensic DNA laboratories utilize different match criteria.

In Dr. Caskey's view, there was nothing unusual in the fact that the match criteria used at his forensics laboratory differed from the match criteria used by the F.B.I.

With regard to questions posed concerning the F.B.I.'s use of molecular weight size markers, human cell line controls, yield gels, test gels, and other quality control measures used by the F.B.I., Dr. Caskey asserted: "It's my . . . opinion that the F.B.I. has set up a . . . very safe and conservative system and that the quality controls that they've put in place at the laboratory level are very adequate." Dr. Caskey stated that the F.B.I. used appropriate match criteria and that the size variations that the F.B.I. obtained when they did their repetitive sampling was about the same as that obtained at his laboratory. According to Dr. Caskey, the concern about false positives is greater than necessary, and that the only real source of potential false positives to be concerned with was possible human error, not system error.

Dr. Caskey asserted that the theory of DNA forensic profiling is generally accepted in the scientific community and there are reliable procedures to implement that theory that have been generally accepted. Dr. Caskey further commented that the F.B.I.'s method constituted an example of a generally accepted implementation of the theories underlying forensic DNA profiling.

In response to questions posed on cross-examination regarding the differences between the diagnostic and the forensic applications of DNA technology, Dr. Caskey stated that he believed that the "methods that are employed . . . overlap considerably," that there was a "greater simplicity" in the forensic application because it is "highly repetitive" and "narrower in its scope of technology." He disagreed that forensic applications were more demanding to interpret.

With regard to the use of highly polymorphic VNTRs for forensic application, Dr. Caskey stated that they were selected for that reason. The various conditions

---

*Editor's note: The opinion identifies Dr. C. Thomas Caskey as "Henry and Emma Meyer Chair in Molecular Genetics at the Baylor College of Medicine. He was Chairman, Advisory Panel, OTA Report, Genetic Witness: Forensic Uses of DNA Tests; Member, National Academy of Sciences Committee on DNA Technology and Forensic Science." Dr. Caskey resigned from the NAS committee after it was suggested that his involvement in developing and commercializing a new class of DNA probes for forensic use constituted a conflict of interest.

imposed on DNA technology, especially those resulting from limited quantities of crime scene samples, do not in his view, call for compromises in the methods used to perform the tests. He stated, it is, "not [a] compromise, but the most optimized analytic method to be able to give you a result from that precious sample."

During cross-examination, the defense attorneys posed a series of questions to Dr. Caskey concerning the potential effects of "expectation bias" on the execution and interpretation of forensic DNA profiling. When the Court asked for clarification on this issue the witness responded, "there's no way to jimmy the system to get an expected result." In response to a series of questions presented to him on cross-examination addressing an issue characterized by the defense as the F.B.I.'s resistance to permitting its DNA laboratory to be evaluated by external agencies through blind external proficiency testing, Dr. Caskey thought that the F.B.I.'s response to such efforts was one of "caution rather than resistance." . . .

Dr. D'Eustachio, the first defense witness,* submitted an expert's report in which he evaluated the F.B.I.'s validation studies on environmental insults and mixed body fluids and experiments from which the F.B.I. derived its quantitative matching rule. The substance of Dr. D'Eustachio's testimony at the hearing is contained in [the] report. Dr. D'Eustachio's opinions were primarily based on his examination of the F.B.I.'s environmental insult validation studies, the F.B.I.'s fixed bin paper, twenty-four autorads and the corresponding laboratory notebooks generated by experiments performed by the F.B.I., and, of course, his own knowledge and expertise as a molecular biologist.

Dr. D'Eustachio cataloged a variety of problems he observed with the F.B.I.'s validation studies on environmental insults and mixed body fluids: multiple gels were scored as successes even though the relevant positive control tracks failed; the sizing standards used by the F.B.I. in casework were not used in these studies, thereby undermining claims as to reproducibility in forensic work; on two occasions band shifts were ignored; most experiments were conducted using only a single probe, thereby suggesting that these studies are inconclusive with respect to other probes because each probe is distinctive. Dr. D'Eustachio concluded that the F.B.I. had not developed a reliable and sensitive procedure for identification of forensic DNA specimens and that the validation procedures were badly flawed.

As to the environmental studies, after noting various discrepancies, Dr. D'Eustachio concluded that the F.B.I. had serious problems with reproducibility. . . . As to the overall quality of the study he concluded that the problems of failed controls, inadequate sizings, failure to assess all probes, and significant misinterpretation or misreporting indicated that the effects of environmental insults and mixed body fluids were unresolved.

Dr. D'Eustachio expounded on the F.B.I.'s quantitative match criteria. He described the standards that a forensic DNA laboratory had to meet in formulating

---

*Editor's note: Dr. Peter D'Eustachio is Associate Professor, Department of Biochemistry, New York University Medical Center.

its match criteria as: 1) understanding the factors that alter band migration, and 2) choosing a match window that does not exceed an acceptable level of risk of false positives. Dr. D'Eustachio asserted that the F.B.I. failed to meet either standard. . . .

He also commented on the size of the F.B.I.'s match window in comparison to the match windows used by other forensic DNA laboratories. Finally, Dr. D'Eustachio concluded that the methods and studies used by the F.B.I. to develop its matching criteria did not reflect good science and that the various studies should be done again and done right.

Dr. Hagerman* initially reviewed the quality and reliability of the F.B.I.'s DNA laboratory by addressing the issues of DNA loading variability and the use of ethidium bromide. . . . Dr. Hagerman stated that the procedures followed by the F.B.I. for isolating and quantifying DNA preclude accurate determination of the amount of DNA present in sample extracts. He also stated that the use of ethidium bromide in the F.B.I.'s analytic gels causes unpredictable effects on the mobility of DNA fragments which in turn compounds the problems that the F.B.I. can have with band shifting. These factors make the F.B.I.'s DNA system unreliable he stated. . . .

Dr. Hagerman indicated that the unpredictability of band shifting at the F.B.I. laboratory adversely affects the population database work, thereby undermining the reliability of these studies. He stated that the autorads comprising the population database are of poor quality, and show many faint bands that are difficult to interpret, lanes in which it is difficult to determine if the probing identified a homozygote or a heterozygote, band positions that are difficult to assess or assign a location to, "doublets," or closely spaced bands, that could easily be mistaken for single banded patterns, and instances of extra bands. Finally, Dr. Hagerman stated that the agarose gels themselves could constitute an additional cause for altered DNA mobility and band shifting if the agarose was not concentrated uniformly throughout the gel.

Dr. Gilliam** stated, in discussing the various differences that distinguish the discrete allele systems generally used in medical diagnostics from the quasi-continuous allele systems used by forensic laboratories, that the forensic laboratories were struggling to come up with a matching rule and that the task of the forensic DNA scientist is "different from the gene mapping community." He considered the problem of developing a quantitative match criteria to be one that has not been dealt with by the medical genetics community, stating, "it's only come up in forensic laboratories."

Addressing the development of matching rules by the various forensic laboratories Dr. Gilliam concluded that the proponents of the forensic application of

---

* Editor's note: Dr. Paul J. Hagerman is Associate Professor of Biochemistry, Biophysics and Genetics, University of Colorado Health Sciences Center.

** Editor's note: Dr. T. Conrad Gilliam is Assistant Professor of Neurogenetics, Department of Genetics and Development, College of Physicians and Surgeons, Columbia University.

DNA technology are, in using a quasi- continuous allele system, taking DNA electrophoresis methods about as far as they can go, and stated that it was a "very technically demanding problem." . . .

On cross-examination Dr. Gilliam indicated that the larger F.B.I. match window would increase the statistical likelihood that a match would be declared. He did state, however, that, "there could be more than one matching rule that applies to a given set of data. In fact, maybe there should be." . . .

On re-direct Dr. Gilliam asserted that he considered ethidium bromide caused band shifting to be a problem that could have an unpredictable effect on casework, and that the validation studies addressing these problems have not yet been done. Dr. Gilliam concluded by asserting that he was sure that investigators could discover probes that identified discrete alleles and that a forensically useful DNA identification technology could be developed based on a discrete allele system and this "would put the forensic scientist laboratories back into the realms of established technology, and it would eliminate, if this . . . line of experimentation proved successful, . . . a lot of problems, matching rules and binning systems that they now have to deal with."

B. Pertinent Scientific Community

. . . In defining the pertinent scientific field, courts must first identify the field in which the underlying principle falls, and next determine whether that principle has been accepted by scientists in that field. In this case neither party has undertaken to define expressly its views about the identity of the pertinent scientific community. The government . . . appears to suggest that DNA testing should be found to meet the *Frye* standard if the F.B.I.'s protocol and procedures enjoy the approval of other forensic scientists. The defendants, by their selection of expert witnesses, implicitly assert that approval must come from a broader scientific community made up of persons familiar with molecular biology and population genetics.

I agree with the perception of the defendants that, in order to meet the *Frye* standard, the F.B.I.'s DNA principles and procedures must be shown to be generally acceptable to scientists beyond the forensic users of such techniques. . . .

[T]he scientific community to which we must turn in order to assess whether general acceptance has been attained is composed of scientists from the fields of molecular biology and population genetics who have expertise in either or both of those fields and a reasonably comprehensive understanding about the F.B.I.'s DNA testing protocol and procedures.

In light of that definition of the pertinent scientific community, it is clear that both parties produced competent and articulate representatives of that community at the hearing in this case. Those witnesses were, moreover, clearly aware of the current views within the pertinent scientific community toward the F.B.I.'s protocol and procedures.

C. Determination of General Acceptance

. . . The issue . . . is, accordingly, whether the proponent has shown by a preponderance of the evidence that the proffered novel scientific evidence is generally accepted in the scientific community. In the context of this case, that requires a finding that the pertinent scientific community generally accepts the ability of the F.B.I.'s protocol and procedures to reliably determine the existence of a match and provide a scientifically acceptable estimate of the relative rarity of the particular pattern in the Caucasian population. . . .

In summary, I have not encountered, and the parties have not cited, a case applying the *Frye* standard rejecting the admissibility of the evidence where a set of experts, such as in this case, have testified that the procedure was generally accepted. Where such experts have testified, the evidence has been admitted despite the firmly held countervailing views of the opponent's experts. . . .

. . . I find that the government has met its burden of showing by a preponderance of the evidence that the general scientific community, but by no means the entire scientific community, accepts the F.B.I. protocol and procedures for determining a match of DNA fragments and estimating the likelihood of encountering a similar pattern.

With regard to the issue of the ability to determine that bands match as provided in the protocol, I am persuaded by the testimony of the prosecution's four principal experts that, in their view and based on their knowledge of the F.B.I.'s practices, the government's laboratory has designed and implemented a program whereby multiple loci matches can reliably be ascertained.

In making my determination, I take note of the relative professional standings of the prosecution witnesses and the defense witnesses regarding the band shift issue. . . . This finding simply reflects my judgment in light of the entire record on the question of which of the experts is more likely to have a better general understanding of the level of acceptance within the scientific community. I find that the stature and professional standing of the government's witnesses on that issue place them in a position in which they are somewhat better able to assess the sense of the scientific community on the ability of the Bureau's ability to make reliable multiple loci matches.

Another important gauge of the general acceptance of the scientific community is the fact that Dr. Caskey, who is the director of one of the country's major genetics laboratories, has adopted the F.B.I. protocol almost in its entirety. The fact that he uses a smaller match window, his own population databases, and may have made some other alterations in the F.B.I. methodology does not detract from the significance of the fact that, after considering the protocols and procedures of the private laboratories, he chose, in light of his knowledge of those practices and those of the F.B.I., and, as well, in light of his expertise, the F.B.I. protocol. . . .

Many times witnesses have an interest in the outcome of the proceeding, and consideration of that fact is an important means of evaluating the accuracy of their testimony. The government's witnesses find themselves in a position of defending a process that is under vigorous attack. As they entered this hearing and throughout their testimony, which touched on all the pertinent subjects of scientific dispute, they had the ability to express reservations about the extent of their colleagues' approval of the Bureau's performance of its casework. In that way, they could minimize the potential damage to their professional reputations and stature that will result if they are ultimately shown to have been in error. They chose not to do so, and that decision on their part is a factor in my determination that they accurately express the views of the general scientific community.

Finally, I find Dr. Kidd's comments about the level of acceptance for the F.B.I.'s methods for determining a match also to be persuasive. He, like the other government experts, has had an opportunity during the course of these proceedings to take the criticisms being made by the defense into account, and has formulated responses that satisfy him that the flaws in the Bureau's system, particularly in regard to band shifting, can and do have no effect on either the ability of the Bureau to make accurate matches or the general acceptance of its procedures among the scientific community.

The fact that other law enforcement laboratories have implemented the F.B.I.'s program and procedures is, as well, some further indication that that program is generally viewed as acceptable by persons concerned with implementing a forensic DNA methodology that can operate reliably. . . . I discount in large part the lengthy listing of courts that have, on the basis of substantially less thorough inquiries than occurred in this case, upheld the admissibility of forensic DNA evidence . . . .

In the last analysis, I am persuaded that the views of the prosecution's witnesses more accurately project the extent to which their professional colleagues would concur that, despite the unfortunate, and to some extent unjustifiable flaws, the F.B.I. is able to declare matches accurately and provide a scientifically acceptable estimate of the resulting probabilities.

D. Alternative Findings re Reliability

Throughout this opinion, I have expressed the firm view, which I believe is mandated by the law of the Sixth Circuit, that this court's function is not to adjudicate the merits of the underlying scientific disputes. . . .

In the event that my interpretation of Sixth Circuit doctrine is in error, I will express the following factual findings on the scientific disputes . . .

With regard to the issues relating to the ability reliably to determine a match, I am persuaded by a preponderance of the evidence that the Bureau's procedures, even with all their flaws and defects, can, in fact, reliably discern matches across multiple loci. I reach this determination despite being also persuaded of the possible occurrence of band shifting.

The defendants argue that the F.B.I.'s procedure is flawed at its very basis, due to the use of a quasi-continuous allele system for forensic DNA typing. I disagree that the Bureau's selection of this form of DNA typing, rather than a discrete allele system, constitutes a systemic flaw that affects its ability reliably to determine matches.

Unquestionably, clinicians who use discrete allele systems for diagnostic work are not confronted with the problems of discerning a match that arise with quasi-continuous allele systems with their high number of genetic fragments per sample and the limitations of the resolution power found in the F.B.I. laboratory.

These objections, in my opinion, go to weight and not admissibility. The F.B.I.'s fixed bin approach accommodates weaknesses in the power of resolution by establishing categories of bands. Use of the fixed bin structure and the +/– 2.5% match window compensate adequately, in my opinion, for the problems caused by the initial decision to use VNTRs. I heard no testimony and have seen no exhibit sufficient to persuade me that selection of the quasi-continuous allele system was such a mistaken choice that, either standing alone or in conjunction with the other problems to which the defendants directed their attention, the system is thereby rendered incapable of producing reliable results.

The defendants raise several challenges to the scientific adequacy of the F.B.I.'s validation studies. It is clear that Dr. D'Eustachio's comparison of the data from Table III of the Fixed Bin Paper and the May, 1990, casework raises troublesome questions about the quality of the Bureau's work with either or both of those sets of gels. Dr. Budowle did not respond persuasively to Dr. D'Eustachio's criticisms, and he refused to acknowledge the potential significance or merit of a competent scientist's critique and to consider the desirability for further experimentation and confirmation. [Nevertheless,] I am persuaded that the defects in the validation study, like the other deficiencies in the operation of the Bureau's laboratory, do not affect its ability reliably to make accurate determinations of matches and avoid false positives. The defects perceived by Dr. D'Eustachio go to weight and not admissibility.

I reach the same determination with regard to the similar criticisms by Dr. D'Eustachio of the Bureau's mixed body fluid and environmental insult studies, although Dr. D'Eustachio's review of the deficiencies with those studies is cogently, comprehensively, and correctly critical of the Bureau's design and implementation of these studies. The issue, with regard to admissibility, is whether this Court can be persuaded, despite the perceived and putative flaws in the implementation of these important studies, that, nonetheless, the Bureau can reliably declare a match with multiple probes. I am persuaded by a preponderance of the evidence that it can.

The defendants challenge the F.B.I.'s selection of a larger match window than other practitioners, including Dr. Caskey, have selected. Particularly in light of the government's acknowledgement that all but a small minority of casework matches fall within a smaller range (85% within a 1.75% range), the F.B.I.'s use of the larger window invites the criticisms made of it by the defendants.

I conclude that those criticisms do not affect the ability of the F.B.I. to make reliable matches and avoid false positives across multiple loci. As I read the record, aside from the obvious fact that the larger window results in a capture of a wider span of alleles, none of the witnesses testified that an unnecessarily large window increased the likelihood of erroneous matches with multiple probes.

Moreover, as I understand the technology, defendants' objections to the match window, and applicable law, defendants who would be outside a smaller window but are within the F.B.I.'s larger window can make that point clear at trial. Thus, the issue of the match window clearly goes to weight and not admissibility.

The problems manifest in the "Repeat Caucasian Database," as outlined in Dr. Hartl's report, are not satisfactorily explained by the government's witnesses.
. . .

But with regard to the impact of this information on the issue of the ability to declare matches across multiple loci, I again conclude that this data and its analysis by Dr. Hartl do not justify a finding that the F.B.I. does not have such ability. The question is whether the government has shown by a preponderance of evidence, where multiple probes are used, that there is no significant risk of a declaration of a false match or positive.

The flaws to be inferred from Dr. Hartl's report show, in contrast, that there may be a likelihood of false exclusion. Such potential for error should be troublesome from a law enforcement standpoint, but in view of the limited issue before this Court — the reliability of multiple loci matches — it is not persuasive from a legal standpoint.

The F.B.I.'s failure to implement a comprehensive program of effective proficiency testing likewise goes at most to weight rather than admissibility, where the issue is the ability reliably to declare matches with multiple probes. The defendants have persuasively established, and the government has not rebutted, the fact that the F.B.I. program of proficiency testing has serious deficiencies, even without consideration of the troubling hint in the record of an impulse at one point to destroy some of the small amount of test data that had been accumulated earlier. The contentions about the absence of a meaningful proficiency testing program seem to be the sort of dispute about "technique" that the Sixth Circuit in United States v. Stifel, 433 F.2d 431, 438 (6th Cir. 1970), stated "went to the quality of the evidence and were for the jury."

With regard to the testimony of Dr. Hagerman about the effects of ethidium bromide, I find that there can be little doubt that there is a likelihood of band shifting that can result from the use of ethidium bromide, just as the defects in the validation, mixed body fluid, and environmental insult studies suggest that band shifts can occur from other causes. However, even accepting the likelihood of band shifting in some instances, I find that the likelihood of multiple shifts resulting in a match to be so slight as to be a matter of weight and not admissibility. . . .

I conclude, therefore, that the government has met its burden of proving by a preponderance of the evidence that its procedures can reliably determine matches over multiple loci. In reaching this finding, I do not either disregard or discount the accuracy of many of the criticisms about the remarkably poor quality of the F.B.I.'s work and infidelity to important scientific principles.

. . .

Upon review of the testimony, exhibits, arguments of counsel, and applicable legal doctrines, it is recommended that the government's motion to admit DNA evidence be granted; and that the defendants' motion to exclude such evidence be denied.

United States v. Bonds
12 F.3d 540 (6th Cir. 1993)

ALICE M. BATCHELDER, Circuit Judge.

On February 27, 1988, David Hartlaub was gunned down in his van as he stopped at a bank near the Sandusky Mall in Perkins Township, Ohio, where he planned to make a night deposit of cash from the music store he helped manage. The killers apparently had no interest in robbery; police found the deposit bag containing some four thousand dollars on the seat of the van. Three individuals — Wayne Yee, Mark Verdi and John Ray Bonds — were indicted in connection with the crime, tried, and convicted on federal firearms offenses and conspiracy. At trial, the Government's theory for the shooting was that the gunmen, members of the Hell's Angels motorcycle gang, had mistaken Mr. Hartlaub's yellow van for an identical van driven by a local member of a rival motorcycle gang, the Outlaws, whom the gunmen had allegedly planned to "hit" in retaliation for the shooting of a Hell's Angels member by an Outlaw the previous year in Joliet, Illinois. The defendants also claim that this is a case of mistaken identity — theirs — and challenge their convictions, claiming the Government's evidence to be either flawed, circumstantial, or both. Among the issues we must confront in this appeal is an issue of first impression for this court: whether the district court erred in admitting expert testimony concerning deoxyribonucleic acid (DNA) evidence in the trial of these defendants. For the reasons set forth below, we affirm the defendants' convictions.

I. Facts

No bystanders saw the shooting, [but various clues led them believe that] Bonds had shot Hartlaub in the van and driven off, that Yee was [seen outside the bank with a gun] after the shooting, and that Verdi had picked the two up in Yee's car . . . after Bonds [drove away] in the van. . . .

[Searches] of Verdi's home [led to the seizure] of items [characterized as a "hit kit"] as well as a MAC-11 of the same type as the murder weapon, with its serial number obliterated, a switchbladetype knife, a .45 caliber pistol, and a shirt matching the description of one worn at the crime scene by one of the gunmen.

In Yee's car, which the agents tracked down a few days later, the agents found, among other things, spent shell casings which experts later determined came from the murder weapon, and blood in the back seat which the FBI eventually matched with John Bonds's blood sample by DNA identification. [Hair and fiber evidence pointing to the murderer also was found.]

Agents [obtained] a search warrant for blood and hair samples from Mr. Bonds . . . These samples were the basis for evidence introduced at trial, including evidence that the DNA in Bonds's blood matched the DNA from the blood found in the back seat of Yee's car. Bonds was subsequently indicted, but fled before he could be brought to trial; he was a fugitive for several months before being discovered in Kentucky.

All three defendants were eventually tried to a jury and convicted; Messrs. Verdi and Yee were each sentenced to a total of fifteen years and Mr. Bonds was sentenced to a total of twenty five years.

II. Admissibility of the DNA Evidence

We first address whether the district court committed reversible error in admitting expert testimony concerning the DNA evidence obtained from the blood sample of defendant Bonds. Although several federal courts have ruled on the admissibility of forensic DNA testimony and evidence, as have numerous state courts, this is a case of first impression for the Sixth Circuit. We find that the district court did not err in admitting the expert testimony in this case. . . .

B. Use of DNA Evidence in this Case

On April 7, 1989, the FBI's DNA laboratory submitted a report stating that there was a "match" of DNA profiles from a bloodstain found in victim David Hartlaub's car and the DNA profiles derived from the blood of defendant Bonds. The FBI then calculated a probability of 1 in 270,000 that an unrelated individual selected randomly from the caucasian population would have a DNA profile matching that of Bonds. In May of 1990, the FBI revised its probability figure to 1 in 35,000. This revised probability estimate was presented to the jury in this case.

Defendants filed a motion to suppress the DNA evidence, and the Government filed a motion to admit the evidence. . . . The magistrate judge then conducted a six-week *Frye* hearing to determine whether the proposed experts' trial testimony about the DNA evidence was based on principles generally accepted in the scientific community. . . .

At the conclusion of the hearing, Magistrate Judge Carr issued a comprehensive 120-page report and recommendation (R & R), recommending that the
Government's motion to admit the DNA evidence be granted and that the defendants' motion to suppress be denied. The district court adopted the magistrate's
R & R . . . . The district court found that the Rule 403 argument must be raised at
trial.

Before trial, defendants moved for an in limine hearing to resolve the Rule
403 ground for exclusion and to expand the *Frye* hearing. The trial court denied
the motion for exclusion of the evidence and for another evidentiary hearing,
again holding that the Rule 403 challenge must be addressed at trial. At trial, the
district court admitted the testimony over the Rule 403 challenge. The district
court's orders denying the motion to suppress are now before us on appeal. . . .

E. Applying Rule 702 to the Expert Testimony in this Case

1. Rulings of the Magistrate Judge and the District Court

We note that although the findings of the magistrate judge and the district
court were based only on the pre-*Daubert Frye* hearing and the general acceptance
test, these findings are relevant to our examination under a *Daubert* analysis, first
because, as the district court noted, neither the defendants nor the Government
challenge the magistrate judge's findings regarding the substance of the expert testimony presented at the *Frye* hearing or his characterization of the testimony, and
second, because general acceptance is still one factor the Supreme Court has said
can impact on a court's scientific validity determination and the defendants' arguments on appeal focus on these findings and their general acceptance determination. After a thorough review of the record, we hold that these findings are not
clearly erroneous, and we adopt the magistrate's findings as conclusive. We briefly
summarize those findings below.

The magistrate judge issued exhaustive findings on the DNA evidence. He
began with a discussion of DNA technology and the procedures used in the FBI's
DNA lab to come up with matches, he proceeded through a very thorough
overview of the experts' testimony at the *Frye* hearing, and he discussed the *Frye*
standard in this Circuit and the general acceptance test, concluding that the
Government must show that the principles and procedures used in formulating the
DNA evidence are generally accepted or that they are in conformity with generally accepted explanatory theories. The magistrate found that the pertinent scientific community was molecular biologists and population geneticists, that the burden
of proof to meet general acceptance is a preponderance of the evidence, and that
the judge's role is limited to determining whether the procedures and principles
are generally accepted and does not extend to determining the reliability or validity of the results. The magistrate then defined general acceptance by stating what
general acceptance is not — it does not require unanimity or consensus, or cer-

tainty, or approval by other courts. He cited factors to consider in determining general acceptance and noted that this Circuit has found the absence of general acceptance only where the evidence "has been manifestly unsupported outside the proponent's own laboratory." Relying on the government witnesses' stature, Dr. Caskey's acceptance of the protocol, the other witnesses' belief that the protocol is generally accepted, other labs' acceptance of the protocol, and the more persuasive testimony of the Government's experts, the magistrate concluded that disputes over the reliability of results went only to the weight of the evidence and that the Government had met its burden of showing that the FBI's protocol and procedures were accepted by "the general scientific community."

The magistrate went on to make alternative findings on the merits of the disputes about the reliability of the results, in the event that a reviewing court disagreed with him that reliability disputes go to weight, not admissibility. He found that the FBI was able to produce reliable results, despite some flaws in the protocol relating to such matters as quasicontinuous allele systems, validation studies, environmental insult studies, proficiency testing, and ethidium bromide use. Notably, he concluded that the prospect of ethnic substructure did not impact on the reliability of results, but went to the weight of the evidence. Finally, the magistrate concluded that he could not make a Rule 403 ruling because this was a fact-specific inquiry for the trial court.

The defendants objected to the R & R on three grounds: (1) that the magistrate's definition of "general acceptance" was flawed and his finding that a consensus is not needed was erroneous; (2) that the magistrate's findings on reliability were flawed; and (3) that the magistrate failed to consider the Rule 403 argument. The district court, in an opinion that thoroughly reviewed the magistrate's report, found no merit in defendants' objections and adopted the report and recommendation.

Although the magistrate judge and the district court in admitting the DNA testimony focused on the general acceptance test that has now been superceded by the Supreme Court's recent *Daubert* decision, we still may affirm the district court on other grounds. We need not ask the parties to rebrief the issues or remand this case to the district court for reconsideration since we have a complete record before us, and, as we shall demonstrate hereinafter, it is clear from this record that the DNA evidence and testimony would have met the more liberal Rule 702 test adopted by the Supreme Court.

2. Daubert's Prongs

a. Relevance requirement

We hold that the expert testimony meets the "relevance" prong of the admissibility test: that the evidence or testimony "assist the trier of fact to understand the evidence or to determine a fact in issue." This requirement merely looks at whether the evidence and testimony is relevant to any issue in the case. The testimony must be "sufficiently tied to the facts of the case that it will aid the jury in resolving a factual dispute." The evidence that Bonds's DNA matched at least to some extent the DNA found in the crime-scene sample clearly is relevant to whether defendant Bonds was present in the victim's van on the night of the murder. Thus, the DNA evidence was helpful to the jury in determining whether defendants were guilty of the charges.

b. Evidentiary reliability requirement

Daubert requires that a preliminary assessment of the proffered testimony be made to determine whether the principles, methodology and reasoning underlying the testimony are scientifically valid. It is important to note that what is being challenged here by the defendants is not the general principle that individuals can be identified by their DNA, the principle that there are tests that can be performed to make these identifications, or the methodology of performing comparative testing by analyzing size and length variations among VNTR alleles in blood samples and calculating the statistical probabilities of a "match." In fact, the defendants presented considerable evidence at the *Frye* hearing about how these tests should have been performed. What the defendants challenge is the particular application of that methodology by the FBI in performing those tests and the results reached by the FBI. Their challenge is essentially that had the tests been performed differently, using a different database for the calculation of the statistical probabilities of the match, and using different materials in performing the test or using a different multiplication rule, the results would have been more accurate and perhaps different. Defendants also challenge the way the methodology was tested, arguing that the reliability of the results would have been greater had a different method of testing been employed. Defendants do not challenge the fact that the specific application of the methodology used by the FBI generated some probability that the DNA sample that "matched" Bonds's sample in fact came from Bonds; they only challenge the precision of that probability estimate. *Daubert* requires only scientific validity for admissibility, not scientific precision.

With this in mind, we now turn to the four factors that the Supreme Court observed would bear on a determination of whether the testimony pertains to scientific knowledge that will assist the trier of fact: (1) whether a theory or technique can be or has been tested; (2) whether the theory or technique has been subjected to peer review and publication; (3) the known or potential rate of error in using a particular scientific technique and the standards controlling the technique's operation; and (4) whether the theory or technique has been generally accepted in the particular scientific field. We note that the first two — can it be or has it been tested? and has it been peer reviewed? — are integral to the former general acceptance analysis and the magistrate judge made specific findings regarding them. The third factor — the known or potential rate of error and the existence and maintenance of standards controlling the technique's operation — is also encompassed in the peer review and testing factors and is implicit in the magistrate's general acceptance findings. The fourth factor is, of course, general acceptance, and the magistrate made explicit findings as to this. Thus, we can look to the magistrate's findings in making our determination.

i. Testing of theory or technique

The *Daubert* Court found that a "key question" is whether the theory or technique can be and has been tested. Evidence credited by the district court establishes that the theory behind matching DNA and calculating probabilities, and the particular technique employed by the FBI lab, can in fact be tested by comparing the results generated from one set of samples with the results reached after repeating the matching and probability estimate process on control samples. It is irrelevant that there are other methods for DNA matching that could also be or have been tested.

Furthermore, the FBI's principles and methodology have in fact been tested. The FBI performed internal proficiency testing as well as validation studies and environmental insult studies to determine whether the lab could produce reliable, reproducible results from samples that had been mixed with contaminants or subjected to environmental insults such as sun. In his report and recommendation, the magistrate made alternative findings on reliability and found that the FBI could reliably determine a match. Specifically, the magistrate addressed the criticisms raised about the FBI's validation studies, finding that the defects in the validation studies "did not affect [the FBI's] ability reliably to make accurate determinations of matches and avoid false positives." The magistrate also addressed the criticisms of the FBI's mixed body fluid and environmental insult studies, and of the "Repeat Caucasian Data base," and concluded that these too did not present a significant risk of false matches. The magistrate considered as well the FBI's failure to implement a "comprehensive" or "meaningful" program of effective proficiency testing, and found that the FBI did have a proficiency testing program — although one with serious deficiencies — and that this dispute was merely a dispute over technique. Therefore, it is clear that the FBI's theories, principles, methods, and techniques can be tested and have in fact been tested.

Finally, it seems clear that this first *Daubert* factor is not really in dispute. The *Daubert* Court found that "the criterion of the scientific status of a theory is its . . . refutability." Defendants vociferously dispute the accuracy of the match results and the adequacy of the testing done, and in refutation have presented evidence about deficiencies in both the results and the testing of the results. Thus, it appears that by attempting to refute the FBI's theory and methods with evidence about deficiencies in both the results and the testing of the results, the defendants have conceded that the theory and methods can be tested. The dispute between the Government and the defendants is over how the results have been tested, not over whether the results can be or have been tested.

ii. Peer review

The Supreme Court has observed that peer review and publication is another consideration in determining whether scientific evidence is admissible under Rule 702. The Court noted that publication — just one element of peer review — is not essential for admissibility or synonymous with reliability.

> [I]n some instances well-grounded but innovative theories will not have been published. Some propositions, moreover, are too particular, too new, or of too limited interest to be published. But submission to the scrutiny of the scientific community is a component of "good science," in part because it increases the likelihood that substantive flaws in methodology will be detected. The fact of publication (or lack thereof) in a peer-reviewed journal thus will be a relevant, though not dispositive, consideration in assessing the scientific validity of a particular technique or methodology on which an opinion is premised.

Id. (citations omitted).

The key here is that the theory and procedures have been submitted to the scrutiny of the scientific community, in part to "increase[ ] the likelihood that substantive flaws in methodology will be detected." Id. It is important, however, to note that "flaws in methodology" uncovered by peer review do not necessarily equate to a lack of scientific validity, since the methods may be based on scientific principles and the alleged flaws go merely to the weight, not the admissibility, of the evidence and the testimony. Instead, peer review and publication should be viewed as evidence that the theory and methodology are scientific knowledge capable of being scrutinized and have in fact been scrutinized by the scientific community.

Here, the FBI's procedures certainly have received "at least some exposure within the scientific peerage to which [they] belong[]." United States v. Kozminski, 821 F.2d 1186, 1201 (6th Cir. 1987) (en banc), aff'd, 487 U.S. 931 (1988). In fact, at the *Frye* hearing, the Government introduced articles on the FBI's techniques, including the FBI's statistical estimates. And the theory behind "matching" DNA itself and the general procedures used to come up with the forensic results clearly have received peer evaluation. In addition, the magistrate in this case anticipated *Daubert* by concluding that expert testimony from experts outside the proponents' lab and acceptance of the proponent's writings in professional journals — in essence peer evaluation or review — were factors to consider in determining general acceptance and thus admissibility. The magistrate concluded that the FBI's methods had received ample acceptance outside the FBI lab.

iii. Rate of error

The *Daubert* Court also observed that the trial court "ordinarily should consider the known or potential rate of error" and "the existence and maintenance of standards controlling the technique's operation." Daubert, 113 S. Ct. at 2797. The FBI did conduct internal proficiency tests to determine a rate of error and calculated a rate of error, although the magistrate found these proficiency tests to have "serious deficiencies." Defendants argued at the *Frye* hearing and on appeal that the scientific community considers indispensable external blind proficiency tests to account for laboratory error.

The deficiencies in calculating the rate of error and the failure to conduct external blind proficiency tests are troubling. We find troubling as well the lack of specific references to the rate of error in the Joint Appendix provided to this Court by the parties. Although we find that on the basis of the record before us the rate of error is a negative factor in the analysis of whether the FBI's procedures are scientifically valid, the error rate is only one in a list of nonexclusive factors that the *Daubert* Court observed would bear on the admissibility question. In addition, as noted in the next subsection, we find that the district court did not err in finding that the FBI's principles and procedures for declaring matches and calculating probabilities are generally accepted by the scientific community; because the magistrate judge's findings underlying general acceptance encompass the "existence and maintenance of standards controlling the technique's operations," id., it is implicit that the rate of error is acceptable to the scientific community as well.

iv. General acceptance

Finally, the *Daubert* Court indicated that the scientific validity analysis "does not require, although it does permit," us to consider the degree to which the FBI's principles and methodology are generally accepted in the relevant scientific community. *Daubert* noted that "[w]idespread acceptance can be an important factor in ruling particular evidence admissible, and 'a known technique that has been able to attract only minimal support within the community' may properly be viewed with skepticism." Id.

The concept of examining the "general acceptance" of a particular scientific theory and procedure stems from Frye v. United States . . . . Before *Daubert,* the *Frye* general acceptance test was the exclusive test in this and several other circuits for determining whether testimony about scientific evidence was admissible. Post-*Daubert,* general acceptance is but one of at least four factors that we may consider in determining whether testimony is admissible under Rule 702. Since the defendants argue extensively that the DNA testimony was not based on generally accepted procedures, since this was the focus of both the magistrate's Frye hearing and the district court's ruling, and since the *Frye* test utilizes to some extent at least two of the *Daubert* factors, we address general acceptance in some detail.

(a) Elements of general acceptance

Under our pre-*Daubert* case law, general acceptance exists when a substantial portion of the pertinent scientific community accepts the theory, principles, and methodology underlying scientific testimony because they are grounded in valid scientific principles. The cases discuss general acceptance in terms of "reliability" but refer only to the reliability of the procedures and process, not the reliability of the results of the procedures. As this Court stated in United States v. Brown, 557 F.2d 541 (6th Cir. 1977):

> [W]e equated general acceptance in the scientific community with a showing that the scientific principles and procedures on which expert testimony is based are reliable and sufficiently accurate. However, "[a]bsolute certainty of result or unanimity of scientific opinion is not required for admissibility."

Id. at 556 (quoting United States v. Baller, 519 F.2d 463, 466 (4th Cir.), cert. denied, 423 U.S. 1019 (1975)). . . . In examining "general acceptance" and in addressing the parties' arguments, we are confronted in this case with the question of what exactly must be generally accepted: whether only the theory of DNA profiling needs to be generally accepted or whether the FBI's methodology for conducting DNA testing need also to be generally accepted. The cases out of this circuit have not been entirely consistent in addressing what needs to be generally accepted.

We find that general acceptance encompasses both. This view is consistent with *Daubert's* requirement that we determine whether the "reasoning or methodology underlying the testimony is scientifically valid," 113 S. Ct. at 2796, and its acknowledgement that a "known technique that has been able to attract only minimal support in the scientific community may properly be viewed with skepticism," id.

Having defined what must be generally accepted, we now must review the defendants' arguments that the magistrate judge and the district court erred in defining general acceptance. The magistrate concluded that general acceptance does not require that there be "unanimity, or consensus within the scientific community concerning such acceptability." He noted, however, that although "neither consensus nor certainty" is needed, an absence of consensus is not immaterial. The district court concurred in the magistrate judge's conclusion. The defendants strenuously object, arguing that a consensus is necessary and that the FBI's procedure is not supported by such a consensus.

A careful review of the case law in this circuit persuades us that the "consensus" question is a red herring. "Consensus" is simply not a term that has been used in this circuit to determine whether the *Frye* general acceptance test has been met. Rather, our precedent demonstrates that while ordinarily the principles and procedures must be accepted by a majority of those in the pertinent scientific community, the absence of a majority does not necessarily rule out general acceptance. The general acceptance test is designed only to uncover whether there is a general agreement of scientists in the field that this scientific data is not based on a novel theory or procedure that is "mere speculation or conjecture." Brown, 557 F.2d at 559. In some instances, there may be several different theories or procedures used concerning one type of scientific evidence, all of which are generally accepted. None may have the backing of the majority of scientists, yet the theory or procedure can still be generally accepted. And even substantial criticism as to one theory or procedure will not be enough to find that the theory/procedure is not generally accepted. Only when a theory or procedure does not have the acceptance of most of the pertinent scientific community, and in fact a substantial part of the scientific community disfavors the principle or procedure, will it not be generally accepted.

Accordingly, we find that the magistrate judge's definition of consensus and his holding in regard to consensus thus defined are immaterial to the resolution of this issue. What is material is that the magistrate judge's findings clearly indicate that the degree of acceptance in the scientific community of the theory of DNA profiling and of the basic procedures used by the lab in this case is sufficient to meet the requirements in this circuit for general acceptance. The Government's experts, some of whom were from outside the FBI lab, clearly indicated that the FBI's DNA procedures were generally accepted. Despite their rebuttal criticism, the defendants' experts did not in fact show that the procedures were not generally accepted; they only showed a substantial controversy over whether the results produced were reliable and accurate.

Defendants argue that the magistrate judge erred in stating that questions about the reliability of the results are not relevant to the general acceptance determination but are only factors for the jury to weigh in considering the evidence at trial. We hold that questions about the accuracy of results are matters of weight, not admissibility.

The decision whether to admit the expert testimony in the first place is a matter of law for the trial judge. Once a court admits the testimony, "then it is for the jury to decide whether any, and if any what, weight is to be given to the testimony." Id. In the context of scientific evidence, this means that "conflicting testimony concerning the conclusions drawn by experts, so long as they are based on a generally accepted and reliable scientific principle, ordinarily go to the weight of the testimony rather than its admissibility." Brown, 557 F.2d at 556. The *Daubert* Court made it explicit that in determining the scientific validity and thus the "evidentiary reliability" of scientific evidence, "[t]he focus, of course, must be solely on principles and methodology, not on the conclusions that they generate." 113 S. Ct. at 2797. Questions about the certainty of the scientific results are matters of weight for the jury. . . .

Accordingly, we hold that general acceptance is required as to the principles and methodology employed. The assessment of the validity and reliability of the conclusions drawn by the expert is a jury question; the judge may only examine whether the principles and methodology are scientifically valid and generally accepted.

Thus in this case, the criticisms about the specific application of the procedure used or questions about the accuracy of the test results do not render the scientific theory and methodology invalid or destroy their general acceptance. These questions go to the weight of the evidence, not the admissibility.

With this in mind, we turn to address the defendants' arguments that the FBI's DNA procedures are not generally accepted by population geneticists and molecular biologists.

(b) Defendants' contentions

Defendants make several arguments to support their contention that the FBI's procedures for making statistical probability estimates are not generally accepted by population geneticists. These arguments focus on the FBI's methods of computing the 1 in 35,000 probability that a caucasian person other than defendant Bonds would have the same DNA pattern that Bonds has.

Defendants first argue that the magistrate's projections that the FBI's statistical method would be generally accepted turned out to be wrong because the NRC Report later showed the FBI's statistical basis to be invalid. Because, as we noted above, we cannot consider the NRC Report, this argument is irrelevant and we do not consider it. However, the particular complaints that defendants have as to erroneous projections by the magistrate judge are addressed below in the context of their objections to the magistrate judge's overall general acceptance finding.

Defendants next argue that general acceptance was not established because the FBI's methods were not published in peer-reviewed journals. As the *Daubert* Court noted, publication is but one element of peer review, is not a sine qua non of admissibility, and is not prerequisite to a finding of scientific validity. As noted above in our discussion of the second *Daubert* factor, we believe that the FBI's procedures have received some peer review. Any shortcomings in the peer review of the FBI's procedures are not sufficient to overcome the other strong evidence that the FBI's principles and procedures were both generally accepted and scientifically valid.

. . .

Besides their contention that the FBI's statistical procedures are not generally accepted among population geneticists, defendants also argue that the FBI's methods for declaring matches and interpreting autorads are not generally accepted among molecular biologists. Defendants allege a number of flaws in these methods including that the FBI's environmental insult studies and match criterion were flawed, that the FBI used ethidium bromide in analytic gels, and that the FBI was unable to type the same DNA samples reliably and reproducibly in its repeat caucasian database.

We addressed some of these concerns in discussing *Daubert* factors number one (can it be tested?) and number three (what is the known or potential rate of error?). We reiterate here that the magistrate and the district court did not err in finding that these flaws in the methods for declaring matching and interpreting autorads were issues of weight and did not pose the risk that the results were based on unaccepted principles or procedures.

Thus, we find that *Daubert* factor number four argues in favor of admissibility because the principles and procedures on which the DNA testimony was based are generally accepted by the relevant scientific communities.

(c) Conclusion as to Daubert prongs

When reviewed in light of the four *Daubert* factors (testing, peer review, rate of error, and general acceptance), we find that the underlying principles and methodology used by the FBI to declare matches and make statistical probabilities are scientifically valid. The methodology was valid in that it "result[ed] from sound and cogent reasoning," Bert Black, A Unified Theory of Scientific Evidence, 56 Ford. L. Rev. 595, 599 (1988), and was "'well grounded or justifiable [and] applicable to the matter at hand,'" id. at 599 n.9. Thus, the methodology clearly had "a grounding in the methods and procedures of science" and was based on "more than subjective belief or unsupported speculation." 113 S. Ct. at 2795.

Daubert sets out a "flexible" and more lenient test that favors the admission of any scientifically valid expert testimony. "Vigorous cross-examination, presentation of contrary evidence, and careful instruction on the burden of proof are the traditional and appropriate means of attacking shaky but admissible evidence." Id. The Court added that if the trial court concludes that the scintilla of evidence supporting a position is insufficient to allow a reasonable juror to conclude that the position is more likely than not true, the court can direct a judgment or grant summary judgment. Id. "These conventional devices, rather than wholesale exclusion under an uncompromising 'general acceptance' test, are the appropriate safeguards where the basis of scientific testimony meets the standards of Rule 702." Id. Thus, it is irrelevant that the FBI's DNA matching and statistical techniques are still being refined or that the results produced may not be wholly accurate since, as the Supreme Court noted, "it would be unreasonable to conclude that the subject of scientific testimony must be 'known' to a certainty; arguably, there are no certainties in science." Id. at 2795. The results of the DNA testing were clearly derived from tests based on methods and procedures of science and not based merely on speculation, and were supported by sound and cogent reasoning, even if these methods and procedures are not perfected.

Daubert requires only that the evidence be scientifically valid to have evidentiary reliability. We have found that the underlying methodology and reasoning are scientifically valid, and it is undisputed that the general principle that individuals can be identified by DNA is scientifically valid. Therefore, we need not examine that issue further. Having found as well that the evidence meets the relevance requirement of being "helpful to the trier of fact," we hold that the testimony proffered by the Government about the DNA matching and probabilities easily met the *Daubert* standard and was admissible under Rule 702.[21] . . .

NOTES

1. *The criticisms of the FBI's DNA typing.* The critics in *Yee* question the use of "the quasi-continuous allele system" of VNTRs, measurement problems produced by the use of ethidium bromide and environmental factors, subjectivity in the declaration of a match, the width of the FBI's match window, lack of proficiency testing, and the FBI's procedure for estimating the frequency of a DNA profile in the relevant population. Evaluating these criticisms demands an understanding of the technology of electrophoresis and the procedures of "matching" and "binning." These are summarized in the 1996 NRC Report — Committee on DNA Forensic Science: An Update, National Research Council, The Evaluation of Forensic DNA Evidence (1996).

2. Yee, Frye, *and* Daubert. A putative advantage of the *Frye* test is that it makes it unnecessary to understand the science. Did the magistrate judge in *Yee* apply the general acceptance test correctly? How can there be "general acceptance" when "[s]cientists of indisputable national and international repute and stature . . . took diametrically opposed views on the issue of general acceptability, and those views reflected the division of opinion on the merits of the underlying scientific disagreements."

Given this division of opinion, is it easier to admit evidence of a DNA match under *Daubert?* Was the court of appeals correct in treating *Daubert* as inherently "more lenient" than *Frye?* The opinion is criticized in Barry C. Scheck, DNA and *Daubert,* 15 Cardozo L. Rev. 1959 (1994).

3. *Subjectivity in declaring matches.* The extent to which subjectivity plays a signficant role in declaring matches of VNTR bands is not entirely clear. Some commentators suggest that it is a serious problem and that analysts sometimes interpret faint bands as real or artifactual so as to produce a match with a suspect's VNTR profile. See, e.g., David J. Balding & Peter Donnelly, How Convincing is DNA Evidence? 368 Nature 285 (1994); William C. Thompson, Subjective Interpretation, Laboratory Error and the Value of Forensic DNA Evidence: Three

---

[21] We note that because we have found that the FBI's DNA principles and procedures are generally accepted by scientists in the field, the FBI's principles and procedures have met the standard the Supreme Court has labelled as "rigid," "at odds with the 'liberal thrust' of the Federal Rules," "austere," and "uncompromising." Daubert, 113 S. Ct. at 2794, 2798. Accordingly, it is difficult to see how the FBI's theory and procedures would not pass muster under the more "liberal" Rule 702 analysis set out in *Daubert.* If under the "rigid" general acceptance standard we would have affirmed the admissibility of the DNA testimony and evidence, we certainly have little problem upholding the admission under this more lenient "scientific validity" test.

Case Studies, 96 Genetica 153 (1995) (urging purely objective determinations of the position of bands or at least "blind scoring," that is, measuring the positions of the bands from one sample without seeing the bands from other samples in the case). On the other hand, the 1996 NRC Report, states that "[g]enetic-typing results . . . are usually unambiguous; one cannot make one genetic type look like another simply by wishing it so. In RFLP analysis, patterns must meet empirically defined objective match crtieria to be said to match." Committee on DNA Forensic Science: An Update, National Research Council, The Evaluation of Forensic DNA Evidence 3-9 (1996) (prepublication copy). Nevertheless, the committee states that "the use of visual inspection other than as a screen before objective measurement . . . should usually be avoided" (id. at 5-16), and it cautions that:

> Laboratory procedures should be designed with safeguards to detect bias and to identify cases of true ambiguity. Potential ambiguities should be documented; in particular, any visual overrides of the computer-assisted imaging devices . . . must be noted and explained. . . .

Id. at 3-9.

4. *Windows.* Defense experts in *Yee* testified that the FBI's "match window" was too large. What scientific or legal criteria are there for determining the size of an acceptable window? If a window is very narrow, won't it exclude many suspects with DNA that actually matches? If it is very broad, won't it include many suspects with DNA that actually does not match? And, won't a very broad window result in very large bins that just raise the frequency of a "match" in the reference population, thereby making the finding of a match less incriminating? Does all this suggest that talk of "matching" is misguided — that it would be better to present the probability of the observed *degree of matching* if the samples come from the same person in comparison to the probability of this observed degree of matching if the samples come from different people? Compare D.H. Kaye, DNA Evidence: Probability, Population Genetics, and the Courts, 7 Harv. J. L. & Tech. 101 (1994), and D.H. Kaye, The Relevance of Matching DNA: Is the Window Half Open or Half Shut?, 85 J. Crim. L. & Criminology 676 (1995), with William C. Thompson, Lessons from the "DNA War," 84 J. Crim. L. & Criminology (1993).

The magistrate judge was concerned about "the F.B.I.'s selection of a wider match window than any other forensic DNA laboratory." There is considerable confusion over the meaning and magnitude of a "match window." Because different laboratories achieve different degrees of reproducibility, comparisons of the windows expressed as percentage differences can be misleading. Some studies suggest that differences in duplicate measurements are "normally distributed" — that the differences occur according to a kind of bell-shaped curve. The width of this curve is indicated by a statistic known as the standard deviation. According to

Eric S. Lander, Invited Editorial: Research on DNA Typing Catching Up with Courtroom Application, 48 Am. J. Hum. Genetics 819, 820 (1991), the FBI's reproducibility study suggests that the Bureau's laboratory has a standard deviation for the difference between two measurements of about 1.5% of the molecular weight of their mean. We may call this standard deviation the "standard error." The ±2.5% window about each band implies that two bands that are within about ±5.0% of their mean will meet the "objective" criterion. If the figures given here are accurate (other values also have been quoted in the literature and in court), then the FBI match window corresponds to ±3.4 standard errors. Commercial laboratories report smaller standard errors — about 0.6%. Lifecodes Corporation uses a match window of ±1.8%. Bruce S. Weir, Review: Population Genetics in the Forensic DNA Debate, 89 Proc. Nat'l Acad. Sci. 11654, 11655 (1992). This means that Lifecodes' window is ±3.0 standard errors. Although the FBI's ±5.0% window may seem much larger than Lifecodes' ±1.8% window, it is only slightly larger relative to the standard error of the respective laboratories — 3.4 for the FBI window versus 3.0 for Lifecodes. The standardized measure is the more apposite. Since more than 99.9% of the area of the normal curve lies within 3.4 standard errors, the FBI can almost always declare matches for alleles that come from the same source. Because 99.7% of the area under the normal curve lies within ±3.0 standard errors, the situation for Lifecodes' window is not very different. For more complete studies of the variability of measurements in different laboratories, see J.L. Mudd et al., Interlaboratory Comparison of Autoradiographic DNA Profiling Measurements, 66 Analytical Chem. 3303 (1994).

   5. *Population structure.* In a portion of the magistrate judge's report that was not included above,

> The defense experts, along with the court's witness, Dr. Lander, contended that the basic design of the F.B.I. Caucasian database was flawed because it failed to take into account the likelihood that there is no such thing as an American Caucasian population. Instead, in the view of the defense experts, there was a significant likelihood of "substructure," whereby the frequency of particular alleles might vary on the basis of the ethnic ancestry of particular subpopulations within the overall American Caucasian population.
>
> Because the impact, in terms of both frequency and magnitude of occurrence, of such substructure on the accuracy of the F.B.I.'s database is unknown, the defense experts asserted that any estimate of probability that might be generated on the basis of the Caucasian database was too speculative to be acceptable scientifically. That speculative quality, the defense witnesses asserted, caused the F.B.I.'s probability estimates to be unacceptable within the general scientific community.

134 F.R.D. at 174-75. What, exactly, is the contention? That is, what does it mean to say that the "database was flawed" or of unknown "accuracy."? A database is a

sample from a population; it is supposed to be representative of that population. An appropriate sample of whites living in the United States can be used to estimate the proportion of all whites in the United States population who will vote for a candidate for the Presidency. Is that sample "flawed" because the candidate's support varies among the ethnic minorities that constitute the white population?

The court of appeals described the population structure issue somewhat differently:

> Defendants' strongest criticism of the FBI's procedures for declaring DNA matches and estimating probabilities is that the database used by the FBI to make a probability estimate of the DNA pattern found in Bonds's blood failed to take into account ethnic substructure. Defendants' argument is based on the fact that the blood samples of the 225 FBI agents which make up the database used in this case were not divided into ethnic subgroups within the caucasian group, such as Polish and Italian. Defendants' experts testified that without accounting for ethnic substructure, the statistics indicating the frequencies with which certain DNA alleles appear in each racial group are exaggerated when the individual allele frequencies are multiplied together using the product or multiplication rule. According to these experts, the FBI should have used a more conservative method of estimating the frequencies of the alleles to take into account the possibility of ethnic substructure.

Bonds, 12 F.3d at 564. This description suggests that the problem caused by population structure lies not with the database, but with the formula that uses the allele frequencies in the white sample to estimate the profile frequency in the white population. The "more conservative" formula favored by some (but not all) of defendant's experts is explained in the next chapter.

Chapter 13
DNA Typing: A Time to Compromise?

Christopher Anderson
DNA Fingerprinting:
Academy Approves, Critics Still Cry Foul
356 Nature 552 (1992)*

Washington — The current procedure for comparing DNA finger prints is "fundamentally sound" and should be considered reliable when done properly, according to a report released this week by the National Academy of Sciences' National Research Council (NRC). But while the report should make the controversial technique more acceptable in the courtroom, it is not expected to end debate about its use.

The report suggests additional standards and measures to improve the standards of laboratories that carry out the tests and to strengthen the statistical basis for making comparisons of DNA samples. The NRC panel recommended that researchers take DNA samples from 100 people in each of 15 to 20 ethnic groups and that they maintain a database of the blood samples to reduce the possibility that ethnic subgroups in populations can distort the chances of finding random matches. It also recommended that the US Department of Health and Human Services establish an accreditation programme to check the quality of forensic laboratories.

None of these suggestions are contentious. But its chapter on population genetics seems likely to renew debate over whether the technique is a good way to identify someone conclusively.

The US Federal Bureau of Investigate (FBI) and many prosecutors have used a "multiplication rule" to determine the odds of random matches. Using that technique, a laboratory comparing DNA at several locations on the chromosome would multiple together the known frequency of each DNA site in available databases. Critics, however, argue that this technique discounts the possibility that the patterns may be related and inherited together. But in the absence of extensive databases on ethnic subpopulations, researchers do not know which patterns are typically inherited together.

The NRC report compares the multiplication rule to multiplying the odds of finding someone with blond hair by the odds of finding someone with blue eyes. That approach is misleading, of course, because blond hair and blue eyes are related; the actual odds of finding them together are much higher. The report cites one occasion in which the multiplication method was compared with an actual counting of matches in the database: the first predicted the odds of a match at 1 in 739,000 million, while the second showed the real odds to be 1 in 500.

The NRC report calls for more samples and better databases to reduce reliance on statistical crutches such as the multiplication rule. But it cautiously

---

endorses the use of a modified multiplication method, using the lowest observed odds for each DNA site.

This compromise, say critics, is just what the DNA fingerprinting advocates wanted. While agreeing with the NRC recommendations on additional measures, the critics claim that the NRC panel acceded to pressure from the US Department of Justice and the FBI, two sponsors of the report. They allege that FBI scientists, to whom a draft copy of the report was leaked last year, convinced the panel that it should delete portions of the population genetics chapter that would have made DNA fingerprinting evidence more difficult to use in court.

Earlier this month a judge in Seattle, Washington, ordered a copy of the earlier draft of the report released as part of a case (State v. Copeland) in which DNA fingerprinting evidence was being challenged. There are substantial changes between the draft (dated 15 October 1991) and the final report, mostly in favour of the use of DNA fingerprinting in court.

In particular, the draft does not recommend the use of the multiplication rule. Instead, it warns that "neglecting population substructure plays the same role in genetics textbooks as neglecting friction and air resistance in physics textbooks." But by eventually accepting the use of a modified multiplication method (even reluctantly and temporarily), that is exactly what the NRC panel has done, says Peter Neufeld, a lawyer who has fought the forensic use of DNA fingerprinting in several court cases. Victor McKusick, a geneticist at Johns Hopkins University who chaired the NRC panel, acknowledges that John Hicks, an FBI scientist, submitted a lengthy criticism of the population genetics chapter to the panel. But the main changes in the final version "came out of the review process, not the Hicks' letter," he says. As a sponsor, the FBI is not supposed to dictate the final product, but it is not inappropriate for FBI scientists to offer expert advice, he says. (In fact, the preface to the report thanks Hicks for his assistance.) "It is, however, unfortunate that the draft got such wide distribution," McKusick adds.

The controversy over the population genetics is unlikely to die with the release of the report. But McKusick hopes that the recommended research on ethnic subpopulations will ease some of the concerns about the multiplication method, if not the suspicion of political meddling in NRC reports.*

People v. Barney
10 Cal. Rptr. 2d 731 (Ct. App. 1992)

CHIN, Associate Justice.

These two appeals challenge the admissibility of deoxyribonucleic acid

---

* Editor's note: For a reply to some of the charges of "tampering" with the NRC Committee Report, see Oscar R. Zaborsky, The NAS-NRC DNA Typing Report: Realities and Miconceptions, in Proceedings of the Fourth International Symposium on Human Identification 1993 101 (1993).

(DNA) analysis evidence. The primary claim is that DNA analysis is a new scientific technique which does not meet the test of general acceptance prescribed by People v. Kelly (1976) 17 Cal. 3d 24, 130 Cal. Rptr. 144, 549 P. 2d 1240 and Frye v. United States (D.C. Cir. 1923) 293 Fed. 1013. We conclude that one element of current DNA analysis — the determination of the statistical significance of a match between a defendant's DNA and the DNA in bodily material found at the crime scene — does not satisfy the *Kelly-Frye* test, but that in both appeals the error in admitting the DNA evidence was harmless.

The two cases are factually unrelated. They were tried separately by two different judges in Alameda County and have been briefed separately. However, we have consolidated them for decision because there is substantial identity of issues presented and underlying scientific principles.

The victim in *Howard,* Octavia Matthews, was found on the floor of her home with a rope wrapped around her neck, bleeding from multiple head wounds. She later died of "[b]lunt trauma to the head associated with asphixia due to blunt trauma to the neck."

Kevin O'Neal Howard was Matthews's tenant in another building. He was behind in his rent payments and was living from paycheck to paycheck, and had previously been served with an eviction notice. Howard's wallet was found at the crime scene under some newspaper on a bloodstained couch. His fingerprint was found on a postcard in an upstairs bedroom. At the time of his arrest he had a fresh cut on one of his fingers. Conventional blood group analysis indicated that Howard's blood and some of the crime scene bloodstains — located on a tile floor, a paper napkin found in a cosmetics case, and a tissue found in a purse — shared an unusual blood type found in approximately 1.2 persons out of 1,000 in the Black population (and not at all in the White population). DNA analysis by the Federal Bureau of Investigation (FBI) indicated that Howard's DNA pattern matched the DNA pattern in those bloodstains, and the frequency of such a pattern is 1 in 200 million in the Black population.

The trial court held a *Kelly-Frye* hearing on the admissibility of the DNA evidence. The court heard expert testimony from both sides, and also admitted transcripts of the previous *Kelly-Frye* hearings in People v. Barney and a Ventura County case, People v. Axell (1991) 235 Cal. App. 3d 836, 1 Cal. Rptr. 2d 411. The court ruled that *Kelly-Frye* was satisfied and that the evidence was admissible.

At trial, Howard testified in his own behalf as follows. He had gone to Matthews's home to discuss his rent and get a receipt for a prior payment. In the course of searching for a receipt already in his possession, he emptied the contents of a pouch filled with his personal items, including his wallet, which he accidentally left at the scene. He never attacked Matthews, and she was alive when he left. He often cuts himself with wire on his job, but his finger was not bleeding on the night of the killing. Howard also presented a defense suggesting that another of Matthews's tenants may have committed the homicide.

A jury convicted Howard of second degree murder with great bodily injury.

The court imposed a prison sentence of 15 years to life.

The victim in *Barney* was accosted in the South Hayward Bay Area Rapid Transit (BART) parking lot as she entered her car. Ralph Edwards Barney forced his way into the car and demanded money, displayed a knife, and forced the victim to drive and park several blocks away, where he penetrated her vagina with his fingers, attempted unsuccessfully to rape her and force her to perform oral copulation, and ejaculated on her clothing. When he left he took her small change in the approximate sum of $2, her BART ticket with $3.80 remaining on it, and her car keys.

The victim found Barney's wallet on the floor of her car. She called the police from a telephone booth. When officers arrived, she identified Barney from a photograph on an identification card in the wallet. Officers were dispatched to the address on the identification card, where Barney was arrested. The police seized a knife, a BART ticket with $2.20 remaining on it, and $1.82 in small change found in Barney's possession and on his front porch. The BART ticket had last been used to enter the transit system at the South Hayward BART station. BART fare between that station and stations near Barney's address was $1.60, the same amount by which the victim's BART ticket was reduced after the assault.

The police took Barney to BART police headquarters, where the victim identified him as her assailant. She subsequently identified him at a lineup, at the preliminary examination, and at trial. At a pretrial display of knives, she identified two knives, one of which was the seized knife. She identified the seized BART ticket at trial. DNA analysis by a commercial entity, Cellmark Diagnostics (Cellmark), indicated that Barney's DNA pattern matched the DNA pattern in semen found on the victim's clothing, and the frequency of such a pattern is 1 in 7.8 million in the Black population.

The trial court held a *Kelly-Frye* hearing on the admissibility of the DNA evidence, at which it heard expert testimony from both sides and also admitted transcripts of the previous *Kelly-Frye* hearing in People v. Axell. The court ruled that *Kelly-Frye* was satisfied and that the evidence was admissible. The court excluded the victim's BART police station identification of Barney on the ground the one-person showup was impermissibly suggestive, but concluded the other identifications were untainted and were therefore admissible.

After a nonjury trial, the court convicted Barney of kidnapping to commit robbery, robbery, vaginal penetration with a foreign object, attempted rape and attempted forcible oral copulation. The court imposed a prison sentence of life with possibility of parole for kidnapping to commit robbery, plus a total of 18 years for the other offenses and enhancements, with the life sentence to be served after completion of the 18-year term. . . .

Howard and Barney raise almost identical issues pertaining to the question whether there is general scientific acceptance of DNA analysis and the adequacy of the *Kelly-Frye* hearing in each case. . . .

We begin with a few basic principles pertaining to admission of the DNA evidence. "[A]dmissibility of expert testimony based upon the application of a new scientific technique traditionally involves a two-step process: (1) the reliability of the method must be established, usually by expert testimony, and (2) the witness furnishing such testimony must be properly qualified as an expert to give an opinion on the subject. Additionally, the proponent of the evidence must demonstrate that correct scientific procedures were used in the particular case." People v. Kelly, 17 Cal. 3d at 30, 130 Cal. Rptr. 144, 549 P. 2d 1240. "[R]eliability" means that the technique "'must be sufficiently established to have gained general acceptance in the particular field in which it belongs.'" Ibid.

The existence of "general acceptance" is subject to limited de novo review on appeal. Ordinarily, the appellate court will confine its review to the record, independently determining from the trial evidence whether the challenged scientific technique is generally accepted. Occasionally, however, it may be necessary for the appellate court to review scientific literature outside the record. The goal is not to decide the actual reliability of the new technique, but simply to determine whether the technique is generally accepted in the relevant scientific community. If the scientific literature discloses that the technique is deemed unreliable by "scientists significant either in number or expertise . . .," the court may safely conclude there is no general acceptance. People v. Reilly (1987) 196 Cal. App. 3d 1127, 1134, 242 Cal. Rptr. 496. Even if the technique was previously determined correctly to have been generally accepted, the converse may subsequently be shown by evidence "reflecting a change in the attitude of the scientific community." People v. Kelly, 17 Cal. 3d at 32, 130 Cal. Rptr. 144, 549 P. 2d 1240. . . .

[The court rejects arguments that] the prosecution failed to meet its *Kelly-Frye* burden because its two expert witnesses were FBI employees and thus were unacceptably biased, [that] there is a current lack of generally accepted standards, guidelines, and controls pertaining to analysis performed by DNA testing laboratories, and the result is a lack of general scientific acceptance of DNA analysis techniques, [that] until recently the FBI laboratory has not been subjected to independent external proficiency testing, and [that] proficiency testing of the Cellmark laboratory has revealed isolated instances in which "false positives" (i.e., incorrect matches) were declared. [It notes that] These points are discussed in a new report on DNA analysis by the National Research Council (NRC). NRC, DNA Technology in Forensic Science (1992). The NRC report concludes there is indeed a need for standardization of laboratory procedures and proficiency testing (as well as appropriate accreditation of laboratories) to assure the quality of DNA laboratory analysis. But the absence of such safeguards does not mean DNA analysis is not generally accepted. To the contrary, the NRC report concludes that "[t]he current laboratory procedure for detecting DNA variation . . . is fundamentally sound. . . ." Id. at 149. Rather, the absence of these safeguards goes to the question whether a laboratory has complied with generally accepted standards in a given case, or, stated in *Kelly-Frye* terms, whether the prosecutor has shown that "correct scientific procedures were used in the particular case." People v. Kelly, 17 Cal. 3d at 30, 130 Cal. Rptr. 144, 549 P. 2d 1240. . . .

Howard and Barney contend there is no general acceptance as to the systems employed by the FBI and Cellmark for declaring a match of DNA patterns. Specifically, they claim there is a lack of consensus regarding (1) match criteria (e.g., the FBI's 2.5 percent match window), (2) the extent to which there is a possibility of declaring false positives, (3) the problem of band shift . . . , and (4) situations where there are missing, extra, or indistinct bands. Barney adds a claim that there was no general acceptance of Cellmark's previous method of using a ruler and a computerized formula to measure bands (Cellmark now uses computer analysis). . . .

The NRC report states there is a need for "an objective and quantitative rule for deciding whether two samples match." NRC Report 54. But, again, the report does not equate the absence of a standardized rule with a lack of general acceptance as to the matching step of DNA analysis. The use of match criteria in a given case is properly addressed as part of the inquiry whether "correct scientific procedures were used in the particular case." People v. Kelly, 17 Cal. 3d at 30, 130 Cal. Rptr. 144, 549 P. 2d 1240.

This brings us to the heart of these appeals, the question whether the third step of DNA analysis — the determination of a match's statistical significance — has received general scientific acceptance.

There is currently a fundamental disagreement among population geneticists concerning the determination of the statistical significance of a match of DNA patterns. The dispute was recently featured in a leading scientific journal, *Science,* in which Richard C. Lewontin of Harvard University and Daniel L. Hartl of Washington University attack the reliability of DNA statistical analysis, while Ranajit Chakraborty of the University of Texas and Kenneth K. Kidd of Yale University defend it. Lewontin & Hartl, Population Genetics in Forensic DNA Typing (Dec. 20, 1991) Science, at 1745; Chakraborty & Kidd, The Utility of DNA Typing in Forensic Work (Dec. 20, 1991), Science, at 1735.

Lewontin and Hartl question the reliability of the current method of multiplying together the frequencies with which each band representative of a DNA fragment appears in a broad data base. The problem, they say, is that this method is based on incorrect assumptions that (1) members of the racial groups represented by the broad data bases — Caucasians, Blacks, and Hispanics — mate within their groups at random, i.e., without regard to religion, ethnicity, and geography, and (2) the DNA fragments identified by DNA processing behave independently and thus are "independent in a statistical sense" — i.e., in the language of population genetics, they are in "linkage equilibrium." Lewontin & Hartl at 1746.

Lewontin and Hartl claim that, contrary to the assumption of random mating, ethnic subgroups within each data base tend to mate endogamously (i.e., within a specific subgroup) with persons of like religion or ethnicity or who live within close geographical distance. Such endogamous mating tends to maintain genetic differences between subgroups — or substructuring — which existed when ancestral populations emigrated to the United States and has not yet had sufficient time to dissipate. As a result, the subgroups may have substantial differences in the frequency of a given DNA fragment — or VNTR allele — identified in the processing step of DNA analysis. A given VNTR allele may be relatively common in some subgroups but not in the broader data base.

There are purportedly two consequences of genetic substructuring and subgroup differences in allele frequencies: (1) it is inappropriate to use broad data bases to which all Caucasians, Blacks, and Hispanics may be referred for estimating frequencies, and (2) it is inappropriate to multiply frequencies together, for want of linkage equilibrium. The current multiplication method, using the Hardy-Weinberg equation (which requires statistical independence within a locus, or Hardy-Weinberg equilibrium) and the product rule (which requires statistical independence across loci, or linkage equilibrium) will be reliable only if there is extensive study of VNTR allele frequencies in a wide variety of ethnic subgroups. Lewontin and Hartl conclude that because the frequency of a given VNTR allele may differ among subgroups, reference to a broad data base may produce an inaccurate frequency estimate for a defendant's subgroup. The current multiplication method may greatly magnify the error. The resulting probability for the defendant's entire DNA pattern may be in error by two or more orders of magnitude (e.g., 1 in 7.8 million could really be 1 in 78,000).

Chakraborty and Kidd strongly disagree. They contend that Lewontin and Hartl exaggerate both the extent of endogamy in contemporary America and the effect of substructuring on the reliability of DNA statistical analysis. They concede there is substructuring (and thus variance of VNTR allele frequencies) within the data bases, but assert its effect on the reliability of frequency estimates is "trivial" and "cannot be detected in practice." Chakraborty & Kidd at 1736-1738.

In an article introducing the Lewontin-Hartl and Chakroborty-Kidd articles, *Science* describes Lewontin and Hartl as "two of the leading lights of population genetics" who "have the support of numerous colleagues." Roberts, Fight Erupts Over DNA Finger printing (Dec. 20, 1991) Science, at 1721 (hereafter Fight Erupts). A population geneticist at the University of California at Irvine is said to agree "that the current statistical methods could result in 'tremendous' errors and should not be used without more empirical data." The introductory article describes the debate as "bitter" and "raging," stating that "tempers are flaring, charges and counter charges are flying. . . . Dispassionate observers, who are few and far between, say that the technical arguments on both sides have merit. . . . [T]he debate is not about right and wrong but about different standards of proof, with the purists on one side demanding scientific accuracy and the technologists on the other saying approximations are good enough." *Science* concludes that the Lewontin-Hartl and Chakraborty-Kidd articles "seem likely to reinforce the notion that the [scientific] community is indeed divided" under the *Frye* standard, although the issue may become moot within a few years "with the expected introduction of even more powerful DNA techniques...."

The NRC report, which was released four months after the *Science* articles, acknowledges there is a "[s]ubstantial controversy" concerning the present method of statistical analysis." The report does not, however, choose sides in the debate, but instead "assume[s] for the sake of discussion that population substructure may exist. . . ."

Briefing in the present appeals predated the appearance of the *Science* articles and the NRC report, on which we have solicited comment from the parties. However, the challenges asserted by Howard and Barney to the third step of DNA analysis, both below and on appeal, are essentially the same as the points raised by Lewontin and Hartl. Howard and Barney claim there is no general scientific acceptance as to (1) use of the Hardy-Weinberg equation in light of genetic substructuring, (2) use of the product rule and the assumption that probed-for DNA fragments are in linkage equilibrium, (3) the size and composition of the FBI and Cellmark data bases, (4) the failure to provide confidence levels (i.e., upper and lower ranges) for frequency estimates, and (5) the degree to which conservative calculation methods employed by the FBI and Cellmark compensate for the possibility of frequency underestimates. They also argue that use of the product rule is precluded by People v. Collins (1968) 68 Cal. 2d 319, 327-329, 66 Cal. Rptr. 497, 438 P. 2d 33, for want of an adequate evidentiary foundation or proof of statistical independence. Barney adds a challenge to the size of Cellmark's bin categories for base-pair lengths. . . .

A threshold issue is whether the *Kelly-Frye* requirement of general scientific acceptance applies at all to the statistical calculation step of DNA analysis. If not, the current scientific debate would go only to the weight of DNA evidence, not its admissibility, and would be a matter for jury consideration. . . . The statistical calculation step is the pivotal element of DNA analysis, for the evidence means nothing without a determination of the statistical significance of a match of DNA patterns. It is the expression of statistical meaning, stated in terms of vanishingly small match probabilities, that makes the evidence so compelling. To say that the frequency of Howard's DNA pattern is 1 in 200 million in the Black population is tantamount to saying his pattern is totally unique, and thus only he could have been the source of the crime scene bloodstains that did not match those of the victim.

To end the *Kelly-Frye* inquiry at the matching step, and leave it to jurors to assess the current scientific debate on statistical calculation as a matter of weight rather than admissibility, would stand *Kelly-Frye* on its head. We would be asking jurors to do what judges carefully avoid — decide the substantive merits of competing scientific opinion as to the reliability of a novel method of scientific proof. We cannot reasonably ask the average juror to decide such arcane questions as whether genetic substructuring and linkage disequilibrium preclude use of the Hardy-Weinberg equation and the product rule, when we ourselves have struggled to grasp these concepts. The result would be predictable. The jury would simply skip to the bottom line — the only aspect of the process that is readily understood — and look at the ultimate expression of match probability, without competently assessing the reliability of the process by which the laboratory got to the bottom line. This is an instance in which the method of scientific proof is so impenetrable that it would "assume a posture of mystic infallibility in the eyes of a jury." United States v. Addison (D.C. Cir. 1974) 498 F.2d 741, 744. It is the task of scientists — not judges, and not jurors — to assess reliability. "The requirement of general acceptance in the scientific community assures that those most qualified to assess the general validity of a scientific method will have the determinative voice. . . ." Id. at 743-744.

Might the statistical calculation step be distinguished from the processing and matching steps for *Kelly-Frye* purposes on the ground that only the first two steps produce novel scientific evidence while the third step is merely interpretative? Again, such an approach would subvert *Kelly-Frye.* The evidence produced by DNA analysis is not merely the raw data of matching bands on autoradiographs but encompasses the ultimate expression of the statistical significance of a match, in the same way that polygraph evidence is not merely the raw data produced by a polygraph machine but encompasses the operator's ultimate expression of opinion whether the subject is telling the truth. Were we to terminate the *Kelly-Frye* inquiry short of the interpretative steps in new methods of scientific proof, *Kelly-Frye* would lose much of its efficacy as a tool of "considerable judicial caution" and of an "essentially conservative nature" that is "deliberately intended to interpose a substantial obstacle to the unrestrained admission of evidence based upon new scientific principles." People v. Kelly, 17 Cal. 3d at 31, 130 Cal. Rptr. 144, 549 P. 2d 1240.

Having concluded that *Kelly-Frye* applies to the statistical calculation step of DNA analysis, we proceed to the *Kelly-Frye* inquiry — whether the process of statistical calculation employed by the FBI and Cellmark has gained general acceptance in the field of population genetics.

The *Science* articles of December 1991 vividly demonstrate not merely a current absence of general acceptance, but the presence of a "bitter" and "raging" disagreement among population geneticists. Fight Erupts, at 1721. According to Lewontin and Hartl, the statistical calculation process is fundamentally flawed because — due to genetic substructuring and linkage disequilibrium — the use of broad data bases and the current multiplication method results in unreliable frequency estimates that may be in error by two or more orders of magnitude. In simple terms, the "bottom line" expression of statistical significance in DNA analysis is claimed to be tremendously unreliable.

Evidently, Lewontin and Hartl — along with their colleagues who agree with them — are significant in both "number" and "expertise." People v. Reilly, 196 Cal. App. 3d at 1134, 242 Cal. Rptr. 496. *Science* describes Lewontin and Hartl as "two of the leading lights of population genetics" who "have the support of numerous colleagues," and quotes a third population geneticist (Francisco Ayala) who agrees with the above criticism. Fight Erupts, at 1721. Lewontin has been described by one of his colleagues as "probably regarded as the most important intellectual force in population genetics alive." United States v. Yee (N.D. Ohio 1991) 134 F.R.D. 161, 181. Similar criticisms of the statistical calculation process of DNA analysis have been leveled by other scientists in previous publications, some of which were admitted in evidence below (e.g., Lander, DNA Fingerprinting on Trial (June 15, 1989) Nature, at 501, 504; Cohen, DNA Fingerprinting for Forensic Identification: Potential Effects on Data Interpretation of Subpopulation Heterogeneity and Band Number Variability (1990) 46 Am. J. Hum. Genetics 358, 367), and in expert testimony at the *Kelly-Frye* hearings in Howard (Laurence Mueller), in *Barney* (Steve Selvin and Laurence Mueller) and in *Axell* (Diane Lavett, Charles Taylor, Seymour Geisser, and Laurence Mueller). People v. Axell, 235 Cal. App. 3d at 850-851.

Of course, Chakraborty and Kidd strongly disagree, and according to *Science* they have "many scientific supporters." Fight Erupts, at 1721; see Risch & Devlin, On the Probability of Matching DNA Fingerprints (Feb. 7, 1992) *Science,* at 717. But the point is not whether there are more supporters than detractors, or whether (as the Attorney General and amicus curiae claim) the supporters are right and the detractors are wrong. The point is that there is disagreement between two groups, each significant in both number and expertise (a "[s]ubstantial controversy," in the words of the NRC report). Even *Science,* which purportedly sought balance in its coverage of this dispute by commissioning the Chakraborty-Kidd article as a rebuttal to the Lewontin-Hartl article (Roberts, Was Science Fair to its Authors? (Dec. 20, 1991) Science, at 1722), recognized that the competing articles "seem likely to reinforce the notion that the [scientific] community is indeed divided" under the *Frye* standard. Fight Erupts, at 1723.

Our task under *Kelly-Frye* is not to choose sides in this dispute over the reliability of the statistical calculation process. Once we discern a lack of general scientific acceptance — which in this instance is palpable — we have no choice but to exclude the "bottom line" expression of statistical significance in its current form.

We do not write on an entirely clean slate. The admissibility of DNA analysis evidence has been litigated in many forums in the past few years. The statistical calculation dispute, however, has not been judicially examined until quite recently.

The few published decisions exploring the question of general acceptance on this point are in conflict. . . .

Whatever the merits of the prior decisions on the statistical calculation process . . . the debate that erupted in Science in December 1991 changes the scientific landscape considerably, and demonstrates indisputably that there is no general acceptance of the current process. . . .

The Lewontin-Hartl article in *Science* concludes with a famous query: "What Is To Be Done?" We confront the same question. More specifically, must the absence of general scientific acceptance as to the current statistical calculation aspect of DNA analysis result in total exclusion of DNA evidence?

DNA analysis is a powerful forensic tool by any standard, and a role for it in the process of criminal justice is inevitable. Even Lewontin and Hartl concede its potential: "Appropriately carried out and correctly interpreted, DNA typing is possibly the most powerful innovation in forensics since the development of finger-printing in the last part of the 19th century." Lewontin & Hartl, supra, at 1746.

Clearly, a match of DNA patterns is a matter of substantial significance. See NRC rep., at 74 ("a match between two DNA patterns can be considered strong evidence that the two samples came from the same source."). The statistical dispute is restricted to the extent of that significance. There must be some common ground, some sufficiently conservative method of determining statistical significance, as to which there is general scientific agreement. See Caldwell v. State, 260 Ga. 278, 393 S.E. 2d at 443-444 (laboratory's calculation of 1 in 24 million held inadmissible, but expert witness's "more conservative" calculation of 1 in 250,000 held admissible).

The NRC report on DNA analysis appears to point the way to such common ground. The report proposes a method of statistical calculation which accounts for the possibility of population substructuring, eliminates ethnicity as a factor in the calculation process, and permits the use of the product rule while ensuring that probability estimates are appropriately conservative. The report proposes a "ceiling frequency" approach, in which DNA samples from 15 to 20 homogeneous populations will be analyzed for allele frequencies. In subsequent analysis of the DNA of a suspect or crime scene sample, each allele will be assigned the highest frequency that appears in the tested populations, or 5 percent, whichever is greater. These frequencies will then be multiplied together using the product rule.

Until the ceiling approach is in place, the report proposes that the following interim methods should be used to report frequencies. (1) Using a "counting principle" approach, the frequency of a DNA pattern (e.g., zero) in an existing data base should be reported. (2) Using a modified ceiling approach, each allele should be assigned a frequency of either the 95 percent "upper confidence limit" for its frequency in existing data bases (wherein the true frequency has only a 5 percent chance of variance), or 10 percent, whichever is larger, and a statistical calculation should then be made using the product rule.

These proposals, however, do not solve the problem in the present cases. The DNA evidence admitted in *Howard* and *Barney* included frequency estimates based on statistical calculations which have not received general scientific acceptance. Even though the trial courts in these cases could not have anticipated the controversy that subsequently arose in the scientific community, this was still error, and no amount of after-the-fact fine tuning of the statistical calculation process can cure the error. The error infects the underlying match evidence, which is incomplete without an interpretation of its significance. Thus, we have no alternative but to hold that the DNA analysis evidence was inadmissible under *Kelly-Frye,* for want of general scientific acceptance of the statistical calculation process employed in these cases.

The question now at hand is whether the interim and future methods of statistical calculation proposed by the NRC report will be generally accepted by population geneticists. If, as appears likely, this question is answered in the affirmative in a future *Kelly-Frye* hearing, then DNA analysis evidence will be admissible in California.

The last DNA issue is whether the trial courts in *Howard* and *Barney* erred by failing to receive evidence and determine, as part of the *Kelly-Frye* inquiry, whether correct scientific procedures were used when the DNA analysis was performed in each particular case.

The California Supreme Court held in *Kelly* that, in addition to establishing the reliability (i.e., general acceptance) of a new scientific technique and the qualifications of expert witnesses, "the proponent of the evidence must demonstrate that correct scientific procedures were used in the particular case." People v. Kelly, 17 Cal. 3d at 30, 130 Cal. Rptr. 144, 549 P. 2d 1240. This latter point is sometimes called the "third prong" of *Kelly-Frye*. . . . We note, however, that . . . third-prong hearings . . . obviously will not approach the level of complexity of a full-blown *Kelly-Frye* hearing in which the question of general acceptance is litigated. All that is necessary in the limited third-prong hearing is a foundational showing that correct scientific procedures were used. . . .

We conclude the admission of the DNA analysis evidence in the present cases was error for two reasons: (1) the absence of general scientific acceptance as to the statistical calculation process, and (2) lack of the third-prong inquiry. The remaining question is whether the errors were prejudicial or harmless. We find in both *Howard* and *Barney* that it is not reasonably probable a different result would have been reached absent the admission of the DNA evidence. . . . [T]he admission of the DNA evidence was superfluous and therefore harmless.

The judgments are affirmed.

NOTES

1. *The ceiling methods.* The *Barney* court wrote that the "ceiling approach" endorsed in the 1992 NRC report might provide "probability estimates [that] are appropriately conservative." As the opinion explained:

> The report proposes a "ceiling frequency" approach, in which DNA samples from 15 to 20 homogeneous populations will be analyzed for allele frequencies. In subsequent analysis of the DNA of a suspect or crime scene sample, each allele will be assigned the highest frequency that appears in the tested populations, or 5 percent, whichever is greater. These frequencies will then be multiplied together using the product rule.

Although the FBI has gathered VNTR data on various populations and localities, this ceiling method has never been implented. Instead, the "modified ceiling method" has been employed. As *Barney* explains:

> Until the ceiling approach is in place, the report proposes that the following interim methods should be used to report frequencies. (1) Using a

"counting principle" approach, the frequency of a DNA pattern (e.g., zero) in an existing data base should be reported. (2) Using a modified ceiling approach, each allele should be assigned a frequency of either the 95 percent "upper confidence limit" for its frequency in existing data bases (wherein the true frequency has only a 5 percent chance of variance), or 10 percent, whichever is larger, and a statistical calculation should then be made using the product rule.

The "existing data bases" are samples from the "major 'races,' e.g., Caucasians, Blacks, Hispanics, Asians, and Native Americans." * National Research Council Committee on DNA Technology in Forensic Science, DNA Technology in Forensic Science 91 (1992). The committee contemplated using as few as three such samples (id.), and we shall illustrate the method with just three. We start with simple "product rule" calculations, then produce the modified ceiling estimates for a given profile.

Suppose that the profile found at the crime scene consists of four "loci," with one allele at the first locus and two alleles at each of the other three, as listed in Table 13.1, where the four loci are abbreviated A though D. Then the profile can be designated $A_6–B_8B_{14}C_{10}C_{13}D_9D_{16}$, the dash indicating the single band at the A locus. The allele frequencies, as estimated from FBI databases, are given in Table 13.1.

Table 13.1. VNTR allele frequencies at four loci by race.

Locus	Allele (Bin)	Frequencies (%)		
		White	Black	Hispanic
A (D2S44)	6	3.5	9.2	10.5
B (D1S7)	8	2.9	3.5	3.1
	14	6.8	6.3	5.6
C (D4S139)	10	7.2	6.6	10.6
	13	13.1	10.3	10.1
D (D10S28)	9	4.7	7.6	4.6
	16	6.5	3.6	5.9

Source: National Research Council Committee on Forensic DNA Science: An Update, The Evaluation of DNA Evidence, Table 4.8 (1996)

---

* When the samples are large and an allele is not too rare, a 95% confidence interval will not diverge very far from the frequency of the allele in the sample. The confidence interval is a rather technical device to account for "sampling error." Contrary to the *Barney* opinion, the "true frequency" does not vary; it is a fixed characteristic of the population. The frequency observed in a random sample of the population is likely to differ from the population value, and the confidence interval is one way to gauge the likely extent of the divergence between the observed sample value and the unknown population figure. If there were not one, but many independent, large, random samples drawn from the same population, and if 95% confidence intervals were drawn around each sample value, then approximately 95% of these intervals would encompass the population value, whatever it may be.

The "product rule" first estimates the frequency of the alleles at each locus (the "single-locus genotypes"), then it combines these figures to estimate the frequency of the combination of single-locus genotypes (the "multilocus genotype").

At the B, C, and D loci, distinct alleles are observed. An individual who inherits different alleles from each parent is said to be "heterozygous" at such loci. One allele is on a chromosome inherited from the individual's mother, and the other is on the paternal chromosome. For the B locus, the product of the estimated allele frequencies in the white population is $0.029 \times 0.068 = 0.002062$. In a large, "randomly mating" population of whites, this is approxmately the fraction who will have an allele B_8 on the paternal chromosome and an allele B_{14} on the maternal chromosome.[3] About the same fraction will have the B_8 on the maternal chromosome and the B_{14} on the paternal one. The laboratory cannot say which of these two possibilities pertains to the evidence sample, so it estimates the frequency of the white population with either arrangement to be $2 \times 0.029 \times 0.068 = 0.004124$. More generally, the formula for the frequency P of a heterozygous single-locus genotype in a large, randomly mating population is $P = 2p_ip_j$ where p_i is the frequency of one allele, and p_j is the frequency of the other.[4] We can apply this formula to the C and D loci to obtain $P_C = 2 \times .072 \times .131 = 0.0189$ and $P_D = 2 \times .047 \times .065 = 0.00611$.

At the A locus, however, only the allele 6 is seen. This might be because the source of the DNA taken from the crime scene has two copies of allele 6 — one inherited from each parent. The frequency of the "homozygous" single-locus genotype in a randomly mating white population is $0.035 \times 0.035 = 0.001225$, about one in a thousand. In a large, randomly mating population, homozygote frequencies are simply p^2. When a population is in what is known as "Hardy-Weinberg equilibrium," the equations $P = 2 \, p_i \, p_j$ for heterozygotes and $P = p_i^2$ for homozygotes describe the relationship between single-locus genotype frequencies and allele frequencies.

But the single allele 6 might really be two bands that are close together, or there might be a second band that is relatively small and has migrated to the edge of the gel during the electrophoresis. In these circumstances, only one band would show up on the autoradiogram. Forensic laboratories therefore make a "conservative" assumption. They act as if there is a second, unseen band, and they use the excessively large value of $q = 100\%$ for the frequency of the unseen allele. With this modification, the genotype frequency $P = p_i^2$ for apparent homozygotes becomes $P = 2p_i$. Thus, the genotype frequency at the A locus is estimated to be $2 \times 0.035 = 0.070$, for whites, $2 \times 0.092 = 0.184$ for Blacks, and $2 \times 0.105 = 0.210$ for Hispanics.

---

[3] "Randomly mating" is a term of art in population genetics. It does not mean that individuals choose their mates at random, but only that the selections are unrelated to the alleles in question.

[4] Oddly, courts and commentators sometimes overlook the factor of two. See David H. Kaye, Editor's Page: Cross-Examining Science, Jurimetrics J., Winter 1996, at vii.

Table 13.2. Single- and multilocus genotype frequencies estimated with the simple "product rule."

Locus	Genotype	Frequency ($2p_i$ or $2 p_i p_j$) White	Black	Hispanic
A	6,–	.0700	.1840	.2100
B	8, 14	.0039	.0044	.0035
C	10, 13	.0189	.0136	.0214
D	9, 16	.0061	.0055	.0054
Profile (per billion)		32	61	85

With the simple "product rule," the four single-locus frequencies are then multiplied together to yield the three multilocus profile frequencies given in Table 13.2. Some 32 out of every billion whites are estimated to have the incriminating profile. The estimates for Blacks and Hispanics are also quite small, but vary by a factor of nearly three. Other examples would give different values and ranges. This multiplication is exactly correct when the single-locus genotypes are statistically independent. When the frequencies of multilocus genotypes are the simple products of the frequencies of single-locus genotypes, the population is said to be in "linkage equilibrium."

If the population is structured, however, so that some subgroups with allele frequencies that differ from the overall frequencies in Table 13.1 mate preferentially among themselves, then the single-locus genotypes are not independent of one another (and neither are the two alleles at each locus). The proportions depart from those expected in Hardy-Weinberg and linkage equilibrium. If structure is severe, then the simple estimates could be appreciably too low or too high.

The modified ceiling method seeks to give an estimate that is on the high side. Here, the largest frequencies of the alleles seen in any of the three races (rounded up to .1) and the resulting ceiling estimates are shown in Table 13.3.

Table 13.3. Modified ceiling frequencies at each locus and their product.

Locus	Allele	Max. freq.	Max. (freq. or 0.10)	Max. single-locus frequency
A	6	0.105	0.105	$2(.105) = 0.2100$
B	8	3.5	0.100	
	14	6.8	0.100	$2(.1)(.1) = 0.0200$
C	10	10.6	0.106	
	13	13.1	0.131	$2(.106)(.131) = 0.0278$
D	9	7.6	0.100	
	16	6.5	0.100	$2(.1)(.1) = 0.0200$
Ceiling multilocus frequency				2,340 per billion

The interim ceiling estimate, using the upper 95% confidence limits, is slightly larger: 3,730 per billion. NRC Committee on DNA Forensic Science: An Update, at 4-29. This quantity is small, but it is some 40 to 120 times greater than the simple "product rule" estimates in Table 13.2. Like the simple product rule, the ceiling method multiplies various alelle frequencies and factors of two together. Unlike the simple product rule, however, it mixes allele frequencies from different races together to arrive at a number that generally will be higher than the profile frequency in any real population or subpopulation.

   2. *The nature and relevance of the population structure objection.* Having seen how the product and interim ceiling methods work, it is important to ask what the "bitter" and "raging" debate is about. In a particular case, what should the forensic scientist be asked to estimate — the profile frequency in the race of the defendant? In the ethnic subgroup of the defendant? In the race or races of possible perpetrators? In the ethnic subgroups of possible perpetrators? Do the experts who point to the possibility of population structure claim that there is more variability in VNTRs within races than across races? That frequency estimates for structured populations are biased against defendants? That estimates obtained from the major races should not be used to estimate frequencies in the subpopulations? That estimates of VNTR frequencies in structured populations should not be used even to estimate frequencies in the overall population? The article excerpted below challenges the result in *Barney* and other cases that suggest that the ceiling method must be used to estimate the probability of a random match when the actual offender is not known to come from some particular, genetically distinctive subpopulation.

D.H. Kaye
DNA Evidence: Probability,
Population Genetics, and the Courts
7 Harvard Journal of Law and Technology 101 (1994)

   . . . In theory, the smallest "genotype" frequency that the interim 10% ceiling procedure can generate for four probes is $1/(200)^4 = 1/1,600,000,000$, and this "one in a billion" figure should be small enough to delight most prosecutors and to convince most jurors that the match is no accident. However, in practice, genotype frequencies computed with "allele" ceilings will be larger than in theory. For example, the "genotype" in *United States v. Yee* had a frequency of 1/35,000 when adjusted upward with big bins. According to some reports, the ceilings expand this figure by a factor of 2,000, to yield the frequency of 1/17.

   Does the hypothetical possibility of substantial population structure warrant requiring such overestimation? At least in jurisdictions that consider the scientific merit of scientific evidence, the answer depends on how hypothetical the population structure argument is and whether the independence method allows an expert to present a reasonable estimate of the population frequency and to quantify the uncertainty in the figure. [S]peculation about the extent of population structure notwithstanding, in many cases a suitable population frequency estimate is obtainable without resort to extreme overestimation. Furthermore, . . . this proposition has not been widely nor directly disputed in the scientific literature.

My analysis builds on a fundamental distinction between what I denote as a general population case and a subpopulation case. A general population case arises when the appropriate reference population is a broad ethnic or racial population, and a representative sample of "allele" frequencies for this general population is available. A subpopulation case arises when the appropriate reference population is itself a subpopulation (or a population or set of subpopulations not represented in the database). The distinction is important because the presence of substructure in general population cases can be expected to cause predominantly one type of error — an overestimate of the population "genotype" frequency — and only relatively small errors in most instances. As a result, the population structure objection does not justify a rule of law that demands drastic overestimation in these cases.

In applying this distinction, it is critical to understand the limited role that the defendant's ethnic or racial status plays in evaluating the evidence of a match. The choice of the reference population for any frequency estimate should be appropriate to the facts of the case. Is the pertinent frequency to be found from a sample drawn from the general population? From a particular geographic area? From people resembling or related to the defendant? These questions are neither new nor special to DNA evidence. One simple principle supplies the answers: The relevant population consists of all people who might have been the source of the evidence sample. In most cases, this will not be people with a defendant's peculiar ancestry, but people of many ethnic groups. . . .

On the other hand, cases do arise where the population of interest is, arguably, a genetically distinct subpopulation, and where little or no data specific to that subpopulation have been collected. *United States v. Two Bulls*[159] may be such a case. Accused of raping a girl on the Pine Ridge Indian reservation in South Dakota, Matthew Two Bulls moved to suppress testimony of a match between DNA extracted from semen on her underwear and his DNA. The FBI estimated the frequency of the matching pattern in "a Native American population base." However, the appropriate reference population is not all Native Americans, but only the Oglala Sioux. If the FBI's "Native American" database is an amalgam of distinct subpopulations, while the suspect population is dominated by one subpopulation, the frequency of matches in the FBI's database might be beside the point.

---

[159] 918 F.2d 56 (8th Cir. 1990), vacated for rehearing en banc but appeal dismissed due to death of defendant, 925 F.2d 1127 (1991).

Population cases. Although courts are coming to appreciate that a defendant's ancestry is, at best, tangentially relevant to the choice of a reference population, the relationship between the reference population and the estimation procedure has yet to be recognized in any reported opinion. Even the NRC Report, commendably lucid and comprehensive in other areas, overlooks the possibility of adapting the computational method to the circumstances of the case. Yet, a simple, numerical example illustrates how the force of the population structure objection depends on the nature of the reference population. To put the example in a forensic context, suppose that there has been a violent robbery and rape at a rest stop on an interstate highway and that the robber and rapist, identified as a Caucasian, left traces of his blood or semen. Suspicion focuses on a particular man. Careful DNA testing demonstrates that he matches at each locus. If, however, this suspect is not the assailant, then we can say only that someone else is. We have no reason to expect the guilty party to be of the suspect's detailed ancestry or ethnicity. Therefore, we are interested in the frequency of the matching "genotype" among all Caucasians who use interstate highways — and not the proportion in the defendant's subpopulation. When the case comes to trial, the prosecution offers an estimate of the frequency of this "genotype" in Caucasians in order to gauge the probative value of the evidence of the match. The prosecution's expert computes the frequency using the independence method with bin widths equal to match windows in a large national database on Caucasian Americans. The defense objects that the estimate is prejudicial because the population may be structured, so the actual frequency could be dramatically larger than the figures computed by the prosecution's expert using equations (1) and (2).

To test the validity of the defense's objection, let us start with the simplest possible case of population substructure — one locus with only two "alleles" and one population composed of two genetically isolated subpopulations. Subpopulation 1 represents 80% of the population, subpopulation 2 represents 20%. The "allele" frequencies are presented in Table 1.

Allele	Freq. in subpop. 1 (80%)	Freq. in subpop. 2 (20%)	Frequency in total population
1	3/5	1/5	(3/5)(80%) + (1/5)(20%) = 13/25
2	2/5	4/5	(2/5)(80%) + (4/5)(20%) = 12/25

Table 1.
Frequencies of two hypothetical alleles
in a structured population.

This population structure implies that equilibrium does not exist for the broad population, but it does not impeach the equilibrium assumptions within each subpopulation. In the two subpopulations, equations (1) and (2) hold and can be used to deduce the "genotype" frequencies within these subpopulations, and hence, in the total population. Table 2 presents these frequencies.

Genotype	Freq. in subpop. 1 (80%)	Freq. in subpop. 2 (20%)	Frequency in total population
1,2	2(3/5)(2/5)	2(1/5)(4/5)	(12/25)(80%) + (8/25)(20%) = 280/625

Table 2.
Frequencies of one genotype
in a structured population.

Of course, the prosecution expert did not know the subpopulation frequencies. Thus, the expert could use only the population allele frequencies 13/25 and 12/25. Using these values in (1) and (2) gives a calculated population genotype frequency of 2(13/25)(12/25) = 312/625. In this example, the population structure objection is not well-taken. While, the simple independence method is slightly inaccurate, reporting 312/625 instead of the true frequency of 280/625, the error favors the defendant.

This result is the consequence of a general mathematical truth rather than the consequence of a clever choice of numbers. As long as a population is composed of two isolated subgroups, each of which is in equilibrium, the frequency for a diallelic locus estimated by ignoring the population structure overstates the true frequency. As a result, the independence procedure is already conservative, and resort to ceilings is unjustified.[167]

Unfortunately, this example is not representative of more complex systems. With more loci or subpopulations, the multilocus frequencies estimated without considering population structure can overstate the true frequencies for populations. Since the number of possible alleles in VNTR systems is typically 20 or more, and considerably more than two subpopulations may be present, an inequality that applies only to the case of two alleles and two subpopulations is of little use. Nevertheless, even in the more realistic situation, on average, the error due to population structure inures to the defendant's benefit, and the differences between the computed and the true single-locus genotype frequencies will rarely be large.

Partly because this point has not been recognized in the legal literature, the population structure objection has proved remarkably powerful in court. . . .

Nevertheless, the concern is largely misplaced when the pertinent frequency is in the general population. In these cases the population structure objection is far less vexing than many opinions and a few articles suggest. There is a corollary to

---

[167]   The frequency that independence with ceilings produces in our example is 2(3/5)(4/5) = 600/625 as compared to the correct value of 280/625. However, the degree of excessive overestimation inherent in the ceiling method will vary with the numbers used in such examples.

this conclusion. The NRC panel's influential call for more conservative methods in these cases is an unnecessary response even to a hypothetical problem. Post-NRC Report cases excluding genotype frequency estimates on the ground that computational methods less conservative than the NRC's version of independence with ceilings are inadmissible should not be followed. Indeed, under the analysis developed in this article, most of the cases should have found the frequency estimates to be admissible because the circumstances of the offenses pointed to no specific subpopulation of suspects. In these cases, the relevant population in which to consider the frequency of the incriminating match is a general population, and existing computational methods work reasonably well for such populations.

Peter Aldous
Geneticists Attack NRC Report as Scientifically Flawed
259 Science 755-56 (1993)*

London — Last April, a committee of the U.S. National Academy of Sciences hoped to end a bitter disagreement among population geneticists — one that had already had major consequences far outside the realm of scientific discourse. The dispute revolved around a deceptively simple question: What are the odds that an apparent match between a suspect's DNA and DNA taken from a sample discovered at a crime scene is, in fact, merely the result of pure chance? Because scientists couldn't agree on this question, DNA fingerprinting evidence had been thrown out of court in a handful of cases across the United States. Then came the National Research Council's (NRC) Committee on DNA Technology in Forensic Science, which proposed a way of calculating the answer that it believed would be acceptable not only to the warring factions in the DNA fingerprinting community but also to the courts. "I don't think anyone will fight it," said committee member Eric Lander, the Whitehead Institute mathematician-turned molecular geneticist, at the time the report was published (*Science*, 17 April 1992, p. 300).

Nine months later, however, it is clear that Lander's judgment was misplaced. At a meeting on forensic DNA typing held here last month, and in a rash of papers now surfacing in the literature — one of which by Bernard Devlin, Neil Risch, and Kathryn Roeder of Yale University, appears on page 748 of this issue — the NRC's proposed method is under attack from a coalition of population geneticists and statisticians. They argue that the NRC erred too far on the side of caution in trying to address concerns about DNA evidence raised by population geneticists such as Richard Lewontin and Daniel Hartl, now both at Harvard. Worse, the critics say, the NRC panel's solution, called the "ceiling principle," is built on erroneous assumptions about population genetics. "If I were asked if there is any scientific justification to the ceiling principle," says Risch, "I'd have to say no."

Such an assault in the scientific literature on an NRC report is, to say the least, highly unusual. The critics contend that the report's conclusions are seriously flawed because the NRC panel lacked the necessary expertise: "The major problem is that there was no population geneticist on that panel," says Risch. Although committee members approached by *Science* last week generally defended the ceiling principle on the grounds that it was designed to reduce the controversy over the admissibility of DNA evidence in court, several acknowledged that Risch has a point. "We probably could have done with more representation in that respect," says Johns Hopkins geneticist Victor McKusick, who chaired the committee.

Faulty product? Before the NRC panel stepped into the debate, forensic scientists generally used a method called the "product rule" to calculate the probability that a match between two DNA profiles is due to chance. Under the product rule, crime labs simply calculate the frequency with which each allele from a matching pair of DNA profiles occurs in a reference database — usually consisting of profiles of individuals from the same ethnic group as the suspect. Then they multiply these individual frequencies together to calculate the frequency with which the suspect's profile as a whole is likely to be present in the general population. The answer is typically a vanishingly small number — so small that lawyers, judges, and juries were increasingly respectful of the novel form of evidence.

But Lewontin and Hartl (who was then at Washington University in St. Louis) threw the field into an uproar when they argued in court testimony — and in an article in *Science* (20 December 1991, p. 1745) — that the product rule ignores the possibility that particular combinations of alleles may show up more frequently in some subpopulations than in the ethnic group as a whole. The result: The rule could greatly underestimate the probability of a chance match, and so bias evidence against a defendant, they said. More detailed knowledge of the genetics of sub-populations is needed, the duo argued, before probabilities can be calculated with confidence. Most geneticists agreed that it would be nice to have such data, but argued that the chances of a false conviction based on the Lewontin/Hartl concern were negligible.

Entering the NRC panel's ceiling principle. The panel urged the creation of a database consisting of DNA profiles of 100 randomly selected individuals from each of 15 to 20 genetically homogeneous reference populations — such as English, German, Navajo, West African, Vietnamese, and Puerto Rican. Crime labs should determine the highest frequency with which each allele in a suspect's DNA profile occurs in any of these reference populations, the panel said, and these "ceiling" frequencies should be multiplied together to give the matching probability for the profile as a whole. In addition, the report recommended that the minimum figure used in the calculation for any individual allele should be 5%. The NRC panel said it wouldn't take long to assemble such a database, but in the meantime, forensic scientists should use maximum allele frequencies found in each of the four major U.S. ethic groups — Caucasian, black, Hispanic and Native American — or 10%, whichever is higher.

But the attempt to find common ground has itself proved controversial. Some critics of the ceiling principle argue that it doesn't even address the potential problem of sub-populations. "They ignore any attempt to describe the substructuring and try to alter the gene frequencies in a way that many of us regard as illogical," says population geneticist Newton Morton of the Cancer Research Campaign's genetic epidemiology unit in Southampton, England. Morton outlines his objections to the NRC report in a forth-coming issue of the *European Journal of Human Genetics.* If the committee simply wanted conservative estimates of match probabilities, says Morton, it could have urged expert witnesses to "move the decimal point a couple of places." Lewontin is not impressed either: "It's just totally irrational," he says, attacking the NRC panel for picking 10% "out of the air" as the minimum allele frequency in the interim version of the ceiling calculation.

Other critics, such as Devlin, contend that the logic that drove the NRC panel to recommend the ceiling principle comes from a single 1972 paper by Lewontin, which suggested that subpopulations within an ethnic group are at least as distinct genetically as are different ethnic groups. The problem, says Devlin, is that the weight of evidence collected since then — but not cited by the NRC — suggests this is not the case. "It's just simply wrong," he says.

Indeed, Risch, and Roeder present evidence in their paper that there's no real problem with using the standard product rule. They add that computer simulations carried out on deliberately substructured databases, made by merging data from different ethnic groups — some of which were presented at the London meeting by statistician Ian Evett of the UK Forensic Science Service — still give adequate results.

Morton isn't prepared to go quite that far. He points out that good defense lawyers will always attack a simple application of the product rule, making it important to account for substructuring. But he argues that there's a population genetic statistic called "kinship," or F_{ST}.

Despite the barrage of criticism, Lander vigorously defends the ceiling principle. "The courts were asking whether there was any method that met the legal standard for 'general acceptance by the scientific community,'" says Lander, not a method that would precisely describe population substructuring. Pointing out that the ceiling principle could still give odds of up to 6 million to 1 for a typical matching profile, Lander says: "I realize that there are some statisticians who are convinced that the odds should be 6 billion or 6 trillion to 1, but I can't see the practical point." The goal, he says, was to find a method conservative enough to win over most critics of the product rule, while still providing impressive enough odds to allow convictions.

In that regard, the report has been at least partially successful: Although Lewontin is still critical, his co-author Hartl is now a strong supporter of the ceiling principle. And even Bruce Budowle, the leading DNA fingerprinting expert with the Federal Bureau of Investigation, concedes that problems with the admissibility of DNA evidence do seem to have eased since the NRC report came out in favor of DNA fingerprinting.

Indeed, some NRC panel members are worried that the current backlash against the report could undermine the progress Budowle describes. "I only worry that renewed controversy about wanting higher odds will confuse the courts into doubting that there is general acceptance that the ceiling principle provides a conservative estimate," says Lander. But Arizona State University professor David Kaye doubts that defense lawyers would succeed in getting evidence ruled inadmissible because of this latest twist to the forensic DNA typing debate, as "nobody's disputing that some number should be presented." Indeed, Kaye predicts that the scientific criticism of the ceiling principle will eventually cause it to be replaced in the courts by less conservative methods. Maybe so, but it won't die a quiet death. Says Morton: "I don't think [we're] going to quit and forget about this."

NOTES

1. *The legal import of the attack on the ceiling methods.* Does the criticism of the NRC Report's "ceiling principle" by many scientists indicate that it too lacks general acceptance or scientific validity as applied in the courtroom? The judge who penned the *Barney* opinion had this reaction:

> Only eight months have passed since our decision in Barney, not enough time to confirm our speculation that the new methods of statistical calculation proposed by the NRC report will likely receive general acceptance resulting in future admissibility of DNA analysis evidence. However, recent developments have shown that general acceptance may not be easily achieved. It appears that some proponents of DNA analysis, rather than attempting to come to terms with the NRC report or some other compromise on statistical calculation, have taken the offensive and attacked the report's proposed new methods of statistical calculation as unsound.
>
> The People claim the position of these proponents is the majority view and is substantively correct, calling for reconsideration of *Barney*. In doing so, the People persist in miscomprehending the issue before us. As we said in *Barney,* "the point is not whether there are more supporters than detractors, or whether (as the Attorney General and amicus curiae claim) the supporters are right and the detractors are wrong. The point is that there is disagreement between two groups, each significant in both number and expertise. . . ." Our inquiry must end with the perception of such disagreement and consequent lack of general acceptance.
>
> While we are in no position to choose sides in this ongoing dispute, we note that its persistence threatens the admissibility of an extremely important forensic tool. This is no time for purist insistence that DNA evi-

dence should be admitted on one's own terms or not at all. . . . Our hope is that the key players in this dispute will take their cue from Dr. Sensabaugh and agree to a compromise on statistical calculation. Otherwise, they risk preventing any general acceptance at all, thus precluding the admissibility of DNA analysis evidence.

People v. Wallace, 17 Cal. Rptr. 2d 721, 725-26 (Ct. App. 1993).

The judicial impact of the NRC report and the debate among scientists over the ceiling method are reviewed in D.H. Kaye, The Forensic Debut of the NRC Committee Report on DNA, 34 Jurimetrics J. 369 (1994) (suggesting that because the disagreement about the ceiling principle is a dispute about legal policy rather than scientific knowledge, the debate among scientists does not justify excluding ceiling frequencies). Beginning in 1995, many courts concluded that a consensus that ceiling estimates are conservative had at last emerged, and other courts concluded that there is sufficient agreement that reasonable estimates can be obtained with the simple product rule. See cases cited, National Research Council Committee on DNA Forensic Science: An Update, National Research Council, The Evaluation of Forensic DNA Evidence ch. 6 (1996). These courts often rely on a provocative article in which Eric Lander (an early proponent of the ceiling principle, a member of the committee that wrote the 1992 NRC report, and the court's expert who questioned the accuracy of the product rule in Yee) joined forces with the FBI's chemist, Bruce Budowle, to defend the product rule. E.g., People v. Miller, No. 78011 (Ill. Aug. 2, 1996). According to Eric S. Lander & Bruce Budowle, DNA Fingerprinting Dispute Laid to Rest, 371 Nature 735 (1994), "the ceiling principle was intended as an ultra-conservative calculation, which did not bar experts from providing their own 'best estimates' based on the product rule."

2. *Alternatives to ceilings.* Kaye proposes confining the ceiling method to, at most, "subpopulation" cases. As noted in the *Science* news story, population geneticists have devised procedures that use estimates of the extent of population structure to account for its effect in computing the probability of a random match in a structured population. See, e.g., David Balding & Richard A. Nichols, DNA Profile Match Probability Calculation: How to Allow for Population Stratification, Relatedness, Database Selection and Single Bands, 64 Forensic Sci. Int'l 125 (1994) (proposed procedure said to be superior to the "complicated, ad hoc and overly-conservative" ceiling principle); National Research Council Committee on DNA Forensic Science: An Update, The Evaluation of Forensic DNA Evidence (1996). These recommendations are described more fully in the next chapter.

Chapter 14
DNA Typing: Lingering and Emerging Issues

The magistrate judge in *Yee* (chapter 12), after listening to the testimony of many experts in genetics, but few population geneticists and no statisticians, concluded that: "the potential effect of substructure cannot be known or even estimated in any given case, and there is no factor that rationally and indisputably will compensate for its presence." 134 F.R.D. at 211. On the heels of that opinion, a committee appointed by the National Research Council but also lacking in population geneticists and statisticians, offered the two ceiling methods as a pragmatic compromise to compensate for any possible population structure. But that method was not well received in the scientific community and found a mixed reaction in the courts (chapter 13). The NRC appointed a second committee to "update" the report. The committee chair was a population geneticist, and its members included two more population geneticists and two statisticians. This second committee offered yet another set of procedures to do what the *Yee* court said was impossible — to account for the effect of population structure in estimates of the probability that a randomly selected, unrelated person would have the same profile as the evidentiary stain (the "random match probability"). This chapter describes these recommendations, then turns to other lingering and emerging issues associated with DNA identification evidence, namely, DNA databanks, the uniqueness or profiles, the interpretation of mixed stains, and PCR-based methods for DNA profiling.

National Research Council
Committee on DNA Forensic Science: An Update
The Evaluation of Forensic DNA Evidence*
Executive Summary (1996)

Recommendations for Estimating
Random-Match Probabilities

4.1. In general, the calculation of a profile frequency should be made with the product rule. If the race of the person who left the evidence-sample DNA is known, the database for the person's race should be used; if the race is not known, calculations for all the racial groups to which possible suspects belong should be made. For systems such as VNTRs, in which a heterozygous locus can be mistaken for a homozygous one, if an upper bound on the

* Reprinted with permission from *The Evaluation of Forensic DNA Evidence,* Copyright 1996 by the National Academy of Sciences, Courtesy of the National Academy Press, Washington D.C.

frequency of the genotype at an apparently homozygous locus (single band) is desired, then twice the allele (bin) frequency, 2p, should be used instead of p^2. For systems in which exact genotypes can be determined, $p^2 + p(1 - p)\theta$-bar should be used for the frequency at such a locus instead of p^2. A conservative value of θ-bar for the United States population is 0.01; for some small, isolated populations, a value of 0.03 may be more appropriate. For both kinds of systems, $2p_i p_j$ should be used for heterozygotes.

Comment: The formulas referred to and the terminology used in this recommendation are explained in [the report]. The product rule, which gives the profile frequency in a population as a product of coefficients and "allele frequencies," rests on the assumption that a population can be treated as a single, randomly mating unit. When there are partially isolated subgroups in a population, the situation is more complex; then a suitably altered model leads to slightly different estimates of the quantities that are multiplied together in the formula for the frequency of the profile in the population.

In most cases, there is no special reason to think that the source of the evidence DNA is a member of a particular ethnic subgroup within a broad racial category, and the product rule is adequate for estimating the frequency of DNA profiles. For example, if DNA is recovered from semen in a case in which a woman hitchhiker on an interstate highway has been raped by a white man, the product rule with the 2p rule can be used with VNTR data from a sample of whites to estimate the frequency of the profile among white males.[1] If the race of the rapist were in doubt, the product rule could still be used and the results given for data on whites, blacks, Hispanics, and East Asians.

4.2. If the particular subpopulation from which the evidence sample came is known, the allele frequencies for the specific subgroup should be used as described in Recommendation 4.1. If allele frequencies for the subgroup are not available, although data for the full population are, then the calculations should use the population-structure equations 4.10 for each locus, and the resulting values should be multiplied.

Comment: This recommendation deals with the case in which the person who is the source of the evidence DNA is known to belong to a particular sub-

---

[1] The 2p rule involves replacing the quantity p^2 for a "single-banded VNTR locus" with the much larger quantity 2p in the product rule. This substitution accounts for cases in which one VNTR band from a heterozygote is not detected, and the person is mistakenly classified as a homozygote. The substitution also ensures that the estimate of the profile frequency will be larger than an estimate from a more precise formula that accounts for population structure explicitly. The technology for "PCR-based systems," however, does not have these problems, and the 2p rule is inappropriate for these systems. Therefore, Recommendation 4.1 calls for using $p^2 + p(1 - p)\theta$-bar (rather than 2p) in place of p^2 for such systems.

group of a racial category. For example, if the hitchhiker was not on an interstate highway but in the midst of, say, a small village in New England and we had good reason to believe that the rapist was an inhabitant of the village, the product rule could still be used (as described in Recommendation 4.1) if there is a reasonably large database on the villagers.

If specific data on the villagers are lacking, a more complex model could be used to estimate random-match probability for the incriminating profile on the basis of data on the major population group (whites) that includes the villagers. The equations referred to in the second sentence of Recommendation 4.2 are derived from this model.

4.3. If the person who contributed the evidence sample is from a group or tribe for which no adequate database exists, data from several other groups or tribes thought to be closely related to it should be used. The profile frequency should be calculated as described in Recommendation 4.1 for each group or tribe.

Comment: This recommendation deals with the case in which the person who is the source of the evidence DNA is known to belong to a particular subgroup of a racial category but there are no DNA data on either the subgroup or the population to which the subgroup belongs. It would apply, for example, if a person on an isolated Indian reservation in the Southwest, had been assaulted by a member of the tribe, and there were no data on DNA profiles of the tribe. In that case, the recommendation calls for use of the product rule (as described in Recommendation 4.1) with several other closely related tribes for which adequate databases exist.

4.4. If possible contributors of the evidence sample include relatives of the suspect, DNA profiles of those relatives should be obtained. If these profiles cannot be obtained, the probability of finding the evidence profile in those relatives should be calculated with formula 4.8 or 4.9.

Comment: This recommendation deals with cases in which there is reason to believe that particular relatives of the suspect committed the crime. For example, if the hitchhiker described in the comment to Recommendation 4.2 had accepted a ride in a car containing two brothers and was raped by one of them, but there is doubt as to which one, both should be tested. If one brother cannot be located for testing and the other's DNA matches the evidence DNA, then the probability that a brother of the tested man also would possess the incriminating profile should be computed.

NOTES

1. *The recommendations for computing random match probabilities and the ceiling method.* The formulae referred to in the recommendations reproduced above are given in the committee report. The arguments behind them are a subtle mix of population genetics theory and empirical analysis. Excerpts from the chapter on genetics, which define the population structure parameter and give the flavor of the argument are presented in Appendix A.

Even assuming that the committee's views reflect a scientific consensus, does the recommendation that forensic experts use the product rule as modified to handle population structure imply that ceiling calculations should be inadmissible? See Clark v. State, No. 95-2638, 1996 WL 470874 (Fla. Ct. App. Aug. 21, 1996) ("the . . . 1996 report . . . effectively demonstrates that the "ceiling principle" has no validity whatever and that, contrariwise, product rule calculations are appropriate as a matter of scientific fact and law."); National Research Council Committee on DNA Forensic Science: An Update, The Evaluation of Forensic DNA Evidence 5-33, 6-23 (1996) (pre-publication copy) ("the interim ceiling principle is not needed, and can be abandoned," but "[t]he ceiling procedure is simply one possible method for producing VNTR profile frequency estimates that are expected to be larger than their true values. If, for courtroom use, advocates desire or courts require probable upper bounds on the true value of the frequency, the ceiling approach should yield a very high upper bound.").

2. *Relatives.* Suppose that a defendant wants to establish, either on cross-examination of the prosecution's statistical expert or by calling another expert, that, according to the formulas provided by the NRC committee, the probability of a matching profile in a relative is substantially greater than the random match probability. What foundation, if any, should be required?

Fred Barbash
Search for Killer Draws Blood;
All Men in Welsh Neighborhood
Face 'Voluntary' DNA Test
The Washington Post
Apr. 14, 1995, at A1

Police are conducting a kind of blood drive in the St. Mellons neighborhood of Cardiff. They are knocking on the doors of male residents, inviting them to the police station to donate. They've got a list, and before they're done, they expect to tap 2,000 to 5,000 doors.

They don't want a lot of blood, just a sample, enough to be sent to a lab for a DNA analysis. The invitation is hard to refuse: The population of St. Mellons has been told that anyone who declines risks calling attention to himself as a possible suspect in the rape and murder of 15-year-old Claire Hood. . . .

The Old World has become the New World, at least when it comes to criminal investigations. Mass DNA screening has been used several times by law enforcement authorities in Britain. They tried it in Cardiff before after a rape a few years ago, Jones said, unsuccessfully. It was successful in a 1986 investigation of a rape and murder in the English Midlands, and the case became the subject of a Joseph Wambaugh book called, "The Blooding." Police in Germany did a mass DNA screening of 1,900 people last year and helped solve the murder of the daughter of a U.S. Army sergeant stationed there.

Experts say they know of no comparable investigation in the United States, where relatively strict constitutional protections against unreasonable searches could stand in the way. While the screening may be "voluntary," technically speaking, the threat of heightened police interest in anyone who declines to volunteer adds a coercive element. . . .

It is a costly technique. [Detective Superintendent Colin] Jones estimates that the full cost of 2,000 analyses will be $150,000. . . .

Jones believes the killer is in the community and that the blooding will flush him out, one way or the other. He recalled — with satisfaction — how in a similar case a few years ago, someone paid a friend 50 pounds to take the test for him. The friend shot his mouth off in a pub, and the culprit was arrested and convicted.

Fred Barbash
British Authorities Launch
1st National DNA Database
The Washington Post
Apr. 11, 1995, at A15

British law enforcement authorities inaugurated the world's first national DNA database today, predicting that in a few years it will contain 5 million DNA "profiles" for use in crime solving. . . .

The computerized database will allow investigators to test crime-scene evidence — such as sperm and blood samples — within 48 hours to determine if it matches samples in the database.

Britain's top law enforcement official, Home Secretary Michael Howard, who dedicated the facility with a publicity blitz, called it the best tool for crime fighting since the advent of fingerprinting. . . .

While the FBI and some states, including Virginia, have established DNA libraries for investigative purposes, Britain's is the first to cover an entire country. Congress has authorized future creation of a nationwide database in the United States.

In concept, the database is no different from a fingerprint database. Crime-scene investigators throughout the country will be given a small kit of sampling tools — such as mouth swabs and bar-coded protective plastic containers for hair or saliva samples. Anyone charged with a serious crime — including burglary, assault and homicide — can be required to provide a sample. When crimes occur and the evidence includes human tissue, blood, semen or saliva, a DNA analysis will be run through the central computer to find a match and perhaps a suspect for the crime. Admissibility in court, which is common now, will be up to trial judges in each case.

Lynne Tuohy
Technology Opens Doors to
Closed Cases: Sex Offenders' DNA in Database
Hartford Courant, June 26, 1996, at A3

Old, unsolved crimes become "cold cases." Most have clues, but no suspects. In the past five years, close to 400 rape cases in Connecticut have fallen into that category.

Connecticut State Police Tuesday announced a new assault on those cases, putting on-line a powerful crime-fighter: the DNA Data Bank for Sex Offenders.

With the DNA profiles of more than 800 convicted sex offenders now entered in the databank and an additional 350 being processed, scientists at the state police forensic laboratory believe they have a large enough database to begin "cold searches."

The scientists will take evidence from unsolved rape cases — principally semen samples — and profile the genetic coding, or DNA, of the unknown assailants. They then will run those DNA codes against those in the sex offender databank in search of a match.

It takes the scientists three to four weeks to fully process a DNA sample. Once the profile is done, it can be entered into the computer and compared electronically with the DNA profiles of all known offenders in the database in less than five minutes.

Henry Lee, chief criminalist and director of the state police forensic laboratory, said the lab would begin cold searches Tuesday and continue working the unsolved cases "one at a time." . . .

Michael Fleeman
First DNA Database "Hit" Leads to Arrest
Orange County Register
Nov. 9, 1995, at A22

California has recorded its first apparent match between a crime and a person listed in a state-run DNA database, resulting in the arrest of a man in the 1992 rape and slaying of a 76-year-old woman in Contra Costa County, sources said. . . .

California, whose DNA lab gained worldwide attention in the O.J. Simpson trial, has now joined other states benefiting from a powerful crime-fighting tool that soon will be used nationally when a countrywide DNA database is established. Currently, 19 states and the District of Columbia have some sort of DNA registry. . . .

The database contains the genetic profiles of about 4,000 violent felons and convicted sex offenders, who are required by law to provide blood samples when they're released from prison or mental hospitals.

The database is expected to swell to about 30,000 genetic profiles by the end of next year as increasingly more blood samples from released inmates are tested and the results stored in the computer . . . .

Laura Vandendorpe
DNA Detectives
Portland Oregonian
Mar. 8, 1995, at B01

. . .

The value of genetic matching was underscored recently when state police helped indict Robert Wayne North Jr. in an unsolved 1993 kidnaping and rape case. North was serving time for first-degree attempted rape at the Oregon State Penitentiary when criminalists matched a sample of his DNA with evidence found at the crime scene. . . .

DNA typing was made admissible as evidence in Oregon state courts in 1991, the same year that the Legislature passed a law requiring criminals convicted of violent crimes to provide blood samples.

These samples, now numbering 6,300, are collected in test tubes, dried onto scraps of white cloth and chilled in an oversized freezer at the Portland Police Bureau before being analyzed and loaded into a database.

"We are at the forefront of what's happening in the nation in forensic science DNA research," said Beth Carpenter, the assistant lab director of the Oregon State Police crime lab. "Oregon is one of 21 states with laws mandating that criminals give samples of blood. So far, we have entered 5,500 genetic codes from the samples into our database." . . .

Three sites on the genetic code from each criminal are stored in the police database and compared with the same sites on the crime scene DNA. If a match is found between the database and the evidence, which carries odds of approximately 10 million to 1, four more sites are compared.

After a match is found between these seven sites, another sample of blood is drawn from the criminal and compared with the blood sample on file and the crime scene evidence. The process is repeated several times to guarantee an accurate correlation and takes up to six months to finish.

The probability of accurately identifying a criminal from genetic evidence depends on the specifics of the case, Humphreys said. In late February, North was indicted when seven sites on his genetic code matched sites from a crime scene sample. The probability that someone other than North committed the 1993 kidnaping and rape was less than 1 in 10 billion, according to forensic scientist Randy Wampler of the Oregon State Police.

"North was Oregon's first cold hit, or conviction based mostly on a match from the database system," Carpenter said. "We're working right now to become incorporated in the national database, which has about 35,000 genetic entries from criminals across the country. Hopefully, this can be used as a valuable tool to catch repeat offenders in violence and sex crimes."

NOTES
DNA Databases
and Search Strategies

1. *Genetic privacy.* It has been said that "DNA analysis and DNA databanking [might] represent the first step toward an Orwellian society . . . ." Jean E. McEwen, Sherlock Holmes Meets Genetic Fingerprinting, Boston Coll. L. Sch. Mag., Spring 1994, at 44; see also E. Donald Shapiro & Michelle L. Weinberg, DNA Data Banking: The Dangerous Erosion of Privacy, 38 Clev. St. L. Rev. 455 (1990). What dangers are there in storing VNTR profiles? In retaining blood samples? Whose samples (if any) should be included in databases for forensic use? See, e.g., National Research Council, DNA Technology in Forensic Science 113-23 (1992); Dan L. Burk, DNA Identification: Assessing the Threat to Privacy, 24 U. Toledo L. Rev. 87 (1992).

2. *Constitutional privacy.* What are the constitutional limitations on taking DNA samples from suspects? See, e.g., State ex rel Juvenile Dep't v. Orozco, 878 P.2d 432 (Or. Ct. App. 1994). From convicted felons? See Jones v. Murray, 763 F. Supp. 842 (W.D. Va. 1991) (Virginia's DNA databanking law for convicted felons held constitutional), modified, 962 F.2d 302 (4th Cir. 1992); Rise v. State, 59 F.3d 1556 (9th Cir. 1995) (Oregon statute providing for warrantless removal of blood from convicted sex offenders for DNA databank held constitutional), cert. denied, 116 S.Ct. 1554 (1996); People v. Calahan, 649 N.E.2d 588 (Ill. Ct. App. 1995) (Illinois DNA databank statute constitutional); State v. Olivas, 856 P.2d 1076 (Wash. 1993) (Washington statute constitutional).

3. *Searches and match probabilities.* Does the fact that a defendant was identified as a result of an exhaustive search through a database reduce the probative value of a match? Should the random match probability be excluded or modified for "cold hits" rather than matches with a single suspect picked for testing on the basis of non-DNA evidence? The two NRC committees and various statisticians have offered conflicting advice, as indicated below:

National Research Council Committee on DNA Technology in Forensic Science
DNA Technology in Forensic Science 124 (1992)

The distinction between finding a match between an evidence sample and a suspect sample and finding a match between an evidence sample and one of many entries in a DNA profile databank is important. The chance of finding a match in the second case is considerably higher, because one does not start with a single hypothesis to test (i.e., that the evidence was left by a particular suspect), but instead fishes through the databank, trying out many hypotheses.

If a pattern has frequency of 1 in 10,000, there would still be a considerable probability (about 10%) of seeing it by chance in a databank of 1,000 people. Although there are statistical methods for correcting for such multiple testing, the committee considers that approach unwise, because it requires that the population frequency estimates of genotypes are accurate to a degree that is unlikely to be achieved (because sample sizes are limited). There is a far better solution: When a match is obtained between an evidence sample and a databank entry, the match should be confirmed by testing with additional loci. The initial match should be used as probable cause to obtain a blood sample from the suspect, but only the statistical frequency associated with the additional loci should be presented at trial (to prevent the selection bias that is inherent in searching a databank). Forensic DNA typing laboratories should recognize that they will require additional loci beyond those used in the databank to prove a case against a suspect. Preparations should be begun now to have additional loci characterized and available for general use before any DNA profile databank comes into common use.

National Research Council Committee on DNA Forensic Science: An Update The Evaluation of Forensic DNA Evidence
5-9 to -10 (1996)

There are different ways to take the search process into account. The 1992 NRC report recommends that the markers used to evaluate a match probability be different from those used to identify a suspect initially. However, . . . [t]o avoid identifying several suspects who must then be investigated, one might need to use a large number of markers in the database search. Then . . . those markers could not also be used in further analysis. If the amount of DNA in the evidence sample is too small, following the recommendation in the 1992 report could leave too few additional loci for computing a match probability . . . .

A correction to account for the database search can be made in computing the match probability. Let Mi denote the event that the i-th DNA profile in the database matches the evidence sample. To decide if the database search itself has contributed to obtaining a match . . . , and event of interest is M, that at least one of the database profiles matches the evidence sample. Suppose that we hypothesize that the evidence sample was not left by someone whose DNA profile is in the database (or a close relative of such a person) and find that under this hypothesis P(M) is small. The usual statistical logic then leads to the rejection of that hypothesis in favor of the alternative that (one of) the matching profile(s) in the database comes from the person who left the evidence sample.

Under the hypothesis that the person leaving the evidence sample is not represented in the database of N persons, a simple upper bound on the probability of M is given by

$$P(M) \leq \Sigma_i P(M_i) = NP(M_i). \tag{5.3}$$

. . .

Equation 5.3 motivates the simple rule sometimes suggested by forensic scientists: multiply the match probability by the size of the database . . . .

David J. Balding & Peter Donnelly
Evaluating DNA Profile Evidence When the Suspect is Identified Through a Database Search*
41 J. Forensic Sci. 603 (1996)

In this paper, we argue that in a situation in which exactly one matching individual is found from a database search, the strength of the DNA evidence against that individual is *not* reduced relative to the setting in which the suspect has been identified on other grounds and subsequently subjected to DNA profiling. (For convenience, . . . we will refer to this scenario as the "probable cause" setting.) In fact, in the database search, under reasonable assumptions, the DNA evidence will be slightly stronger than in the probable cause setting. . . .

There is a broad consensus that the appropriate method for quantifying the strength of DNA evidence is through likelihood ratios. The DNA evidence relates directly to the question of whether the suspect is the source of the crime stain. In

---

*Extracted with permission from the *Journal of Forensic Sciences,* Vol. 41, No. 4, copyright American Society for Testing and Materials, 100 Barr Harbor Drive, West Conshohocken, PA.

this context, the likelihood ratio can be written:

$$LR = \frac{P(\text{DNA evidence} \mid \text{suspect is source})}{P(\text{DNA evidence} \mid \text{suspect is not source})}. \tag{1}$$

In the database search scenario that we are considering, the DNA evidence consists of the measured DNA profiles of the suspect and the crime stain (including the observation that they match) and the fact that particular other individuals do not match the crime stain profile. . . .

We now consider the likelihood ratio in more detail. Write E_s and E_c for the measured genotypes of respectively, the suspect and the source of the crime stain, O for the event that none of the other individuals in the database match E_c, and G for the hypothesis that the suspect is the source of the crime stain. Then,

$$LR = \frac{P(E_s, E_c, O \mid G)}{P(E_s, E_c, O \mid G^c)} = \frac{P(O \mid G)}{P(O \mid G^c)} \quad \frac{P(E_s, E_c \mid G, O)}{P(E_s, E_c \mid G^c, O)}, \tag{2}$$

in which we introduce the notation G^c for "not G." In considering the first factor in (2), it may be easier to compare $P(O^c \mid G)$ and $P(O^c \mid G^c)$. Under hypothesis G^c, there are two ways in which O^c might occur. It may be that one of these individuals is the source of the crime stain. Alternatively, none of them may be the source but at least one happens by chance to match E_c. Under hypothesis G, only the second of these explanations is possible. It follows that $P(O^c \mid G) < P(O^c \mid G^c)$, so that $P(O \mid G) > P(O \mid G^c)$, and the first factor in (2) is larger than unity. . . .

In the probable cause setting, the likelihood ratio for DNA evidence is

$$\frac{P(E_s, E_c \mid G)}{P(E_s, E_c \mid G^c)}. \tag{3}$$

In the match-binning framework, this likelihood ratio is often taken to be the reciprocal of the relative frequency of the profile in some population. In ignoring positive correlations of the genotypes of distinct individuals, such an equation rests on independence assumptions that may not be appropriate. Nevertheless, we note that if these correlations are ignored, the second factor in (2) will be equal to the likelihood ratio (3) in the probable cause setting. More generally, in the light of (positive) genetic correlations, knowledge that certain individuals do not share the profile in question may warrant a revision downward of estimates of its frequency, and thus the second factor in (2) will be larger than (3).

In summary, the strength of the DNA evidence, as measured by the likelihood ratio, is greater when the evidence results from a database search than in the probable cause setting. One source of intuition for this conclusion is that the database search has served to eliminate some individuals as possible sources of the crime stain. Although the difference in strength is difficult to quantify in general, it seems likely that (2) will be only slightly larger than (3), and hence, it may be convenient and not unfavorable to the defendant, to calculate and report (3). . . .

. . . Consider two cases. In one, the suspect is identified through weak and unreliable eye-witness identification. Subsequent DNA testing reveals that he matches the crime stain profile. In the second case, a DNA database search identifies a match between an individual (who then becomes the suspect) and the crime stain, and subsequent investigation unearth the weak and possibly unreliable eye-witness identification evidence. Assuming that the DNA evidence is identical in each case, and similarly for the identification evidence, and that the different types of evidence are independent in each case, the jury will be presented with identical information from the eyewitness and from the forensic scientist in describing the DNA match. . . .

It is, of course, true that (in the absence of other information about the individuals concerned) the searching of a database is more likely to result in the finding of a match than if a single individual were tested. . . . This probability is, however, not relevant to the strength of the DNA evidence against the (unique) individual found to match. In particular, we do not accept the claim . . . that in the database search case the strength of the DNA evidence is reduced, approximately by a factor of N.

. . . [A] particular individual is on trial. The DNA evidence against him is that his DNA profile matches the crime stain profile while the profiles of certain other individuals do not. The individuals in the database are not collectively on trial, and the chance that at least one (or exactly one) of them would match if all were innocent is therefore not relevant.

NOTE

Revealing a database search. The defendant is charged with murder. He was identified as a suspect as a result of a search of a database of 10,000 previous violent felony offenders. No other profile in the database matched the crime stain DNA from the presumed murderer. An expert is prepared to testify that the random match probability for the matching genotype is 1/1,000,000. The accuracy of this figure is not contested. The defendant objects to introduction of the estimate, however, on the ground that the laboratory did not follow the procedure of searching the database on a subset of loci, then deriving the match probability from a further, independent set of loci. Should the objection be sustained?

If the objection is overruled, should the expert, in an effort to be complete, reveal how the defendant's DNA profile was obtained? Would mentioning the fact of the database search over defendant's objection conflict with the rule that evidence of prior offenses is generally inadmissible?

If the expert were to follow the recommendation of the 1996 NRC report to use NP in place of P, what figure would be presented and how would it be characterized?

State v. Bloom
516 N.W.2d 159 (Minn. 1994)

KEITH, Chief Justice.

Agreeing with the state on the central issue in each of three separate criminal appeals decided today, we hold . . . that if the evidentiary foundation provided by the proponent of the evidence is sufficient, a properly qualified expert may express the opinion that, to a reasonable degree of scientific certainty, the defendant is (or is not) the source of the bodily evidence found at the crime scene. . . .

The appeal in this case is an accelerated appeal by the state of a pretrial suppression order in a rape prosecution. . . . The alleged facts in this case are as follows: Shortly after 1:00 a.m. on November 23, 1992, J.L.P., a 34-year-old woman, was entering her home in Brooklyn Park when she was grabbed from behind by a Caucasian man. The man, whom she did not see well enough to identify, forced her into her car, pulling a stocking cap over her face. . . . After assaulting her, he drove her home and dropped her off, then abandoned her car nearby. After preserving semen samples taken from the victim in the sexual assault examination and other semen samples found in the car, the BCA, prepared a DNA profile of the samples. This consisted of six separate probes and resulting autorads for comparison with autorads made from probes of known DNA. James Liberty, who does forensic work at the BCA and has attended an FBI course on forensic aspects of DNA technology, testified that using information from two of the six probes to make a computer search of the BCA's sex-offender DNA database, he came up with five potential suspects, including defendant, whose DNA matched at those two loci. Comparing the probe data of the five potential suspects found in this manner, he determined that one of them, defendant, "stood out." Then, by comparing the database pattern at all five loci available in defendant's prior database profile he determined that there was a match with the pattern at all five loci on the autorads made from the assailant's semen. Liberty then did another complete DNA test on both the assailant's semen and on a new sample of defendant's blood, taken after his arrest, as well as on blood from the victim's boyfriend and from another individual, and he produced new autorads. The victim's boyfriend and the other individual were excluded as possible sources. The defendant's DNA profile matched the crime scene sample at all nine loci tested. After using five loci and finding a match at each, Liberty made some calculations and concluded that there was a 1 in 93,700 chance that a randomly selected person would match at all five points. Professor Daniel Hartl, a Professor of Biology at Harvard and an earlier critic of some of the statistical computations that forensic scientists were making based on FBI databases, testified (by telephone) for the state at the suppression hearing that, using the "interim ceiling method" recommended by the National Research Council, there was a 1 in 634,687 chance of a random match across the five loci. He testified that Liberty had obtained the less-impressive 1 in 93,700 figure by making some "adjustments" that were not needed because the interim ceiling approach, which Liberty too had used, had those adjustments built into it. Dr. Hartl, if permitted, would further testify at trial that in fact there was a nine-loci match and that in his opinion the nine-loci match constituted "overwhelming evidence that, to a reasonable degree of scientific certainty, the DNA from the victim's vaginal swab came from [defendant], to the exclusion of all others." The trial court, . . . ruled (1) that the jury could be told (a) that defendant's DNA was consistent with crime scene samples on each of the nine bands tested, (b) the frequency of each individual band and (c) nonstatistical opinion testimony that defendant's DNA profile is consistent with that of the assailant, but (2) the jury could not be told (a) that the frequency of the profile in the population based on five tests is 1 in 634,687 (or, for that matter, 1 in 93,700) or (b) that the opinion of Dr. Hartl is as just quoted. . . .

[T]he issue in this case is not the admissibility of DNA evidence but the form that the presentation of the evidence takes. . . . We have concluded that the DNA expert should be allowed to express the opinion that there is a "match" between the defendant's DNA profile and that left by the assailant at the scene or on the victim. The strength of the expert's opinion is something the jury should be told; it will depend in part on the degree of the expert's confidence in the opinion and in part on the underlying statistical foundation for the opinion. [T]he expert should be allowed to phrase the opinion this way: that given a reliable multi-locus match, the probability that the match is random or coincidental is extremely low.

The expert should not, of course, be allowed to say that a particular profile is unique. Nor should the expert be allowed to say that defendant is the source to the exclusion of all others or to express an opinion as to the strength of the evidence. But should a properly qualified expert, assuming adequate foundation, be allowed to express an opinion that, to a reasonable scientific certainty, the defendant is (or is not) the source? We believe so. In reaching this conclusion, we merely are saying, as we intended all along, that the admissibility in a criminal trial of qualitative expert opinion testimony on DNA identification techniques be governed by the same basic rules of admissibility that historically have applied to qualitative expert opinion testimony based on other scientific identification techniques. See, e.g., State v. Rean, 353 N.W.2d 562, 564 (Minn. 1984) (where there was expert opinion testimony that it was "highly probable" that shoe prints found at scene were made by defendant's shoes).

We believe that allowing this sort of verbal, qualitative, non-statistical presentation of the underlying statistical evidence will lead to more agreement among reputable experts at trials and may decrease the likelihood of there being a battle of experts (over the reliability of the random match probability figure), with one expert cancelling out or discrediting the other. . . .

Reversed in part and remanded for trial.

NOTES

1. Bloom's *holding.* Under the Minnesota Supreme Court's opinion, should Dr. Hartl be permitted to testify at trial that the nine-loci match constitutes "overwhelming evidence that, to a reasonable degree of scientific certainty, the DNA from the victim's vaginal swab came from [defendant], to the exclusion of all others"?

2. *The probability of uniqueness.* The proposed testimony just quoted would render the debate over match probabilities and database searches — not to mention the controversy over the product and ceiling rules — academic. But the court states that "[t]he expert should not, of course, be allowed to say that a particular profile is unique." Why not? The 1992 NRC report stated, without further elaboration: "Regardless of the calculated frequency, an expert should — given with [sic] the relatively small number of loci used and the available population data — avoid assertions in court that a particular genotype is unique in the population." National Research Council Committee on DNA Technology in Forensic Science DNA Technology in Forensic Science 92 (1992). Not long after the report, a member of the committee who reported that she wrote part of the chapter in which this admonition appears, testified in an Arizona case involving a three-locus match that "one can . . . uniquely identify every person with just a sample of . . . DNA," and in a Washington case that "there's absolutely no doubt those two samples came from the same human being." Her testimony prompted appellate courts to reverse the convictions in those cases. State v. Hummert, 905 P.2d 493 (Ariz. Ct. App. 1994), review granted, (1995); State v. Buckner, 890 P.2d 460 (Wash. 1995).

Likewise, the 1996 NRC report, which noted the growing number of loci and greater availability of population data, was more willing to countenance testimony such as that proposed in *Bloom:*

> How small must [the probabilities] be before a suspect profile can be considered unique? The match probability computed in forensic analysis refers to a particular evidentiary profile. That profile might be said to be unique if it is so rare that it becomes unreasonable to suppose that a second person in the population might have the same profile. More precisely suppose that a given genetic profile, G, occurs with probability [P] and has been observed exactly once, namely, in the evidence sample. In a population of N unrelated persons, the probability, before a suspect has been profiled, that at least one G occurs among the N−1 unobserved profiles is $1 − (1 − P)^{N-1} \leq NP$. . . . Suppose that the profile frequency, P, is one in ten billion. Then, for the US population of about 250 million, the product is 1/40. It could be argued that if the probability of finding another person with this profile is such a small fraction, probably no other person in the United States has it. Clearly, if the fraction is very small, the profile is almost certainly unique. But we leave it to the courts to decide just how small this fraction should be in order to declare a profile to be unique.

National Research Council Committee on DNA Forensic Science: An Update, The Evaluation of Forensic DNA Evidence 5-11 (1996) (pre-publication copy). The committee also gave a formula for the probability that no two profiles in a population are unique. Id. at 5-12.

    3. *The admissibility of warm and fuzzy words over cold and hard numbers.* The Bloom court endorsed "allowing . . . verbal, qualitative, non-statistical presentation of the underlying statistical evidence . . . ." In Commonwealth v. Daggett, 622 N.E.2d 272, 275 n.4 (Mass. 1993), a plurality of the Massachusetts Supreme Judicial Court disparaged an expert's testimony that used phrases like "highly likely" but did not include numbers because the commonwealth "cited no authorities and presented no testimony . . . that the use of such terms is generally accepted by the scientific community in evaluating the significance of a match." "The point is," the plurality insisted, "not that this court should require a numerical frequency, but that the scientific community clearly does." Id. Is whether a scientist may describe the implications of a DNA match in qualitative rather than quantitative terms a question of scientific practice or legal policy? See D.H. Kaye, The Forensic Debut of the National Research Council's DNA Report: Population Genetics, Ceiling Frequencies, and the Need for Numbers, 34 Jurimetrics J. 369, 381-82 (1994).

B.S. Weir
Statistical Interpretation of the DNA Evidence
June 21, 1995

    The jury in this trial is being asked to determine the guilt or innocence of a defendant. They are being asked to make this determination, in part, on the DNA evidence to be described below. It is now widely recognized that the appropriate way to assign weight to such evidence is by means of a likelihood ratio. This ratio is the probability of evidence of matching DNA profiles from the defendant and the evidentiary sample if the sample were contributed by the defendant, divided by the probability of the evidence if the evidentiary sample was not contributed by the defendant.

    Likelihood ratio methodology has been described and used by statisticians, academic lawyers, forensic scientists, statisticians who have appeared as experts for the prosecution and for the defense, as well as defense attorneys. . . .

    The DNA from various items of evidence is consistent with Orienthal James Simpson (OS) having had contact with the Bundy scene where the bodies of Nicole Brown Simpson (NB) and Ronald Goldman (RG) were found. These notes are concerned with assessing the strength of that DNA evidence E by determining the probabilities of the evidence under the alternative hypotheses that either C: OS had contact with the Bundy scene or [*not-C*]: OS did not have contact with the Bundy scene. There are some items of evidence for which OS is excluded as a possible contributor, and then statements can be made about probabilities of the evidence under hypotheses involving NB or RG. The likelihood ratio L is defined as the probability of the evidence under hypothesis C (Pr($E \mid C$) — read as "probability of E given C") divided by the probability of the evidence under hypothesis *not-C*.

$$L = \frac{\mathrm{Pr}(E \mid C)}{\mathrm{Pr}(E \mid not\text{-}C)}$$

The assignment of prior odds in favor of C, and the determination of posterior odds through multiplication by L, is not addressed in these notes. A Bayesian viewpoint is not being adopted. In particular, statements about the chances of any of the evidentiary items contain DNA from someone other than OS will not be made. . . .

Notice of Objections to Testimony Concerning DNA Evidence and Memorandum in Support Thereof
People v. Simpson
No. BA097211, 1995 WL 126286
(Cal. Super. Ct. Mar. 20, 1995)

A report prepared by prosecution expert Prof. Bruce Weir declares that "[t]he appropriate way of presenting the extent to which the evidence of matching DNA profiles favors one scenario over another is by means of a likelihood ratio. This ratio is formed by dividing the probability of the evidence under the first scenario by the probability of the evidence under the second scenario." The two "scenarios" that Weir evaluates are (1) that defendant was the source of a particular sample, and (2) that some other person was the source of the sample. He concludes that evidence of a match between defendant and two samples "is at least 270 million times more likely to have arisen" if defendant is the source of the samples than if some person unrelated to defendant is the source of the samples.

The use of likelihood ratios to characterize the value of DNA evidence is novel. Although the appropriateness of using likelihood ratios in connection with DNA evidence has been debated in the academic literature, defense counsel have found no previous cases in which likelihood ratios were used in this manner. Defendant contends that the use of likelihood ratios is an unacceptable deviation from the standard practice of presenting data on the frequency of matching genotypes and the rate of laboratory error.

First, defendant contends that likelihood ratios are not generally accepted in the scientific community as a method for characterizing DNA evidence and are therefore inadmissible under Kelly. Second, defendant contends that likelihood ratios are difficult to understand and are likely to confuse the jury. Although a careful expert can present DNA statistics in the form of a likelihood ratio without committing the prosecutor's fallacy, the line between correct and fallacious statements of the evidence is quite subtle when the statistics are presented in this format. Consequently, when likelihood ratios are used there is a strong danger that the expert will slip over the line into fallacious misstatement, and an even greater danger that jurors will slip over the line into fallacious conclusions regardless of what the expert says. Defendant therefore objects to likelihood ratios in general under Evidence Code Section 352 [the analog of Federal Rule of Evidence 403].

If the prosecution chooses to contest defendant's position on this matter, then a hearing under Evidence Code Section 402 may be necessary to establish, as a matter of preliminary fact, whether it is misleading and prejudicial to use likelihood ratios to characterize the value of DNA evidence. At such a hearing, defendant would present testimony from leading experts in the psychology of human judgment and decision making to support his position. . . .

NOTES
Likelihood Ratios
and Mixed Stains

1. *Likelihood ratios in court.* Simpson's counsel were unable to locate "previous cases in which likelihood ratios were used . . . ." Are you aware of any? See chapter 10. For a previous case involving serologic markers, see State v. Klindt, 389 N.W.2d 670 (Iowa 1986); Russell Lenth, On Identification by Probability, 26 J. Forensic Soc'y 197 (1986). For a subsequent case, see United States v. Thomas, 43 M.J. 626 (A.F. Ct. Crim. App. 1995) (in the prosecution of a serviceman stationed in Germany for killing his Filipino girlfriend, a population geneticist testified that "conservatively, it was 76.5 times more likely that the samples tested by Dr. Pflug . . . came from the victim than from someone else in the Filipino population. Dr Prenger also concluded that it was 843.2 times more likely that the DNA fragments found by Dr. Pflug in the samples from the rental car and the ax . . . came from the victim than from anyone else in the general population.").

2. *Likelihood ratios in statistics.* Likelihood functions and ratios are a fundamental and well-established concept in statistics. See, e.g., H. Cramer, Mathematical Models of Statistics ch. 33 (1946); C. Rao, Linear Statistical Inference and Its Applications ch. 5 (2d ed. 1973).

3. *Likelihood ratios for DNA evidence.* If VNTR profiles are considered either to match or not to match, if it is certain that the same profile will match when measured a second time, and if the probability of a coincidental match is some number P, then the likelihood ratio for a match is 1/P. For a profile such that P is say, 1 in a million, the likelihood ratio is one million, and an expert might testify that the match is one million times as probable under the hypothesis that the defendant's DNA is present in both samples than under the hypothesis that the DNA comes from two unrelated people who just happen to have matching DNA profiles.

But the line between a "match" and something less than a "match" in VNTR fragment lengths is a construct that is forced upon the data (see chapter 12), and more complicated VNTR-profile likelihood ratios do not use match windows and bins, but rather consider the extent of matching at each allele. These ratios have been termed "similarity likelihood ratios" and advocated on the ground that they make better use of the DNA data. See authorities cited, National Research Council Committee on DNA Forensic Science: An Update, The Evaluation of Forensic DNA Evidence 6-30 (1996) (pre-publication copy). The first NRC committee choose not to address the use of likelihood ratios to describe the strength of DNA evidence. The second committee remarked that "[n]one of the [likelihood ratios] that have been devised for VNTRs can be dismissed as clearly unreasonable or based on principles not generally accepted in the statistical community." Id.

In *Simpson,* Dr. Weir sought to use match-binning likelihood ratios to interpret mixed stains — those with DNA fragments from more than one person. The defendant never "present[ed] testimony from leading experts in the psychology of human judgment and decision making to support his position" because the prosecution insisted that Dr. Weir confine himself to describing certain frequencies appearing in the denominators of the ratios. The defense argued that a rather different statistic was appropriate. Appendix B describes the two different approaches. By using only part of the likelihood ratio, the evidentiary strength of the mixed stains was overstated, but Simpson never raised that objection.

4. *The prejudicial effect of likelihood ratios.* Is the objection that likelihood ratios are inherently prejudicial well-taken? Is it supported by the work of "leading experts in the psychology of human judgment and decision making"? Which do you think is more likely to be misconstrued: (a) the probability that a randomly selected person would have matching DNA is one in a million, or (b) the match is one million times as probable under the hypothesis that the defendant's DNA is present in both samples than under the hypothesis that the DNA comes from two unrelated people who just happen to have matching DNA profiles? The second NRC committee had this reaction:

[p]rejudice might exist because the proposed LRs [likelihood ratios] do not account for laboratory error, and a jury might misconstrue even a modified

version that did account for it as a statement of the odds in favor of S. As for the possible misinterpretation of LRs as the odds in favor of identity, that too is a question of jury ability and performance to which existing research supplies no clear answer.

Id. at 6-31. The committee explained:

No research has as yet tested the reactions of triers of fact to the detailed presentations of evidence on DNA profiling that are encountered in the courtroom. We do know that people can make frequent and systematic errors in tasks that require them to assess probabilities or to draw inferences using probabilistic information. Yet, despite this plethora of research into information processing in other contexts, we know very little about how laypersons respond to DNA evidence and how to minimize the risk that they will give DNA evidence inappropriate weight. . . .

Id. at 6-32. The committee therefore recommended further research into these questions. Id. at 6-34.

State v. Russell
882 P.2d 747 (Wa. 1994)

MADSEN, Judge.

George W. Russell was convicted by a King County jury of the first degree murder of Mary Ann Pohlreich and the aggravated first degree murders of Carol Beethe and Andrea Levine.

Russell appealed, and the Court of Appeals certified his appeal to this court . . . .

Russell first challenges the trial court's conclusion that PCR testing of DNA has gained sufficient scientific acceptance to admit the results of such testing in court. The PCR tests pertained to count 1, and were conducted on a vaginal swab taken from Mary Ann Pohlreich's body and a piece of stained upholstery removed from Smith McLain's truck [that Russell had borrowed on the night of the murder]. . . .

The AmpliType DQ alpha test kit is one of the few PCR test systems sufficiently developed for forensic use, and was used to conduct the PCR tests in this case. This kit was developed by the Cetus Corporation and will be referred to hereafter as the Cetus kit. The Cetus kit uses probes that identify the six different alleles present in the HLA DQ alpha genetic marker system. . . . The six alleles present in this system are denominated as 1.1, 1.2, 1.3, 2, 3, and 4. These alleles are combined in pairs in each person, because one is received from each parent. There are 21 possible pairs of these traits, and each pairing is called a "genotype". . . .

PCR testing at the DQ alpha locus provides a power of discrimination of approximately 83 to 94 percent. This compares favorably to that of the ABO red cell typing system. By itself, however, PCR testing can neither provide individual identification nor the very high power of discrimination possible with RFLP methods of DNA typing. PCR analysis has proven useful, though, in including or excluding criminal suspects in circumstances where conventional typing has failed or insufficient DNA was available for RFLP testing. RFLP analysis requires relatively large samples of DNA, whereas PCR testing is capable of analyzing minute and degraded samples. Other advantages of the PCR technique are that it takes much less time to achieve results than RFLP, is less expensive, and achieves results that are easier to interpret.

The PCR test results in this case indicated that the sperm on the vaginal swab contained Russell's DQ alpha genotype, and that the DQ alpha type recovered from the blood-stained upholstery was consistent with Pohlreich's blood but inconsistent with Russell's and McLain's. Prosecution witnesses concluded that Russell's DQ alpha genotype occurs in approximately 5 to 10 percent of the population. Therefore, 90 to 95 percent of the population (but not Russell) could be excluded as sources of the sperm in Pohlreich's body. Since Pohlreich's DQ alpha genotype is shared by 4 to 9 percent of the population, approximately 91 to 96 percent of the population (including Russell), could be excluded as sources of the bloodstain in McLain's truck. This exclusion was significant since Russell had told McLain that his (Russell's) vomit was the source of the upholstery stain.

The trial court admitted these test results after a lengthy pretrial *Frye* hearing. . . .

The core concern of *Frye* is whether the evidence being offered is based on an established scientific methodology. This involves both an accepted theory and general acceptance of the technique used to implement that theory. The *Frye* inquiry does not require acceptance of the laboratory testing procedures used in the case before the court. If the methodology is sufficiently accepted in the scientific community at large, concerns about the possibility of error or mistakes made in the case at hand can be argued to the factfinder.

This reference to the scientific community at large is important — a court looks not only to the technique's acceptance in the forensic setting but also to its acceptance by the wider scientific community familiar with the theory and underlying technique. Under *Frye,* the court looks for "general acceptance in the appropriate scientific community", that is, acceptance by the community of scientists familiar with the challenged theory. Furthermore, *Frye* requires only general acceptance, not full acceptance, of novel scientific methods. This only makes sense since full acceptance would obviate the necessity of a *Frye* hearing. . . .

During the 2-week *Frye* hearing in this case, the State introduced four experts to support its position that PCR analysis meets the scientific acceptance required by *Frye*. These experts included Dr. Rebecca Reynolds, a Cetus employee; Dr. Daniel Geraghty, a molecular geneticist employed by Fred Hutchinson Cancer Research Center; Dr. Cecelia Von Beroldingen, forensic DNA specialist at the Oregon State police crime laboratory; and Dr. Edward Blake of Forensic

Science Associates, a forensic serologist who conducted the PCR tests at issue. The defense presented Dr. John Gerdes, DNA analysis director at Immunological Associates of Denver; Dr. Kristin Skogerboe, a clinical chemist at the Laboratory of Pathology; and Dr. Glenn Evans, associate molecular laboratory professor at the Salk Institute.

Dr. Reynolds acknowledged that PCR testing received attention first from biomedical researchers, but she added that over 30 laboratories were either in the process of implementing DQ alpha typing, using the Cetus kit, or already using it on casework. She regarded the PCR technique as a useful and reliable source of genetic markers.

Dr. Von Beroldingen also testified to the growing use of the Cetus kit by both private and governmental laboratories. She further stated that the forensic application of PCR testing in this case met with generally accepted scientific principles and practices.

Dr. Daniel Geraghty testified that PCR analysis was the major technical development of the last 10 years in molecular immunology and that it met with no pockets of resistance. He saw no serious dispute regarding the scientific principles involved in PCR testing. Fred Hutchinson uses the Cetus kit to help determine compatibility for bone marrow transplants. The same technology is used by Dr. Blake and Fred Hutchinson, with the only difference being the method of seeing the result. Dr. Blake uses an enzymatic color change which turns blue if the enzyme is present, while Fred Hutchinson uses a chemifluorescent method. Dr. Geraghty described them both as "perfectly reasonable and well established methods". . . . Fred Hutchinson uses the same amplification method as Dr. Blake, with all reagents coming from Cetus, and also has approximately 50 thermal cyclers, which the doctor termed "very reliable".

Dr. Geraghty stated that PCR was now used by almost every molecular biologist in the world, and added that he had heard no criticisms of the Cetus kit. Dr. Geraghty said that Dr. Blake's tests in this case were conducted properly and he expressed confidence in the results even though Dr. Blake conducted only one test on the swab. (The blood stain sample was performed in triplicate).[4]

Defense expert Dr. John Gerdes testified that while RFLP has been used by research labs for 15 to 20 years, PCR is a newer method. Dr. Gerdes felt it was too early for the Cetus kit to produce reasonable results in a forensic setting because of the danger of typing a contaminant, the low power of discrimination, and the lack of independent validation of laboratories other than Dr. Blake's. On cross examination, Dr. Gerdes stated that he saw no evidence of contamination in the present case.

Dr. Skogerboe was concerned that insufficient validation studies had been

---

[4] Following Dr. Geraghty's testimony, the State moved to have him retest the vaginal swab at state expense, with a defense witness observing. The defense opposed the motion and the court denied it as untimely.

performed on the use of the Cetus kit for crime-scene evidence. On cross examination, however, she acknowledged that her current laboratory had been using PCR on clinical samples for diagnosis for 1 1/2 years, and she regarded the benefits of using PCR as outweighing any problems associated with the test.

Dr. Evans regarded the Cetus kit as unreliable for use in a forensic setting. He added, however, that he believed PCR analysis would "revolutionize society, particularly forensics", and saw no resistance to the techniques of enzymatic amplification of DNA in general.

Following this testimony, the trial judge found the results of PCR testing at the HLA DQ alpha locus admissible under the *Frye* standard. The judge found that the underlying principle and techniques of PCR had been generally accepted by the scientific community, and added that DQ alpha testing and typing had gone sufficiently beyond the experimental stage to gain general acceptance in the scientific community. She observed further that the DQ alpha gene has been subjected to considerable scientific study, especially in the fields of immunology and medicine. The variations of the gene are well known, readily identified, and easily distinguished, making this gene an appropriate genetic marker for forensic use. She also noted that the population frequencies of the various genotypes occurring at the DQ alpha locus were not contested. The judge concluded that the fact that a scientific procedure might yield a false result if not performed properly did not render it inadmissible and that any problems associated with PCR testing at the DQ alpha locus went to the weight to be given the evidence.

On appeal, Russell challenges these conclusions, and argues that the State failed to demonstrate that PCR analysis has gone through the extended period of use and testing in the forensic community necessary to achieve the general scientific acceptance required under the *Frye* standard.

Russell derives most of his support for this position from a recent report prepared by the Committee on DNA Technology in Forensic Science, under the auspices of the National Academy of Sciences. The Committee was formed in 1990 to address the general applicability and appropriateness of the use of DNA technology in forensic science, the need to develop standards for data collection and analysis, aspects of the technology, management of DNA typing data, and legal, societal and ethical issues surrounding DNA typing. Nat'l Research Coun., DNA Technology in Forensic Science 1-2 (1992) (hereinafter DNA Technology). While most of the resulting report focuses on the RFLP method of DNA identification, it also discusses the PCR technique.

The Committee found no scientific dispute about the validity of the general principles underlying DNA typing. The Committee apparently found less agreement, however, over whether a given DNA method might be scientifically appropriate for forensic use. "Before a method can be accepted as valid for forensic use, it must be rigorously characterized in both research and forensic settings to determine the circumstances under which it will and will not yield reliable results."

The basic thrust of the report was the need to standardize forensic DNA typing to the extent possible (realizing that the lack of control over crime-scene evidence makes standardization problematic). To achieve such standardization, the report recommended quality-assurance programs, individual certification, laboratory accreditation, and state or federal regulation. With regard to PCR testing, the Committee observed that one commercial kit for forensic PCR analysis has been marketed. While the report voiced no criticisms of the existing kit, it saw a potential for the introduction of unreliable kits and the misuse of kits. The committee believes that nonexpert laboratories will run a significant chance of error in using kits.

> We therefore recommend that a standing committee . . . consider the issue of regulatory approval of kits for commercial use in forensic DNA analysis. Even though no precedent exists for regulation of tests in forensic applications, we believe that it might be necessary for a government agency to test and approve kits for DNA analysis before their actual forensic use.

The report then summarized its findings regarding the forensic use of PCR analysis:

> PCR analysis is extremely powerful in medical technology, but it has not yet achieved full acceptance in the forensic setting. The theory of PCR analysis . . . is scientifically accepted and has been accepted by a number of courts. However, most forensic laboratories have invested their energy in development of RFLP technology and have left the development of forensic PCR technology to a few other laboratories. Thus, there is no broad base of experience in the use of the technique in identity testing. Forensic PCR-based testing is now limited for the most part to analysis of genetic variation at the DQ-alpha locus in the HLA complex. . . . [F]urther experience should be gained with respect to PCR in identity testing. Information on the extent of the contamination problem in PCR analysis and the differential amplification of mixed samples needs to be further developed and published. A great deal of this information can be obtained when a number of polymorphic systems are available for PCR analysis. . . . Considerable advances in the use of PCR in forensic analysis can be expected soon; the method has enormous promise.

Russell points to this language as evidence of the lack of general scientific acceptance of PCR testing. In a subsequent chapter on the use of DNA in the legal system, however, the report acknowledges the admissibility of DNA evidence, without distinguishing between the PCR and RFLP methodology, so long as the precautions outlined are taken (as discussed later in this opinion):

> It is not necessary, at this stage of development of DNA typing, to hold extensive admissibility hearings on the general validity of the scientific techniques, although cases will still arise in which the procedures used to report a match will be questioned. . . . As a general matter, so long as the safeguards we discuss in this report are followed, admissibility of DNA typing should be encouraged. There is no substantial dispute about the underlying scientific

principles. However, the adequacy of laboratory procedures and of the competence of the experts who testify should remain open to inquiry.

The report's message regarding the forensic use of DNA typing has been interpreted contrarily to Russell's position both by experts in the scientific community and a number of court decisions. On April 14, 1992, a New York Times article stated that courts should cease to admit DNA evidence until laboratory standards have been tightened and the technique is established on a stronger scientific basis. Gina Kolata, U.S. Panel Seeking Restriction on Use of DNA in Courts, N.Y. Times, Apr. 14, 1992, at A1. In response, the chairman of the DNA Committee stated that "'[w]e think that DNA can be used in court without interruption.'" Gina Kolata, Chief Says Panel Backs Courts' Use of a Genetic Test, N.Y. Times, Apr. 15, 1992, at A1. A statement included in the Committee's final report referred to the Times articles and provided this clarification:

> We recommend that the use of DNA analysis for forensic purposes, including the resolution of both criminal and civil cases, be continued while improvements and changes suggested in this report are being made. There is no need for a general moratorium on the use of the results of DNA typing either in investigation or in the courts. We regard the accreditation and proficiency testing of DNA typing laboratories as essential to the scientific accuracy, reliability, and acceptability of DNA typing evidence in the future. Laboratories involved in forensic DNA typing should move quickly to establish quality-assurance programs. After a sufficient time for implementation of quality-assurance programs has passed, courts should view quality control as necessary for general acceptance.

A California Court of Appeal described the final NRC report as concluding that "there is indeed a need for standardization of laboratory procedures and proficiency testing (as well as appropriate accreditation of laboratories) to assure the quality of DNA laboratory analysis". People v. Barney, 8 Cal.App.4th 798, 812, 10 Cal.Rptr.2d 731 (1992). The absence of such safeguards does not mean, however, that DNA analysis is not generally accepted. Rather, the question becomes whether a laboratory has complied with generally accepted standards in a given case. Barney, at 812-13, 10 Cal. Rptr.2d 731.

The Colorado State Supreme Court also concluded that concerns about the forensic use of a given scientific theory bear on the weight accorded DNA typing evidence rather than its admissibility. Fishback v. People, 851 P.2d 884, 893 (Colo.1993) . . . . Similarly, a federal district court held that concerns about the forensic applications of RFLP did not bar its admissibility in United States v. Jakobetz, 747 F.Supp. 250, 256-58 (D.Vt.1990), aff'd, 955 F.2d 786 (2d Cir.), cert. denied, 113 S.Ct. 104 (1992).

In addition to citing the *DNA Technology* report, Russell points more specifically to the absence of accreditation of forensic laboratories, the lack of published literature and professional testing of PCR, and the small number of forensic laboratories doing PCR work to demonstrate that PCR testing has not yet endured sufficient scientific analysis for general acceptance and thus admissibility under *Frye*.

As we evaluate these challenges it is important to reiterate that our inquiry is not confined to an examination of PCR testing in the forensic laboratory setting. Rather, we are concerned with the extent of peer review and acceptance as manifested in the general scientific community.

PCR analysis is in routine use in many settings. PCR testing has been used in HIV detection and diagnosis; in identifying microorganisms in the aquatic environment, as well as in food, dairy, soil, and clinical samples; in neonatal screening for cystic fibrosis and sickle cell anemia; in detecting chromosomal abnormalities and mutations; in gene replacement therapy; in human pedigree analysis; in studying the epidemiology of Lyme disease; and in the new fields of molecular anthropology and molecular paleontology. PCR analysis also is being used to monitor environmental contamination, to establish the new field of diagnostic molecular pathology, and to help identify those killed in the Persian Gulf War. In this case, Dr. Geraghty testified for the State that PCR is used by nearly every molecular biologist in the world, and defense expert Dr. Evans stated that he saw no resistance to the techniques of enzymatic amplification in general. Moreover, we do not agree with Russell's contention that only a few forensic laboratories are using PCR analysis. Cetus reported that over 30 forensic labs were performing DQ alpha typing as of March 1991. Cetus also reports that the FBI began using the Cetus kit in 1992. Dr. Reynolds testified that the British Home Office has adopted DQ alpha as its screening test. As of December 1989, the HLA DQ alpha typing system reportedly had been used in 106 forensic cases involving the analysis of over 1,000 evidence samples. Rhea Helmuth et al., HLA-DQ-Alpha Allele and Genotype Frequencies in Various Human Populations, Determined by Using Enzymatic Amplification and Oligonucleotide Probes, 47 Am. J. Hum. Genetics 515, 521 (1990). As of October 1991, PCR-based DQ alpha typing methods were used in biological evidence in over 250 cases.

Russell is correct that the National Research Council report cites accreditation and governmental regulation of forensic laboratories as potential external mechanisms needed to ensure quality science. However, the report also observed that no precedent exists for regulation of forensic testing. Furthermore, Dr. Geraghty stated that Fred Hutchinson, a medical research institute, had not yet received accreditation to perform DNA testing. While accreditation and regulation may be desirable in the medical as well as the forensic setting, it is not necessary to bar the use of DNA technology until such safeguards are in place. "Although the court is not the ideal forum for ensuring quality science, the adversary process is a means by which those who practice 'bad' science may be discredited, while those who practice 'good' science may enjoy the credibility they deserve."

Russell also states that PCR testing lacks sufficient validation studies for admissibility. We disagree and conclude that extensive validation studies have been conducted on PCR testing. Following repeated validation experiments, the

FBI found that typing of the DQ alpha gene by PCR and detection of specific alleles can be accomplished, when the typing is done using proper protocols, without producing false positive or false negative results. Catherine T. Comey & Bruce Budowle, Validation Studies on the Analysis of the HLA DQ alpha Locus Using the Polymerase Chain Reaction, 36 J. Forensic Sci. 1633 (1991). An Oregon Court of Appeals found "no dispute" that scientific articles concerning the PCR method exist and that peer-reviewed journals publish many of the articles. State v. Lyons, 124 Or.App. 598, 608-09, 863 P.2d 1303 (1993). The court also noted that the Cetus Corporation has published a bibliography listing more than a thousand scientific articles on PCR analysis. Lyons, at 608-09, 863 P.2d 1303.

Russell next argues that the problems with using PCR in the forensic setting are so serious that this method of DNA testing fails to meet the standard of general acceptance required under Frye. The areas of concern that he identifies include differential amplification, misincorporation, and contamination.

Again, we note that whether these problems occur in the forensic setting does not affect the general scientific acceptance of PCR methodology. Rather, these problems bear on the question of the reliability of the individual test . . . . Once the general underlying principles are accepted, as they are here, then both the proponents and opponents of a particular test should be able to garner the necessary information to present both sides of the issue to the factfinder. Any remaining questions about the reliability of the particular tests in this case should be examined under the standards for admissibility of expert testimony, which is within the trial court's discretion. . . .

It is important at this point to explain the relationship between *Frye* and ER 702 and how it affects this case. As stated earlier, the concern of *Frye* is whether the evidence being offered is based on generally accepted scientific theory and methodology. *Frye* is not concerned with the acceptance of the results of a particular study or of the particular testing procedures followed in the case before the court. These concerns are addressed under the ER 702 inquiry of whether the expert testimony would be helpful to the trier of fact. If the testing before the trial court shows that the testing procedure as performed was so flawed as to be unreliable, the results may be inadmissible because they are not helpful to the trier of fact. If the evidence survives an ER 702 challenge, however, these questions then are considered by the trier of fact in assessing the weight to be given the evidence.

The problems that Russell now raises do not affect the general acceptance of the underlying PCR methodology. The possibility that differential amplification, contamination, or misincorporation affected the test results in a given case can be assessed by a trial court pursuant to ER 702, as the following discussion illustrates.[5] . . .

---

[5] Russell does not contend that any of these problems occurred here. Furthermore, none of the experts who testified either for the defense or the prosecution raised any of the concerns that Russell now mentions in connection with the tests performed in this case.

Thus, the potential testing problems that Russell cites are either detectable or preventable. Expert witnesses may assist the trial court in determining whether the testing procedures are so flawed that exclusion of the results are warranted under ER 702. If the results are admitted, the same experts can assist the trier of fact in determining what weight to give the test results in light of the perceived problems.

Adherence to proper laboratory procedure is essential in assessing the reliability of PCR test results and thus their admissibility under ER 702. As one commentator notes, it will be advisable for attorneys to be extremely familiar with the laboratory and with the person who conducts the PCR tests. Thus, if the opponent to the test procedure raises issues regarding contamination, the well-prepared proponent of the evidence should be able to counter the arguments with specific descriptions, photographs or other documentation of the care and diligence with which samples are handled and tested in the laboratory. On the other side of the fence, if the opponent of the evidence is aware of sloppy technique, the lack of controls and/or unsuitable laboratory design which could foreseeably lead to contamination, this would be an important argument against the evidence.

We see no question that the principles and methodology underlying PCR analysis at the DQ alpha locus have been generally accepted by the scientific community. We hold that the Cetus kit test results in this case were the product of generally accepted scientific theory and technique and were properly admitted under *Frye.* In so holding, however, we caution that this conclusion by no means assures the automatic admission of PCR DQ alpha test results. Serious flaws in a given test may render PCR evidence unreliable and thus inadmissible pursuant to ER 702. In seeking to admit PCR evidence, counsel must be prepared to establish adherence to proper laboratory procedures and protocols.

It is also important to note that while both parties have assumed here that *Frye* requires the general acceptance of the Cetus kit as well as DQ alpha testing, that is not the case. The trial court properly determined that the issue here was the admissibility of PCR testing at the DQ alpha locus. The Cetus kit is one means by which such testing is performed; there undoubtedly will be others. The Cetus kit is simply one tool for carrying out generally accepted PCR methodology, and any concerns about its implementation in a given case are matters to be addressed to the trial court under ER 702. . . .

ANDERSEN J., dissenting.

. . .

The [1992 NRC] report recommends that before a new DNA typing procedure can be used, it must have not only a solid scientific foundation but also a solid base of experience. Since the report concludes that there is no broad base of experience in the use of the PCR technique in identity testing, I cannot conclude that the report is endorsing the use of PCR at this time.

The majority also relies upon the NRC's response to a *New York Times* newspaper article which had opined that the report had advocated a moratorium on the use of DNA evidence in courts until better accreditation and protocols were in place. While the Council did deny that sweeping characterization of its report, that response certainly does not give the committee's endorsement to every method of DNA analysis. . . . The NCR report points out that before any particular DNA typing method is used for forensic purposes, precise and scientifically reliable procedures for performing the steps must be established. "It is meaningless to speak of the reliability of DNA typing in general — i.e., without specifying a particular method."

Additionally, and perhaps most importantly to me, is that it is the job of the judiciaries, and not the job of scientists, to make the legal decision whether evidence is admissible in a court of law. We look to the NRC report to demonstrate general scientific acceptance, or lack thereof, and not to make the determination of legal admissibility. Admissibility depends upon a particular state's law regarding the standards for admissibility of novel scientific evidence. If the report demonstrates a lack of general acceptance by the relevant scientists (which I believe to be the case) then we should decide as a matter of state law that the evidence is not yet admissible in Washington under the *Frye* test. . . .

The majority opinion cites to three cases apparently to support its conclusion that the NRC report says that PCR evidence should be admissible. . . . All three cases so cited concern only the admissibility of RFLP evidence and address the issue of whether the present lack of laboratory accreditation and established protocols, which could cause errors in a given case, should go to the admissibility or the weight of the evidence. . . . None of these three cited cases are relevant to the issue of whether the PCR technique is sufficiently accepted for use in a forensic setting. To the date this opinion is written, no appellate court in a *Frye* jurisdiction has allowed the admission of PCR evidence!

. . .

I disagree with the majority's conclusion that the reliability of the test due to contamination and unknown mixed samples goes to the weight of the evidence; it goes instead to the critical issues of the validity and reliability of the test when used in the forensic laboratory. At the *Frye* hearing, Dr. John Gerdes also explained some of the differences between DNA testing in the medical setting and in the forensic setting. He testified that the forensic specimens are generally contaminated, or mixed specimens, meaning that they are from a crime scene where they are contaminated with either bacteria or other DNA, that they are not controlled samples and are usually in very small amounts. He testified that for these reasons the specimen itself introduces an order of complexity in the testing. Dr. Gerdes testified that there is definitely a difference between applying PCR technology in a research or clinical setting and applying it to the examination of crime scene evidence in a forensic laboratory because the forensic source introduces inhibitors, and degradation and variability in terms of predictable outcome. . . .

In spite of such testimony, the majority opinion concludes that "extensive validation studies have been conducted on PCR testing" and cites to Kamrin T.

MacKnight, Comment, The Polymerase Chain Reaction (PCR): The Second Generation of DNA Analysis Methods Takes the Stand, 9 Santa Clara Computer & High Tech.L.J. 287, 344 (1993). Although this law student article does make this statement, it cites to just one study to support this statement. That study is described in a 1991 article published by the FBI. This FBI validation study was published a year before the NRC published its exhaustive report on DNA testing which concluded that PCR has not yet achieved full acceptance in the forensic setting and that information on the extent of the contamination problem in PCR analysis and the differential amplification of mixed samples needs to be further developed and published. Dr. Gerdes testified that the FBI study was a first step but does not go far enough. Dr. Evans testified that he would not recommend the FBI study be accepted for publication in the scientific journals for which he reviews because some of the studies could not be reproduced and because he knew that some of the test results regarding contamination were wrong.

Dr. Evans testified that the RFLP test is reliable and accepted for use on crime scene evidence. Report of Proceedings, at 1506. However, with regard to PCR, he testified that it was difficult to ensure that a PCR test is amplifying DNA from the forensic sample and not from a contaminant. . . .

Based upon the *Frye* hearing record in this case, the case law and the literature . . . I would conclude that PCR DNA testing is not yet generally accepted by the scientific community for use on crime scene evidence and hence should not have been admissible at the trial of this case. [T]he NRC . . . report's conclusion that PCR in the forensic setting has not yet gained full acceptance in the scientific community can only be ignored at our peril. . . .

. . . I have no doubt that this kind of evidence, in some form, is the wave of the future — at the present moment in scientific history, however, that is where it belongs — in the future.

Thus, I dissent.

JOHNSON, SMITH, and UTTER, JJ., concur.

NOTES

Emerging Methods
of DNA Profiling

1. *Framing the issue. Russell* revisits the perennial question of *Frye* and other special tests for scientific evidence: What must be generally accepted (or scientifically valid, reliable, or the like)? The Cetus kit? The ability of the polymerase chain reaction to replicate DNA fragments accurately? How much testing of a specific protocol must be completed before a court should deem that protocol sufficiently accepted or validated? Is the answer to be found in the opinions of scientists or in the uses to which they put the procedure or others like it? Is the possibility of error due to laboratory contamination or lack of proficiency of the purchasers of a kit a bar to its use in all cases, or is only a subject for case-by-case inquiry? Does the wording of Rule 702 offer much guidance?

2. *The growing use of PCR-based methods.* PCR is not a single, forensic technique for identifying DNA. Indeed, in itself, PCR identifies nothing. It merely "amplifies" the quantity of DNA to permit subsequent analysis. The extent to which the various analytic techniques have been validated and the population genetics of the various genotypes have been studied varies widely. In the final excerpt for this chapter, the 1996 NRC report describes the PCR-based systems in use and under study. Although the report seems to approve of several systems, it does not suggest that all are ready for forensic use. And, it concludes: "We expect continued development of new and better methods and hope for prompt validation so that they can quickly be brought into use." National Research Council Committee on DNA Forensic Science: An Update The Evaluation of Forensic DNA Evidence 2-14 (1996) (pre-publication copy).

National Research Council
Committee on DNA Forensic Science: An Update
The Evaluation of Forensic DNA Evidence*
2-11 to -16 (1996) (pre-publication copy)

. . . PCR-based typing is widely and increasingly used in forensic laboratories in this country and abroad. Many forensic laboratories carry out PCR-based typing along with VNTR typing. Some laboratories, particularly smaller ones, have gone exclusively to PCR techniques.

Once the amount of DNA is amplified by PCR methods, the analysis proceeds in essentially the same way as with VNTRs. There are minor procedural modifications, but the general procedures are the same — identification of fragments of different size by their migration in an electric field.

Another class of repeated units is STRs, short tandem repeats of a few nucleotide units. . . . Because the total length is short, STRs can be amplified with PCR. Alleles differing in size can be resolved to the scale of single bases with both manual and automated sequencing technologies. Moreover, it has proved possible to co-amplify STRs at multiple loci, allowing significant increases in test throughput. They do not have as many alleles per locus as VNTRs, but that is compensated by the very large number of loci that are potentially usable. As more STRs are developed and validated, this system is coming into wide use.

Any procedure that uses PCR is susceptible to error caused by contamination

---

* Reprinted with permission from *The Evaluation of Forensic DNA Evidence,* Copyright 1996 by the National Academy of Sciences, Courtesy of the National Academy Press, Washington D.C.

leading to amplification of the wrong DNA. The amplification process is so efficient that a few stray molecules of contaminating DNA can be amplified along with the intended DNA. Most such mistakes are readily detected after the PCR analysis is completed because the contaminating DNA yields a weak pattern that differs from the predominant pattern. Most undetected contamination is likely to lead to a false-negative result; that is, a nonmatch might be declared when a match actually exists. Nevertheless, false-positive results are also possible, in which the profile from an evidence sample is falsely declared to match the genetic type of another person. That could happen, for example, if by mistake the same amplified sample were used twice in a given analysis, instead of two different samples. Procedures for minimizing the occurrence of errors are discussed [elsewhere].

A second disadvantage of most markers used in PCR-based typing is that they have fewer alleles than VNTRs and the distribution of allele frequencies is not as flat. Hence, more loci are required to produce the same amount of information about the likelihood that two persons share a profile. Furthermore, some of these loci are functional (they are genes, not just markers). Those are more likely to be subject to natural selection and therefore might not conform strictly to some of the population-genetics assumptions used in evaluating the significance of a match. In future, loci that are brought on as markers should be chosen so as not to be linked to important disease-producing genes, so that the markers can more confidently be treated as neutral and to provide greater assurance of genetic privacy. In fact, some 3-base repeating units are the cause of severe human diseases, and even some VNTRs might have disease associations. These are not used in forensics, however.

One application of PCR in forensic work has used the DQA locus (the gene is called DQA, its product, DQα. In distinction to VNTRs, the alleles at this locus code for a protein. This locus is part of the histocompatibility complex, a group of highly variable genes responsible for recognizing foreign tissue. Eight alleles at the DQA locus have been identified, although only six are commonly used in forensic work. The different alleles can be distinguished by specific probes. With these six alleles there are 21 possible genotypes; six homozygous and 15 heterozygous.

Analysis of DQA uses the same DNA hybridization technique as VNTR analysis. In this case, probes specific for individual alleles are placed in designated locations on a membrane (because the probes, rather than the DNA to be typed, are fixed on the membrane, this is called a *reverse* blot). The amplified DNA is then added, and the DNA from whatever DQA alleles are present hybridizes with the appropriate probe. A stain reaction specific for double-stranded DNA shows up as a colored spot on the membrane wherever specific hybridization occurs. The positions of the colored spots on the membrane strip indicate which alleles are present.

The DQA system has several advantages. It is quick and reliable, so it is useful as a preliminary test. It can also be used, with other markers, as part of a more detailed DNA profile. In practice, a substantial fraction of suspects are cleared by DNA evidence, and prompt exclusion by the DQA test is obviously preferable to waiting months for results of a VNTR test. On the average, the DQA genotype of a given person is identical with that of about 7% of the population at large, so an innocent person can expect to be cleared in short order 93% of the time. This high probability might not be achieved if the sample includes DNA from more than one individual.

Another system that is beginning to be widely used is the Amplitype polymarker (PM) DNA system. This system analyzes six loci simultaneously: DQA, LDLR (low-density-lipoprotein receptor), GYPA (glycophorin A, the MN blood-groups), HBGG (hemoglobin gamma globin), D7S8 (an anonymous genetic marker on chromosome 7), and Gc (group-specific component). There are two or three distinguishable alleles at each locus. The system has been validated with tests for robustness with respect to environmental insults, and there is substantial information on population frequencies . . . .

Other PCR-based techniques have been or are being developed. For example, D1S80 is a VNTR in which the largest allele is less than 1,000 bp long. Its value for forensic analysis has been validated in a number of tests. The locus consists of a 16-base unit that is repeated a variable number of times. There are more than 30 distinguishable alleles. The size classes are fully discrete, so usually each allele can be distinguished unambiguously. However, some ambiguous alleles are caused by insertion or deletion of a single base and these complicate the analysis.

Another class of genetic marker is mitochondrial DNA. Mitochondria are microscopic particles found in the cell, but outside the nucleus, so they are not associated with the chromosomes. The transmission of mitochondria is from mother to child; the sperm has very little material other than chromosomes. Ordinarily, all the many mitochondrial particles in the cell are identical. There is no problem distinguishing heterozygotes from homozygotes, since only one kind of DNA is present. Since mitochondrial DNA is always transmitted through the female, all the children of one woman have identical mitochondrial DNA. Therefore, siblings, maternal half-siblings, and others related through female lines are as much alike in their mitochondrial DNA as identical twins. Mitochondrial DNA is particularly useful for associating persons related through their maternal lineage, for example, for associating skeletal remains to a family.

A highly variable region of mitochondrial DNA is used for forensic analysis. The techniques have been validated and there is a growing body of frequency data. A disadvantage for forensic use is that siblings cannot be distinguished, nor can other maternally related relatives, such as cousins related through sisters. Since mitochondria are inherited independently of the chromosomes, mitochondrial information can be combined with nuclear data to yield probabilities of a random match.

A promising technique is minisatellite repeat mapping, or digital typing, which, apart from length variation, detects sequence differences within the base sequences repeated in VNTRs. Although technical limitations still need to be overcome before this system can be used in forensic analysis, it could have a particular advantage, in that it uses the same loci that have already been extensively studied in various populations and subpopulations.

Table 2.1 summarizes the most widely used systems.

Table 2.1 Genetic Markers Used in Forensic Identification

Nature of Variation at Locus

Locus Example	Method of Detection	Number of Alleles	Diversity[5]
Variable Number Tandem Repeat (VNTR) — Loci containing repeated core sequence elements, typically 15- 35 bp in length. Alleles differ in number of repeats and are differentiated on the basis of size.			
D2S44 (core repeat 31 bp)	Intact DNA digested with restriction enzyme producing fragments that are separated by gel electrophoresis. Alleles detected by Southern blotting followed by probing with locus specific radioactive or chemiluminescent probe.	At least 75 (size range 700-8500 bp); allele size distribution continuous.	ca. 95% in all populations studied
D1S80 (core repeat 16 bp)	Amplification of allelic sequences by PCR; discrete allelic products separated by electrophoresis and visualized directly.	ca. 30 (size range 350-1000 bp); alleles can be discretely distinguished.	80-90%, depending on population.
Short Tandem Repeat (STR) — Like VNTR loci except that the repeated core sequence elements are 2-6 bp in length. Alleles differ in number of repeats and are differentiated on the basis of size.			
HUMTHO1 (tetranucleotide repeat)	Amplification of allelic sequences by PCR; discrete allelic products separated by electrophoresis on sequencing gels and visualized directly.	8 (size range 179-203 bp); alleles can be discretely distinguished.	70-85%, depending on population.

---

[5] In a randomly mating diploid population, diversity is the same as heterozygosity. In general, including haploid mitochondria, the value is $\sum_{ij} p_i p_j$.

Table 2.1, cont.

Simple Sequence Variation — Nucleotide substitution in a defined segment of sequence.			
DQA (an expressed gene in the histo-compatibility complex)	Amplification of allelic sequences by PCR; discrete alleles detected by sequences specific probes.	8 (6 used in DQA kit)	85-95%, depending on population
Polymarker (a set of 5 loci)	Amplification of allelic sequences by PCR; discrete alleles detected by sequences specific probes.	Loci are bi- or tri-allelic; 972 genotypic combinations	37-65%, depending on locus and population
Mitochondrial DNA Control Region (D-loop)	Amplification of control region sequence and sequence determination	Hundreds of sequence variants known	Greater than 95%

APPENDIX A

National Research Council
Committee on DNA Forensic Science: An Update
The Evaluation of Forensic DNA Evidence*
ch. 4 (1996)

To assess the probability that DNA from a randomly selected person has the same profile as evidence DNA, we need to know the frequency of that profile in the population. That frequency is usually determined by comparison with some reference data set. A very small proportion of the trillions of possible profiles are found in any data-base, so it is necessary to use the frequencies of individual alleles to estimate the frequency of a given profile. That approach necessitates some assumptions about the mating structure of the population, and that is where population genetics comes in.

In the simplest population structure, mates are chosen at random. . . . We use *random mating* to refer to choice of mates independently of genotype at the relevant loci and independently of ancestry. With random mating, the proportion of a genotype in a population is the simple product of the frequencies of the constituent alleles. The expected proportions with random mating are called the Hardy-Weinberg (HW) proportions . . . .

Clearly, the HW assumption is hardly ever exactly correct. The issue in

---

forensic DNA analysis is whether the departures are large enough to be important. . . . We explicitly assume that departures from HW proportions exist and use a theory that takes them into account.

Departures from HW proportions in populations can occur for three principal reasons. First, parents might be related, leading to inbreeding. Inbreeding decreases the proportion of heterozygotes, with a compensatory increase in homozygotes.

Second, the population can be subdivided, as in the United States. There are major racial groups (black, Hispanic, American Indian, East Asian, white). Allele frequencies are often sufficiently different between racial groups that it is desirable to have separate databases. Within a race, there is likely to be subdivision. The blending in the melting pot is far from complete, and in the white population, for example, some groups of people reflect to a greater or lesser extent their European origins. A consequence of population subdivision is that mates might have a common origin. Translated into genetic terms, that means that they share some common ancestry — that they are related. Thus, the consequences of population structure are qualitatively the same as those of inbreeding: a decrease of heterozygotes and an increase of homozygotes.

Third, persons with different genotypes might survive and reproduce at different rates. That is called selection. We shall not consider this possibility, however, because the VNTR and other loci traditionally used in forensic analysis are chosen specifically because they are thought to be selectively neutral or nearly so. Some, such as DQA, are associated with functional loci that are thought to be selected, but show no important departures from HW expectations.

Inbreeding means mating of two persons who are more closely related than if they were chosen at random. The theory of inbreeding was worked out 75 years ago by Sewall Wright, who defined the *inbreeding coefficient,* F. . . . With inbreeding, the expected proportion of heterozygotes is reduced by a fraction F; that of homozygotes is correspondingly increased. Thus, with inbreeding,

$$A_iA_i: \quad P_{ii} \ = \ p_i^2 + p_i(1 - p_i)F, \quad\quad\quad\quad (4.2a)$$
$$A_iA_j: \quad P_{ij} \ = \ 2p_ip_j(1 - F). \quad\quad\quad\quad\quad (4.2b)$$

Because F for first cousins is 1/16, a population in which everybody had married a first cousin in the previous generation would be 1/16 less heterozygous than if marriages occurred without regard to family relationships.

The white population of the United States is a mixture of people of various origins, mostly European. The black and Hispanic populations also have multiple origins. Matings tend to occur between persons who are likely to share some common ancestry and thus to be somewhat related. Homozygotes are somewhat more common and heterozygotes less common than if mating were random.

The related problem of greatest concern in forensic applications is that profile frequencies are computed (under the assumption of HW proportions) from the population-average allele frequencies. If there is subdivision, that practice will always lead to an underestimate of homozygous genotype frequencies and usually to an overestimate of heterozygous genotype frequencies. . . .

We can deal with a structured population by using a theory that is very similar to that of inbreeding. . . . The following formulae, which are analogous to those for inbreeding, define a parameter θ_{ij} for each genotype A_iA_j. These formulae do not require that the subpopulations mate at random or even that they be distinct.

$$A_iA_i: \quad P_{ii} = p_i^2 + p_i(1 - p_i)\theta_{ii} \ , \tag{4.4a}$$
$$A_iA_j: \quad P_{ij} = 2p_ip_j(1 - \theta_{ij}) \ , \ i \neq j \ . \tag{4.4b}$$

. . .

The average of the parameter θ_{ij} over all genotypes [can be designated θ-bar. [I]f the local populations are mating at random or if there is local inbreeding, then the true value of θ-bar is positive. In empirical data . . . θ-bar is almost always positive or very small. . . .

. . . Instead of estimating θ_{ij}, we assume only that it is positive for all pairs of alleles. We know that for heterozygotes the HW calculation is generally an overestimate, because from Equation 4.4b the true value includes $(1 - \theta_{ij})$. The assumption of HW proportions always gives overestimates of heterozygotes when $\theta_{ij} > 0$. Therefore, even if we do not know the actual value of each θ_{ij}, we can obtain conservative estimates of match probabilities for all heterozygotes by assuming HW proportions. Negative estimates of θ_{ij} are observed for some data, but these are usually very close to zero and are almost certainly the consequence of sampling errors.

That is not the case with homozygotes, as is clear from Equation 4.4a, because with small allele frequencies, a small value of θ_{ii} can introduce a large change in the genotype frequency. However, . . . [i]t can be shown that if $2p_i$ is assigned to the frequency of a single band at the position of allele A_i, then this simple formula gives an estimate that is necessarily larger than the true frequency. The upper bound always holds, but it is necessary only if some single bands represent heterozygotes. . . .

We arrive at a remarkable simplifying procedure for obtaining a conservative estimate, that is, one that generally underestimates the weight of the evidence against a defendant: *Assign the frequency $2p_i$ to each single band and $2p_ip_j$ to each double band.* In arriving at this important conclusion we have made only one assumption: that θ_{ij} ($i \neq j$) is positive. Then the HW rule is conservative, because in a structured population, heterozygote frequencies are overestimated and, with this adjustment, so are homozygote frequencies.

Empirical data show that with VNTRs departures from HW proportions are small enough for the HW assumption to be sufficiently accurate for forensic purposes. For example, a θ-bar value of 0.01, larger than most estimates, would lead to an error in genotype estimates of about 1%. Nevertheless, to be conservative, we recommend that the HW principle, with the value $2p_i$ for a single band at allele A_i, be used.

With random mating (and in the absence of selection), the population approaches a state in which the frequency of a multilocus genotype is the product of the frequencies at the separate loci. When the population has arrived at such a state, it is said to be in *linkage equilibrium, LE* . . . .

[An] important difference between HW and LE is that whereas a population broken into subgroups has a systematic bias in favor of homozygosity, departures from LE increase some associations and decrease others in about equal degrees. Although there might be linkage disequilibrium, we would expect some canceling of opposite effects. [Considering] the small amount of linkage disequilibrium (see below), . . . multiplying together the frequencies at the several loci will yield roughly the correct answer. An estimated frequency of a composite genotype based on the product of conservative estimates at the several loci is expected to be conservative for the multilocus genotypes.

The main cause of linkage disequilibrium is incomplete mixing of different ancestral populations. We can get an idea of the extent of this in the U.S. white population by asking what would happen in a mixed population derived from two different European countries. There are abundant VNTR data from Switzerland and Spain, so we shall use them for illustration (FBI 1993). . . .

Many more examples could be chosen, but the general conclusion is that departures from LE are not likely to be large, a few percent at most. The cause of uncertainty in using population averages as a substitute for local data is mainly allele-frequency differences, not departures from HW and LE.

. . .

In the great majority of cases, very little is known about the person who left the DNA evidence, and the procedures just discussed are appropriate. It might be known that the DNA came from a white person, in which case the white database is appropriate. If the race is not known or if the population is of racially mixed ancestry, the calculations can be made with each of the appropriate databases and then presented to the court. Alternatively, if a single number is preferred, one might present the calculations for the major racial group that gives the largest probability of a match.

If it is known that the contributor of the evidence DNA and the suspect are from the same subpopulation and there are data for that subpopulation, this is clearly the set of frequencies to use to obtain the most-accurate estimate of the genotype frequency in the set of possible perpetrators of the crime. Of course, the database should be large enough to be statistically reliable (several hundred persons) and rare alleles rebinned so that no allele has a frequency less than five. The product rule is appropriate, in that departures from random mating within a subgroup are not likely to be important . . . . The use of the 2p rule makes the product rule conservative.

. . .

To continue with the assumption that the person contributing the evidence and the suspect are from the same subgroup, an appropriate procedure is to write the conditional probability of the suspect genotype, given that of the perpetrator. As before, we measure the degree of population subdivision by θ-bar, although a single parameter θ-bar is not sufficient to describe the situation exactly. A number of formulae have been proposed to deal with this. They depend on different assumptions and methods of derivation but agree very closely for realistic values of θ-bar and [the allele frequencies] . . . .

Nothing in population genetics theory tells us that θ_{ij} should be independent of genotype. In fact, there is likely to be a different θ_{ij} for each pair of alleles A_i and A_j. Since individual genotypes are usually rare, these values are inaccurately measured and ordinarily unknown. The best procedure is to use a conservative (large) value of θ-bar in Equations 4.10, knowing that the true individual values are likely to be smaller. . . .

The value of θ-bar has been estimated for several populations. [T]ypical values for white and black populations are less than 0.01, usually about 0.002. Values for Hispanics are slightly higher, as expected because of the greater heterogeneity of this group, defined as it is mainly by linguistic criteria. . . .

For urban populations, 0.01 is a conservative value. A higher value — say, 0.03 — could be used for isolated villages. . . .

APPENDIX B

National Research Council
Committee on DNA Forensic Science: An Update
The Evaluation of Forensic DNA Evidence*
5-4 to 5-5 (1996) (pre-publication copy)

Mixed samples are sometimes found in crime situations — for instance, blood from two or more persons at the scene of a crime . . . . [W]hen the contributors to a mixture are not known or cannot otherwise be distinguished, a likelihood-ratio approach offers a clear advantage and is particularly suitable.

Consider a simple case of a VNTR analysis in which, for a particular locus, there are four bands in the lane, known to be contributed by two persons. If alleles from the two persons are known and correspond to the set of four in the lane, there is usually no problem of interpretation, since two of the bands will match one suspect and the other two bands will match the other. However, two of the bands might match the alleles of only one suspect, and the source of the other two might be unknown. The 1992 report says: "If a suspect's pattern is found within the

---

* Reprinted with permission from *The Evaluation of Forensic DNA Evidence,* Copyright 1996 by the National Academy of Sciences, Courtesy of the National Academy Press, Washington D.C.

mixed pattern, the appropriate frequency to assign to such a 'match' is the sum of the frequencies of all genotypes that are contained within (i.e., that are a subset of) the mixed pattern." Suppose the four bands correspond to alleles (bins) that A1, A2, A3, and A4, whose frequencies are p1, p2, p3, and p4. This procedure recommended in the 1992 report would calculate the match probability as

$$2(p_1p_2 + p_1p_3 + p_2p_3 + p_2p_4 + p_3p_4),$$

that is, the probability that a randomly selected person would have two alleles from the set of possibilities $\{A_1, A_2, A_3, A_4\}$. [T]he reciprocal of the probability can be interpreted as a likelihood ratio.

That calculation is hard to justify, because it does not make use of some of the information available, namely, the genotype of the suspect. The correct procedure, we believe, was described by [Ian W.] Evett et al., [A Guide to Interpreting Single Locus Profiles of DNA Mixtures in Forensic Cases, 31 J. Forensic Sci. Soc'y 41] (1991). Suppose that the suspect's genotype is A1A2. The hypothesis we wish to test is that the samples came from the suspect and one other person. The probability under this hypothesis of finding the profile shown by the evidence sample is $2p_3p_4$, because under this hypothesis it is certain that two of the bands are A_1 and A_2. If the samples came from two randomly selected persons, the probability of any particular pair of profiles, such as A_1A_3 and A_2A_4, is $(2p_1p_3)(2p_2p_4) = 4p_1p_2p_3p_4$. There are six possible pairs of two-band profiles corresponding to the four bands, so the total probability is $24p_1p_2p_3p_4$. The likelihood ratio . . . is

$$\text{LR} = \frac{2p_3p_4}{24p_1p_2p_3p_4} = 1/12p_1p_2.$$

This LR, compared with that derived from the recommendation of the 1992 NRC report, is larger when the suspect bands are relatively rare and smaller when the suspect bands are relatively common. The reason is that we have taken advantage of the information in the genotype of the suspect rather than averaging over the set of possible genotypes consistent with the four-band evidence-sample profile. . . .

Part V

FORENSIC PSYCHIATRY AND PSYCHOLOGY

Chapter 15
Sanity and Other Things

Edwards v. State
540 S.W.2d 641 (Tenn. 1976)

COOPER, CHIEF JUSTICE.

Petitioner, George S. Edwards, was indicted for . . . the killing of his sister . . . . The jury found petitioner guilty of murder in the second degree and fixed his punishment at ten years in the penitentiary . . . .

The record is replete with testimony, both expert and lay, on the issue of insanity. Petitioner . . . became a patient of Dr. Walker in October, 1971. The doctor testified that petitioner had a schizophrenic personality and was suffering from schizophrenia. He further testified that petitioner responded to anti-depressant drugs and his condition improved. Petitioner was still under the care of Dr. Walker at the time of the homicide in June, 1972 . . . .

Lay testimony showed petitioner's personality quirks became more pronounced during the spring of 1972, particularly after petitioner quit taking his tranquilizers. . . .

[Edwards' wife] testified that petitioner . . . pulled a pistol out of a bureau drawer and, without saying a word, fired a single shot at his sister. His wife ran from the house, and the petitioner fired two shots at her, narrowly missing her. . . .

Immediately after the shooting and before the police arrived on the scene, petitioner called his mother and told her that he had shot his sister and was sorry. When the police arrived, he at first told them that his wife had shot herself. Later, he told the investigating officers that his "sister" had shot herself. He gave a third statement to the officers within fifteen minutes of the killing stating that he had killed his sister because she had sinned too much and that she was better off dead. He further stated that she was scolding him for mistreating his wife and that when he could not take it anymore, he shot her.

Following the homicide, Dr. Walker engaged the services of Dr. Garo Aivazian, Chairman of the Department of Psychiatry at the University of Tennessee Medical School, and they together evaluated the petitioner over the next several months. Both diagnosed petitioner's condition as schizophrenia. Both testified that in their opinion on the date of the shooting the petitioner was insane within the definition of the *M'Naughten* rule. Both expressed the opinion that petitioner was sane at the time of the trial. Both admitted that there were times when petitioner would know right from wrong. And, on cross-examination, Dr. Aivazian testified that petitioner was not psychotic when he first saw him on June 12, 1972, and also expressed the opinion that petitioner knew what was going on around him during the day of the homicide on June 7, 1972. There was also evidence of a history of mental illness in petitioner's family, going back several generations on both sides.

Mrs. Nona Owensby, a licensed psychological examiner employed at Central State Hospital, was called as a rebuttal witness by the state. She testified that based upon her observation of the petitioner and study of his records she was of the opinion that petitioner was not psychotic or mentally deranged at the time of the shooting, and did know right from wrong. She expressed the further opinion that petitioner was feigning mental illness in an effort to avoid criminal responsibility, and testified to observations and conversations with petitioner which led her to this belief. . . .

Petitioner insists . . . that the evidence preponderated against the jury's finding that petitioner was sane at the time of the killing. Implicit in petitioner's argument is the insistence that the testimony of the psychiatrists on this issue must be accepted over lay testimony. Petitioner also stresses the testimony of his wife and family concerning his disturbed mental condition in the days before the killing and the history of mental illness in his family, and the lack of an apparent motive for his actions.

The jury is not required to accept testimony of a psychiatrist on the issue of sanity to the exclusion of lay testimony or to the exclusion of evidence of the actions of the petitioner inconsistent with sanity. If it were, "[it] would effectively preempt our jury trial system on sanity issues and replace it with a system of trial by psychiatrists' opinions. We are unwilling, even if we had the power, to saddle society with so basic a change in our system of criminal jurisprudence."

In this state, "it is settled beyond question that the weight and value of expert testimony is for the jury and must be received with caution." This applies to the expert opinions of medical men. Where there is any conflict between expert testimony and the testimony as to the facts, the jury is not bound to accept expert testimony in preference to other testimony, and must determine the weight and credibility of each in the light of all the facts shown in case. Expert medical opinion regarding the functioning of the human body must always be more or less speculative. . . .

Petitioner's conviction is sustained . . . .

NOTES

1. *The insanity defense.* For centuries courts and legislatures have struggled with the problem of excusing criminal conduct on the part of an "insane" person. The standard the jury was asked to apply in *Edwards* was, in the words of a dissenting Justice, "the ancient and archaic M'Naghten Rule." This rule arose from an attempt by Daniel McNaughten to assassinate Robert Peel, the Prime Minister of England. Apparently believing that the Prime Minister and his political party was persecuting him, McNaughten came to London. There, he shot and killed a man riding in Peel's carriage, whom he thought was Peel, but who was in fact Peel's secretary. A jury found McNaughten "not guilty by reason of insanity," and an irate Queen Victoria summoned the House of Lords to "take the opinion of the Judges on the law governing such cases." The fifteen judges of the common law courts found themselves required to answer prolix and obtuse questions on the status of criminal responsibility in England. In this politically charged atmosphere, they announced that "to establish a defence on the ground of insanity, it must be clearly proved that, at the time of the committing of the act, the party accused was labouring under such a defect of reason, from disease of the mind, as not to know the nature and quality of the act he was doing; or, if he did know it, that he did not know he was doing what was wrong." M'Naghten's Rule, 10 Cl. & F. 200, 8 Eng.Rep. 718, 722 (H.L. 1843). For discussions of and citations to the extensive literature on this rule and its more modern competitors, see Modern Scientific Evidence § 6-1.2 (David Faigman et al. eds., 1997); Michael L. Perlin, Jurisprudence of the Insanity Defense (1994); Saleem A. Shah, Criminal Responsibility, in Forensic Psychiatry and Psychology 167 (William J. Curran et al. eds., 1986); Michael Moore, Law and Psychiatry: Rethinking the Relationship (1984); By Reason of Insanity: Essays on Psychiatry and the Law (Lawrence Z. Freedman ed., 1983); Richard Moran, Knowing Right from Wrong: The Insanity Defense of Daniel McNaughton (1981); Alan Stone, Mental Health and Law: A System in Transition 218-31 (1976); Alexander D. Brooks, Law, Psychiatry and the Mental Health System 135-233 (1974).

Like the jury verdict in *M'Naughten,* the acquittal of John Hinckley for his attempted assassination of President Ronald Reagan provoked reflections on the status of insanity defense. The psychiatric testimony in this case, and some of the political and professional reactions to it, are discussed in Alan Stone, Law, Psychiatry and Morality: Essays and Analysis 77-98 (1984). In the wake of the *Hinckley* trial, some states limited the scope of the insanity defense and the evidence admissible to establish it. See, e.g., State v. Searcy, 798 P.2d 914 (Idaho 1990) (abolition of defense constitutional); Henry J. Steadman et al., Before and After *Hinckley:* Evaluating Insanity Defense Reform (1993). However, remarkably few defendants plead insanity, and fewer still prevail in their claims. Lisa Callahan et al., The Volume and Characteristics of Insanity Defense Pleas: An Eight-State Study, 19 Bull. Am. Acad. Psychiatry & L. 331 (1991) (insanity is claimed in about 1% of felony cases and is successful about one quarter of the time).

2. *Diminished Capacity.* The insanity defense rests on the premise that it is wrong to punish people who suffer from diseases or defects that prevent them from understanding, appreciating, or conforming to the criminal law. Someone can be insane, as the law uses the term, yet possess the requisite state of mind to commit a crime. Defenses of diminished capacity, on the other hand, are directed at negating some or all of the *mens rea* requirements for committing the alleged crime. Well-founded clinical testimony that a defendant could not have had the purpose, intent, or knowledge required to commit the crime therefore should be admissible regardless of the status and nature of the insanity defense in a particular jurisdiction. See, e.g., Modern Scientific Evidence § 6-1.3 (David Faigman et al. eds., 1997).

3. *Psychiatrists for the indigent.* Psychiatric evaluation is so crucial to establishing the insanity defense that "when [an indigent] defendant demonstrates to the trial judge that his sanity at the time of the offense is to be a significant factor at trial, the State must, at a minimum, assure the defendant access to a competent psychiatrist who will conduct an appropriate examination and assist in evaluation, preparation, and presentation of the defense." Ake v. Oklahoma, 463 U.S. 880, 83 (1985). In implementing this requirement of due process, two major issues have surfaced: (1) the standard that trial courts should apply to determine when sanity will be a significant factor and (2) the effect of determinations of sanity by psychiatrists at state hospitals. See generally David A. Harris, *Ake* Revisited: Expert Psychiatric Witnesses Remain Beyond Reach for the Indigent, 68 N. Car. L. Rev. 763 (1990); Mark P. Goodman, Note, The Right to a Partisan Psychiatric Expert: Might Indigency Preclude Insanity? 61 NYU L. Rev. 703 (1986). On the extension of *Ake* to the provision of expert services in non-capital cases, see David A. Harris, The Constitution and Truth Seeking: A New Theory on Expert Services for Indigent Defendants, 83 J. Crim. L. & Criminology 469 (1992); John M. West, Note, Expert Services and the Indigent Criminal Defendant, 84 Mich. L. Rev. 1326 (1986).

4. *Executing the insane.* The constitution also prevents the state from executing an insane prisoner. Ford v. Wainwright, 477 U.S. 399 (1986). The logic underlying this decision is questioned in Jonathan L. Entin, Psychiatry, Insanity and the Death Penalty: A Note on Implementing Supreme Court Decisions, 79 J. Crim. L. & Criminology 218 (1988). The problem of defining appropriate procedures for determining the sanity of death row inmates is pursued in Gordon L. Moore, Note, *Ford v. Wainwright:* A Coda in the Executioner's Song, 72 Iowa L. Rev. 1461 (1987).

5. *Competency. Edwards* also illustrates a very common use of psychiatric expertise in the criminal justice system — to assess the competency of a defendant to stand trial. Indeed, "far more persons are confined on the basis of incompetence than because they have been found not guilty by reason of insanity." Alan Stone, Mental Health and Law: A System in Transition 203 (1976). Whereas the defense of insanity focuses on the ability of the defendant to have formed the requisite intent or on the desirability of punishing a person who is not considered responsible for his actions at the time of the alleged offense, competency refers to the defendant's ability to understand the subsequent legal proceedings and to participate in his defense. See id. at 199-217; Thomas Grisso & Sandra K. Siegel, Assessment of Competency to Stand Trial, in Forensic Psychiatry and Psychology 145 (William J. Curran et al. eds., 1986); Benjamin J. Vernia, Note, The Burden of Proving Competency to Stand Trial: Due Process at the Limits of Adversarial Justice, 45 Vand. L. Rev. 199 (1992). Questions of mental competency arise in many other areas as well, including testamentary capacity, contract formation, commission of torts, and, of course, competence to manage one's affairs, to consent to medical treatment, to care for children, and to waive legal rights. See Daniel W. Shuman, Psychiatric and Psychological Evidence (2d ed. 1994); Robert L. Sadoff, Forensic Psychiatry: A Practical Guide for Lawyers and Psychiatrists (2d ed. 1988); Gary B. Melton et al., Psychological Evaluations for the Courts: A Handbook for Mental Health Professionals and Lawyers (1987); Thomas Grisso, Evaluating Competencies: Forensic Assessment and Instruments (1986); Thomas G. Gutheil & Paul S. Appelbaum, Clinical Handbook of Psychiatry and the Law 210-303 (1982); Alexander Brooks, Law, Psychiatry and the Mental Health System 971-1035 (1974).

6. *Psychiatric opinions on ultimate issues.* The psychiatrists in *Edwards* testified that Edwards was legally insane when he shot and killed his sister.* Does psychiatric expertise extend to diagnosing insanity, as the criminal law uses the term? Should psychiatric testimony be limited to diagnoses and prognoses for psychiatrically meaningful mental diseases or conditions? See Fed. R. Evid. 704(b); Abraham Goldstein, The Insanity Defense 97-105 (1967); Maury R. Olicker, Note, The Admissibility of Expert Witness Testimony: Time to Take the Final Leap? 42 U. Miami L. Rev. 831 (1988).

Edwards does not question the propriety of expert testimony on an "ultimate issue" like insanity or competence, but rather deals with the effect that a judge or jury must give such testimony. It applies the general rule that a jury may disbelieve expert testimony even when that testimony goes uncontradicted by other bona fide experts.**

---

* After describing the symptoms and characteristics of schizophrenia, Dr. Parks testified that at the time of the killing the defendant was laboring under such a defect of reasoning from disease of mind as not to know the nature and quality of his act, or if he did know it, that he did not know what he was doing was wrong. Dr. Aivazian also expressed his opinion in legal as well as medical terms. He testified that "at the time of the shooting [defendant] was psychotic to a degree whereby his ability to recognize what was around him as the environment and to test the environment and its realities was impaired to a degree whereby he was not capable of deciding between right or wrong and was not capable of adhering to any decision because he could not decide between right and wrong."

** Why does the appellate court not place more emphasis on the opinion of the "psychological examiner" that Edwards was feigning insanity? The answer may be that this expert could provide little or no basis for her opinion and misled the trial court as to her qualifications. She began her testimony by describing herself as "the psychologist at the Forensic Services Division of Central State Psychiatric Hospital." On appeal, the state confessed that this was a "misrepresentation." It called the court's attention to a report finding, among other things, that "she exceeded her authority in testifying before courts regarding matters of probation, parole, suspension of sentence, leniency, and insanity," that "she furnished courts, attorneys for patients and district attorneys with . . . inaccurate and misleading" information on her qualifications as an expert witness, and "that she held herself out to be a psychologist . . . , tending to mislead courts before whom she gave testimony, attorneys representing patients, district attorneys, patients, and staff at FSD." But if the jury was misinformed as to this expert's qualifications, can the verdict in *Edwards* be upheld on the theory that the lay testimony as to Edward's behavior and state of mind could have persuaded the jury that he was sane, notwithstanding the psychiatric opinions?

In the principal case of chapter 16, Barefoot v. Estelle, the United States Supreme Court considers psychiatric testimony introduced to satisfy a requirement in Texas for imposing capital punishment: that "there is a probability that the defendant would commit criminal acts of violence that would constitute a continuing threat to society." *Barefoot* is a mirror image of *Edwards*. The jury credited the predictions of two psychiatrists, and the convicted defendant argued that such predictions were so invalid that the jury's reliance on them deprived him of due process of law.

NOTES

Other Uses of Psychiatry in the Legal System

1. *Personal injury litigation.* Psychiatric assessments have obvious application in tort suits, workers' compensation and similar claims. E.g., Herbert Modlin, Civil Law and Psychiatric Testimony, in Forensic Psychiatry and Psychology 469 (William J. Curran et al. eds. 1986). The use of the "psychological autopsy" to help differentiate between suicide and accident is described supra at chapter 3.

2. *Child custody.* Psychological evaluations of children and parents can be extremely influential when a marriage dissolves and both parents seek custody of a child, or when the fitness of parents is called into question. A survey of the Indiana Trial Lawyer's Association seeking information on the type of cases in which psychologists are employed found that

> the psychologist was most frequently called upon in cases that involved children. Sixty-nine percent of the respondents had used the psychologist in a child custody case, 42% in cases involving child visitation rights, 27% in cases involving abuse of child, and 14% in cases involving termination of parental rights. Overall, 58% of the reported total of 5,632 cases in which the psychologist was employed involved children.

Albert Levitt & Albert Lawlor, Employment of the Psychologist as an Expert Witness, 1 Forensic Rep. 133, 135 (1988). In light of the difficulty of decisions profoundly affecting parents and children, courts may be especially willing to defer to expert judgments. See generally Benjamin M. Shutz et al., Solomon's Sword: A Practical Guide to Conducting Child Custody Evaluations (1989); Robert L. Sadoff, Forensic Psychiatry: A Practical Guide for Lawyers and Psychiatrists (2d ed. 1988); Thomas Grisso, Evaluating Competencies: Forensic Assessments and Instruments 188-267 (1986); Daniel W. Shuman, Psychiatric and Psychological Evidence (2d ed. 1994); A.L. McGarry, Child Custody, in Forensic Psychiatry and Psychology 247 (William J. Curran et al. eds., 1986).

3. *Veracity of witnesses.* The courts are more chary of psychiatric or psychological opinions on the veracity of witnesses. See infra chapter 16.

4. *Further references.* Some practice-oriented texts on psychiatric testimony and related topics are Kenneth S. Pope et al., The MMPI, MMPI-2 and MMPI-A in Court: A Practical Guide for Expert Witnesses and Attorneys (1994); Daniel W. Shuman, Psychiatric and Psychological Evidence (2d ed. 1994); Robert J. Simon, Clinical Psychiatry and the Law (1993); Jay Ziskin & David Faust, Coping with Psychiatric and Psychological Testimony (4th ed. 1988); Robert L. Sadoff, Forensic Psychiatry: A Practical Guide for Lawyers and Psychiatrists (2d ed. 1988); Martin G. Blinder, Psychiatry in the Everyday Practice of Law (2d ed. 1982). See also Paul S. Appelbaum & Thomas G. Gutheil, Clinical Handbook of Psychiatry and the Law (2d ed. 1991); Raymond L. Spring et al., Patients, Psychiatrists and Lawyers: Law and the Mental Health System (1989).

Chapter 16
Predicting Violence

Barefoot v. Estelle
463 U.S. 880 (1983)

JUSTICE WHITE delivered the opinion of the Court.

On November 14, 1978, petitioner was convicted of the capital murder of a police officer in Bell County, Texas. A separate sentencing hearing before the same jury was then held to determine whether the death penalty should be imposed. . . .

Petitioner [submits] that his death sentence must be set aside because the Constitution of the United States barred the testimony of the two psychiatrists who testified against him at the punishment hearing. There are several aspects to this claim. First, it is urged that psychiatrists, individually and as a group, are incompetent to predict with an acceptable degree of reliability that a particular criminal will commit other crimes in the future and so represent a danger to the community. Second, it is said that in any event, psychiatrists should not be permitted to testify about future dangerousness in response to hypothetical questions and without having examined the defendant personally. Third, it is argued that in the particular circumstances of this case, the testimony of the psychiatrists was so unreliable that the sentence should be set aside. As indicated below, we reject each of these arguments.

A

The suggestion that no psychiatrist's testimony may be presented with respect to a defendant's future dangerousness is somewhat like asking us to disinvent the wheel. In the first place, it is contrary to our cases. If the likelihood of a defendant committing further crimes is a constitutionally acceptable criterion for imposing the death penalty, which it is, and if it is not impossible for even a lay person sensibly to arrive at that conclusion, it makes little sense, if any, to submit that psychiatrists, out of the entire universe of persons who might have an opinion on the issue, would know so little about the subject that they should not be permitted to testify. . . .

Acceptance of petitioner's position that expert testimony about future dangerousness is far too unreliable to be admissible would immediately call into question those other contexts in which predictions of future behavior are constantly made. For example, in O'Connor v. Donaldson, 422 U.S. 563, 576 (1975), we held that a non-dangerous civil committee could not be held in confinement against his will. Later, speaking about the requirements for civil commitments, we said:

There may be factual issues in a commitment proceeding, but the factual aspects represent only the beginning of the inquiry. Whether the individual is mentally ill and dangerous to either himself or others and is in need of confined therapy turns on the meaning of the facts which must be interpreted by expert psychiatrists and psychologists.

In the second place, the rules of evidence generally extant at the federal and state levels anticipate that relevant, unprivileged evidence should be admitted and its weight left to the fact finder, who would have the benefit of cross-examination and contrary evidence by the opposing party. Psychiatric testimony predicting dangerousness may be countered not only as erroneous in a particular case but as generally so unreliable that it should be ignored. If the jury may make up its mind about future dangerousness unaided by psychiatric testimony, jurors should not be barred from hearing the views of the State's psychiatrists along with opposing views of the defendant's doctors.

Third, petitioner's view mirrors the position expressed in the *amicus* brief of the American Psychiatric Association (APA). . . . We are not persuaded that such testimony is almost entirely unreliable and that the factfinder and the adversary system will not be competent to uncover, recognize, and take due account of its shortcomings.

The *amicus* does not suggest that there are not other views held by members of the Association or of the profession generally. Indeed, as this case and others indicate, there are those doctors who are quite willing to testify at the sentencing hearing, who think, and will say, that they know what they are talking about, and who expressly disagree with the Association's point of view. Furthermore, their qualifications as experts are regularly accepted by the courts. If they are so obviously wrong and should be discredited, there should be no insuperable problem in doing so by calling members of the Association who are of that view and who confidently assert that opinion in their *amicus* brief. Neither petitioner nor the Association suggests that psychiatrists are always wrong with respect to future dangerousness, only most of the time. Yet the submission is that this category of testimony should be excised entirely from all trials. We are unconvinced, however, at least as of now, that the adversary process cannot be trusted to sort out the reliable from the unreliable evidence and opinion about future dangerousness, particularly when the convicted felon has the opportunity to present his own side of the case.

We are unaware of and have been cited to no case, federal or state, that has adopted the categorical views of the Association. Certainly it was presented and rejected at every stage of the present proceeding. . . .

B

Whatever the decision may be about the use of psychiatric testimony, in general, on the issue of future dangerousness, petitioner urges that such testimony must be based on personal examination of the defendant and may not be given in response to hypothetical questions. We disagree. Expert testimony, whether in the form of an opinion based on hypothetical questions or otherwise, is commonly admitted as evidence where it might help the factfinder do its assigned job. As the Court said long ago, Spring Co. v. Edgar, 99 U.S. 645, 657 (1878):

> Men who have made questions of skill or science the object of their particular study, says Phillips, are competent to give their opinions in evidence. Such opinions ought, in general, to be deduced from facts that are not disputed, or from facts given in evidence; but the author proceeds to say that they need not be founded upon their own personal knowledge of such facts, but may be founded upon the statement of facts proved in the case. Medical men, for example, may give their opinions not only to the state of a patient they may have visited, or as to cause of the death of a person whose body they have examined or as to the nature of the instruments which caused the wounds they have examined, but also in cases where they have not themselves seen the patient, and have only heard the symptoms and particulars of his state detailed by other witnesses at the trial. Judicial tribunals have in many instances held that medical works are not admissible, but they everywhere hold that men skilled in science, art, or particular trades may give their opinions as witnesses in matters pertaining to their professional calling.

Today, in the federal system, Federal Rules of Evidence 702-706 provide for the testimony of experts. The advisory committee notes touch on the particular objections to hypothetical questions, but none of these caveats lends any support to petitioner's constitutional arguments. Furthermore, the Texas Court of Criminal Appeals could find no fault with the mode of examining the two psychiatrists under Texas law . . . .

. . . Although cases such as this involve the death penalty, we perceive no constitutional barrier to applying the ordinary rules of evidence governing the use of expert testimony.

C

As we understand petitioner, he contends that even if the use of hypothetical questions in predicting future dangerousness is acceptable as a general rule, the use made of them in his case violated his right to due process of law. For example, petitioner insists that the doctors should not have been permitted to give an opinion on the ultimate issue before the jury, particularly when the hypothetical questions were phrased in terms of petitioner's own conduct; that the hypothetical questions referred to controverted facts; and that the answers to the questions were so positive as to be assertions of fact and not opinion. These claims of misuse of the hypothetical questions, as well as others, were rejected by the Texas courts, and neither the District Court nor the Court of Appeals found any constitutional infirmity in the application of the Texas Rules of Evidence in this particular case. We agree.

In sum, we affirm the judgment of the District Court. There is no doubt that the psychiatric testimony increased the likelihood that petitioner would be sentenced to death, but this fact does not make that evidence inadmissible, any more than it would with respect to other relevant evidence against any defendant in a criminal case. . . .

NOTES

1. *Validity of clinical predictions of violence.* The dissenting opinion of Justice Blackmun, joined by Justices Brennan and Marshall, emphasizes that "psychiatric testimony about a defendant's future dangerousness . . . is wrong two times out of three," 463 U.S. at 916, making it "less accurate than the flip of a coin." Id. at 931. "[W]hen a person's life is at stake," they insist, "a requirement of greater reliability should prevail." Id. at 916. This figure for the accuracy of dangerousness predictions can be traced to John Monahan, The Clinical Prediction of Violent Behavior 47 (1981). Monahan summarizes his metastudy as follows:

> In reviewing the research literature as of 1981 on clinical risk assessment of violence among the mentally disordered — most of it conducted on criminal or "forensic" patient populations I [concluded]:
>
> 1. The upper bound of accuracy that even the best risk assessment technology could achieve was on the order of .33. That is, of every three disordered persons predicted by psychiatrists or psychologists to be violent, one will be discovered to commit a violent act, and two will not.
> 2. The best predictors of violence among the mentally disordered are the same demographic factors that are the best predictors of violence among non-disordered offender populations (e.g., age, gender, social class, history of prior violence).
> 3. The poorest predictors of violence among the mentally disordered are psychological factors such as diagnosis or severity of disorder, or personality traits.

John Monahan, Risk Assessment of Violence Among the Mentally Disordered: Generating Useful Knowledge, 11 Int'l J. L. & Psychiatry 249, 250 (1988). Although research conducted after this 1981 review "could be seen as challenging each of these conclusions," Monahan observes that "[t]he most striking characteristic of recent risk assessment research . . . is that the research is so inconsistent. For every study that reports increases in predictive accuracy, there is another that finds clinical risk assessments no better than chance. . . ." Id. at 251-52. See also

Violence and Mental Disorder: Developments in Risk Assessment (John Monahan & Henry Steadman eds., 1994). But see Charles Lidz et al., The Accuracy of Predictions of Violence to Others, 269 JAMA 1007, 1010 (1993); Douglas Mossman, Assessing Predictions of Violence: Being Accurate About Accuracy, 62 J. Consulting & Clinical Psych. 783, 790 (1994); G. Palmero et al., On the Probability of Violent Behavior: Considerations and Guidelines, 36 J. Forensic Sci. 1435 (1991).

The Blackmun dissent in *Barefoot* implied that a psychiatric prediction of dangerousness might even be taken as evidence of non-dangerousness: "Psychiatric predictions of future dangerousness *are not accurate;* wrong two times out of three, their probative value, and therefore any possible contribution they might make to the ascertainment of truth, is virtually nonexistent. . . . Indeed, given a psychiatrist's prediction that an individual will be dangerous, it is more likely than not that the defendant will *not* commit further violence." 463 U.S. 928. However, the two-out-of-three figure should not be confused with the probative value of the evidence. To the extent that the rate of violence is higher among those people predicted to be violent than those predicted to be nonviolent, the predictions are probative. Cf. D.H. Kaye, The Validity of Tests: Caveant Omnes, 27 Jurimetrics J. 349 (1987). The two-out-of-three figure, on the other hand, is a posterior probability of non-dangerousness given a prediction of dangerousness; it depends on the base rate, or prevalence, of dangerousness in the population on which predictions are made. When the prevalence of a condition is low, even an exquisitely sensitive and specific test for that condition — a test with undeniable probative value — will result in many false positive errors. As Christopher Slobogin, Dangerousness and Expertise, 133 U. Pa. L. Rev. 97, 111-12 (1984), explains:

> While it cannot be denied that mental health professionals using clinical prediction techniques are not very accurate at determining who is violence-prone, they are not nearly as inept at that task as many would suggest. In fact, knowledgeable clinicians are much better at predicting dangerousness than the random selection process suggested by the coin-flipping analogy.
>
> To understand why this is so, it is helpful to focus at the outset on a study conducted in Massachusetts by Dr. Kozol and his associates. This investigation is chosen for illustrative purposes because it is usually cited as representative of clinical prediction at its best. Each prediction made in the study was based on independent examinations by at least five clinicians, a battery of psychological tests, and "a meticulous reconstruction of the life history [of the subject] elicited from multiple sources."
>
> Four hundred and thirty-five male offenders evaluated in this manner were released into the community after being confined for various lengths of time. During the follow-up period, only eight percent of those predicted nondangerous (thirty-one out of 386) were found to have committed a

serious assaultive act. Yet of those offenders predicted dangerous, 34.7% (seventeen out of forty-nine) were found to have committed such an act. More than sixty-five percent of the individuals identified as dangerous, therefore, were false positives. Given the results of this and other studies, it has become the accepted wisdom that at best only one out of every three clinical predictions of dangerousness will be correct.

On its face, this finding appears singularly unimpressive. But in evaluating what it means about the ability of mental health professionals to predict future dangerousness, one must take into account the fact that very few people commit violent acts. In the United States, for instance, only one person out of every 500 commits a seriously violent act (murder, rape, robbery, or assault) each year. Thus if one were to label a randomly selected American citizen dangerous, one would have one chance in five hundred of being right. Were Kozol and his associates able to maintain their one out of three accuracy rate when evaluating a random population, their predictions would thus be about 165 times better than chance.

Of course, most of the dangerousness studies, including Kozol's, do not involve randomly selected populations. They usually focus on male offenders, a group that has a much higher base rate for violence than the population as a whole. In Kozol's group, for example, the base rate was one out of nine; forty-eight of the 435 offenders studied committed violent acts during the time period of the study. Even so, Kozol and his associates produced predictions that were three times better than chance. Although their absolute accuracy was low, their relative accuracy could be called commendable.

In addition to the confusion over the meaning of the two-out-of-three figure, there are other reasons to think that "[c]ontrary to the 'nearly universal' view of academic and professional communities, the available evidence does not support the claim that predictions of future criminality are inherently or even usually inaccurate." Albert W. Alshuler, Preventive Pretrial Detention and the Failure of Interest-Balancing Approaches to Due Process, 85 Mich. L. Rev. 510, 539 (1986); Slogobin, supra, at 114-17.

2. *Legal significance of high error rates.* The *Barefoot* majority is painfully aware of the misgivings of many mental health professionals about their ability to make valid predictions of future dangerousness. Somewhat feebly, the Court notes that "[n]either petitioner nor the [American Psychiatric] Association suggests that psychiatrists are always wrong with respect to future dangerousness, only most of the time." 463 U.S. at 899. Hoping that "the factfinder and the adversary system will . . . be competent to uncover, recognize and take due account of its shortcomings," the Court resists any "constitutional rule barring an entire category of expert testimony." Id. Can juries "separate the wheat from the chaff"? Id. at 901 n.7. How?

If behavioral scientists have been unable to validate expert predictions of dangerousness, should judges or juries — with or without the benefit of mental health professionals — rely on this factor in deciding who should receive capital punishment? See Jurek v. Texas, 428 U.S. 262 (1976). Even if the constitution permits expert as well as lay predictions of dangerousness, should the general acceptance test (see supra chapter 6) or other evidentiary rules for scientific evidence be applied to exclude expert clinical predictions of dangerousness? See United States v. Kozminski, 821 F.2d 1186 (6th Cir. 1987) (psychologist's testimony that pressures on mentally retarded farm workers resulted in an "involuntary conversion" to dependency inadmissible without proof that the theory was scientifically recognized); Bert Black, Evolving Legal Standards for the Admissibility of Scientific Evidence, 239 Science 1508, 1509-10 (1988); Christopher Slobogin, Dangerousness and Expertise, 133 U. Pa. L. Rev. 97, 130-48 (1984).

Is there a defensible middle ground between the wholesale exclusion of predictions of dangerousness and the widespread comforting but questionable reliance on expert assessments? Should expert involvement be limited to providing "actuarial" rather than clinical predictions? Compare Jay Faust & David Ziskin, The Expert Witness in Psychology and Psychiatry, 241 Science 31 (1988), with Slobogin, supra. Keep in mind yet another concern with predictions of dangerousness, a concern that did not surface in *Barefoot*:

> The invidious aspect of testimony about sociopaths and their future dangerousness has to do with racial and social implications of the diagnosis of sociopath as defined by DSM-III [Am. Psychiatric Ass'n, Diagnostic and Statistical Manual (3d ed. 1980)] rather than with the ethics and expertise of the particular psychiatrists. The diagnostic criteria for antisocial personality in DSM-III might apply to the vast majority of those who face a death sentence as well as many black men who have grown up in inner cities. These criteria include the following characteristics . . . inability to establish consistent work behavior, lack of ability to function as a responsible parent, failure to accept social norms, e.g., holding an illegal occupation (pimping, prostitution, fencing, selling drugs), failure to honor financial obligations, failure to plan ahead, disregard for truth, and recklessness. . . .
>
> Whatever scientific value the diagnosis of sociopath may have, there can be little question that the urban poor and racial minorities will be swept into this diagnostic category.

Alan Stone, Law, Psychiatry and Morality 110 (1984). See also Sheri L. Johnson, The Politics of Predicting Criminal Violence, 86 Mich. L. Rev. 1322 (1988) (reviewing The Prediction of Criminal Violence (F.N. Dutile & C.H. Foust ed., 1987)).

3. *The psychiatric testimony against Barefoot.* The psychiatrists who testified at Barefoot's trial were John Holbrook and James Grigson. Neither had examined Barefoot nor requested an opportunity to do so. Presented with a hypothetical question about Barefoot, both diagnosed him as a sociopath. Dr. Holbrook testified to "a reasonable psychiatric certainty" that there was "a probability that the Thomas A. Barefoot in that hypothetical will commit criminal acts of violence in the future." Dr. Grigson's predictions were less guarded. He declared that on a scale of one to ten for sociopaths, Barefoot was "above ten," that there was no known cure for this condition, and that there was a "one hundred percent and absolute" chance that Barefoot would commit future acts of criminal violence. 463 U.S. at 918-19.

Known to some as "Dr. Death," Dr. Grigson has testified in well over 100 death-penalty cases for the prosecution. "[H]e gives similar convincing testimony in almost every case, diagnosing the defendant as an antisocial personality (a 'sociopath' or 'psychopath'). Since sociopaths do not learn from experience and show no remorse, they are essentially untreatable people who would certainly commit further criminal violence. The jury, after hearing this psychiatrist, almost never fails to impose the death penalty." Alan Stone, Law, Psychiatry and Morality 107 (1984). Does such testimony exceed the boundaries of ethical behavior for psychiatrists? See id. at 70-71, 107 (1984); 463 U.S. at 881 n.6 (dissenting opinion).

4. *Other limitations on psychiatric predictions of violence.* In some circumstances the privilege against self-incrimination and the right to counsel may prevent the state from introducing clinical predictions of dangerousness. See Estelle v. Smith, 451 U.S. 454 (1981); Satterwhite v. Texas, 486 U.S. 249 (1988).

5. *Other uses of psychiatric predictions of violence.* The Supreme Court has held that it is not unconstitutional to keep dangerous people accused of criminal conduct in jail pending trial. See United States v. Salerno, 481 U.S. 739 (1987); Schall v. Martin, 467 U.S. 253, 264-66 (1984); Keith E. Hansen, When Worlds Collide: The Constitutional Politics of United States v. Salerno, 14 Am. J. Crim. L. 155 (1987). What are the implications of *Barefoot* on the use of clinical psychiatric predictions in this context? See Albert W. Alschuler, Preventive Detention and the Failure of Interest-Balancing Approaches to Due Process, 85 Mich. L. Rev. 510 (1986).

Defendants acquitted of criminal charges by reason of insanity and people never even accused of or prosecuted for crimes may be confined to mental institutions as a result of commitment proceedings. As a constitutional matter, *must* involuntary hospitalization be predicated on a finding of danger to others? See O'Connor v. Donaldson, 422 U.S. 563 (1975); Alan Stone, Law, Psychiatry and Morality 111-17 (1984). Is a need for medical treatment enough? See Alan Stone, Mental Health and Law: A System in Transition (1976). If the threat of harm to others is a basis for involuntary commitment, what is the burden of persuasion that the state should shoulder? See Addington v. Texas, 441 U.S. 418 (1979) (due process requires "clear and convincing evidence" for civil commitment); Jones v. United States, 463 U.S. 354 (1983) (mere "preponderance of the evidence" enough for indefinite commitment of insanity acquittee). If the majority of predictions of dangerousness are false positives, how can the state ever meet these burdens? See John Monahan & David Wexler, A Definite Maybe: Proof and Probability in Civil Commitment, 2 Law & Hum. Behav. 37 (1978).

Chapter 17
Testing for Truth

Frye v. United States
293 F. 1013 (D.C. Cir. 1923)

[See supra chapter 6]

NOTE

The defense expert in *Frye,* William M. Marston, developed the theory of a "specific lie response" while a Harvard law student. In later years, Marston created the comic strip heroine, Wonder Woman. 2 Who Was Who in America 347 (1950). Although he and others have asserted that subsequent investigations proved Frye's innocence (and the accuracy of the early lie detector test), this claim appears to be baseless. James Starrs, "A Still-Life Watercolor": *Frye v. United States,* 27 J. Forensic Sci. 684, 690 (1982). For more on the early history of "scientific" lie detection, see David Lykken, A Tremor in the Blood: Uses and Abuses of the Lie Detector (1981).

State v. Valdez
371 P.2d 894 (Ariz. 1962)

UDALL, VICE CHIEF JUSTICE.

Defendant was tried for and convicted of possession of narcotics. Pursuant to a written stipulation entered into by defendant, his counsel and the county attorney before trial defendant submitted to a polygraph (lie-detector) examination. The stipulation also provided that the results of such examination would be admissible at the trial. Accordingly, the polygraph operator was permitted, over objection by defendant to testify to the results of the examination (unfavorable to defendant) at defendant's jury trial. After the jury returned a verdict of guilty and before sentence was entered, the trial court . . . certified the following question to this court:

> In a criminal case, if prior to trial the defense attorney, on behalf of his client and with his client's consent, and the deputy county attorney agree in a written stipulation that the results of a polygraph test, to be taken by the defendant, will be admissible as evidence at the trial, on behalf of either the State of Arizona or the accused, may the trial court admit the results of the test over the objection of defense counsel? . . .

The polygraph or lie-detector is a pneumatically operated device which simultaneously records changes in a subject's blood pressure, pulse, respiration rate and depth, psychogalvanic skin reflex (skin resistance to electrical current) and, in some cases, muscular activity. "The basis for the use of the so-called lie-detector . . . is the hypothesis that conscious deception can be deduced from certain involuntary physiological responses in the same manner as physicians diagnose various diseases. The thesis is that lying engenders emotional disturbances which are transmuted into tangible bodily manifestations." The machine itself reflects and records only the subject's physiological responses to the questions propounded by the operator. He then interprets the polygraph (meaning, literally, 'many pictures') and determines whether the subject is lying.

I. Admissibility in General

The first reported American case involving admissibility of lie-detector evidence was Frye v. United States . . . . In affirming the conviction and in upholding the trial court's refusal of the proffered testimony the Circuit Court observed:

> We think the systolic blood pressure deception test has not yet gained such standing and scientific recognition among physiological and psychological authorities as would justify the courts in admitting expert testimony deduced from the discovery, development, and experiments thus far made.

Ten years later the Supreme Court of Wisconsin reached the same result in State v. Bohner, 210 Wis. 651, 246 N.W. 314 (1933). Bohner's conviction for robbery was affirmed and it was held that the trial judge had correctly excluded defendant's offer of lie-detector results. The Wisconsin court added the following:

> We are not satisfied that this instrument, during the ten years that have elapsed since the decision in the *Frye* Case, has progressed from the experimental to the demonstrable stage.

And the judicial attitude toward lie-detector evidence expressed in *Bohner* has not changed markedly in the numerous cases decided since 1933. Thus, in 1961 a New Jersey appellate court was correct in pointing out:

> . . . that there is not a single reported decision where an appellate court has permitted the introduction of the results of a polygraph or lie detector test as evidence in the absence of a sanctioning agreement or stipulation between the parties.

Consistent with this approach appellate courts have reversed convictions in cases where lie-detector results unfavorable to defendants were placed before the juries inferentially. Further, it is uniformly held that a defendant is not permitted to introduce evidence of his willingness to take a lie-detector test. Nor can a defendant's refusal to submit to polygraphic interrogation be shown by the state directly or indirectly.

But judicial reluctance to recognize generally the worth of lie-detector evidence in the court room has not been due to mere inertia. For, in affirming a first degree rape conviction, the Oklahoma Criminal Court of Appeals quoted from two leading authorities the following "factors which occasion the chief difficulties in the diagnosis of deception by the lie-detector technique . . . ."

(1) Emotional tension — "nervousness" — experienced by a subject who is innocent and telling the truth regarding the offense in question, but who is nevertheless affected by

(a) fear induced by the mere fact that suspicion or accusation has been directed against him, and particularly so in instances where the subject has been extensively interrogated or perhaps physically abused by investigators prior to the time of the interview and testing by the lie-detector examiner; and

(b) a guilt complex involving another offense of which he is guilty.

(2) Physiological abnormalities, such as

(a) excessively high or excessively low blood pressure;

(b) diseases of the heart;

(c) respiratory disorders, etc.

(3) Mental abnormalities, such as

(a) feeblemindedness, as in idiots, imbeciles, and morons;

(b) psychoses or insanities, as in manic depressives, paranoids, schizophrenics, paretics, etc.;

(c) psychoneuroses, and psychopathia, as among so-called "peculiar" or "emotionally unstable" persons — those who are neither psychotic nor normal, and who form the borderline between these two groups.

(4) Unresponsiveness in a lying or guilty subject, because of

(a) lack of fear of detection;

(b) apparent ability to consciously control responses by means of certain mental sets or attitudes;

(c) a condition of "sub-shock" or "adrenal exhaustion" at the time of the test;

(d) rationalization of the crime in advance of the test to such an extent that lying about the offense arouses little or no emotional disturbance;

(e) extensive interrogation prior to the test.

(5) Unobserved muscular movements which produce ambiguities or misleading indications in the blood pressure tracing.

And in addition to the above enumerated scientific shortcomings of the polygraph technique the following objections to the unrestricted use of its results in the court room have been registered:

(1) The supposed tendency of judges and juries to treat lie-detector evidence as conclusive on the issue of defendants' guilt.

(2) Lack of standardization of test procedure, examiner qualifications and instrumentation.

(3) Difficulty for jury evaluation of examiners' opinions.

Finally, it appears "that at the present time the technique is not an 'accepted' one among the scientists whose approval is a prerequisite to judicial recognition." Of course absolute infallibility is not the standard for admissibility of scientific evidence. But at this time it seems wise to demand greater standardization of the instrument, technique and examiner qualifications and the endorsement by a larger segment of the psychology and physiology branches of science before permitting general use of lie-detector evidence in court. Accordingly, in the absence of a stipulation lie detector evidence should not be received in an Arizona court for the present.

II. Admissibility Upon Stipulation

[The court's summary of the conflicting and generally inconclusive decisions from 1943 to 1962 "involving stipulated admissibility of lie-detector results" is omitted.]

Generally speaking, even [some of] those experts who warn against admissibility in the absence of a stipulation favor admission of lie-detector evidence upon a proper stipulation. And although polygraphic interrogation has not attained that degree of scientific acceptance in the fields to which it belongs to be admissible at the instance of either the state or defendant . . . it has been considerably improved since Frye v. United States was decided in 1923. A conservative estimate of the accuracy of such tests is as follows:

(1) In 75-80 per cent of the cases the examination correctly indicates the guilt or innocence of the accused;

(2) in 15-20 per cent of the cases the results are too indefinite to warrant a conclusion by the examiner one way or the other; and

(3) 5 per cent or less is the margin of proven error.

With improvement in and standardization of instrumentation, technique and examiner qualifications the margin of proven error is certain to shrink. "Modern court procedure must embrace recognized modern conditions of mechanics, psychology, sociology, medicine, or other sciences, philosophy, and history. The failure to do so will only serve to question the ability of courts to efficiently administer justice." Although much remains to be done to perfect the lie-detector as a means of determining credibility we think it has been developed to a state in which its results are probative enough to warrant admissibility upon stipulation.

Accordingly, and subject to the qualifications announced herein, we hold that polygraphs and expert testimony relating thereto are admissible upon stipulation in Arizona criminal cases. And in such cases the lie-detector evidence is admissible to corroborate other evidence of a defendant's participation in the crime charged. If he takes the stand such evidence is admissible to corroborate or impeach his own testimony.

The "qualifications" are as follows:

(1) That the county attorney, defendant and his counsel all sign a written stipulation providing for defendant's submission to the test and for the subsequent admission at trial of the graphs and the examiner's opinion thereon on behalf of either defendant or the state.

(2) That notwithstanding the stipulation the admissibility of the test results is subject to the discretion of the trial judge, i.e. if the trial judge is not convinced that the examiner is qualified or that the test was conducted under proper conditions he may refuse to accept such evidence.

(3) That if the graphs and examiner's opinion are offered in evidence the opposing party shall have the right to cross-examine the examiner respecting:

a. the examiner's qualifications and training;

b. the conditions under which the test was administered;

c. the limitations of and possibilities for error in the technique of polygraphic interrogation; and

d. at the discretion of the trial judge, any other matter deemed pertinent to the inquiry.

(4) That if such evidence is admitted the trial judge should instruct the jury that the examiner's testimony does not tend to prove or disprove any element of the crime with which a defendant is charged but at most tends only to indicate that at the time of the examination defendant was not telling the truth. Further, the jury members should be instructed that it is for them to determine what corroborative weight and effect such testimony should be given.

The case as certified is remanded for action consistent with this opinion.

NOTES

1. *The rationale of the stipulation-only rule.* What is the theory of the *Valdez* stipulation-only rule? That scientists generally accept the modern polygraph as a valid device for detecting deception? That when the parties agree to use "scientific" evidence that is not generally accepted by scientists, the court should not stand in their way?

2. *The improvement in lie detection technology.* The improvement that the *Valdez* court discerned in polygraphy consisted of a "conservative estimate" derived from "experiments" that established that "5 per cent or less is the margin of error." 371 P.2d at 900. The accompanying footnote reads: "These statistics are taken from Dean Wicker's discussion of Inbau's experiments regarding accuracy of the polygraph. See 22 Tenn. L. Rev. at 713." Inspection of the *Tennessee Law Review* article reveals that the sole support for this "conservative estimate" comes from a 1953 article by an attorney describing the remarks in a 1948 book by another attorney who served also as director of a crime laboratory. There is no indication in the article of a single experiment. The 5% figure comes from the director's impression of "several thousand examinations" covering "a period of sixteen years." Wicker, The Polygraphic Truth Test and the Law of Evidence, 22 Tenn. L. Rev. 711, 713 (1953).

State v. Lyon
744 P.2d 231 (Or. 1987)

CAMPBELL, JUSTICE.

In State v. Brown, 297 Or. 404, 445, 687 P.2d 751 (1984), we held that polygraph evidence is not admissible, over proper objection, in any civil or criminal trial in this state. We reserved opinion as to the admissibility of such evidence pursuant to a pre-examination stipulation. . . .

Defendant was convicted of murder in the shooting death of Mr. Terry Reiser. At defendant's trial, the court permitted the state to introduce into evidence against defendant the results of a polygraph examination administered by detective Michael Plester. Before taking the examination, defendant had received Miranda warnings and had read and signed a "polygraph stipulation form." Defendant had not yet been charged with the crime and was not represented by counsel when he signed the stipulation and took the examination. The results of the examination were not favorable to defendant. . . .

The issue presented in this case is one of first impression in this court. However, an impressive body of precedent from other jurisdictions is available to aid us in our resolution of this issue. Though the available authority is almost unanimous in holding that polygraph results may not be introduced into evidence upon the motion of either party, the jurisdictions appear to be almost evenly split on the question of admissibility of polygraph evidence pursuant to the parties' stipulation. The momentum does not discernibly favor either stance.

Those courts that admit polygraph evidence under stipulation typically rely upon one or the other of two basic rationales. A few courts maintain that the stipulation enhances the reliability of the polygraph by permitting the parties "to control . . . those variables deemed significant to fairness and reliability." However, most courts that permit the introduction of polygraph results pursuant to stipulation hold that by entering into the stipulation the parties waive the right to object or are estopped to object to the introduction of the proffered evidence. . . .

We noted in *Brown* that the leading case on stipulations for the admission of polygraph evidence is State v. Valdez, 91 Ariz. 274, 371 P.2d 894 (1962). . . .

. . . A number of courts have adopted the *Valdez* "qualifications" in whole or in part in concluding that polygraph results are admissible as evidence pursuant to the parties' stipulation. The imposition of these elaborate procedures and preconditions to admission appears to reflect judicial recognition that the volatile mixture of uncertain reliability and extreme persuasiveness represented by polygraph results must be handled gingerly, if at all.

At least two states that initially adopted the *Valdez* criteria later reversed field and held stipulated polygraph results inadmissible. One state that initially adopted *Valdez* later wholly abandoned the requirement of a stipulation and now admits polygraph evidence upon either party's initiative subject only to foundational requirements of the polygraph operator's expertise, the reliability of the particular testing procedure used and the validity of the tests made on the subject.

Those courts that reject the admissibility of stipulated polygraph evidence do so on the grounds (1) that the stipulation does not improve the reliability of the polygraph results, (2) that juries are likely to be unduly persuaded by the polygraph evidence, (3) that the parties can stipulate to facts but cannot by stipulation change the law regarding the admissibility of polygraph evidence, and (4) that it is logically inconsistent to hold polygraph evidence inadmissible when one party seeks to introduce it but admissible by the parties' stipulation. Even commentators who champion the general admissibility of polygraph results question the basis in logic of admitting pursuant to stipulation evidence that it is otherwise inadmissible. . . .

We find particularly instructive the experiences of two states that recently ended prolonged experiments with the *Valdez* requirements and concluded that stipulated polygraph evidence is no longer admissible in evidence.

In 1974 the Supreme Court of Wisconsin adopted the *Valdez* criteria for admission of stipulated polygraph evidence. Seven years later, the court overruled [itself] and held inadmissible polygraph evidence submitted pursuant to stipulation. The court [stated]:

> We recognize . . . that the science and art of polygraphy have advanced and that the polygraph has a degree of validity and reliability. We are, nevertheless, not persuaded that the reliability of the polygraph is such as to permit unconditional admission of the evidence. Our analysis of and our experience with the [stipulation] rule lead us instead to conclude that the . . . conditions are not operating satisfactorily to enhance the reliability of the polygraph evidence and to protect the integrity of the trial process as they were intended to do. . . .

Two years [later], North Carolina joined Wisconsin in abandoning *Valdez*. In State v. Grier, 307 N.C. 628, 300 S.E. 2d 351 (1983), the North Carolina Supreme Court ended its nine-year experiment with *Valdez* . . . . The court emphasized, as the Wisconsin court had, that:

> [a]dmissibility of this evidence has not been based on the validity and accuracy of the lie detector, but rather that by consenting to the evidence pursuant to stipulation, the parties have waived any objections to the inherent unreliability of the test. The stipulation itself and the other conditions [to admissibility] were to operate as a compromise between total rejection and complete acceptance of polygraph evidence.

The court was "forced to conclude that the stipulation accomplishes little toward enhancing the reliability of the polygraph," and that subjecting admissibility to the discretion of the trial judge is not "a sufficient safeguard to ensure reliability of the polygraph test results in a particular case." The court was "also disturbed by the possibility that the jury may be unduly persuaded by the polygraph evidence," and was not convinced that the cautionary instructions required by *Valdez* sufficiently meliorated this possibility. The court concluded "that the admission by stipulation approach does not resolve some of the more perplexing problems attendant to the use of polygraph evidence," and that consequently "in North Carolina, polygraph evidence is no longer admissible in any trial."

In State v. Brown, we held that upon proper objection, polygraph test results are not admissible into evidence in any trial or other legal proceeding subject to the rules of the Oregon Evidence Code. We concluded that though "under proper conditions polygraph evidence may possess some probative value and may, in some cases, be helpful to the trier of fact," "the probative value of polygraph evidence is far outweighed by reasons for its exclusion." We conclude that the stipulation of the parties does not cure these difficulties, and that these same considerations necessitate the exclusion of polygraph evidence even when the parties stipulate to its admission.

In determining whether we will admit polygraph evidence introduced pursuant to the parties' stipulation, we first consider the terms of the stipulation and what the stipulation purports to do. We note that certain items in the stipulation form are simply not proper subjects of stipulation. That defendant, having had the operation of the polygraph explained to him by the police, "believe[s] it to be a scientifically reliable instrument and . . . stipulate[s] that it is so reliable" is testament to the officer's powers of persuasion but is not binding upon the courts of this state. Like the Alaska Supreme Court, we concluded in *Brown* that "no judgment of polygraph testing's validity or potential rate of error can be established based on available scientific evidence." The parties' stipulation to the polygraph's reliability does not change this. Nor does defendant's "stipula[tion] that these results are admissible evidence" vitiate our pronouncement that "polygraph evidence shall not be admissible" over objection in Oregon's courts.

The parties may stipulate to facts. Where the admissibility of an item of evidence is conditioned upon the satisfaction of certain foundational requirements, the parties may stipulate to the satisfaction of those requirements and will be bound by that stipulation. However, they may not by stipulation change the law to render admissible that which we have concluded is not admissible. As other courts have recognized, the "stipulation" to the admissibility of polygraph results constitutes the parties' mutual waiver of the right to object to the introduction into evidence of those results. The Washington Supreme Court, in the course of adopting the *Valdez* requirements, characterized such stipulations as follows:

> When there is a stipulation as in this case, the prosecution and the defense, knowing that the degree of reliability is open to question, in effect gamble that the test will prove favorable to them.

We have determined that we will not permit this gamble in Oregon's courts. Because of the importance of the institutional values implicated by the admission of polygraph results into evidence, we hold that we will not recognize a stipulation between the parties to the admissibility of polygraph evidence.

In *Brown* we were concerned with the "undue delay in administering justice that would occur if we were to allow the admission of polygraph evidence in all cases." We are not convinced that the admission of the evidence pursuant to stipulation significantly reduces the risk of such delay. We are particularly concerned with consumption of time and potential confusion of issues resulting from challenges to the accuracy of the test. Even if the stipulation at issue were read as foreclosing challenges to the qualifications of the examiner and the reliability of the polygraph test, or the introduction of opposing test results, it cannot be argued that defendant would be foreclosed from challenging the manner in which his or her test was conducted, the form of the questions asked, or inquiring into any of the myriad factors that affect the accuracy of a particular test. . . .

> [A]lthough the inquiry was far from complete, the experience of this case has amply shown that, as of now, the validity of a polygraphic test is dependent upon a large number of variable factors, many of which would be very difficult, and perhaps impossible, to assess. In a given case, the time required in order to explore and seek to adjudicate such factors would be virtually incalculable . . . . Accordingly, this court is impelled to the conclusion that the administration of justice simply cannot tolerate the burden of litigation inherently involved in such a process.

Nor is it likely that a "stipulation" that would adequately address all these factors could be drafted or, if successfully drafted, withstand judicial scrutiny. The North Carolina Supreme Court, in overturning its own prior adoption of *Valdez* and holding stipulated polygraph evidence inadmissible, stated:

> The validity of the polygraphic process is dependent upon such a large number of variable factors, many of which are extremely difficult, if not impossible, to assess, that we feel the stipulation simply cannot adequate-

ly deal with all situations which might arise affecting the accuracy of any particular test.

Of greater concern even than the possibility of undue delay is the potential for misuse and over-valuation of the polygraph evidence by the jury. We stated in *Brown:*

> Polygraph evidence may well divert the trier of fact from the direct and circumstantial evidence presented in a case to a distorted valuation of the polygraph evidence. Polygraph evidence is not just another form of scientific evidence presented by experts such as ballistics analysis, fingerprint and handwriting comparisons, blood typing and neutron activation analysis. These other tests do not purport to indicate with any degree of certainty that the witness was or was not credible. By its very nature the polygraph purports to measure truthfulness and deception, the very essence of the jury's role.

This is certainly no less true when the evidence is introduced pursuant to stipulation than when the evidence is introduced by one or other of the parties. In fact, that the parties stipulated to its introduction and to its "reliability" may only exacerbate the prejudicial impact of the polygraph evidence. Our primary considerations in reaching our conclusion in *Brown* were the probable effect of polygraph evidence upon the integrity of the trial process and our respect for the traditional role of the jury. The parties cannot by private agreement "waive" these vital institutional concerns.

A stipulation neither enhances the uncertain reliability of the polygraph examination nor blunts the prejudicial effect of polygraph results upon the jury. The same considerations that compelled us to conclude in Brown that polygraph results are inadmissible over the objection of either party compel us now to conclude that polygraph evidence is inadmissible for any purpose in any legal proceeding subject to the rules of evidence under the Oregon Evidence Code, and henceforth its admission, pursuant even to the parties' stipulation, is error. On retrial, the court will exclude from evidence the proffered polygraph test results. . . .

The Court of Appeals remanded the case for a new trial because of the admission of inadmissible hearsay. We agree that the conviction should be reversed and the case remanded for the reasons stated by the Court of Appeals and for the additional reasons set forth above. The decision of the Court of Appeals is affirmed. The case is remanded to the trial court for a new trial.

LINDE, JUSTICE, concurring.

While I fully concur in the court's opinion, a few words may be added to ask whether there perhaps are wider reasons for the result.

This court, like others, has rejected the use of polygraph evidence on grounds that this means of attacking or supporting the truthfulness of a person's declarations is too unreliable, too prone to error and conscious or unconscious manipulation, to have evidentiary value. The court set forth the reasons for that conclusion in Justice Jones's extensive review of the literature on polygraphy in State v. Brown. Today's decision is based on the same premises and conclusion.

These are reasons enough for the present case. Yet it seems worth raising a question whether more is involved in the widespread uneasiness about electrical lie detectors, reasons that are masked by the common law courts' characteristic professional emphasis on trial procedures and rules of evidence. In fact, the question whether more is involved than unreliability suggests itself in this case, because the holding goes beyond normal procedures for excluding unreliable evidence over an opposing party's objection and instructs courts not to admit polygraph evidence even without objection or when the parties expressly stipulate to its admission. These are extraordinary strictures against questionable evidence.

I think more is involved. I doubt that the uneasiness about electrical lie detectors would disappear even if they were refined to place their accuracy beyond question. Indeed, I would not be surprised if such a development would only heighten the sense of unease and the search for plausible legal objections.

Published accounts, not of record here, report that submission to polygraph tests is widely demanded in public as well as in private employment, not without resentment by employees. It was not only a concern about inaccuracy that caused the current Secretary of State to protest White House plans to demand such tests in a drive to discover and to inhibit unauthorized disclosures of information. In part, of course, the Secretary's protest and the resentment of many civil servants and private employees arise from the implication that their word may not be trusted; but trust, too, is not the ultimate issue.

There are many contexts in which one person — a lender, a reporter, or a careful police officer — does not take another's word about an important fact at face value without checking the credibility of the speaker and the believability of the information against other sources. The principle is familiar in the law governing warrants for a search or seizure. Sometimes a person will be required to undergo a physical examination that may contradict his verbal assertions (for instance, that he consumed no more than two beers), or without even obtaining or considering any verbal statements from him. That, too, may be resented, but it is different from a polygraph examination.

What is that difference? The heart of the matter, I suspect, is that the polygraph seeks to turn the human body against the personality that inhabits it in a way that other tests do not.

The polygraph differs in principle from other physical examinations. Tests of one's breath, blood, or urine to detect the presence of illicit substances or a communicable disease may be perceived as an insult or an infringement of one's privacy. They also may prove one a liar. But even when employed to confirm or to contradict a verbal assertion, the immediate object of the test itself is to determine an independently relevant fact, the actual condition of the organism. Whether the tested person's stated belief is proved correct or erroneous is a secondary consequence, even when it is important.

The polygraph does not independently establish any past, present, or future fact. It purports neither to replace nor to supplement the assertions of the tested person with other evidence on the matter in question. The polygraph is indifferent to what the assertions are about and whether they are factually correct. As its popular name suggests, the lie detector only purports to detect whether a person is uttering a lie.

Beyond doubt that often is a useful thing to know. There is no general right to lie, as civil, criminal, and administrative sanctions in many contexts show, although it is interesting to recall that as late as the time of Oregon's statehood it was disputed whether a defendant could be sworn to the truth as well as permitted to address the jury, and knowingly false statements do not invariably forfeit the guarantees of free expression. Doubtless, also, it often is in one's interest to be able to overcome suspicion and "prove" one's truthfulness.

Legal systems have sought truthful testimony by various means. The solemn oath to speak the truth "so help me God" invoked religious obligation and fear for one's soul. Temporal punishment for perjury was added when conscience or fear of damnation would not suffice. Both forms of admonition prompt the witness as a free agent to choose truth over falsehood and its consequences. The law also has experience with compelling disclosure by turning the human body against the human will. For five hundred years torture was a judicially administered instrument of criminal procedure to obtain confessions when reliable eyewitness testimony was lacking, because no conviction could rest only on inferences from circumstantial evidence. Even without that legal rationale (and without its accompanying legal restraints), coercion of disclosures by pain remains a widespread though officially disavowed practice. Indefensible as it is, it still is addressed to human volition, as instances of failure to break the victim's resistance show. Coercion of the will by threat or by force confirms rather than denies traditional conceptions of personality.

Of course the polygraph is not torture, no more than an electrocardiogram, for instance. Also unlike torture, however, the polygraph is unconcerned with personal choice. Purporting only to detect lies, it is as indifferent to persuading the subject to tell the truth (though it may produce that effect) as it is to the substance of the questions asked and answered. The polygraph turns its subject into an object.

So do many diagnostic tests, as I have said. The same approach also may correspond to one theory of human behavior and human relationships. But is it consistent with the theory underlying our legal and social institutions? This seems doubtful. Inconsistency of physiological lie detection with fundamental tenets about human personhood has been important in European objections to the polygraph, reflecting Christian and Kantian philosophical traditions as much as doubts of its accuracy.

The institution of the trial, above all, assumes the importance of human judgment in assessing the statements of disputing parties and other witnesses. The cherished courtroom drama of confrontation, oral testimony and cross-examination is designed to let a jury pass judgment on their truthfulness and on the accuracy of their testimony. The central myth of the trial is that truth can be discovered in no better way, though it has long been argued that the drama really serves symbolic values more important than reliable factfinding. One of these implicit values surely is to see that parties and the witnesses are treated as persons to be believed or disbelieved by their peers rather than as electrochemical systems to be certified as truthful or mendacious by a machine.

What would be the effect if some such machine were proved 100 percent effective? It could be the ultimate 21st-Century refinement of the medieval Anglo-Saxon oath-helpers, who, of course, were only human.[3] A machine improved to detect uncertainty, faulty memory, or an overactive imagination would leave little need for live testimony and cross-examination before a human tribunal; an affidavit with the certificate of a polygraph operator attached would suffice. There would be no point to solemn oaths under threat of punishment for perjury if belief is placed not in the witness but in the machine.

Compulsion to take polygraph examinations would hardly be necessary; the present somewhat pathetic urge of previously unfaithworthy prisoners and suspects to prove their statements by volunteered polygraph tests would likely be emulated by other witnesses who want to be believed. Volunteered certificates of truthfulness could be expected to spread from legal procedures to employment, credit, and more personal relationships, and their absence thereafter would appear as grounds for suspicion. Would a perfect detector enhance people's capacity to test for truth only at the cost of diminishing their common humanity?

These questions go beyond doubts of the polygraph's accuracy. I do not speculate what legal issues beyond the rules of evidence they may raise; here none has been briefed. For the present case, I am satisfied to join in the court's opinion.

NOTES

1. *The varied applications of polygraphic lie detection.* Even after *Lyon,* the efforts of polygraphers to detect lies are admitted in Oregon in probation revocation hearings and administrative disciplinary hearings on state prison inmates. James R. Wygant, And Nothing But the Truth: The Current Status of Polygraph, Ore. Bar J., Nov. 1988, at 27, 29. See also Anne M. Payne, Annotation, Propriety of Conditioning Probation on Defendant's Submission to Polygraph or Other Lie Detector Testing, 86 A.L.R. 4th 709 (1991).

In the private sector, employers have used polygraphy for job screening and

---

[3] Oath-helpers were persons who swore on oath that they believed the oaths of a party to a suit, thus helping to prove that the assertions made by that party were true.

investigations of misconduct by employees, but state and federal legislation curtails these applications of polygraphy. See Brad V. Driscoll, Note, The Employee Polygraph Protection Act of 1988: A Balance of Interests, 75 Iowa L. Rev. 539 (1990); Note, Lie Detectors in the Workplace: The Need for Civil Actions Against Employers, 101 Harv. L. Rev. 806 (1988).

For still other possible uses of polygraphy, see Steven J. Gaynor, Annotation, Admissibility of Evidence of Polygraph Test Results, or Offer or Refusal to Take Test, in Action for Malicious Prosecution, 10 A.L.R. 5th 663 (1993); Lisa K. Gregory, Annotation, Admissibility of Polygraph or Similar Lie Detector Results, or Willingness to Submit to Test, on Issues of Coverage Under Insurance Policy, or Insurer's Good-Faith Belief that Claim was not Covered, 7 A.L.R. 5th 143 (1992).

2. *Validity of polygraphic lie detection.* The ability of polygraphers to detect lies remains controversial. No known physiological response or pattern of responses is unique to deception. David Raskin, The Polygraph in 1986: Scientific, Professional and Legal Issues Surrounding Applications and Acceptance of Polygraph Evidence, 1986 Utah L. Rev. 29, 31. Consequently, as it is usually used to detect deception, the polygraph is not a lie detector; it is a fear detector. Testimony of Leonard Saxe, Hearings on H.R. 1524 and H.R. 1924 Before the Subcomm. on Employment Opportunities, House Comm. on Education and Labor, 99th Cong., 1st sess., 1986, at 109. To detect deception, the polygraph operator must ensure that the subject believes that his lies can be detected (so that the subject feels fear when he speaks falsely) and that the subject believes that his truthful statements will be recognized as such (so that he feels less fear when he speaks truthfully). In addition, other sources of anxiety that would produce responses characteristic of fear when the subject is being truthful must be eliminated. Achieving these conditions is difficult. Raskin, supra, at 31.

Nevertheless, the polygraph industry claims that the tests are very accurate, both in specific incident investigations and in job screening. The vice president of the American Polygraph Association maintains that:

> Over the past 15 years, at least 100 studies have been conducted by scholars, scientists and polygraph practitioners concerning the accuracy of the polygraph technique. Based on a responsible reading of these results, the polygraph has been shown to have an accuracy of 85-95%.

Testimony of Lawrence W. Talley, 1986 Hearings, supra, at 358. In contrast, the most prominent academic critic of the polygraph, insists that:

> We can summarize the available evidence as follows: When scored without knowledge of the case facts or clues based on the suspect's behavior or demeanor, the modern polygraph test can be expected to be wrong about one-third of the time. The polygraph test is strongly biased against the innocent person; truthful suspects failed the polygraph 39%, 49% and 55%

of the time in the three scientific investigations [that meet reasonable standards of scientific research].

David T. Lykken, Detecting Deception in 1984, 27 Am. Behav. Scientist 481, 493 (1984). For still other descriptions and differing assessments of the empirical research, see Modern Scientific Evidence § 14-2.0 to 14-7.0 (David Faigman et al. eds., 1997); Gershon Ben-Shakar & John J. Furedy, Theories and Applications in the Detection of Deception (1990); The Polygraph Test: Lies, Truth and Science (Anthony Gale ed., 1988); U.S. Dep't of Defense, The Accuracy and Utility of Polygraph Testing (1984); Office of Technology Assessment, U.S. Cong., Scientific Validity of Polygraph Testing: A Research Review and Evaluation — A Technical Memorandum (1983); Charles R. Honts & Bruce D. Quick, The Polygraph in 1995: Progress in Science and the Law, 71 N.D. L. Rev. 987 (1995); William J. Yankee, The Current Status of Research in Forensic Psychophysiology and and Its Application in the Psychophysiological Detection of Deception, 40 J. Forensic Sci. 63 (1995); Charles R. Honts, The Psychophysiological Detection of Deception, 3 Current Directions Psych. Sci. 77 (1994); James R. McCall, Misconceptions and Reevaluation — Polygraph Admissibility after *Rock* and *Daubert,* 1996 U. Ill. L. Rev. 363 (1994); Leonard Saxe, Detection of Deception: Polygraph and Integrity Tests, 3 Current Directions Psych. Sci. 69 (1994); Robert Steinbrook, The Polygraph Test — A Flawed Diagnostic Procedure, 327 New Eng. J. Med. 122 (1992) (editorial); John C. Kircher et al., Meta-Analysis of Mock Crime Studies of the Control Question Polygraph Technique, 12 Law & Hum. Behav. 79 (1988). For a review of studies of the impact of polygraph testimony on jurors, see Steven M. Egesdal, Note, The *Frye* Doctrine and Relevancy Approach Controversy: An Empirical Evaluation, 74 Geo. L.J. 1769 (1986).

3. *Admissibility. Lyons* holds polygraph evidence inadmissible, whether offered as substantive evidence or to impeach the credibility of a witness. Most jurisdictions follow this per se rule. See 1 McCormick on Evidence § 206 (John Strong ed., 4th ed. 1992). Following *Valdez,* a substantial minority of jurisdictions give the trial court discretion to admit the evidence if, prior to the testing, the parties have stipulated to its admission. Id. A handful of jurisdictions allow the judge to admit the evidence even without a prior stipulation. See Modern Scientific Evidence § 14-1.2.2 (David Faigman et al. eds., 1997). Is the stipulation-only rule compatible with *Daubert?* See id. at § 14-1.2.3. Post-*Daubert* cases are reviewed in James R. McCall, Misconceptions and Reevaluation — Polygraph Admissibility after Rock and Daubert, 1996 U. Ill. L. Rev. 363 (concluding that a "profound" change toward greater use of polygraphy is underway).

4. *Impeachment.* If a jurisdiction does not exclude polygraph evidence under its rules as to the soundness or acceptance of scientific evidence, then the expert opinion that the defendant (or another witness) lied during the examination might be offered to impeach the credibility of the witness. Federal (and Uniform) Rule of Evidence 608 governs the use of evidence of character for truthfulness. Rule 608(a) provides that "[t]he credibility of a witness may be attacked or supported by evidence in the form of opinion or reputation . . . ." Ordinarily, the attack would consist of testimony that the witness has a reputation for lying or that, in the opinion of the person testifying about the witness, the witness characteristically lies. In other words, Rule 608(a) normally deals with evidence of the propensity to lie. Does it extend as well to the opinion of the polygrapher that the witness lied during the examination?

If the answer is in the negative, then the impeachment consists of evidence about a specific, past act of lying. Rule 608(b) states that "[s]pecific instances of the conduct of a witness for the purpose of attacking or supporting a witness's credibility . . . may not be proved by extrinsic evidence. They may, however, . . . be inquired into on cross-examination of the witness . . . concerning the witness' character for truthfulness or untruthfulness . . . ." This might be read to imply that the polygrapher cannot be called to testify that the witness lied during the examination, but the witness can be asked on cross-examination whether he failed the polygraph test. Id. at § 14-1.2.4.

Nevertheless, does Rule 608 really apply to this kind of specific-act testimony? The cross-examination must concern "the witness' *character* for truthfulness or untruthfulness." Rule 608(b) (emphasis added). Is the rule limited to evidence that invites reasoning of the form "the witness has a tendency to lie, therefore the witness is lying now"? Is that the reasoning that proponent of the testimony about the polygraph examination wants the jury to use?

5. *Bolstering.* If a jurisdiction does not exclude polygraph evidence under its rules as to the soundness or acceptance of scientific evidence, then the expert opinion that the defendant (or another witness) spoke truthfully during the examination might be offered to bolster the credibility of the witness. Again, there is a real question as to whether the past act is introduced to prove a "character for truthfulness," but if it is, then Rule 608(a)(2) prohibits this "evidence of truthful character" unless and until "the character of the witness has been attacked . . . ."

United States v. Solomon
753 F.2d 1522 (9th Cir. 1985)

EUGENE A. WRIGHT, CIRCUIT JUDGE:

The defendants appeal their convictions arising from the robbery and murder by arson of a woman on the Yakima Indian Reservation. We have reviewed the evidentiary rulings and constitutional arguments raised on appeal and we affirm the convictions.

While drinking at a tavern on the night of July 25, 1983, defendants Louella Solomon and her brother, John Wesley, met Katherine Piel Heath and offered her a ride. At 2:00 on the morning of the 26th, the three joined Peter George, defendants' 17-year-old nephew, who was waiting in a car. Solomon eventually drove them all to a residence on Progressive Road. All the actors were Yakima Indians and the house was on Indian National Tribal trust land on the Yakima Indian Reservation.

The three surviving participants gave conflicting testimony as to the events preceding the fire. Wesley and George each changed his account of the events during the course of investigation and trial. The following account of that night's events is presented in the light most favorable to the government.

Solomon suggested that Wesley and George obtain Heath's purse. Inside the house Wesley either struck Heath or held her while George struck her, knocking her unconscious. Her purse was taken outside to Solomon who took money from it (at least $2.00). At Solomon's suggestion, the purse was burned in a wood stove inside the house.

At some point Solomon stated that Heath had to be killed. Wesley and George returned inside and one of them started a fire in some curtains. Solomon had agreed to the burning of the house. The defendants and George left the house and drove away, leaving Heath inside.

The fire was discovered at 4:00 a.m. and allowed to burn itself out. Heath's remains were found later during a check of the scene by a firefighter. An autopsy identified carbon monoxide poisoning as the probable cause of death.

Wesley was arrested and detained by Tribal authorities on July 28th. He was federally indicted on October 24th and remained in custody until trial. George was granted complete immunity by federal and state authorities in return for his cooperation.

On December 22, 1983, at Wesley's request, a psychiatrist administered sodium amytal and interviewed him under its influence. On January 20, 1984, at the government's request, George was interviewed while under the influence of sodium amytal. A new indictment was returned, charging Solomon also.

A jury trial resulted in Solomon's conviction for first degree murder and robbery and Wesley's conviction for first degree murder and arson endangering life. Both were sentenced on the murder count to life imprisonment with the possibility of parole and each received a concurrent sentence on the other charge. . . .

Dr. Frederick Montgomery, a psychiatrist, conducted the separate interviews of Wesley and the witness George while they were under the influence of sodium amytal, administered intravenously. Such interviews are referred to as "narcoanalysis." Both interviews were attended by an Assistant United States Attorney and Wesley's attorney. George's attorney also witnessed his interview.[2]

---

[2] These procedures were undertaken at the suggestion of and with the cooperation of all counsel. At oral argument, we complemented [sic] the attorneys for their professional attitudes in their search for the truth.

A. Taint of Witness George

Solomon contends that George's testimony should have been excluded from the trial because his testimony could not be reliable after he underwent a sodium amytal interview. In response, the government asserts that the trial court scrutinized George's sodium amytal interview and carefully applied the teachings of the hypnosis cases in this circuit. Moreover, Solomon was not precluded from presenting evidence to the jury that George's testimony was enhanced by the use of sodium amytal.

The only Ninth Circuit case addressing narcoanalysis excluded a recording of and psychiatric testimony supporting an interview conducted under the influence of sodium pentathol, a precursor of sodium amytal. Lindsey v. United States, 16 Alaska 268, 237 F.2d 893 (9th Cir. 1956). The case at bar is distinguishable because no testimony concerning the narcoanalysis was offered at trial. Only George's current recollection of events was presented.

In an analogous situation, this circuit has held that the current recollections of witnesses whose memories have been refreshed by hypnosis are admissible, with the fact of hypnosis relevant to credibility only. United States v. Adams, 581 F.2d 193, 198-99 (9th Cir.), cert. denied, 439 U.S. 1006 (1978). We have cautioned, however, that "[g]reat care must be exercised to insure" that statements after hypnosis are not the product of hypnotic suggestion.

We find no abuse of discretion in the trial court's ruling to admit the testimony of the witness George. The court's order denying Solomon's Motion to Suppress reflects a careful balancing of reliability against prejudicial dangers:

> The sodium amytal examination of George was performed at a Yakima hospital by Dr. Fred Montgomery, a board certified psychiatrist with training and experience in narco-analysis and hypnosis. Dr. Montgomery had completed a residency in psychiatry and had used sodium amytal on at least fifteen to twenty occasions in civil and criminal cases during his fifteen years of practice. Also present at the George examination were his attorney, [the] Assistant United States Attorney, . . . and defendant Wesley's attorney. There is no evidence to support an inference that George's examination was in any way suggestive or leading. The evidence establishes the contrary. All questions were propounded by Dr. Montgomery in a hospital setting pursuant to medically accepted standards. Questions from attorneys during the examination were written and then forwarded to Dr. Montgomery.[2]

---

[2] While we do not endorse specific procedures to ensure that statements made under narco-analysis are not the product of suggestion, we believe that a complete stenographic record is desirable for purposes of judicial review. See Adams, 581 F.2d at 199 n. 12 (suggested procedural safeguards to be followed in hypnosis cases).

The trial court did not err in refusing to exclude George's testimony. Solomon's conviction is affirmed.

B. Wesley's Statements During Narcoanalysis

Wesley wanted to introduce expert testimony by Dr. Montgomery explaining the effects of sodium amytal and relating the statements that Wesley made while under its influence. The testimony was to rehabilitate Wesley's credibility after the government impeached it with an earlier confession. The trial court held that narcoanalysis was not reliable enough to admit into evidence, but that Dr. Montgomery could testify to the statements made to him by Wesley, without an explanation of the circumstances.

Expert testimony is admissible if the jury may receive "appreciable help" from it. The necessary balancing of the probative value of the evidence against its prejudicial effect is committed to the discretion of the trial court.

Evidence based on a novel scientific technique is admissible if it is generally accepted as a reliable technique among the scientific community. Frye v. United States, 293 F. 1013, 1014 (D.C. Cir. 1923). The admission of a tape recording of narcoanalysis with an expert's explanation of the technique was held prejudicial error by this court in 1956. Lindsey, 237 F.2d at 898.

Dr. Montgomery testified in the absence of the jury that narcoanalysis is now a generally accepted investigative technique. He stated that safeguards against suggestion of memories by the examiner are essential. He opined that Wesley's interview was safeguarded adequately by production of a transcript, the presence of prosecuting and defense attorneys, and having the examining psychiatrist pose all of the questions.

Dr. Montgomery testified also that narcoanalysis is useful as a source of information that can be valuable if verified through other sources. At one point he testified that it would elicit an accurate statement of subjective memory, but later said that the subject could fabricate memories. He refused to agree that the subject would be more likely to tell the truth under narcoanalysis than if not so treated.

Wesley wanted to use the psychiatric testimony to bolster the credibility of his trial testimony that George started the fatal fire. Wesley's statement shortly after the fire was that he himself set the fire. The probative value of the statement while under narcoanalysis that George was responsible was the drug's tendency to induce truthful statements.

Montgomery admitted that narcoanalysis does not reliably induce truthful statements. The judge's exclusion of the evidence concerning narcoanalysis was not an abuse of discretion. The prejudicial effect of an aura of scientific respectability outweighed the slight probative value of the evidence. . . .

The convictions are affirmed.

NOTE

"Truth Sera." The *Solomon* opinion notes that:

> The only Ninth Circuit case addressing narcoanalysis excluded a recording of and psychiatric testimony supporting an interview conducted under the influence of sodium pentathol, a precursor of sodium amytal. Lindsey v. United States, 16 Alaska 268, 237 F.2d 893 (9th Cir. 1956). The case at bar is distinguishable because no testimony concerning the narco-analysis was offered at trial. Only George's current recollection of events was presented.

What would the proper outcome have been had the government informed the jury that George's recollections came from a narcoanalytic session? The court observes that even if this session may have implanted erroneous memories, "Solomon was not precluded from presenting evidence to the jury that George's testimony was enhanced by the use of sodium amytal." As defense counsel, would you have chosen to bring this fact to the attention of the jury? In *Lindsey,* the court had this to say about the operation of "truth sera":

> Although narcoanalysis in general, and the sodium-pentothal inter-view in particular, may be a useful tool in the psychiatric examination of an individual, the courts have not generally recognized the trustworthiness and reliability of such tests as being sufficiently well established to accord the results the status of competent evidence.
>
> In prosecutions where the defendant has voluntarily submitted him-self to drug tests, and the results have indicated his innocence, the courts have rejected the evidence on the ground that it is "self serving."
>
> The expected effect of the drug is to dispel inhibitions so the subject will talk freely, but it seems scientific tests reveal that people thus prompt-ed to speak freely do not always tell the truth. [Citations omitted.] In an article jointly prepared by two of the faculty of Yale Medical School and two of the faculty of Yale Law School, the authors conclude:
>
> > In summary, experimental and clinical findings indicate that only individuals who have conscious and unconscious reasons for doing so are inclined to confess and yield to interrogation under drug influence. On the other hand, some are able to with-hold information and some, especially character neurotics, are able to lie. Others are so suggestible they will describe, in response to suggestive questioning, behavior which never in fact occurred . . . . But drugs are not 'truth sera'. They lessen inhibitions to verbalization and stimulate unrepressed expres-sion not only of fact but of fancy and suggestion as well. Thus the material produced is not 'truth' in the sense that it conforms to empirical fact.

Dession et al., Drug Induced Revelation and Criminal Investigation, 62 Yale L.J. 315, 319 (1953). Another writer on the subject has gone so far as to state that: "The intravenous injection of a drug by a physician in a hospital may appear more scientific than the drinking of large amounts of bourbon in a tavern, but the end result displayed in the subject's speech may be no more reliable . . . ." MacDonald, Truth Serum, 46 J. Crim. L., C. & P.S. at 259.

Whatever may be the value as an aid to psychiatric examination or otherwise, we cannot affirmatively say that the sodium-pentothal interview is generally vouched for by scientific authority and so entitled to judicial recognition, through having gained "general acceptance in the particular field in which it belongs," as a trustworthy truth-extracting procedure, which is reliably so in all cases. Hence it was error to admit the recording of the sodium-pentothal interview, even as a prior consistent statement for the limited purpose of rehabilitating the impeached witness.

See also State v. Pitts, 562 A.2d 1320 (N.J. 1989) (psychiatrist's testimony about sodium amytal interview used to arrive at an opinion concerning defendant's state of mind during the murder was properly excluded).

Chapter 18
Enhancing Memory

Rock v. Arkansas
483 U.S. 44 (1987)

JUSTICE BLACKMUN delivered the opinion of the Court.

The issue presented in this case is whether Arkansas' evidentiary rule prohibiting the admission of hypnotically refreshed testimony violated petitioner's constitutional right to testify on her own behalf as a defendant in a criminal case.

I

Petitioner Vickie Lorene Rock was charged with manslaughter in the death of her husband, Frank Rock, on July 2, 1983. A dispute had been simmering about Frank's wish to move from the couple's small apartment adjacent to Vickie's beauty parlor to a trailer she owned outside town. That night a fight erupted when Frank refused to let petitioner eat some pizza and prevented her from leaving the apartment to get something else to eat. When police arrived on the scene they found Frank on the floor with a bullet wound in his chest. Petitioner urged the officers to help her husband, and cried to a sergeant who took her in charge, "please save him" and "don't let him die." The police removed her from the building because she was upset and because she interfered with their investigation by her repeated attempts to use the telephone to call her husband's parents. According to the testimony of one of the investigating officers, petitioner told him that "she stood up to leave the room and [her husband] grabbed her by the throat and choked her and threw her against the wall and . . . at that time she walked over and picked up the weapon and pointed it toward the floor and he hit her again and she shot him."

Because petitioner could not remember the precise details of the shooting, her attorney suggested that she submit to hypnosis in order to refresh her memory. Petitioner was hypnotized twice by Doctor Betty Back, a licensed neuropsychologist with training in the field of hypnosis. Doctor Back interviewed petitioner for an hour prior to the first hypnosis session, taking notes on petitioner's general history and her recollections of the shooting.[2] Both hypnosis sessions were

---

[2] Doctor Back's handwritten notes regarding petitioner's memory of the day of the shooting read as follows:

Pt states she & husb. were discussing moving out to a trailer she had prev. owned. He was 'set on moving out to the trailer — she felt they should discuss. She bec[ame] upset & went to another room to lay down. Bro. came & left. She came out to eat some of the pizza, he wouldn't allow her to have any. She said she would go out and get [something] to eat he wouldn't allow her — He pushed her against a wall an end table in the corner [with] a gun on it. They were the night watchmen for business that sets behind them. She picked gun up stated she didn't want him hitting her anymore. He wouldn't let her out door, slammed door & 'gun went off & he fell & he died' [pt looked misty eyed here — near tears]" (additions by Doctor Back).

recorded on tape. Petitioner did not relate any new information during either of the sessions, but, after the hypnosis, she was able to remember that at the time of the incident she had her thumb on the hammer of the gun, but had not held her finger on the trigger. She also recalled that the gun had discharged when her husband grabbed her arm during the scuffle. As a result of the details that petitioner was able to remember about the shooting, her counsel arranged for a gun expert to examine the handgun, a single action Hawes .22 Deputy Marshal. That inspection revealed that the gun was defective and prone to fire, when hit or dropped, without the trigger's being pulled.

When the prosecutor learned of the hypnosis sessions, he filed a motion to exclude petitioner's testimony. The trial judge held a pretrial hearing on the motion and concluded that no hypnotically refreshed testimony would be admitted. The court issued an order limiting petitioner's testimony to "matters remembered and stated to the examiner prior to being placed under hypnosis." At trial, petitioner introduced testimony by the gun expert, but the court limited petitioner's own description of the events on the day of the shooting to a reiteration of the sketchy information in Doctor Back's notes.[4] The jury convicted petitioner on the manslaughter charge and she was sentenced to 10 years imprisonment and a $10,000 fine.

On appeal, the Supreme Court of Arkansas rejected petitioner's claim that the limitations on her testimony violated her right to present her defense. The court concluded that "the dangers of admitting this kind of testimony outweigh whatever probative value it may have," and decided to follow the approach of States that have held hypnotically refreshed testimony of witnesses inadmissible per se. Although the court acknowledged that "a defendant's right to testify is fundamental," it ruled that the exclusion of petitioner's testimony did not violate her constitutional rights. Any "prejudice or deprivation" she suffered "was minimal and resulted from her own actions and not by any erroneous ruling of the court." We granted certiorari, to consider the constitutionality of Arkansas' per se rule excluding a criminal defendant's hypnotically refreshed testimony.

---

[4] When petitioner began to testify, she was repeatedly interrupted by the prosecutor, who objected that her statements fell outside the scope of the pretrial order. Each time she attempted to describe an event on the day of the shooting, she was unable to proceed for more than a few words before her testimony was ruled inadmissible. For example, she was unable to testify without objection about her husband's activities on the morning of the shooting, about their discussion and disagreement concerning the move to her trailer, about her husband's and his brother's replacing the shock absorbers on a van, and about her brother-in-law's return to eat pizza. She then made a proffer, outside the hearing of the jury, of testimony about the fight in an attempt to show that she could adhere to the court's order. The prosecution objected to every detail not expressly described in Doctor Back's notes or in the testimony the doctor gave at the pretrial hearing. The court agreed with the prosecutor's statement that "ninety-nine percent of everything [petitioner] testified to in the proffer" was inadmissible.

II

Petitioner's claim that her testimony was impermissibly excluded is bottomed on her constitutional right to testify in her own defense. At this point in the development of our adversary system, it cannot be doubted that a defendant in a criminal case has the right to take the witness stand and to testify in his or her own defense. . . .

The right to testify on one's own behalf at a criminal trial has sources in several provisions of the Constitution. [The Court finds this right to be implicit in] the Fourteenth Amendment's guarantee that no one shall be deprived of liberty without due process of law . . . , the Compulsory Process Clause of the Sixth Amendment, which grants a defendant the right to call "witnesses in his favor," . . . the Sixth Amendment, [which] "grants to the accused *personally* the right to make his defense," . . . , [and] the Fifth Amendment's guarantee against compelled testimony. . . .

III

The question now before the Court is whether a criminal defendant's right to testify may be restricted by a state rule that excludes her post-hypnosis testimony. This is not the first time this Court has faced a constitutional challenge to a state rule, designed to ensure trustworthy evidence, that interfered with the ability of a defendant to offer testimony. In Washington v. Texas, 388 U.S. 14 (1967), the Court was confronted with a state statute that prevented persons charged as principals, accomplices, or accessories in the same crime from being introduced as witnesses for one another. The statute, like the original common-law prohibition on testimony by the accused, was grounded in a concern for the reliability of evidence presented by an interested party . . . .

Just as a State may not apply an arbitrary rule of competence to exclude a material defense witness from taking the stand, it also may not apply a rule of evidence that permits a witness to take the stand, but arbitrarily excludes material portions of his testimony. In Chambers v. Mississippi, 410 U.S. 284 (1973), the Court invalidated a State's hearsay rule on the ground that it abridged the defendant's right to "present witnesses in his own defense." Chambers was tried for a murder to which another person repeatedly had confessed in the presence of acquaintances. The State's hearsay rule, coupled with a "voucher" rule that did not allow the defendant to cross-examine the confessed murderer directly, prevented Chambers from introducing testimony concerning these confessions, which were critical to his defense. This Court reversed the judgment of conviction, holding that when a state rule of evidence conflicts with the right to present witnesses, the rule may "not be applied mechanistically to defeat the ends of justice," but must meet the fundamental standards of due process. In the Court's view, the State in *Chambers* did not demonstrate that the hearsay testimony in that case, which bore "assurances of trustworthiness" including corroboration by other evidence, would be unreliable, and thus the defendant should have been able to introduce the exculpatory testimony.

Of course, the right to present relevant testimony is not without limitation. The right "may, in appropriate cases, bow to accommodate other legitimate interests in the criminal trial process." But restrictions of a defendant's right to testify may not be arbitrary or disproportionate to the purposes they are designed to serve. In applying its evidentiary rules a State must evaluate whether the interests served by a rule justify the limitation imposed on the defendant's constitutional right to testify.

IV

The Arkansas rule enunciated by the state courts does not allow a trial court to consider whether posthypnosis testimony may be admissible in a particular case; it is a per se rule prohibiting the admission at trial of any defendant's hypnotically refreshed testimony on the ground that such testimony is always unreliable. Thus, in Arkansas, an accused's testimony is limited to matters that he or she can prove were remembered before hypnosis. This rule operates to the detriment of any defendant who undergoes hypnosis, without regard to the reasons for it, the circumstances under which it took place, or any independent verification of the information it produced.[13]

In this case, the application of that rule had a significant adverse effect on petitioner's ability to testify. It virtually prevented her from describing any of the events that occurred on the day of the shooting, despite corroboration of many of those events by other witnesses. Even more importantly, under the court's rule petitioner was not permitted to describe the actual shooting except in the words contained in Doctor Back's notes. The expert's description of the gun's tendency to misfire would have taken on greater significance if the jury had heard petitioner testify that she did not have her finger on the trigger and that the gun went off when her husband hit her arm.

In establishing its per se rule, the Arkansas Supreme Court simply followed the approach taken by a number of States that have decided that hypnotically enhanced testimony should be excluded at trial on the ground that it tends to be unreliable. Other States that have adopted an exclusionary rule, however, have done so for the testimony of *witnesses,* not for the testimony of a *defendant.* The Arkansas Supreme Court failed to perform the constitutional analysis that is nec-

---

[13] The Arkansas Supreme Court took the position that petitioner was fully responsible for any prejudice that resulted from the restriction on her testimony because it was she who chose to resort to the technique of hypnosis. . . . It should be noted, however, that Arkansas had given no previous indication that it looked with disfavor on the use of hypnosis to assist in the preparation for trial and there were no previous state-court rulings on the issue.

essary when a defendant's right to testify is at stake.

Although the Arkansas court concluded that any testimony that cannot be proved to be the product of prehypnosis memory is unreliable, many courts have eschewed a per se rule and permit the admission of hypnotically refreshed testimony.[16] Hypnosis by trained physicians or psychologists has been recognized as a valid therapeutic technique since 1958, although there is no generally accepted theory to explain the phenomenon, or even a consensus on a single definition of hypnosis. See Council on Scientific Affairs, Scientific Status of Refreshing Recollection by the Use of Hypnosis, 253 J.A.M.A. 1918, 1918-1919 (1985) (Council Report).[17] The use of hypnosis in criminal investigations, however, is controversial, and the current medical and legal view of its appropriate role is unsettled.

Responses of individuals to hypnosis vary greatly. The popular belief that hypnosis guarantees the accuracy of recall is as yet without established foundation and, in fact, hypnosis often has no effect at all on memory. The most common response to hypnosis, however, appears to be an increase in both correct and incorrect recollections.[18] Three general characteristics of hypnosis may lead to the introduction of inaccurate memories: the subject becomes "suggestible" and may try to please the hypnotist with answers the subject thinks will be met with approval; the subject is likely to "confabulate," that is, to fill in details from the imagination in order to make an answer more coherent and complete; and, the subject experiences "memory hardening," which gives him great confidence in both true and false memories, making effective cross-examination more difficult. See generally M. Orne et al., Hypnotically Induced Testimony, in Eyewitness Testimony: Psychological Perspectives 171 (G. Wells and E. Loftus, eds., 1985); Diamond, Inherent Problems in the Use of Pretrial Hypnosis on a Prospective Witness, 68 Calif. L. Rev. 313, 333-342 (1980). Despite the unreliability that hypnosis concededly may introduce, however, the procedure has been credited as instrumental

---

[16] Some jurisdictions have adopted a rule that hypnosis affects the credibility, but not the admissibility, of testimony. Other courts conduct an individualized inquiry in each case. In some jurisdictions, courts have established procedural prerequisites for admissibility in order to reduce the risks associated with hypnosis. Perhaps the leading case in this line is State v. Hurd, 86 N.J. 525, 432 A.2d 86 (1981).

[17] Hypnosis has been described as "involv[ing] the focusing of attention; increased responsiveness to suggestions; suspension of disbelief with a lowering of critical judgment; potential for altering perception, motor control, or memory in response to suggestions; and the subjective experience of responding involuntarily." Council Report, 253 J.A.M.A., at 1919.

[18] "[W]hen hypnosis is used to refresh recollection, one of the following outcomes occurs: (1) hypnosis produces recollections that are not substantially different from nonhypnotic recollections; (2) it yields recollections that are more inaccurate than nonhypnotic memory; or, most frequently, (3) it results in more information being reported, but these recollections contain both accurate and inaccurate details. . . . There are no data to support a fourth alternative, namely, that hypnosis increases remembering of only accurate information." Id., at 1921.

in obtaining investigative leads or identifications that were later confirmed by independent evidence.

The inaccuracies the process introduces can be reduced, although perhaps not eliminated, by the use of procedural safeguards. One set of suggested guidelines calls for hypnosis to be performed only by a psychologist or psychiatrist with special training in its use and who is independent of the investigation. See Orne, The Use and Misuse of Hypnosis in Court, 27 Int'l J. Clinical & Experimental Hypnosis 311, 335-336 (1979). These procedures reduce the possibility that biases will be communicated to the hypersuggestive subject by the hypnotist. Suggestion will be less likely also if the hypnosis is conducted in a neutral setting with no one present but the hypnotist and the subject. Tape or video recording of all interrogations, before, during, and after hypnosis, can help reveal if leading questions were asked. Id., at 336. Such guidelines do not guarantee the accuracy of the testimony, because they cannot control the subject's own motivations or any tendency to confabulate, but they do provide a means of controlling overt suggestions.

The more traditional means of assessing accuracy of testimony also remain applicable in the case of a previously hypnotized defendant. Certain information recalled as a result of hypnosis may be verified as highly accurate by corroborating evidence. Cross-examination, even in the face of a confident defendant, is an effective tool for revealing inconsistencies. Moreover, a jury can be educated to the risks of hypnosis through expert testimony and cautionary instructions. Indeed, it is probably to a defendant's advantage to establish carefully the extent of his memory prior to hypnosis, in order to minimize the decrease in credibility the procedure might introduce.

We are not now prepared to endorse without qualifications the use of hypnosis as an investigative tool; scientific understanding of the phenomenon and of the means to control the effects of hypnosis is still in its infancy. Arkansas, however, has not justified the exclusion of all of a defendant's testimony that the defendant is unable to prove to be the product of prehypnosis memory. A State's legitimate interest in barring unreliable evidence does not extend to per se exclusions that may be reliable in an individual case. Wholesale inadmissibility of a defendant's testimony is an arbitrary restriction on the right to testify in the absence of clear evidence by the State repudiating the validity of all posthypnosis recollections. The State would be well within its powers if it established guidelines to aid trial courts in the evaluation of posthypnosis testimony and it may be able to show that testimony in a particular case is so unreliable that exclusion is justified. But it has not shown that hypnotically enhanced testimony is always so untrustworthy and so immune to the traditional means of evaluating credibility that it should disable a defendant from presenting her version of the events for which she is on trial.

In this case, the defective condition of the gun corroborated the details petitioner remembered about the shooting. The tape recordings provided some means to evaluate the hypnosis and the trial judge concluded that Doctor Back did not suggest responses with leading questions. Those circumstances present an argument for admissibility of petitioner's testimony in this particular case, an argument that must be considered by the trial court. Arkansas' per se rule excluding all posthypnosis testimony infringes impermissibly on the right of a defendant to testify on his or her own behalf.

The judgment of the Supreme Court of Arkansas is vacated and the case is remanded to that court for further proceedings not inconsistent with this opinion.

It is so ordered.

CHIEF JUSTICE REHNQUIST, with whom JUSTICE WHITE, JUSTICE O'CONNOR, and JUSTICE SCALIA join, dissenting.

In deciding that petitioner Rock's testimony was properly limited at her trial, the Arkansas Supreme Court cited several factors that undermine the reliability of hypnotically induced testimony. Like the Court today, the Arkansas Supreme Court observed that a hypnotized individual becomes subject to suggestion, is likely to confabulate, and experiences artificially increased confidence in both true and false memories following hypnosis. No known set of procedures, both courts agree, can insure against the inherently unreliable nature of such testimony. Having acceded to the factual premises of the Arkansas Supreme Court, the Court nevertheless concludes that a state trial court must attempt to make its own scientific assessment of reliability in each case it is confronted with a request for the admission of hypnotically induced testimony. I find no justification in the Constitution for such a ruling.

In the Court's words, the decision today is "bottomed" on recognition of Rock's "constitutional right to testify in her own defense." While it is true that this Court, in dictum, has recognized the existence of such a right, the principles identified by the Court as underlying this right provide little support for invalidating the evidentiary rule applied by the Arkansas Supreme Court.

As a general matter, the Court first recites, a defendant's right to testify facilitates the truth-seeking function of a criminal trial by advancing both the "detection of guilt" and "the protection of innocence." Such reasoning is hardly controlling here, where advancement of the truth-seeking function of Rock's trial was the sole motivation behind limiting her testimony. The Court also posits, however, that "a rule that denies an accused the opportunity to offer his own testimony" cannot be upheld because, "[l]ike the truthfulness of other witnesses, the defendant's veracity . . . can be tested adequately by cross-examination." But the Court candidly admits that the increased confidence inspired by hypnotism makes "cross-examination more difficult," thereby diminishing an adverse party's ability to test the truthfulness of defendants such as Rock. Nevertheless, we are told, the exclusion of a defendant's testimony cannot be sanctioned because the defendant "above all others may be in a position to meet the prosecution's case." In relying on such reasoning, the Court apparently forgets that the issue before us arises only by virtue of Rock's memory loss, which rendered her less able "to meet the prosecution's case."

In conjunction with its reliance on broad principles that have little relevance here, the Court barely concerns itself with the recognition, present throughout our decisions, that an individual's right to present evidence is subject always to reasonable restrictions. Indeed, the due process decisions relied on by the Court all envision that an individual's right to present evidence on his behalf is not absolute and must often times give way to countervailing considerations. Similarly, our Compulsory Process Clause decisions make clear that the right to present relevant testimony "may, in appropriate cases, bow to accommodate other legitimate interests in the criminal trial process." The Constitution does not in any way relieve a defendant from compliance with "rules of procedure and evidence designed to assure both fairness and reliability in the ascertainment of guilt and innocence." Surely a rule designed to exclude testimony whose trustworthiness is inherently suspect cannot be said to fall outside this description.

This Court has traditionally accorded the States "respect . . . in the establishment and implementation of their own criminal trial rules and procedures." One would think that this deference would be at its highest in an area such as this, where, as the Court concedes, "scientific understanding . . . is still in its infancy." Turning a blind eye to this concession, the Court chooses instead to restrict the ability of both state and federal courts to respond to changes in the understanding of hypnosis.

The Supreme Court of Arkansas' decision was an entirely permissible response to a novel and difficult question. See National Institute of Justice, Issues and Practices, M. Orne et al., Hypnotically Refreshed Testimony: Enhanced Memory or Tampering with Evidence? 51 (1985). As an original proposition, the solution this Court imposes upon Arkansas may be equally sensible, though requiring the matter to be considered res nova by every single trial judge in every single case might seem to some to pose serious administrative difficulties. But until there is a much more general consensus on the use of hypnosis than there is now, the Constitution does not warrant this Court's mandating its own view of how to deal with the issue.

NOTES

1. *The usual rule for memories evoked under hypnosis.* Hypnotically induced memories have provoked a variety of judicial responses. Statements made while under hypnosis, offered as substantive evidence or as bearing on credibility, are almost universally inadmissible. See cases cited, Paul C. Giannelli & Edward J. Imwinkelried, Scientific Evidence 271 n.173 (2d ed. 1993); cf. id. at 271 n.174 (same rule for statements made under narcoanalysis); but see Modern Scientific Evidence § 12-1.3.4 (David Faigman et al. eds., 1997) ("majority" rule). As the opinions in *Rock* recognize, however, posthypnotic testimony as to recollections enhanced or evoked under hypnosis have triggered more divergent rulings. Compare the U.S. Supreme Court's characterization of the current legal environment with the description in the Arkansas Supreme Court's opinion, Rock v. State, 708 S.W.2d 78, 79-80 (Ark. 1986):

> While it was said in State v. Hurd that a majority of courts have held hypnotically induced testimony admissible, the cases cited for that conclusion are from the previous decade. The more recent trend is toward exclusion of such testimony. Typical of this trend is Maryland, which in 1968 permitted the testimony, treating the issue as one of weight rather than admissibility. Harding v. State, 5 Md. App. 230, 246 A.2d 302 (1968). *Harding* was the leading opinion on this point, yet in 1982 Maryland reversed its position and held that a witness who has been hypnotized may not testify to induced recollections. Polk v. State, 48 Md. App. 382, 427 A.2d 1041 (1981) . . . . [E]ven in those jurisdictions that previously held post-hypnotic testimony generally admissible, there is a trend toward insisting that rigorous safeguards be observed before the hypnotically refreshed memories are admissible, and "[t]he more prevalent view is that testimony about the post-hypnotic memories is not admissible.

Although the weight of opinion now favors the per se rule, at least as applied to hypnotic subjects other than the defendant, even in these jurisdictions, untainted, prehypnotic statements are usually admissible. Indeed, this was the rule that the Arkansas courts applied in *Rock*. According to the state supreme court,

> The trial court in this case chose the course of excluding testimony induced by hypnosis and admitting testimony of the appellant based on pre-hypnotic recollection. The difficulty was determining what that recollection was, based only on a record from the pre-hypnotic session with Dr. Back, a record admittedly incomplete. In this situation the trial court limited the appellant to what she could recall without the benefit of hypnosis, as evidenced by Dr. Back's notes and enlarged by Dr. Back's memory of her discussions with appellant before she was placed in a hypnotic state. Appellant argues the court misapplied the rule employed by courts where hypnotically induced testimony is inadmissible and was too restrictive. Appellant, however, never demonstrated how the rule was violated. The rule simply limits the hypnotized subject's testimony to those matters demonstrably recalled prior to testimony. Any other testimony on the topic runs all the risks discussed earlier in hypnotically refreshed memories. Here, the court was in a difficult position as the defense supplied only partial notes of the pre-hypnotic session. Nevertheless, the appellant was allowed to testify to those items referred to in the notes and given considerable latitude in explaining them in her own words. The trial court also allowed testimony on matters Dr. Back had previously testified were covered in the pre-hypnotic session. The burden was on appellant to establish

a reliable record of the testimony. She cannot now claim error because the court restricted her to the record she offered.

Dr. Back testified that during the hypnotic session she took appellant back to her childhood and brought her forward to the shooting incident. Under these circumstances, in order to avoid testimony on topics covered in the sessions that were not previously preserved, the trial court could have limited appellant entirely to the notes and testimony of Dr. Back. However, to give appellant as much latitude as possible, the trial court applied that order only to the day of the shooting.

In contrast to this approach, for a time California rigorously excluded *all* testimony of a hypnotized witness, even that which is unrelated to the hypnotic session. People v. Brown, 709 P.2d 440, 446 (Cal. 1985); People v. Guerra, 690 P.2d 635, 663-65 (Cal. 1984). Exclusion of prehypnotic statements follows from the concern that the hypnotic session enhances the witness' confidence in all his recollections, thereby insulating him from meaningful cross examination. It also obviates the need to inquire into taint, but at the obvious cost of excluding sometimes untainted testimony. California retreated from this absolute ban in People v. Hayes, 783 P.2d 719 (1989) (rape victim not barred from testifying as to events the court found she recalled and related prior to the hypnotic session).

2. *Limits of the* Rock *right to present evidence.* What are the implications of *Rock* for a civil litigant with hypnotically "refreshed" memories? For criminal defendants who want to introduce various kinds of scientific evidence considered too unreliable for use by the state? In the light of *Rock,* how should the following case be decided on appeal?

> Cogburn was charged with rape for allegedly engaging in sexual intercourse with his seven-year-old daughter. He was convicted by a jury of carnal abuse and sentenced to ten years imprisonment. Prior to the trial, the defense took the deposition of Dr. Gregory S. Kaczenski. The doctor testified that he conducted a neuropsychiatric evaluation of Cogburn and an amytal interview to look for evidence of a mental disorder. The doctor stated that the amytal interview, otherwise known as administering "truth serum," lowers the inhibitions in the conscious mind and allows the person to speak freely. While under the influence of the truth serum, the doctor said that Cogburn achieved a hypnotic state and denied having sexual contact or experience with the victim. The doctor testified that, in his opinion, the test is good evidence against Cogburn having abused his daughter. The state filed a motion in limine to suppress the doctor's testimony, which was granted by the trial court.

After *Rock,* what showing must the state make to prevent an accused from introducing memories influenced by non-drug induced hypnosis? Should the same standard be applied to all witnesses who have undergone such hypnosis?

Consider the view attributed in David O. Stewart, Hypnotized Witnesses, Loaded Jurors, A.B.A.J., Oct. 1, 1987, at 54, 56-57, to Dr. Martin Orne, a psychiatrist at the University of Pennsylvania, whose work was cited in all the opinions in *Rock:*

> Orne stressed that laboratory experiments have not been able to demonstrate an increase in accurate memory through hypnosis. The subject often "remembers" more after hypnosis, but much of the additional information is wrong.
>
> Nevertheless, Orne agrees that a criminal defendant should be allowed to testify after hypnosis because he is entitled to state his case and because "the judge or jury takes into account that he is putting his best foot forward."
>
> "But if you change the memory of an unbiased witness or a victim [through hypnosis], it is a catastrophe, because you can convict anyone," he said.

3. *Costs of the procedural guidelines.* The majority opinion of the U.S. Supreme Court suggested that procedural safeguards along the lines suggested by Dr. Martin Orne might permit introduction of the defendant's memories induced under hypnosis. The Arkansas Supreme Court also considered these safeguards:

> One of the more significant studies . . . is that of Dr. Martin T. Orne (Orne, et al, Hypnotically Induced Testimony, In Eyewitness Testimony: Psychological Perspectives, Wells & Loftus, edits. 1984). Orne is widely cited on this issue, and it was his guidelines for the use of hypnotic testimony that were adopted by the New Jersey court in Hurd v. State. [Yet,] Orne's current position [is that]:
>
>> The present state of scientific knowledge is consistent with the rules of a number of state supreme courts that memories retrieved through hypnosis are sufficiently unreliable that their use is precluded as eyewitness testimony in criminal trials . . . . There is no way, however, by which anyone (including an expert with extensive experience in hypnosis) can for any particular piece of information obtained in hypnosis determine whether it is an actual memory or a confabulation. For these reasons, hypnotically induced testimony is not reliable and ought not be permitted to form the basis of testimony in court. . . .
>
> Appellant urges that if we do not allow hypnotically refreshed testimony unconditionally, we should adopt the guidelines of State v. Hurd. We note that appellant has not fully complied with those guidelines, but we are not inclined to follow *Hurd* in any case. The cases which have rejected *Hurd* have noted that some of the dangers of hypnotically induced testi-

mony are not eliminated by the *Hurd* guidelines and others are not even addressed.[2]

Of equal importance, to adopt the guidelines would further burden the pretrial process with no off-setting benefit: the guidelines require that the opposing party be notified of the intent to use hypnosis and be furnished a recording of any sessions; only a psychologist or psychiatrist experienced in hypnosis, and independent of either the state or the defense, may be used; all sessions must be recorded and the trial court in a pretrial or chambers hearing must decide a number of issues determinative of whether the induced testimony should be received, such as the presence of cues or suggestions by the hypnotist. The burden of proof is by clear and convincing evidence.

In light of the questionable probative value of such proof and the risks inherent in the means by which it is retrieved, we think it would be a serious mistake to further encumber the pretrial process with the steps outlined in Hurd. We agree with the comment in People v. Shirley [641 P.2d 775 (Cal. 1982)]:

> On the other hand, it takes little prescience to foresee that these and related issues would provide a fertile new field for litigation. There would first be elaborate demands for discovery, parades of expert witnesses, and special pretrial hearings, all with concomitant delays and expense. Among the questions our trial courts would then be expected to answer are scientific issues so subtle as to confound the experts. Their resolution would in turn generate a panoply of new claims that could be raised on appeal, including difficult questions of compliance with the "clear and convincing" standard of proof. And because the hypnotized subject would frequently be the victim, the eyewitness, or a similar source of crucial testimony against the defendant, any errors in ruling on the admissibility of such testimony could easily jeopardize otherwise unimpeachable judgments of conviction. In our opinion, the game is not worth the candle.

---

[2] In deciding to discard the *Hurd* approach, the *Shirley* court noted initially that it was not persuaded that the requirements adopted in *Hurd* and other cases would eliminate each of the dangers at which they were directed.

> For example, one of the requirements . . . is that all contacts between the hypnotist and the subject must be recorded for the stated purpose of enabling the trial court to determine what "cues" the hypnotist may have conveyed to the subject by word or deed; and the opinion strongly encouraged the use of videotape to make such recordings. Yet as the same opinion recognizes elsewhere, "Because of the unpredictability of what will influence a subject, it is difficult even for an expert examining a videotape of a hypnotic session to identify possible cues." If even an expert cannot confidently make that identification, it is vain to believe that a layman such as a trial judge can do so.

The court points out that certain dangers of hypnosis are not even addressed by the *Hurd* requirements recognized elsewhere in that opinion, such as the subject losing his critical judgment and crediting memories that were formerly viewed as unreliable, confusing actual recall with confabulation and the unwarranted confidence in the validity of his ensuing recollection.

4. *Significance of the hypnotic memory in* Rock. How important was the alleged memory to which Mrs. Rock was precluded from testifying? Compare the majority opinion set forth above with the Arkansas Supreme Court's analysis:

> [A]ppellant . . . was allowed to relate the substance of her version of the shooting to the jury, which she had remembered prior to hypnosis. Appellant's defense was that the shooting was an accident and this she was able to adequately relay to the jury. She testified that she and her husband were quarreling, that he pushed her against the wall, that she wanted to leave because she was frightened, and her husband wouldn't let her go. She said her husband's behavior that night was unusual, and the shooting was an accident, that she didn't mean to do it and that she would not intentionally hurt her husband.
>
> In reality nothing was excluded that would have been of much assistance to appellant, or would have enlarged on her testimony to any significant degree. . . .

5. *Accuracy of hypnotically enhanced memories.* The courts generally recognize that false memories are easily evoked under hypnosis. For studies of the accuracy of hypnotically evoked memories, see, e.g., Nancy Mehrkens Steblay & Robert K. Bothwell, Evidence for Hypnotically Refreshed Testimony: The View from the Laboratory, 18 Law & Hum. Behav. 635 (1994); G.S. Sanders & W.L. Simmons, Use of Hypnosis to Enhance Eyewitness Accuracy: Does It Work? 69 J. App. Psych. 70 (1983); J.C. Yulle & N.H. McEwan, Use of Hypnosis as an Aid to Eyewitness Testimony, 70 J. App. Psych. 389 (1985).

6. *Repressed memories.* Some testimony involving "repressed memories," particularly in cases where witnesses seem to remember being abused as children, has been devastating and dubious. Thus, concern has been expressed over the "memories" that surface after sessions with therapists or counselors. Mark Pendergrast, Victims of Memory: Incest Accusations and Shattered Lives (1995); Richard Ofshe & Ethan Watters, Making Monsters: False Memories, Psychotherapy, and Sexual Hysteria (1994); Elizabeth Loftus & Katherine Ketcham, The Myth of Repressed Memories: False Memories and Allegations of Sexual Abuse (1994); Minouche Kandel & Eric Kandel, Flights of Memory, Discover, May 1994, at 32-38; Gary M. Ernsdorff & Elizabeth F. Loftus, Let Sleeping Memories Lie? Words of Caution About Tolling the Statute of Limitations in Cases of Memory Repression, 84 J. Crim. L. & Criminology 129 (1993); Elizabeth Loftus & R.A. Rosenwald, Buried Memories, Shattered Lives, 79 A.B.A.J. 70 (1993). Indeed, it has been argued that the entire concept of memory repression lacks scientific validity. Frederick Crews, The Revenge of the Repressed, N.Y. Rev. Books, Nov. 17, 1994, 1994, at 54-60; Frederick Crews, The Revenge of the Repressed: Part II, N.Y. Rev., Dec. 1, 1994, at 49-58, discussed in "Victims of Memory": An Exchange, N.Y. Rev., Jan. 12, 1995, at 42-48.

At the other end of the spectrum, see Ellen Bass & Laura Davis, The Courage to Heal: A Guide for Women Survivors of Child Sexual Abuse (1992). The psychologists and other therapists or counselors who have been instrumental in encouraging their patients to find the apparently repressed memories have become the targets of tort actions by the family members or others accused of child abuse. See, e.g., Mark Hansen, More False Memory Suits Likely, A.B.A.J., Aug. 1994, at 36.

For discussions of the admissibility of repressed memories, see, e.g., Modern Scientific Evidence § 13-1 (David Faigman et al. eds., 1997); Jacqueline Hough, Recovered Memories of Childhood Sexual Abuse: Applying the *Daubert* Standard in State Courts, 69 So. Cal. L. Rev. 855 (1996); Jacqueline Kanovitz, Hypnotic Memories and Civil Sexual Abuse Trials, 45 Vand. L. Rev. 1185 (1992); Matthew J. Eisenberg, Comment, Recovered Memories of Childhood Sexual Abuse: The Admissibility Question, 68 Temple L. Rev. 249 (1995); Monica L. Hayes, The Necessity of Memory Experts for the Defense in Prosecutions for Child Sexual Abuse Based Upon Repressed Memory, 32 Am. Crim. L. Rev. 69 (1994); Julie M. Kosmond Murray, Comment, Repression, Memory, and Suggestibility: A Call for Limitations on the Admissibility of Repressed Memory Testimony in Sexual Abuse Trials, 66 U. Colo. L. Rev. 477-522 (1995).

7. *Expert opinions on credibility and memory.* Unlike polygraphy or narco-analysis, hypnosis rarely is proffered as a device for verifying or extracting the truth of a witness' statements. Instead, its alleged forensic value lies in enhancing the recall of cooperative subjects. See People v. Hughes, 453 N.E.2d 484 (N.Y. 1983). In some cases, however, individuals with psychological training profess the ability to discern when a witness is telling the truth. The courts are reluctant to allow experts to express such opinions, whether based on clinical experience, statistical profiles, polygraphy, narcoanalysis or hypnosis. See supra chapter 17; infra chapter 20.

Chapter 19
Generalizations About Eyewitnesses

United States v. Downing
753 F.2d 1224 (3d Cir. 1985)

BECKER, CIRCUIT JUDGE. . . .

I

Appellant, John W. Downing, was indicted for mail fraud, wire fraud, and interstate transportation of stolen property. All counts of the indictment arose from a scheme to defraud numerous vendors conducted in 1978 and 1979 by a group of individuals calling themselves the Universal League of Clergy (U.L.C.). . . . Its modus operandi was essentially as follows. U.L.C. representatives at national trade shows made contact with manufacturers' representatives by expressing an interest in their product line. When the representative took an order for his product, U.L.C. furnished the vendor with the list of supposed credit references. In fact, U.L.C. had compiled a list of non-existent trade and bank references; the trade addresses were actually the addresses of mail-drops, and the bank reference was a foreign post office box. Later, when the credit department of the manufacturer investigated the "references" — usually by mail — it received favorable reports concerning U.L.C.'s payment history with other corporate creditors and assurances from the "bank" that U.L.C.'s account was substantial. These reports, the government established, were actually supplied by U.L.C. itself after collecting the credit inquiries from the various mail-drops. These positive credit references usually induced the manufacturer to ship goods to U.L.C. on credit. U.L.C. then disposed of the goods, without making payment to the manufacturers.

U.L.C. was represented in these dealings by men identifying themselves as U.L.C. clergy, including "Reverend" or "'Doctor' Claymore," "Malcolm Sloane," "Reverend Olson," "Paul Eaton," and "Richard Thomas." The government contended that the individuals acting as the U.L.C. clergy were actually appellant and his co-defendants, James A. Silva and Richard Piazza. The central issue at the trial was the identification of appellant as Reverend Claymore. Silva and Piazza admitted setting up U.L.C., but denied knowing that the suppliers were going to be defrauded. They asserted that they were innocent dupes of Reverend Claymore, who masterminded the entire scheme. They (along with appellant) further asserted that appellant was not Claymore, and that if the government could only find the real Claymore, their innocence would be proved.

The government's case against appellant consisted primarily of the testimony of twelve eyewitnesses who, with varying degrees of confidence, testified that

appellant was the man they knew as Reverend Claymore. These witnesses testified on the basis of their personal observations of Reverend Claymore for periods
ranging from 5 to 45 minutes during the course of business dealings that later were
discovered to be fraudulent. Appellant contended at trial that these eyewitnesses
were mistaken and that their testimony was unreliable because of the short period
of time in which the witnesses had to view Claymore, the innocuous circumstances of their meetings with him, and the substantial lapse of time between the
meetings and the subsequent identifications.

In an effort to overcome the substantial weight of twelve eyewitness identifications in the jury's mind, appellant's counsel . . . inquired whether the court
would permit expert testimony on the unreliability of eyewitness testimony. . . .
On the tenth day of trial, following an off-the-record side-bar discussion, the court
briefly summarized the parties' positions and then denied appellant's motion:

> The Court: There is a discussion at side bar.
> Mr. Concannon offered Robert Weisburg, Ph.D. of Temple
> University, who is a cognative [sic] psychologist. He is an assistant pro-
> fessor of psychology at Temple University.
> Mr. Concannon wants to offer him as an expert witness in order to
> present him to the Jury as a person who would be able to help them deal
> with the problem of identification of the defendants or any witnesses.
> He also would want him to answer a hypothetical question which
> would be related to the evidence presented in this case.
> The U.S. Attorney's position is this would usurp the function of the
> Jury, and he opposes the witness appearing.
> Mr. Concannon said the objection the U.S. Attorney has could be
> dealt with as of cross examination.
> Anything else you want to add to that summary?
> Mr. Concannon: This is basically it, Your Honor.
> The Court: Anything you want to add to what has been said?
> Mr. Schenck: No, but I have case law.
> The Court: Do you want to cite any cases?
> Mr. Schenck: The United States versus Focher [sic], 590 Fed. 2d 381,
> 1979 case by the Third Circuit [sic]. In a recent case with Judge Green of
> this court he declined to admit the same type of evidence.
> The Court: Anything else?
> Mr. Schenck: No.
> The Court: It is the ruling of this court that the motion to have the
> psychologist testify is denied because this is a function of the jury to deal
> with the credibility of the witness[es] that have appeared here and give
> whatever weight to that testimony that they see fit and also determine if
> their evidence is credible. What we have in this case is not only a matter
> of identification, but we have as an [sic] additional evidence such as fin-
> gerprints, handwriting, which is also for the jury and the credibility of the
> experts that appeared.

This dialogue represents the total on-the-record discussion concerning the admissibility of defendant's expert testimony. The case went to the jury without the expert's testimony and appellant was convicted. . . .

II

As the transcript of the colloquy indicates, the district court articulated two reasons for refusing to permit appellant's expert witness to testify: (1) the witness would usurp the "function of the jury"; and (2) there was additional evidence "such as fingerprints [and] handwriting." We note at the outset, and the government concedes, that the court was in error as to the second ground: no fingerprint or handwriting evidence was offered against appellant; rather, the government's case rested almost exclusively on the eyewitness identifications.

The first ground for the court's decision does not proceed from a similar misapprehension of the record, but the court's reasoning in this regard does lack clarity. Initially, it would appear that the court was concerned that the expert witness would testify as to the "ultimate issue of fact," Fed. R. Evid. 704. Were this so, the first ground of decision would also be erroneous. As the advisory committee's note on Rule 704 points out, the basic approach to opinion testimony in the federal rules is one of helpfulness. "In order to render this approach fully effective and to allay any doubt on the subject, the so-called 'ultimate issue' rule is specifically abolished by [Rule 704]." The rule rejects as "empty rhetoric" the notion that some testimony is inadmissible because it usurps the "province of the jury."

In light of this clear mandate of Fed. R. Evid. 704, it appears rather that the district court based its ruling on an interpretation of Fed. R. Evid. 702, in effect concluding that expert testimony concerning the reliability of eyewitness identifications is never admissible in federal court because such testimony concerns a matter of common experience that the jury is itself presumed to possess. Under this approach, an expert's testimony on the reliability of eyewitnesses can never meet the test for the admissibility of expert testimony contained in Fed. R. Evid. 702. . . . This rule invests trial courts with broad discretion to admit expert testimony over the objection that it would improperly invade the province of the jury. Under Rule 702, "an expert can be employed if his testimony will be helpful to the trier of fact in understanding evidence that is simply difficult, [though] not beyond ordinary understanding."

Notwithstanding the fact that the Rule 702 standard usually favors admissibility, several courts of appeals have upheld the exclusion of expert testimony on eyewitness perception and memory because the testimony would involve questions that "can be adequately addressed in cross examination and that the jury can adequately weigh . . . through common-sense evaluation."

We have serious doubts about whether the conclusion reached by these courts is consistent with the liberal standard of admissibility mandated by Rule 702. Instead, we find persuasive more recent cases in which courts have found that, under certain circumstances, this type of expert testimony can satisfy the helpfulness test of Rule 702. For example, in State v. Chapple, 135 Ariz. 281, 660 P.2d 1208 (1983), the Supreme Court of Arizona set aside a jury's guilty verdict and ordered a new trial on the ground that the trial court had erroneously excluded an expert on eyewitness identification offered by the defendant. In addressing the question whether the expert's testimony would have been "helpful" to the jury in reaching an *informed* decision, the court noted several specific factual "variables" that were present in that case which, the defendant's expert was prepared to testify, reduced the eyewitnesses' ability to perceive and remember accurately.

The proffer stated that the expert would testify concerning: (1) the "forgetting curve," i.e., the fact that memory does not diminish at a uniform rate; (2) the fact that, contrary to common understanding, stress causes inaccuracy of perception and distorts one's subsequent recall; (3) the "assimilation factor," which indicates that witnesses frequently incorporate into their identifications inaccurate information gathered after the event and confused with the event; (4) the "feedback factor," which indicates that where identification witnesses discuss the case with each other they can unconsciously reinforce their individual identifications; and (5) the fact that studies demonstrate the absence of a relationship between the confidence a witness has in his or her identification and the actual accuracy of that identification. Each of these "variables" goes beyond what an average juror might know as a matter of common knowledge, and indeed some of them directly contradict "common sense." For this reason, the Arizona Supreme Court concluded that the expert's testimony would have assisted the jury in reaching a correct decision.

In another case, United States v. Smith, 736 F.2d 1103 (6th Cir. 1984) (per curiam), the Sixth Circuit held that expert testimony on the reliability of eyewitness identification met the "helpfulness" test of Rule 702 and therefore had been improperly excluded. The excluded testimony would have focused on "a hypothetical factual situation identical" to the facts of the case, and would have explained (1) that a witness who does not identify the defendant in a first line-up may "unconsciously transfer" his visualization of the defendant to a second line-up and thereby incorrectly identify the defendant the second time; (2) that studies demonstrate the inherent unreliability of cross-racial identifications; and (3) that an encounter during a stressful situation decreases the eyewitness' ability to perceive and remember and decreases the probability of an accurate identification. In concluding that this evidence would have assisted the jury in reaching an accurate decision, the court emphasized that the expert's proffered testimony was based upon "the exact facts before the court and not only might have assisted the jury, but might have refuted their otherwise common assumptions about the reliability of eyewitness identification."

The California Supreme Court has recently adopted this view. In People v. McDonald, 37 Cal. 3d 351, 208 Cal. Rptr. 236, 690 P.2d 709 (1984), the Court held that, under certain narrow circumstances, it will be error for trial courts to exclude qualified expert testimony on eyewitness perception and memory.[8] After surveying the "impressive" professional literature in the area, the *McDonald* court rejected the prosecution argument that section 801(a) of the California Evidence Code, which "limits expert testimony to subjects beyond the range of common experience," cf. Fed. R. Evid. 702, suffices to bar this type of testimony. While conceding the proposition that all jurors know that certain factors, such as lighting, distance, and duration, may affect the accuracy of identifications, the court went on to point out that "[i]t appears from the professional literature, however, that [certain] factors bearing on eyewitness identifications may be known only to some jurors, or may be imperfectly understood by many, or may be contrary to the intuitive beliefs of most."

We agree with the courts in *Chapple, Smith,* and *McDonald* that under certain circumstances expert testimony on the reliability of eyewitness identifications can assist the jury in reaching a correct decision and therefore may meet the helpfulness requirement of Rule 702. For example, most people, and hence most jury members, probably believe that stress increases the accuracy of one's perception. The expert in the *Chapple* case, however, proposed to testify that studies reveal precisely the opposite effect. The sole evidence against the defendant in *Chapple* consisted of the eyewitness identification testimony of two people who viewed the murders under the belief that they might soon become victims as well. In such a setting, the effect of stress on the eyewitnesses was certainly relevant to an evaluation of the reliability of their identifications, and the expert's testimony, if itself reliable, clearly would have assisted the jury.

Judicial resistance to the introduction of this kind of expert testimony is understandable given its innovativeness and the fear of trial delay spawned by the spectre of the creation of a cottage industry of forensic psychologists. The logic of Fed. R. Evid. 702 is inexorable, however, and requires, as the *Smith, Chapple* and *McDonald* courts recognized, that expert testimony on eyewitness perception and memory be admitted at least in some circumstances. We therefore conclude that the district court erred as a matter of law when it in effect decided that expert testimony on the subject is simply not admissible. . . .

V

The Rule 702 analysis we have outlined incorporates to some extent a consideration of the dangers, particularly the danger of unfair prejudice, enumerated

---

[8] The precise holding of the court is as follows: When an eyewitness identification of the defendant is a key element of the prosecution's case but is not substantially corroborated by evidence giving it independent reliability, and the defendant offers qualified expert testimony on specific psychological factors shown by the record that could have affected the accuracy of the identification but are not likely to be fully known to or understood by the jury, it will ordinarily be error to exclude that testimony.

in Fed. R. Evid. 403. On remand, however, even if the proffered evidence satisfies Rule 702, the district court may decide nonetheless to invoke Rule 403 to exclude the evidence if the court finds its probative value to be substantially outweighed by other dangers, e.g., confusion of the issue or waste of time. The availability of Rule 403 is especially significant when there is evidence of a defendant's guilt other than eyewitness evidence, e.g., fingerprints, or other physical evidence. There is no such evidence in this case, however.

The availability of other methods that would serve the purposes for which the appellant seeks to introduce expert testimony may also serve to justify exclusion under Rule 403, though we do not perceive the viability of such an alternative in this case. Moreover, as an abstract proposition, it would seem anomalous to hold that the probative value of expert opinion offered to show the unreliability of eyewitness testimony so wastes time or confuses the issue that it cannot be considered even when its putative effect is to vitiate the only (eyewitness) evidence offered by the government. We understand the government to argue, however, that, because the eyewitness encounters in this case were more than brief in duration and because there are so many eyewitnesses who identified appellant, the offered expert testimony would be of no utility. In exceptional circumstances this, too, might concededly constitute a Rule 403 balancing factor. In any event, because the district court did not mention Rule 403 on the record or conduct the balancing required by that rule, we decline to decide the Rule 403 question at this stage of the litigation.[27]

VI

[T]he judgment of conviction will be vacated and the case will be remanded to the district court for an evidentiary hearing concerning the admissibility of appellant's proffered expert testimony. If the court determines that the expert testimony should have been admitted, it is directed to grant a new trial. If the court decides that the testimony is not admissible under Rule 702 (or should be excluded under Rule 403), then the judgment of conviction against appellant should be reinstated.

---

[27] Some courts, concerned with the prospect of creating a new "cottage industry" of psychological experts who will be asked to testify in every case involving eyewitness testimony, and with the spectre of criminal cases turning into a "battle of the experts" that misleads the jury and confuses the issues, have excluded this expert testimony on the grounds that its prejudicial effect outweighs its probative value. We are sympathetic to these concerns but are not moved by the legal point. There will be cases in which the Rule 403 balancing will serve to justify exclusion. Moreover, we do not doubt that the district court has the discretionary authority to limit the number of experts who may testify and the length of their testimony. At all events, if the testimony is highly probative and meets the conditions set forth above concerning reliability, the likelihood of misleading the jury, and the requisite specificity in the offer of proof, the parties are entitled to present it, whether or not it adds to the length of the trial; presumably such evidence will add clarity and enhance the truth-seeking function of the trial, thereby offsetting the disadvantage of delay.

Michael McCloskey and Howard E. Egeth
Eyewitness Identification:
What Can a Psychologist Tell a Jury?
18 American Psychologist 550, 560-62 (1983)*

[W]e present a hypothetical cross-examination of a defense psychologist by a prosecutor who has been thoroughly briefed by his or her own expert. We ask the reader to consider whether this sort of occurrence would benefit either the psychological profession or the justice system.

Prosecutor: Are you suggesting that it is impossible for an eyewitness to accurately identify a criminal?

Psychologist: No, but accurate identification is quite difficult.

Prosecutor: In the studies conducted by yourself and your colleagues, do any of the participants do very well at identifying people?

Psychologist: Yes, some subjects do quite well, but others do very poorly.

Prosecutor: Dr. Smith, are you aware of studies showing that subjects made accurate identifications over 90% of the time?

Psychologist: Yes, there are such studies. Usually, however, the performance of witnesses is worse than that.

Prosecutor: Isn't it true that the accuracy rates in identification studies depend heavily on the conditions of the experiment, such as how many faces each subject sees, how long each face is seen, and so forth?

Psychologist: Yes, that is obviously true of any experiment.

Prosecutor: Isn't it also the case that conditions in most experiments are deliberately arranged so that accuracy is low?

Psychologist: Well, yes, in a way that's true. If none of the subjects make any errors we don't learn anything from an experiment. For example, if we wanted to see whether poor lighting makes identification harder, we would do an experiment where subjects see people under good and poor lighting conditions. We would then look to see whether accuracy was lower with poor lighting. If the task were too easy, most or all of the subjects might make accurate identifications and we wouldn't learn anything about the effects of lighting. To find out whether lighting is important, we have to have a situation in which subjects make some errors. So to ensure that errors occur, we might let the subjects view people for only a short period of time, from some distance away, and so forth.

Prosecutor: Isn't it true, Dr. Smith, that even in tests giving low overall accuracy, some witnesses identify the right person?

Psychologist: Yes.

Prosecutor: Is there any way you can tell beforehand which witnesses will make an accurate identification and which witnesses will be inaccurate?

Psychologist: No, at the present time we have no good way of telling in a particular situation which witnesses will be accurate and which ones will be inaccurate. All we can say is that certain conditions yield lower accuracy than others.

Prosecutor: You have testified, Dr. Smith, that in your psychological tests, the accuracy of witnesses varies widely according to the conditions of the test. You have also stated that in conducting tests, psychologists deliberately create situations that produce low accuracy. Finally, you have said that there is no way you can tell whether a particular individual will make an accurate or inaccurate identification in a particular situation. How, then, can your tests be applied to the present case, in which a bank teller looked at a single bank robber for a much longer time than in most research studies? How can the results of experiments be used to suggest that the witness is inaccurate in his identification?

Psychologist: I cannot comment on the accuracy of any particular witness. All I can do is explain what sorts of conditions lead to a good or poor eyewitness performance.
    . . .

Prosecutor: I would like to ask you about your testimony concerning cross-racial identifications. Are you saying that a white person could never identify a black person?

Psychologist: No, I merely said that it is more difficult for a white person to identify a black person than a white person.

Prosecutor: Are you suggesting that most cross-racial identifications are wrong?

Psychologist: No, I did not say that.

Prosecutor: Well, then, are cross-racial identifications often incorrect?

Psychologist: I cannot say exactly how often cross-racial identifications are erroneous, only that cross-racial identifications are less likely to be correct than within-racial identifications.

Prosecutor: Does that mean that there might be a difference about 80% in the accuracy of within- versus cross-racial identifications?

Psychologist: No, the difference in accuracy is not that large.

Prosecutor: Would 50% be a more reasonable figure?

Psychologist: No, the difference is somewhat smaller than that.

Prosecutor: Well, Dr. Smith, can you estimate for the jury just how much less likely a cross-racial identification is to be correct than a within-racial identification?

Psychologist: I can't be sure of the exact figures, but I believe that most studies show about 10% difference in the accuracy between within- and cross-racial identifications would represent the average performance of a group of subjects.

Prosecutor: So it is probably the case that some people in these studies did just as well at cross-racial identification as within-racial identification?

Psychologist: That's possible.

Prosecutor: So you can't say for any individual that you haven't tested whether that individual is less likely to be correct in a cross-racial or a within-racial identification?

Psychologist: All I can say it that, in general, cross-racial identifications are more difficult than within-racial identifications.

Prosecutor: I would like to ask you a few questions about your testimony on the effects of stress on performance. You testified, I believe, that people under a moderate amount of stress are better at remembering and perceiving than people under very high or very low stress.

Psychologist: That's right. As I said before, the relationship between stress and performance is expressed by what is called the Yerkes-Dodson law, which is a well-known principle of psychology.

Prosecutor: How much stress, Dr. Smith, is moderate stress? That is, what level of stress leads to the best performance, and how much stress must a person be under before his or her performance deteriorates?

Psychologist: That depends on the type of task involved. Some tasks can be performed well under a fair amount of stress, and in other tasks the same amount of stress would impair performance. In general, the more complex the task, the lower the level of stress that gives the best performance.

. . .

Prosecutor: Let me ask you one other thing about stress, Dr. Smith. Would the effects of stress in a task be the same for everyone? In other words, would the level of stress at which performance begins to be impaired be the same for all individuals?

Psychologist: Not necessarily. It is quite possible that a level of stress that impaired performance for one person might have little effect on another.

Prosecutor: According to your testimony, the level of stress at which performance begins to be impaired is different for different situations and for different people. Would you agree, then, that for a particular person in a particular situation, it would be impossible to tell how much stress would be necessary to impair perception and memory without testing that person directly in the situation?

Psychologist: Yes, but as I have said, in general high stress impairs performance.

Prosecutor: How much time have you spent testing Mr. Robinson, the eyewitness in this case?

Psychologist: I have not tested him at all. I have never even met him.

Prosecutor: Then how can you testify about the effects of stress on his ability to identify the person who robbed him?

Psychologist: I cannot make any judgment about whether Mr. Robinson as an individual is an accurate or inaccurate witness. I can only describe the principles concerning eyewitness identifications that have been discovered through psychological research.

Prosecutor: How can these vague principles be of help to the jury, Dr. Smith, when you, with all your knowledge and experience, cannot use them to tell whether a witness was accurate or not?

Psychologist: It is not my function to decide that.

NOTES

1. *The criticism.* Where in the legal framework for admitting evidence does the McCloskey-Egeth criticism belong? Is it indicative of a lack of general acceptance of the research into the determinants of eyewitness errors? The validity of the research? The helpfulness of the research? See Modern Scientific Evidence § 11-1.4 (David Faigman et al. eds., 1997).

2. *Literature on eyewitness testimony.* The commentary on expert testimony about the factors influencing the accuracy of eyewitness identifications is vast. E.g., Brian L. Cutler & Steven D. Penrod, Mistaken Identity: The Eyewitness, Psychology, and the Law (1995); Elizabeth F. Loftus & James M. Doyle, Eyewitness Testimony: Civil and Criminal (2d ed. 1992); Elizabeth Loftus & Katherine Ketcham, Witness for the Defense: The Accused, the Eyewitness, and the Expert who Puts Memory on Trial (1991); Gary L. Wells, The Scientific Status of Research on Eyewitness Identification, in Modern Scientific Evidence § 11-2 (David Faigman et al. eds., 1997); Wayne T. Westing, The Case of Expert Witness Assistance to the Jury in Eyewitness Identification Cases, 71 Or. L. Rev. 93 (1992); Cindy J. O'Hagan, Note, When Seeing is Not Believing: The Case of Eyewitness Expert Testimony, 81 Geo. L.J. 741 (1993). Criticism like that by McCloskey and Egeth triggers sharp retorts. Compare Rogers Elliott, Expert Testimony About Eyewitness Identification (A Critique), 17 Law & Hum. Behav. 423 (1993), with Saul M. Kassin et al., Smith, Déjà Vu All Over Again: Elliott's Critique of Eyewitness Experts, 18 Law & Hum. Behav. 203 (1994).

3. *Procedures for educating jurors.* If the expert on eyewitness identification does not give judgments on the accuracy of the identifications at bar, what is his or her role? To identify the variables that experimenters have shown to affect accuracy and to estimate their importance? Is courtroom testimony an efficient and effective way to achieve this educational mission? What are the alternatives? Consider John Monahan & Laurens Walker, Social Frameworks: A New Use of Social Science in Law, 73 Va. L. Rev. 559, 559-60 (1987):

> Over the past half-century it has become commonplace for courts and commentators to distinguish two uses of social science in law. Social science is said either to prove "legislative facts" that concern general questions of law and policy, or to prove "adjudicative facts" that pertain only to the case at hand. The choice of procedures to introduce research findings has depended heavily on the assignment of the research to one of these two categories. In this article, we identify a new generic use of social science in law that is emerging from recent cases. In this third use, research

findings presented in court are neither legislative nor adjudicative facts themselves. Rather, empirical information is being offered that incorporates aspects of both of the traditional uses: general research results are used to construct a frame of reference or background context for deciding factual issues crucial to the resolution of a specific case. We call this new use of social science in law the creation of *social frameworks*.

In Part I we describe the novel and rapidly increasing use of social research as a social framework. The accepted distinction between legislative and adjudicative facts is recalled and illustrated. We then relate several recent and seemingly anomalous cases where the application of social science does not correspond to either of the two established categories. These cases involve eyewitness identification, assessments of dangerousness, battered women, and sexual victimization. The application of social science in these disparate areas does not concern legislative fact, since no rule of law is at issue. Neither does it concern adjudicative fact, since the research does not involve the parties before the court. We propose the concept of social frameworks to refer to these uses of general conclusions from social science research in determining factual issues in a specific case. . . .

Currently, a social framework is typically offered by one of the parties through the oral testimony of expert witnesses for evaluation and application by a jury. In Part III, we present a theory that suggests a very different procedural scheme for dealing with social science used as a social framework: the research either may be offered by one of the parties in a brief or located by the trial judge; it should be evaluated by the judge according to accepted common law principles; and only then should it be conveyed to the jury, by instruction from the judge. As the same frameworks are brought to bear in an increasing number of cases, we propose that attention be given to establishing standard instructions, either by the common law process of taking them from prior cases or by creating pattern instructions.

Chapter 20
Post Traumatic Stress Disorder,
Syndromes, and Profiles

State v. Saldana
324 N.W. 227 (Minn. 1982)

SCOTT, JUSTICE.

Camilo Saldana appeals from his conviction of criminal sexual conduct in the first degree . . . . At trial appellant admitted that sexual intercourse had occurred but claimed it was consensual. To rebut appellant's claim, the state presented an expert witness who described the typical post-rape symptoms and behavior of rape victims, and gave her opinion that the complainant was a victim of rape . . . . We find that the admission of such testimony requires the reversal of appellant's conviction, and we remand for a new trial.

Our concern is directed toward the testimony of Lynn Dreyer, a counselor for sexual assault victims, who testified for the state. Dreyer, the director of the Victim Assistance Program in Mankato, holds a bachelor's degree in psychology and social work. Dreyer testified that she met Martha Fuller, the complainant, 10 days after the alleged rape and that she counseled Fuller for approximately a 10-week period. In her testimony, Dreyer explained the stages that a rape victim typically goes through and discussed typical behavior of victims after a rape. She then described Fuller's reactions as she had observed them. In response to a question, Dreyer testified that it was not unusual that Fuller did not report the incident until the following day and that many rape victims never report a rape. Dreyer stated that Fuller was the victim of "acquaintance rape," that she definitely believed Fuller was a victim of sexual assault and rape, and that she did not think Fuller fantasized or "made it up." . . .

To be admissible, expert testimony must be helpful to the jury in reaching its decision . . . . If the jury is in as good a position to reach a decision as the expert, expert testimony would be of little assistance to the jury and should not be admitted. Expert testimony may also be excluded if its probative value is substantially outweighed by the danger of unfair prejudice, confusion, or misleading the jury. Under this test of admissibility, we must examine each segment of Dreyer' testimony.

Dreyer's discussion of the stages a rape victim typically goes through was essentially an explanation of "rape trauma syndrome,"[1] although she did not so

---

[1] Ann Burgess and Lynda Holmstrom coined the term in their seminal 1974 article to describe the recurring pattern of post-rape symptoms. Burgess & Holmstrom, Rape Trauma Syndrome, 131 Am. J. Psychiatry 981 (1974). . . .

label it. On the facts of the case before us, such testimony is of no help to the jury and produces an extreme danger of unfair prejudice. The factual question to be decided by the jury is whether the alleged criminal conduct occurred. It is not necessary that Fuller react in a typical manner to the incident. Fuller need not display the typical post-rape symptoms and behavior of rape victims to convince the jury that her view of the facts is the truth.

Rape trauma syndrome is not the type of scientific test that accurately and reliably determines whether a rape has occurred. The characteristic symptoms may follow any psychologically traumatic event. American Psychiatric Association, Diagnostic and Statistical Manual of Mental Disorders 236 (3d ed. 1980). At best, the syndrome describes only symptoms that occur with some frequency, but makes no pretense of describing every single case. The jury must not decide this case on the basis of how most people react to rape or on whether Fuller's reactions were the typical reactions of a person who has been a victim of rape. Rather, the jury must decide what happened in this case, and whether the elements of the alleged crime have been proved beyond a reasonable doubt.

The scientific evaluation of rape trauma syndrome has not reached a level of reliability that surpasses the quality of common sense evaluation present in jury deliberations. As we stated in refusing to permit introduction of "battering parent" syndrome, the evidence may not be introduced "until further evidence of the scientific accuracy and reliability of syndrome or profile diagnoses can be established." State v. Loebach, 310 N.W. 2d 58, 64 (Minn. 1981). Permitting a person in the role of an expert to suggest that because the complainant exhibits some of the symptoms of rape trauma syndrome, the complainant was therefore raped, unfairly prejudices the appellant by creating an aura of special reliability and trustworthiness. Since jurors of ordinary abilities are competent to consider the evidence and determine whether the alleged crime occurred, the danger of unfair prejudice outweighs any probative value. To allow such testimony would inevitably lead to a battle of experts that would invade the jury's province of fact-finding and add confusion rather than clarity.

Rape trauma syndrome is not a fact-finding tool, but a therapeutic tool useful in counseling. Because the jury need be concerned only with determining the facts and applying the law, and because evidence of reactions of other people does not assist the jury in its fact-finding function, we find the admission of expert testimony on rape trauma syndrome to be error.

The second segment of Dreyer's testimony of questionable admissibility is her opinion that Fuller was raped.[4] The issue is whether the state may introduce

---

[4] The prosecutor elicited the following testimony from Dreyer: . . .

Q From your professional involvement with Martha Fuller, do you have an opinion Miss Dreyer, as to whether or not this incident actually took place?

A I definitely believe that Martha was a victim of assault.

Q Of a sexual assault?

A Sexual assault and rape.

expert testimony in a rape prosecution that, in the expert's opinion, a rape in fact occurred. [Noting that the witness was not a physician and that she did not conduct a physical examination of the complainant, the court concluded] that the admission of Dreyer's testimony was error. Because the jurors were equally capable of considering the evidence and determining whether a rape occurred, Dreyer's opinion was not helpful. Her testimony was a legal conclusion which was of no use to the jury. Furthermore, the danger of unfair prejudice outweighed any probative value. Dreyer's testimony "gave a stamp of scientific legitimacy to the truth of the complaining witness's factual testimony."

The final segment of Dreyer's testimony was her opinion that Fuller had not fantasized the rape. Once a victim is deemed competent, expert opinions concerning the witness's reliability in distinguishing truth from fantasy are generally inadmissible because such opinions invade the jury's province to make credibility determinations. Expert testimony concerning the reliability of a witness should be received only in "unusual cases." An example of such an unusual case is a sexual assault case where the alleged victim is a child or mentally retarded. See Commonwealth v. Carter, 9 Mass. App. 680, 403 N.E.2d 1191 (1980), aff'd, 417 N.E. 2d 438 (Mass. 1981) (examining pediatrician may give opinion relating to the ability of a retarded child to differentiate between reality and fantasy but not concerning whether the child was telling the truth about an alleged sexual assault).

We hold that in this prosecution for criminal sexual conduct where the defendant claimed consent it was reversible error for an expert to testify concerning typical post-rape symptoms and behavior of rape victims and give opinions that the complainant was a victim of rape and had not fantasized the rape. Our holding is necessary to ensure accuracy in the truth-seeking process and to guarantee fairness to the accused. . . .

Reversed and remanded.

NOTES

1. *Value of expert testimony about "rape trauma syndrome."* The majority opinion in *Saldana* asserts that "rape trauma syndrome" testimony is "of no help to the jury." Why not? Because jurors already appreciate the range and types of normal responses to rape? Because the "syndrome" is not specific to rape, but may follow other traumatic experiences? (The medically accepted label for the diagnostic category is "post-traumatic stress disorder." E.g., John E. Helzer et al., Post-Traumatic Stress Disorder in the General Population, 317 New Eng. J. Med. 1630 (1987).) Because the reactions do not occur "in every single case"? Because "how most people react to rape" is logically irrelevant? How convincing are these arguments of the *Saldana* court? See, e.g., Patricia A. Frazier & Eugene Borgida, Juror Common Understanding and the Admissibility of Rape Trauma Syndrome Evidence in Court, 12 Law & Hum. Behav. 101 (1988); Toni M. Massaro, Experts, Psychology, Credibility and Rape: The Rape Trauma Syndrome Issue and its

Implications for Expert Psychological Testimony, 69 Minn. L. Rev. 395 (1985); David McCord, The Admissibility of Expert Psychological Testimony Regarding Rape Trauma Syndrome in Rape Prosecutions, 26 B.C. L. Rev. 1143 (1985); Susan Murphy, Note, Assisting the Jury in Understanding Victimization: Expert Psychological Testimony on Battered Woman Syndrome and Rape Trauma Syndrome, 25 Colum. J.L. & Soc. Probs. 277 (1992); Bridget A. Clarke, Note, Making the Woman's Experience Relevant to Rape: The Admissibility of Rape Trauma Syndrome Evidence in California, 39 UCLA L. Rev. 251 (1991); Karla Fischer, Note, Defining the Boundaries of Admissible Expert Testimony on Rape Trauma Syndrome, 1989 U. Ill. L. Rev. 691.

    2. *Probative value of the absence of the syndrome.* If proof of the syndrome were allowed to show lack of consent, would the absence of the syndrome be admissible to prove that there was consent? Should a defendant be permitted to argue that the prosecution's failure to introduce evidence of post traumatic stress disorder (PTSD) in a rape case indicates that the alleged victim really consented? See McCormick on Evidence § 206 (John W. Strong ed., 4th ed. 1992).

    3. *General acceptance standard. Saldana* maintains that PTSD is not generally accepted in the scientific community as an indicator of rape, and that expert testimony about the syndrome therefore violates the general acceptance rule announced in Frye v. United States (see supra chapter 6). Is this true? Compare Patricia A. Frazier & Eugene Borgida, Rape Trauma Syndrome: A Review of Case Law and Psychological Research, 16 Law & Human Behav. 293 (1992), and Deborah A. Dwyer, Expert Testimony on Rape Trauma Syndrome: An Argument for Limited Admissibility, 63 Wash. L. Rev. 1063 (1988), with Robert R. Lawrence, Checking the Allure of Increased Conviction Rates: The Admissibility of Expert Testimony on Rape Trauma Syndrome in Criminal Proceedings, 70 Va. L. Rev. 1657 (1984). Does the general acceptance standard even apply to this type of behavioral symptom evidence? Compare State v. Black, 745 P.2d 12 (Wash. 1987), with People v. Hampton, 746 P.2d 947 (Colo. 1987).

    4. *Scientific soundness.* It has been said that "[a]lthough most of the caselaw concerning RTS predates *Daubert,* the specific standard of admission . . . does not appear to affect the conclusion," but "few courts have seriously evaluated the underlying scientific foundation. . . ." Modern Scientific Evidence § 10-1.3 (David Faigman et al. eds., 1997). That research is reviewed in, e.g., Patricia A. Frazier & Eugene Borgida, The Scientific Status of Research on Rape Trauma Syndrome, in id, at § 10-2.

    5. *Distinction between explanations of PTSD as a general phenomenon and expert opinion testimony.* In jurisdictions where PTSD testimony is admissible in rape prosecutions, the psychological expert may be barred from offering an opinion as to whether the stress disorder diagnosed in the alleged victim resulted from rape. In the words of one state supreme court:

> We, therefore, must draw a distinction between an expert's testimony that an alleged victim exhibits post-rape behavior consistent with rape-trauma syndrome and expert opinion that bolsters the credibility of the alleged victim by indicating that she was indeed raped.

State v. McCoy, 366 S.E.2d 731, 737 (W. Va. 1988). Can this distinction be maintained in practice? What if the expert testifies that the victim was "still traumatized by this experience"? Id. What if the following exchange occurs:

> Based on the work you have done . . . and the literature and . . . your background and training, did you have an opinion as to what proportion of victims in these sorts of cases . . . are lying about this happening . . . ?
>
> Well, there aren't too many statistics on that. The one statistic that I have found came from this Santa Clara [project]. . . . [T]heir figures were that it was possibly one percent that lied. But I don't know that that's totally accurate. But in general, most people in the field feel that it's a very small proportion that lie.

Does such testimony amount to "[q]uantification of the percentage of witnesses who tell the truth [which] is nothing more than the expert's overall impression of truthfulness"? State v. Lindsey, 720 P.2d 73 (Ariz. 1986).

State v. Hall
406 N.W. 2d 503 (Minn. 1987)

AMDAHL, CHIEF JUSTICE.

On October 25, 1985, a jury found respondent Mark Steven Hall guilty of criminal sexual conduct in the first degree; Hall was sentenced to a 43-month term of imprisonment. The Court of Appeals reversed Hall's conviction and remanded for a new trial on the ground that the trial court committed reversible error by admitting expert testimony concerning the common behavioral characteristics of sexually abused adolescents. We granted the state's petition for further review to determine whether, under the facts of this case, the admission of such expert testimony was reversible error. We reverse and reinstate the judgment of conviction.

On June 28, 1985, Hall sexually assaulted the complainant; at that time, the complainant was 14 years old and Hall was 30 years old. On the day of the assault, the complainant was babysitting for the Halls, as she had been doing on an almost daily basis for the prior month. Around 8 p.m. that evening, Mark Hall came home and put his children to bed; meanwhile, the complainant, expecting that Hall would take her home, collected her purse and shoes and sat on a couch. After Hall had put his children to bed, he came into the living room where the complainant was seated, grabbed her around the wrists, and took her into his bedroom. As he was taking the complainant into the bedroom, Hall told her to be quiet or he would kill her. Once inside the bedroom, Hall sexually assaulted the complainant; the sexual assault included an act of sexual penetration. Either during or immediately after the assault, Hall told the complainant that if she told anyone about the incident, he had 46 acres behind his house and her body would never be found. Hall then took the complainant home; she did not immediately report the assault. The testimony at trial indicates that during the weeks following the assault, the complainant told some of her friends about the assault; however, none of these people nor the complainant reported the assault to the police. Also, in the weeks following the assault, the complainant continued to babysit for the Halls.

About 1 month after the assault, the complainant was again babysitting for the Halls. During the evening, Hall returned home with two friends. Prior to their leaving, Hall said something to the complainant which made her fear that she might be assaulted again. Shortly after Hall and his friends had left, the complainant called her sister and told her about the earlier assault and her fear of being assaulted again. The complainant's sister picked up the complainant and drove her home. The police were then notified. At trial, the complainant testified that she did not immediately report the June 28 assault because she was scared and thought that Hall meant what he said about killing her. She also testified that she continued to babysit for the Halls because she was afraid that if she stopped, Hall would think she had told someone about the assault.

Mark Hall testified at trial. He denied sexually assaulting the complainant, and he claimed that on the evening of June 28, 1985, from 8 p.m. until 9:30 p.m., he had been at the restaurant where his wife was working. Hall's wife also testified that Hall was at the restaurant that night from 8 until 9:30. Another employee of the restaurant also testified that she remembered seeing Hall in the restaurant at around 8:30 p.m. on June 28.

The concern in this case is directed toward the testimony of Dr. Clare Bell, a clinical psychologist at the Range Mental Health Center. Over defense objection, the trial court allowed Dr. Bell, an expert in the area of sexual abuse, to testify. Dr. Bell testified that experts are able to identify behavioral characteristics commonly exhibited by sexually abused adolescents. Dr. Bell testified that one of the characteristics displayed by an adolescent sexual abuse victim is a delay in reporting; the principal reason for the delay, she stated, is the victim's fear of being harmed. Dr. Bell also testified that when the victim knows the assailant, it is not uncommon for the victim to have continued contact with the assailant; one of the reasons for the continued contact, stated Dr. Bell, is the victim's fear of retaliation if she avoids the assailant.

The main issue is whether the trial court committed reversible error by admitting the testimony of Dr. Bell. We hold that under the facts of this case, the trial court's admission of this testimony did not constitute an abuse of discretion.

The admissibility of expert testimony concerning the characteristics typically displayed by victims of sexual assault has been addressed by this court on three previous occasions. In State v. Saldana, 324 N.W. 2d 227 (Minn. 1982), and its companion case, State v. McGee, 324 N.W. 2d 232 (Minn. 1982), we held that the admission of such testimony was error. In both *Saldana* and *McGee*, the victim of the sexual assault was an adult, and the expert in each case discussed the stages a rape victim typically goes through, i.e., explained "Rape trauma syndrome." We reversed the convictions in both cases, holding that it was reversible error to allow an expert to testify about the characteristics typically displayed by sexual assault victims and to give an opinion either that the complainant had been raped (*Saldana*) or that the complainant's behavior after the assault was consistent with rape trauma syndrome (*McGee*).

In State v. Myers, 359 N.W.2d 604 (Minn. 1984), we held that it is within the trial court's discretion to admit expert testimony describing the traits and characteristics typically observed in sexually abused children. In *Myers,* the victim was 7 years old. The expert was allowed to give an opinion that the complainant's allegations were truthful; we allowed this testimony not because the complainant was a child, but because the defendant had opened the door to this opinion testimony. In fact, we commented that as a general rule, "we would reject expert opinion testimony regarding the truth or falsity of a witness' allegations about a crime . . . ." This case, in terms of the age of the complainant, falls between *Saldana* and *Myers;* here the complainant, at the time of the assault and at trial, was a 14-year-old adolescent — neither an adult as in *Saldana,* nor a child as in *Myers.* This case is also different from *Saldana* and *Myers* in that the testimony of Dr. Bell was limited in scope. Dr. Bell did identify several specific characteristics commonly exhibited by adolescent victims of sexual assault who are abused outside the family context but by someone they knew; however, the focus of her testimony was that when the victim is an adolescent, neither a delay in reporting nor continued contact with the assailant is unusual. Dr. Bell had not examined the complainant, so she did not attempt to describe the characteristics or conditions observed in or exhibited by the complainant.

The admissibility of expert testimony lies within the sound discretion of the trial court. In determining whether expert testimony should be admitted, the basic consideration is whether it will be helpful to the jury. The trial court must also remain cognizant that even if expert testimony is helpful, its probative value must be balanced against the danger of unfair prejudice, confusion, or misleading the jury, and if its probative value is substantially outweighed by any of these considerations, it may be excluded.

Our review of the record leads us to conclude that the trial court did not abuse its discretion by admitting the testimony of Dr. Bell concerning the behavioral characteristics typically displayed by adolescent victims of sexual assault.

While we hold that in cases where a sexual assault victim is an adolescent, expert testimony as to the reporting conduct of such victims and as to continued contact by the adolescent with the assailant is admissible in the proper exercise of discretion by the trial court, we caution that we do not intend to establish a categorical rule that expert testimony concerning all characteristics typically displayed by adolescent sexual assault victims is admissible. . . .

Reversed; judgment of conviction reinstated.

[The concurring opinions of two justices are omitted.]

State v. J.Q.
617 A.2d 1196 (N.J. 1993)

O'HERN, J.

This appeal concerns the use of expert opinion testimony to aid jurors in the criminal trial of a child-sexual-abuse case. The specific issue concerns expert-opinion evidence premised on the Child Sexual Abuse Accommodation Syndrome (CSAAS), and whether there is a reliable scientific explanation for certain exhibited characteristics of an abused child, such as acceptance of the abuse or delayed reporting, that would help jurors understand why a child victim would not complain to a parent or other authority figure about the abuse. We hold that CSAAS has a sufficiently reliable scientific basis to allow an expert witness to describe traits found in victims of such abuse to aid jurors in evaluating specific defenses. In this case, the expert's opinion went beyond that limited scope and included opinions on commonplace issues, such as credibility assessments derived from conflicting versions of an event and not-yet scientifically established opinions on the ultimate issues that are for jury resolution. Although the evidentiary questions arise as a matter of plain error, we agree with the Appellate Division that the introduction of such evidence was clearly capable of producing an unjust result and we thus affirm the Appellate Division's judgment ordering a new trial.

I. Facts and Procedural History

The background to the case is regrettably familiar, a story of childhoods unhinged by events so traumatic that even the participants cannot contemplate them. When first confronted with the possibility that defendant might have sexually abused his daughters, their mother was incredulous. After the girls first told their mother of the alleged abuse, she cautioned them that it was important to tell the truth about their father. The girls said that they were telling the truth. Their mother testified that she had warned her daughters never to let a stranger touch them but had never told them about sexual abuse from a father, because she never thought it could happen to her children. Defendant was equally insistent that committing sexual acts with children and, in particular, his daughters is unimaginable. He testified that anybody who engaged in sexual relations with his own children would have to be "sick" and that he did not believe he was sick. Whether defendant is sick or not, the jury has found that abuse occurred.

Rather than use the initials mandated by law, we shall use fictitious names to describe the parents and children involved. We shall refer to the mother as "Karen," the father as "John," and the two children as "Connie" and "Norma." The parents appear to be of different cultures — Karen is from the midwest and John is a recent arrival to the continental United States. They met in Indiana in 1973 or 1974 and started their life together there when Karen was thirteen and John was nineteen or twenty. John already had a child at that time. They soon moved to Brooklyn and later settled in Newark. Connie and Norma were born in 1977 and 1979, respectively. John and Karen never married. Although John worked as an auto mechanic and a golf-greens attendant during their years in New Jersey, he did not provide sufficient financial support for the household; thus, Karen received public assistance for the two children. Theirs was a tempestuous union marked by recriminations that each had been unfaithful. Their relationship deteriorated in late 1984 when John separated from Karen. During the separation, which lasted approximately four months, Karen became pregnant by another man. The breakup became final in late 1985 or early 1986 when John went to Brooklyn to live in an apartment with his brother. At the time of the breakup, Connie and Norma were approximately eight and six years old, respectively.

After the breakup, John customarily picked up the children and took them to Brooklyn for weekend visits. John was then living in a one-room apartment with another woman, whom he married in 1987. About two years after the separation, Karen learned that Norma, during play, had attempted to pull down her younger sister's underwear and touch her buttocks. Karen asked Norma where she had ever learned of such things and Norma reluctantly identified the person who had initiated her into such conduct by spelling out the word "D-A-D."

Although at first disbelieving, Karen consulted a family counsellor and eventually reported the incident to the police. Both Connie and Norma reported that they had been the victims of repeated acts of sexual abuse by their father in the Newark apartment in 1984 as well as during their visits to Brooklyn. An Essex County grand jury returned an indictment charging John with acts of criminal sexual abuse in New Jersey on his children between January 1, 1984, and December 31, 1984.

Before trial, the prosecutor moved to have Connie's and Norma's testimony taken on closed-circuit television. In ruling on the motion, the trial court heard testimony from Madeline Milchman, a Ph.D. in psychology with a concentration in developmental or child psychology. Dr. Milchman had interviewed the children and had reviewed other information on them as well. The court first qualified Dr. Milchman, without objection, as an expert witness in the areas of child psychology and child sexual abuse. Dr. Milchman essentially testified that both infant witnesses would suffer severe emotional distress if forced to testify before spectators, jurors, and especially their father in the courtroom setting. The trial court granted the motion, ordering that Norma and Connie testify through a closed-circuit system outside the presence of jurors, spectators, and defendant.

At trial, both Connie and Norma described, in graphic detail, the abuses committed on them involving sexual penetration and oral sexual contact. A pediatric resident who conducted a genital examination of Norma testified that she found that the child had a stretched hymenal opening, an abnormal condition for a seven-year- old girl. The medical evidence relating to Connie, entered by way of stipulation, also revealed a stretched hymen. Karen described discharges that she had observed on Norma's underwear but said that she had attributed them to Norma's not changing her underwear.

Dr. Milchman was called to the stand again at trial and qualified, without objection, as an expert witness on child sexual abuse. She identified the child sexual abuse accommodation syndrome "as a pattern of behavior that is found to occur again and again in children who are victims of incest." She described the various aspects of CSAAS and related them to behavior she had observed in Connie and Norma. Dr. Milchman also testified about how she assesses the veracity of an alleged victim of child sexual abuse. At the conclusion of her direct testimony, Dr. Milchman stated that in her expert opinion, Connie and Norma had been sexually abused.

The theory of the defense was that Karen had put the children up to this story to avenge her loss of John. Defendant offered evidence that the Newark apartment housed eight people and that there was no isolated occasion during which such abuse could have occurred.

The jury convicted defendant [and the] court sentenced defendant to thirty years' imprisonment . . . . The Appellate Division reversed the convictions, finding that the trial court had committed plain error in permitting the use of the CSAAS testimony to establish the credibility of the witnesses rather than for other limited purposes for which it is generally reliable, i.e., to explain secrecy, belated disclosure, and recantation by a child-sexual-abuse victim. The Appellate Division specifically held that

> syndrome evidence, including CSAAS, is not reliable to prove the occurrence of sexual abuse, and that absent a question of capacity, a social science expert lacks the qualifications to render an opinion as to the truthfulness of a statement by another witness. Because the expert in this case testified before the jury as to syndrome evidence to prove that sex abuse occurred; opined as to the truthfulness of the children (and their mother), and rendered the opinion that the children were abused based in great measure upon these two interdicted classes of evidence, we are satisfied that the admission of her testimony was error clearly capable of producing an unjust result. . . .

II. Types of Expert Testimony in
Child-Sexual-Abuse Prosecutions

In recent terms of Court we have had to consider various evidentiary problems in criminal prosecutions of child-sexual-abuse cases. Whether society has changed or whether society is finally confronting its deepest flaws is something that we cannot answer. Freud mistakenly believed that his female patients' experiences of sexual abuse as children were merely fantasies and attributed their complaints to hysteria. Chandra Lorraine Holmes, Child Sexual Abuse Accommodation Syndrome: Curing the Effects of a Misdiagnosis in the Law of Evidence, 25 Tulsa L.J. 143, 144 (1989) [hereinafter Holmes]. We know now, from the many accounts, that such abuse in the home is regrettably all too real. "Since the 1970s * * *, there has been a growing awareness of child sexual abuse and reports of it have skyrocketed." Diana Younts, Evaluating and Admitting Expert Opinion Testimony in Child Sexual Abuse Prosecutions, 41 Duke L.J. 691, 693 (1991) [hereinafter Younts]. At the same time, we know that moving from the child's world into the courtroom presents legal issues of varying dimension. . . .

A

At the outset, we must carefully distinguish the issues presented in this case from those that are not presented. There are various categories of expert testimony on child sexual abuse. For purposes of this analysis, we draw on the survey of issues by John E.B. Myers et al., Expert Testimony in Child Sexual Abuse Litigation, 68 Neb. L. Rev. 1 (1989).

The authors point out that some expert testimony is routinely accepted and presents no genuine evidentiary problem. For example, expert medical testimony plays an important role in child-sexual-abuse litigation. Such testimony is based on a physician's clinical diagnostic examination and the child's medical history. Courts have permitted expert medical witnesses to describe the results of the examination and to offer opinions as to the cause of any injuries, to establish penetration, and to answer questions whether injuries could have been inflicted in a particular way or whether a caretaker's explanation for an injury is reasonable.

In the behavioral-science field, the authors identify one type of expert testimony that describes behaviors commonly observed in sexually-abused children. By way of background, the authors describe a wealth of literature that documents general patterns of behavioral and emotional reactions found in clinical samples of sexually-abused children, typically victims of incest. The authors' review of the literature, however, leads them to conclude that the effects of sexual abuse vary among children. Furthermore, children who exhibit symptoms of fear, anxiety, or avoidance are probably suffering the effects of some traumatic experience, of which sexual abuse is only one of many possible causes. Nevertheless, some behaviors, such as age-inappropriate sexualized responses, are more associated with sexual abuse than others. Thus, the authors assert that situations in which sexual abuse is likely can be identified. Given the prevalence of sexual abuse, and its documented association with anxiety symptoms, however, abuse should be considered and evaluated through direct inquiry. When symptoms of fear, anxiety, or avoidance accompany a credible report of sexual abuse, sexual abuse must be seriously considered. While no symptom or set of symptoms is conclusive proof of sexual abuse, when symptoms evidencing abuse are present in conjunction with a report that bears indicia of reliability, the clinician is justified in forming a clinical opinion that a child has been sexually abused.

Despite the considerable basis for this behavioral-science evidence, "most courts do not approve such testimony as substantive evidence of abuse." Myers, supra, 68 Neb. L. Rev. at 65, 68. However, this type of testimony has an important nonsubstantive purpose of which the majority of courts approve. It can be used on rebuttal "to rehabilitate" the victim's testimony when the defense asserts that the child's delay in reporting the abuse and recanting of the story indicate that the child is unworthy of belief.

Another area of behavioral-science testimony seeks to address the ultimate question of whether a child was in fact sexually abused. Such testimony would be based on the clinical observations of a professional "trained in the patterns, effects, and dynamics of child sexual abuse." Id. at 73. The authors say that many experts now believe that the study of child sexual abuse has advanced to such a point as to enable "qualified professionals" to "determine whether a child's symptoms and behavior are consistent with sexual abuse." Id. at 73-75. For example, in 1985 the Council on Scientific Affairs of the American Medical Association published a set of guidelines that listed, in particular, physical and behavioral signs identified with child sexual abuse. Id. at 74 (citing AMA Diagnostic and Treatment Guidelines Concerning Child Abuse and Neglect, 254 J.A.M.A. 796 (1985) [hereinafter Guidelines]). The behavioral signs listed include:

— Overt or subtle and indirect disclosures to a relative, friend or teacher
— Highly sexualized play
— Withdrawal and excessive daydreaming
— Low self esteem, feelings of shame or guilt
— Falling grades
— Pseudomature personality development
— Sexual promiscuity
— Poor peer relationships
— Suicide attempt
— Positive relationship exhibited toward the offender
— Frightened or phobic, especially towards adults.

[Guidelines, supra, 254 J.A.M.A. at 798.]

Although the Myers article points to only two instances in which courts have approved the actual use of such testimony at a criminal trial for the purpose of establishing that sexual abuse had occurred, we do not rule out the possibility that a qualified behavioral-science expert could demonstrate a sufficiently reliable scientific opinion to aid a jury in determining the ultimate issue that the abuse had occurred. This record does not support the conclusion.

The scientific community does not yet exhibit a consensus that the requisite degree of scientific reliability has been shown. Although some argue that "'under no circumstances should a court admit the opinion of an expert about whether a particular child has been abused * * * [,]' [t]he majority of professionals believe qualified mental health professionals can determine whether abuse occurred; not in all cases, but in some." 1 John E.B. Myers, Evidence in Child Abuse and Neglect Cases § 4.31, at 283-84 (2d ed. 1992) [hereinafter Myers, Evidence in Child Abuse and Neglect Cases] (footnote omitted). In evaluating the qualifications of a witness who seeks to offer substantive evidence of sexual abuse, the trial court may wish to consider the criteria suggested in Myers, supra, Evidence in Child Abuse and Neglect Cases § 4.31, at 284-85. Assessing children for possible sexual abuse is a complex task requiring skill and experience. The expert must possess specialized knowledge of child development, individual and family dynamics, patterns of child sexual abuse, the disclosure process, signs and symptoms of abuse, and the use and limits of psychological tests. The expert is familiar with the literature on child abuse, and understands the significance of developmentally inappropriate sexual knowledge. The expert is able to interpret medical reports and laboratory tests. The expert also is trained in the art of interviewing children, and is aware of the literature on coached and fabricated allegations of abuse. Of tremendous importance is the expert's clinical experience with sexually abused children. Obviously, the more limited the purpose for which the evidence is to be used, e.g., were it not for a substantive but for a rehabilitative purpose, the less demanding need be the qualifications of the witness.

Still another category of expert testimony, not presented in this case, concerns inferences to be drawn from a child's interaction with anatomically-detailed dolls during the investigative interview. In many child-sexual-abuse trials, the expert's testimony is wholly or partially based on this methodology. However, the social-science literature questions whether proponents of doll use have yet demonstrated that the dolls are a valid assessment tool for diagnosing abuse. Younts suggests that before the reliability of this methodology can be established, researchers must show at least that children can be accurately categorized as abused or nonabused based on their interaction with the dolls. Obviously, the use of the anatomical dolls may help a child in reciting the history of the event and that demonstration may be of aid to jurors.

B

We must examine the scientific premises supporting the expert's testimony and the purpose for which the testimony was used. We note first that testimony on the child sexual abuse accommodation syndrome has been placed within the category of behavioral-science testimony that describes behaviors commonly observed in sexually-abused children. Courts rarely permit the testimony for the purpose of establishing substantive evidence of abuse, but allow it to rehabilitate the victim's testimony. Roland C. Summit, M.D., has authored the most concise and seemingly most authoritative statement of CSAAS. Roland C. Summit, The Child Sexual Abuse Accommodation Syndrome, 7 Child Abuse & Neglect 177 (1983) [hereinafter Summit].[3] Dr. Summit explained in 1983 that although "[c]hild sexual abuse has exploded into public awareness during a span of less than five years," the awakening of interest creates new hazards for the child victim because it increases the likelihood of discovery "but fails to protect the victim against the secondary assaults of an inconsistent intervention system." Id. at 178 (emphasis omitted). Dr. Summit believed that most adults who hear a distraught child accuse a "respectable" adult of sexual abuse will fault the child. The "[d]isbelief and rejection by potential adult caretakers," which in Dr. Summit's view were the too-frequent responses to reports of child sexual abuse, "increase the helplessness, hopelessness, isolation and self-blame that make up the most damaging aspects of child sexual victimization."[4]

To remedy the systemic injury to the child that results from disbelief, Dr. Summit undertook a scientific study of child-sexual-abuse victims.[5] In publishing his results, Dr. Summit hoped "to provide a vehicle for a more sensitive, more therapeutic response to legitimate victims of child sexual abuse and to invite more active, more effective clinical advocacy for the child within the family and within the systems of child protection and criminal justice." In other words, the purpose of his study was to improve the health of the child, ensure that children receive adequate treatment for what they had suffered, and guarantee that society's response be not flawed by misperceptions.

Dr. Summit's study drew upon correlations and observations that "emerged as self-evident within an extended network of child abuse treatment programs and self-help organizations" and he tested the validity of his theory over a four-year period of his own practice. The child sexual abuse accommodation syndrome, or CSAAS, "represents a common denominator of the most frequently observed vic-

---

[3] At the time of the article's publication, Dr. Summit was Head Physician, Community Consultation Service, and Clinical Assistant Professor of Psychiatry, Harbor-UCLA Medical Center.

[4] Although scholars report the existence of some fabricated allegations of child sexual abuse, the highest incidence of fabrication tends to occur in custody cases. Myers, supra, Evidence in Child Abuse and Neglect Cases § 4.4, at 225. Furthermore, when fabrication does occur, an adult, not the child, is usually responsible. "[F]alse complaints made by children are very rare.'" Id. at 229 (quoting J. Spencer & R. Flin, The Evidence of Children: The Law and the Psychology 269 (1990)).

[5] Dr. Summit limited his study to the most typical victim; i.e., a young, female molested by an adult male entrusted with her care. Summit, supra, 7 Child Abuse & Neglect at 180. At the time he conducted his study, most of the victims available fit this description. However, Dr. Summit observed that young male victims are at least as prevalent, although there is a greater probability that a boy will be molested by someone outside his immediate family. Ibid.

tim behaviors." CSAAS includes five categories of behavior, each of which contradicts "the most common assumptions of adults." Of the five categories, he described two as "preconditions" to the occurrence of sexual abuse and the remaining three as "sequential contingencies" to the abuse "which take on increasing variability and complexity." Obviously, the "preconditions" continue into and characterize the period of abuse.

The first of the preconditions is secrecy: child abuse happens only when the child is alone with the offending adult, and the experience must never be disclosed. That secrecy is frequently accompanied by threats: "'This is our secret; nobody else will understand.'" "'Don't tell anybody.'" "'Nobody will believe you.'" "'Don't tell your mother; (a) she will hate you, * * * (c) she will kill you,'" and the like. From the secrecy, the child gets the impression of danger and fearful outcome. In this case, Norma and Connie testified that they had not reported the alleged abuse because defendant had told them that if they did, he would hit them and they would get into more trouble than he.

The second precondition is helplessness. Dr. Summit explains that the abused child's sense of helplessness is an outgrowth of the child's subordinate role in an authoritarian relationship in which the adult is entrusted with the child's care, such as the parent-child relationship. The prevailing reality for the most frequent victim of child sexual abuse is a sense of total dependence on this powerful adult in the face of which the child's normal reaction is to "play possum."

The third aspect of the syndrome, also the first of what Dr. Summit identifies as a sequential contingency, is a combination: the child feels trapped by the situation (entrapment), and that perception results in the behavior of accommodating the abuse (accommodation). Because of the child's helplessness, the only healthy option left is to survive by accepting the situation. "There is no way out, no place to run." Adults find that hard to believe because they lack the child's perspective, but "[t]he child cannot safely conceptualize that a parent might be ruthless and self-serving; such a conclusion is tantamount to abandonment and annihilation." The roles of parent and child become reversed: it is the child who must protect the family. The abuser warns, "'If you ever tell, they could send me to jail and put all you kids in an orphanage.'"

The fourth aspect, then, is delayed, conflicted and unconvincing disclosure. Most victims never disclose the sexual abuse — at least not outside the immediate family. Dr. Summit found that family conflict triggers disclosure, if ever, "only after some years of continuing sexual abuse and an eventual breakdown of accommodation mechanisms."

Allegations of sexual abuse seem so unbelievable to most that the natural reaction is to assume the claim is false, especially because the victim did not complain years ago when the alleged abuse was ongoing. Dr. Summit surmises that

> [u]nless specifically trained and sensitized, average adults, including
> mothers, relatives, teachers, counselors, doctors, psychotherapists, investi-

gators, prosecutors, defense attorneys, judges and jurors, cannot believe that a normal, truthful child would tolerate incest without immediately reporting or that an apparently normal father could be capable of repeated, unchallenged sexual molestation of his own daughter. There are very few clues to such abuse. Most women (indeed, even this mother) do not believe it possible that a man whom she loved would ever be capable of molesting his or her own children.

The fifth and final aspect is retraction. Although this case does not involve retraction, that "[w]hatever a child says about sexual abuse, she is likely to reverse it" appears to be a fact. The post-disclosure family situation tends to confirm the victim's worst fears, which encouraged her secrecy in the first place, i.e., her mother is disbelieving or hysterical, her father threatened with removal from the home, and the blame for this state of affairs placed squarely on the victim. Once again, because of the reversed roles, the child feels obligated to preserve the family, even at the expense of his or her own well being. The only "good" choice, then, is to "capitulate" and restore a lie for the family's sake.

Dr. Summit analogizes the gradual acceptance of the reality of child sexual abuse to society's changing attitude towards adult rape with the emergence of the rape trauma syndrome theory (RTS). Women were assumed to cause rape, in the absence of a consistent clinical understanding of the "psychological climate," and reactions to such sexual attacks. Thus, "Those who reported often regretted their decision as they found themselves subjected to repeated attacks on their character and credibility." The gradual departure from the mythology of women and rape so recently outlined by our Court in In re M.T.S., 129 N.J. 422, 432-33, 443-45, 609 A.2d 1266 (1992) (dispelling myth that victim's silence in response to sexual assault equals consent), and State v. Hill, 121 N.J. 150, 157-66, 578 A.2d 370 (1990) (dispelling myth that victim's failure immediately to report an alleged sexual assault tends to show that she was not assaulted at all), has slowly been extended to child-abuse victims.

Hence, the behavioral studies of CSAAS are designed not to provide certain evidence of guilt or innocence but rather to insure that all agencies, including the clinician, the offender, the family, and the criminal justice system, offer "the child a right to parity with adults in the struggle for credibility and advocacy." CSAAS achieves that by providing a "common language" for analysis and a more "recognizable map" to the understanding of child abuse.

III. Standards Governing the Admission of Expert Opinion Evidence of CSAAS in Criminal Trials

We need not retrace the development of these standards in any extensive detail. In a long series of cases, we have outlined the general standards that govern the admissibility of such evidence. . . . As provided in the Rules of Evidence and reiterated by many cases, the testimony of an expert is allowed when it relates to a subject-matter beyond the understanding of persons of ordinary experience, intelligence, and knowledge. This applies as well to the field of child sex-abuse offenses. As we have seen, such testimony may be allowed to explain generally the behavior, feelings, and attitudes of such victims when it is shown that their condition is not readily understood by persons of average intelligence and ordinary experience; an expert or scientific explanation of their condition, one accepted as reliable by the scientific community that is involved in the diagnosis, treatment, and care of such individuals, can assist a jury in understanding the evidence.

Acceptance within a scientific community can sometimes be an elusive premise to prove. There will always be some detractors to any theory or clinical approach. State v. Kelly, supra, 97 N.J. 178, 208-14, 478 A.2d 364, illustrates the kind of inquiry that must be made concerning the definition of the scientific community, the degree of acceptance within that community, and the method of proof of that acceptance. Some courts have admitted expert testimony that a child has been sexually abused without any reference to scientific reliability. However, even a qualified expert's opinion must have a reliable basis. Landrigan v. Celotex Corp., 127 N.J. 404, 417, 420, 605 A.2d 1079 (1992) (stating that whether an expert may testify to cancer causation depends on degree of acceptance within relevant scientific community of the methodology of analysis). Certainly, we should be even more hesitant to depart from the general-acceptance requirement in a criminal case.

Finally, we have consistently recognized that juries have exclusive responsibility in the determination of criminal guilt or innocence. Hence, in State v. Odom, 116 N.J. 65, 560 A.2d 1198 (1989), we permitted a State's expert witness to testify that, in his opinion, based on his experience and specialized knowledge, the quantity of drugs was there possessed with the intent to distribute them. We therefore concluded that "as long as the expert does not express his opinion of defendant's guilt but simply characterizes defendant's conduct based on the facts in evidence in light of his specialized knowledge, the opinion is not objectionable." We realize that the line drawn in *Odom* may be thin at times but believe that properly charged juries can see the distinction.

There does not appear to be a dispute about acceptance within the scientific community of the clinical theory that CSAAS identifies or describes behavioral traits commonly found in child-abuse victims. The most pointed criticism of the theory is that the same traits may equally appear as the result of other disorders. Even extreme poverty or psychological abuse can produce the sense of entrapment or accommodation. In other words, the existence of the symptoms does not invariably prove abuse.

That would be a valid criticism if the CSAAS evidence were offered for a purpose beyond the scope of the scientific theory. An analogy may be drawn from State v. Cavallo, supra, 88 N.J. 508, 443 A.2d 1020 (1982). In that case, defense counsel offered to prove that the defendant did not have the characteristics common to all or most rapists and thus to disprove the fact of rape. After reviewing the literature and cases in other jurisdictions, the Court was convinced that the medical or legal communities do not generally accept the view that psychiatrists possess the knowledge or capability to state the likelihood that an individual behaved in a particular manner on a specific occasion.

In contrast, State v. Kelly, supra, 97 N.J. 178, 478 A.2d 364, explained that expert scientific evidence concerning "battered-woman's syndrome" does not aid a jury in determining whether a defendant had or had not behaved in a given manner on a particular occasion; rather, the evidence enables the jury to overcome common myths or misconceptions that a woman who had been the victim of battering would have surely left the batterer. Thus, the evidence helps the jury to understand the battered woman's state of mind. Because the State in *Kelly* had reinforced those myths by repeatedly asking the victim why she had taken her husband back after the battering, the Court ruled such evidence admissible to counter the myths if reliability of the evidence of a counter-intuitive behavioral pattern were established within the scientific community.

IV. The Use of CSAAS Expert Testimony in This Case

Turning then to the application of the standards to the record of this trial, we find that the CSAAS evidence was not presented to the jury in accordance with its scientific theory, i.e., the evidence was not offered to explain the conflicting behavioral traits in this case either of accommodation or delayed disclosure. Rather, the evidence was presented to the jury as though it were to prove directly and substantially that sexual abuse had occurred. Dr. Milchman, the prosecution's expert witness on child sexual abuse, described CSAAS as a pattern of behavior found to occur consistently in children who are victims of incest, and she outlined Dr. Summit's five-part syndrome: secrecy, helplessness, entrapment and accommodation, delayed disclosure, and retraction.

The prosecutor asked whether she had examined Connie and Norma and whether, in the course of examination, Dr. Milchman had found the children to "suffer symptoms of the child sexual abuse accommodation syndrome." (Recall that Dr. Summit describes two aspects of CSAAS, secrecy and helplessness, as "preconditions.") Dr. Milchman said that Norma had exhibited four of the symptoms: secrecy, helplessness, accommodation, and delayed disclosure. She said that Norma's crying, shaking, rubbing her hands in her eyes, and covering her face during the interview were manifestations of her feeling of helplessness towards the abusive situation and her fears, anxieties and anger which she had to suppress in order to accommodate the abuse. Technically, these interview observations do not seem to be the symptoms that Dr. Summit describes. Rather, they appear to us to be generic post-traumatic symptoms. Dr. Milchman pointed out that Norma had revealed the abuse only after questioning initiated by her mother. She also explained that Norma had stuck to her story, instead of recanting it, because nobody was pressuring or threatening her. Connie, on the other hand, had presented herself differently as a "very brassy, very assertive, very outgoing child on the surface" but "[u]nderneath there was a lot of fear and anxiety." Dr. Milchman described Connie as being entrapped and accommodating to the abuse — she complied and accepted the abuse for a long time. She also believed Connie had given a delayed disclosure. Dr. Milchman believed that Connie had kept the abuse a secret for a long time because John had threatened her and her mother with physical violence, a threat she believed because she had seen her father be violent with her mother.

The prosecution then made a transition into areas not covered by CSAAS. Dr. Milchman was presented with a series of questions based on a child's testimony concerning (1) the experience of feeling someone putting a finger inside the child's vagina, (2) the experience of feeling someone putting his tongue inside the child's mouth, and (3) graphic details concerning oral sexual contact. She was asked whether that testimony would be consistent with a child who had been sexually abused or would reflect a child's exposure to outside sources, such as watching others or watching an adult movie. Dr. Milchman said that such testimony was consistent with sexual abuse and added that the graphic details concerning oral sexual contact are not within a child's normal imagination.

The three questions presented to Dr. Milchman obviously had no relationship to CSAAS. They pose evidentiary difficulties in the absence of a more detailed record.[7] Yet counsel did not object to them. Perhaps counsel in such cases prefer to give a wide latitude to expert testimony rather than to appear to shield the jury from such opinion evidence. . . .

However, Dr. Milchman then proceeded to describe how one could "tell whether a child is lying." For example, a child's speaking in a mechanical way, "like it was by rote memory rather than by their own feelings," could raise the suspicion that the child was trying to remember what someone else had told him or her, thereby undermining the child's credibility. Or a child's perfectly consistent narration of all details of the story would be inconsistent, she said, with a child's natural tendency to forget minor detail. Certainly the prefatory basis of CSAAS has nothing to do with those areas of opinion.

This type of testimony equates with the kind of expertise said to relate to eyewitness testimony. Courts are frequently requested to permit expert opinion testimony on the reliability of eyewitness identification. Although People v. McDonald, 37 Cal.3d 351, 208 Cal. Rptr. 236, 690 P.2d 709 (1984), allowed expert testimony from a psychologist concerning the ability of eyewitnesses to

---

[7] For example, was expert testimony needed at all to answer these questions? Arguably at least, the questions do not relate "to a subject-matter beyond the understanding of persons of ordinary experience, intelligence, and knowledge." State v. R.W., supra, 104 N.J. at 30, 514 A.2d 1287. In a similar vein, we have expressed concern about the use of expert testimony "'to interpret matters that could be considered commonplace or conduct that could be accounted for commonsensically.'" State v. Zola, supra, 112 N.J. at 415, 548 A.2d 1022.

perceive, remember, and relate accurately and the distorting effects of fear and excitement, courts have sometimes hesitated to allow such testimony because it may interfere in the truthfinding function or create an unwarranted aura of expertise. Thus, if the child-sexual-abuse expert testifies that the child is "believable" or "truthful," the "courts will most likely exclude the evidence." Linda E. Carter, Admissibility of Expert Testimony in Child Sexual Abuse Cases in California: Retire Kelly-Frye and Return to a Traditional Analysis, 22 Loyola L. Rev. 1103, 1118 (1989).

Yet, in this case Dr. Milchman was asked, "How can you tell when a child or a victim is telling the truth about the fact that they have been sexually abused?" Although the court cautioned the jurors that it was up to them ultimately to determine that, the expert proffered a theory — again unrelated to CSAAS:

> Okay. I look for — I look for many different things. I look for whether the child appears to be sincere. I look for whether or not the feeling that they have at the time goes with what they are saying or whether it contradicts what they are saying. I go for whether there are a lot of different behaviors that all point to the same conclusion. For example, is what the child saying, does that match the demonstrations that they give when they try to explain it with their hands or with dolls, does it match the pictures that they draw for me? Does it match what they told the mother; does it match what they told the DYFS worker; does it match what they told the Prosecutor or investigator; or does it match what they told me? I look for consistency across a lot of different kinds of behaviors. * * * I look for * * * realistic, concrete, specific, kinds of details that are not the kinds of things that you would tend to see on a television so that any kid could pick up or any cable T.V. or movie that any kid could just pick up * * *.

The final question to the witness was: "Doctor, based on your examinations of the girls can you give this jury your expert opinion as to whether or not both [Connie] and [Norma] were sexually abused?" Answer: "I believe that they were sexually abused."

At this point, whether Dr. Milchman had reached that opinion on the basis of her credibility assessments or on the basis of her understanding of CSAAS evidence is not clear to us and could not have been clear to the jury. If it were the former, it would be improper opinion evidence because it would introduce an unwarranted aura of scientific reliability to the analysis of credibility issues. If it were the latter, it would be improper opinion evidence because CSAAS is not relied on in the scientific community to detect abuse.

There has not been a showing . . . of a general acceptance that would allow the use of CSAAS testimony to establish guilt or innocence. Such use of CSAAS evidence would present the analog to State v. Cavallo, supra, 88 N.J. 508, 443 A.2d 1020, and would require a study of the reliability of psychiatric or psychological testimony on the likelihood that the traits found in the victim will establish that another had engaged in the conduct that had caused the symptoms. It strikes us that the premise would be strained, at least on the basis of the Summit studies. As Myers noted:

> Summit did not intend the accommodation syndrome as a diagnostic device. The syndrome does not detect sexual abuse. Rather, it assumes the presence of abuse, and explains the child's reactions to it. Thus, child sexual abuse accommodation syndrome is not the sexual abuse analogue of battered child syndrome, which is diagnostic of physical abuse. With battered child syndrome, one reasons from type of injury to cause of injury. Thus, battered child syndrome is probative of physical abuse. With child sexual abuse accommodation syndrome, by contrast, one reasons from presence of sexual abuse to reactions to sexual abuse. Thus, the accommodation syndrome is not probative of abuse. Unfortunately, a number of mental health professionals, lawyers, and commentators drew unwarranted comparisons between battered child syndrome and child sexual abuse accommodation syndrome. This error led to considerable confusion. First, some professionals misinterpreted Summit's article, believing Summit had discovered a "syndrome" that could diagnose sexual abuse. This mistake is understandable, if not forgivable. Mental health and legal professionals working in the child abuse area had long been accustomed to thinking in terms of syndrome evidence to prove physical abuse. Battered child syndrome was an accepted diagnosis by the time Summit's accommodation syndrome came along in 1983. It was natural for professionals to transfer their understanding of battered child syndrome to this new syndrome, and to conclude that the accommodation syndrome, like battered child syndrome, could be used to detect abuse. . . .
>
> [T]he accommodation syndrome was being asked to perform a task it could not accomplish. The accommodation syndrome has a place in the courtroom. The syndrome helps explain why many sexually abused children delay reporting their abuse, and why many children recant allegations of abuse and deny that anything occurred. If use of the syndrome is confined to these rehabilitative functions, the confusion clears, and the accommodation syndrome serves a useful forensic function.

This we believe is the most concise summary of the proper use of CSAAS and will serve as a useful road map in the trial of such cases. . . .

The California Court of Appeals has thus refused to admit testimony about the general characteristics of molested children for the purpose of allowing the jury to conclude that a particular child is a victim of abuse. People v. Bowker, supra, 203 Cal. App. 3d 385, 249 Cal. Rptr. 886. Instead, because CSAAS has a limited, therapeutic purpose and not a predictive one, "the evidence must be tailored to the purpose for which it is being received." Id. at 891, 203 Cal. App. 3d 385. "[A]t a minimum the evidence must be targeted to a specific 'myth' or 'misconception' suggested by the evidence" and limited to explaining why "the victim's reactions as demonstrated by the evidence are not inconsistent with having been molested." Id. at 891-92, 203 Cal. App. 3d 385. The court must also explain to the jury that the expert's testimony is not intended to address the ultimate question of whether the victim's molestation claims are true and must admonish the jury not to use the testimony for that purpose. That use of CSAAS testimony is consistent with the use to which we put the battered-woman-syndrome evidence in Kelly, supra, 97 N.J. 178, 478 A.2d 364.

Other jurisdictions follow that approach. See State v. Reser, 244 Kan. 306, 767 P.2d 1277, 1283 (1989) (qualifying clinical specialist with training in child sexual abuse to testify to "common patterns of behavior" resulting from abuse and that this victim had symptoms consistent with those patterns); People v. Beckley, 434 Mich. 691, 456 N.W.2d 391, 407 (1990) (finding appropriate expert testimony limited to providing jury with background information, relevant to specific aspect of child's conduct at issue, which it could not otherwise bring to its evaluation of child's credibility); State v. Middleton, 294 Or. 427, 657 P.2d 1215, 1220 (1983) (explaining "superficially bizarre behavior" of victims of abuse helps jury to assess credibility). But see State v. Bachman, 446 N.W.2d 271, 276 (S.D. 1989) (allowing opinion testimony that victim's allegations were truthful).

Such use accords with the use now generally afforded to rape trauma syndrome (RTS) evidence most often in the context of adult rape. RTS describes symptoms frequently experienced by rape victims, e.g., phobic reactions and sexual fears. Because RTS was developed as a therapeutic tool, not as a test to determine the existence of a past event, the California Supreme Court in People v. Bledsoe, 36 Cal.3d 236, 203 Cal. Rptr. 450, 681 P.2d 291 (1984), questioned the reliability of RTS in determining whether a rape has occurred. Thus, the court held that, given the history, purpose and nature of RTS, testimony on the concept was inadmissible to prove that a rape occurred, but recognized that RTS testimony has been admitted in cases in which the alleged rapist suggests that the victim's conduct after the incident was inconsistent with her claim of rape. In the latter context, expert testimony of RTS may play a particularly useful role by disabusing the jury of widely-held myths and misconceptions about rape and rape victims.

V. Conclusion

Expert opinion testimony has a vital role to play in the trial of child-sexual-abuse cases. At one end of the spectrum is the clearly admissible evidence of the qualified expert with respect to the physical manifestations of sexual abuse or the child's out-of-court statements relating to a sexual offense under Evidence Rule 63(33) (the tender-years exception). As courts and counsel proceed further from that clearly admissible end of the spectrum, they must focus on the research basis for the proposition that the expert witness seeks to establish.

The State has argued before us that it is appropriate to admit Dr. Milchman's testimony describing CSAAS and concluding that Norma's and Connie's symptoms were consistent with sexual abuse and rendering an expert opinion that they had been sexually abused. Obviously, scientific evidence exists to aid a jury in determining whether sexual abuse has occurred. As we understand CSAAS, however, it does not purport to establish sexual abuse but helps to explain traits often found in children who have been abused. Hence we believe that in this case the "accommodation syndrome was being asked [by the State] to perform a task it could not accomplish." Myers, supra, 68 Neb. L. Rev. at 68.

In this case the theory of the defense was that the children had been put up to their stories by a vengeful scorned lover. The CSAAS evidence would have served well to counter the mythology that if the abuse had occurred, the children surely would have complained sooner and would not have put up with repeated visits to the apartment in Brooklyn. However, when the expert, without a reliable foundation, went on to offer opinions with respect to the basic factual issues, including truth-telling, she transgressed the purpose for which CSAAS testimony is admissible.

We realize that these cases are extremely difficult to prosecute. They should not be made more difficult by evidentiary issues that surface in the midst of trial. Our rules permit a criminal defendant to have access to the contents of a State expert's report in advance of trial. We understand that the State routinely furnishes defendants with such discovery. Speedy-trial practice contemplates that the defendant will have the report by arraignment. If there is to be objection to the testimony, a defendant may request a Rule 8 hearing in advance of the trial at which the court will assess the qualifications of the witness as well as the research basis for the expert proposition to be stated. For example, in a case such as this the trial court should have been given the opportunity before trial to determine the qualifications of the witness and whether under any of the three methods of establishing reliability, i.e., expert testimony, authoritative literature, or decisional law, the research (here only CSAAS was mentioned) sustains an expert opinion that the children were telling the truth or were reliably diagnosed as victims of sexual abuse.

At such a Rule 8 hearing, the court will conduct an inquiry into whether the witness possesses the "education, knowledge, training, and experience" necessary to render an opinion on the proposition to be presented to the jury. Rubanick, supra, 125 N.J. at 449-53, 593 A.2d 733. If qualified, the witness should then establish at a minimum that the methodology used to form his or her opinion is generally accepted within the relevant scientific community to establish the proposition to be stated by the witness. In this case, the only scientific basis or methodology referred to by the witness was CSAAS and as we have seen, qualified mental health professionals do not regard CSAAS as a sufficiently reliable scientific indicator of the substantive fact of abuse. Obviously, a qualified witness may wish to incorporate the CSAAS research into the totality of his or her methodology for assessing the substantive fact of abuse.

In setting forth these requirements, we do not intend in any sense to mystify the trial of child-sexual-abuse cases. All that is required is close attention to existing precedent: (1) are the factual matters "beyond the ken" of the jurors, State v. Kelly, supra, 97 N.J. at 208, 478 A.2d 364, and will expert testimony aid the jury in resolution of the matter?; (2) is the proposed expert witness qualified by education, training, experience, and knowledge to express an opinion on the factual matter in dispute?; (3) is there general acceptance of the scientific theory or even the methodology used to establish the factual proposition?; and (4) will the jury be given proper instructions limiting the evidence to the purpose for which it is offered? The study of child sexual abuse is rapidly evolving, and we may expect that behavioral scientists will continue their efforts to develop reliable criteria to detect child sexual abuse.

Because this is the first time that our Court has addressed those issues, we affirm the judgment of the Appellate Division. In future cases, we shall assume that the failure of informed defense counsel to object to such expert testimony may reflect a tactical decision by the defense to let the jury hear all available information pertaining to the case. . . .

The judgment of the Appellate Division is affirmed.

NOTES

1. *The caselaw.* What distinguishes *Saldana* and *McGee* from *Myers* and *Hall?* The age of the alleged victims? The content of the testimony? The extent of scientific knowledge of PTSD in children as opposed to adults? A jury's need for the evidence? An increased willingness to convict possible child abusers? May the evidence be used to prove the fact of abuse as well as to explain a child's delay in reporting the abuse or his or her retraction of an accusation?

For conflicting views on the usefulness of testimony about the child sexual abuse syndrome, see State v. Floody, 481 N.W.2d 242 (S.D. 1992), *noted,* 38 S.D. L. Rev. 189 (1993); Lisa R. Askowitz & Michael H. Graham, The Reliability of Expert Psychological Testimony in Child Sexual Abuse Prosecutions, 15 Cardozo L. Rev. 2027 (1994); Mary Ann Mason, A Judicial Dilemma: Expert Witness Testimony in Child Sex Abuse Cases, 19 J. Psychiatry & Law 185 (1991); Diana Younts, Evaluating and Admitting Expert Opinion Testimony in Child Sexual Abuse Prosecutions, 11 Duke L.J. 691 (1991); Maureen Mundt-Larsh, *State v. Rimmasch*: Utah's Threshold Admissibility Standard for Child Sexual Abuse Profile Evidence, 1990 Utah L. Rev. 641; John E.B. Myers et al., Expert Testimony in Child Sexual Abuse Litigation, 68 Neb. L. Rev. 1 (1989); David McCord, Expert Psychological Testimony About Child Complainants in Sexual Abuse Prosecutions: A Foray Into the Admissibility of Novel Psychological Evidence, 77 J. Crim. L. & Criminology 1 (1986); Lisa R. Askowitz, Comment, Restricting the Admissibility of Expert Testimony in Child Sexual Abuse Prosecution: Pennsylvania Takes it to the Extreme, 47 U. Miami L. Rev. 201 (1992); Andrew Cohen, Note, The Unreliability of Expert Testimony on the Typical Characteristics of Sexual Abuse Victims, 74 Geo. L.J. 429 (1985); authorities cited, 1 McCormick on Evidence § 206(D), at 925-26, n.15, 927 n.26, 928 n.30 (John W. Strong 4th ed., 1992).

2. *Research on PTSD in abused children.* Empirical research on PTSD in abused children is reviewed in, e.g., Regina A. Schuller & Neil Vidmar, Battered Woman Syndrome Testimony in the Courtroom: A Review of the Literature, 16 Law & Human Behav. 273 (1992); Regina Schuller & Patricia A. Hastings, The Scientific Status of Research on the Physical and Sexual Abuse of Children, in Modern Scientific Evidence § 9-2 (David Faigman et al. eds., 1997). These psychologists report that:

> For the most part, research on PTSD . . . involving children is only in its infancy. [T]he studies conducted to date vary in their definition and measurement of PTSD . . . . [T]he studies involve . . . small samples, with children representing a wide range of age levels (e.g., 4 to 14), different types of abuse, and various victim-perpetrator relationships. Without properly controlling for these variables, their relationship to PTSD cannot be clearly determined. Finally, the children assessed may also be unrepresentative of the general population of abused children, since the samples . . . have been based on children admitted to hospitals for treatment or whose abuse has been officially reported.

Id. at § 9-2.1.1. Which of these criticisms of the research should bear on the admissibility of testimony about PTSD in sexually abused children?

3. *"Battered Woman Syndrome."* Another controversial category of testimony pertains to the tendency of victims of physical abuse to remain with the abuser and to attack the abuser outside the confines of the traditional justification of self-defense. See, e.g., Modern Scientific Evidence § 8 (David Faigman et al. eds., 1997); Robert F. Schopp et al., Battered Woman Syndrome, Expert Testimony, and the Distinction Between Justification and Excuse, 1994 U. Ill. L. Rev. 45; Erich D. Andersen & Anne Read-Andersen, Constitutional Dimensions of the Battered Woman Syndrome, 53 Ohio St. L.J. 363 (1992); Holly Maguigan, Battered Women, 140 U. Pa. L. Rev. 379 (1991); John Monahan & Laurens Walker, Legal Doctrines Governing the Admissibility of Expert Testimony Concerning Social Framework Evidence, 52 Law & Contemp. Probs. 85 (1989); Susan Murphy, Note, Assisting the Jury in Understanding Victimization: Expert Psychological Testimony on Battered Woman Syndrome and Rape Trauma Syndrome, 25 Colum. J. L. & Soc. Probs. 277 (1992); Joan M. Schroeder, Note, Using Battered Woman Syndrome in the Prosecution of a Batterer, 76 Iowa L. Rev. 553 (1991); Rick Brown, Note, Limitations on Expert Testimony on the Battered Woman Syndrome in Homicide Cases: The Return of the Ultimate Opinion Rule, 32 Ariz. L. Rev. 665 (1990); David L. Faigman, Note, The Battered Woman Syndrome and Self-Defense: A Legal and Empirical Dissent, 72 Va. L. Rev. 619 (1986).

4. *Other syndromes and profiles.* In the cases described in this chapter, the findings of behavioral scientists are admissible on the theory that the expert serves to educate the jury about these experimental or other findings so that the jurors may use this background information to evaluate the trial testimony more accurately. However, when psychological experts go beyond the presentation of such general knowledge and offer clinical judgments about the accuracy of a particular eyewitness, the lack of consent in an alleged rape, the credibility of a child witness, the tendency of battered women to remain with the man who abuses them, and so on, many courts will find the testimony should be excluded. The crucial distinction, then, is between statistical, experimental, or clinical data that support a generalization about human behavior or performance, and the expert's application of these data or this generalization to a specific person. It has been argued that the former testimony should be admissible because it provides a useful "social framework" for evaluating the trial evidence, John Monahan & Laurens Walker, Social Frameworks: A New Use of Social Science in Law, 73 Va. L. Rev. 559 (1987), but that once the expert supplies these generalizations, "the jury needs nothing further from the expert." State v. Lindsey, 720 P.2d 73 (Ariz. 1986).

Other examples of such testimony include "profiles" of certain types of offenders — characteristics statistically associated with an offense. May the prosecution prove that a defendant fits the "profile" of a rapist, arsonist, a drug courier, or the like? Consider Rule 404(b) of the Federal (and Uniform) Rules of Evidence:

> Evidence of other crimes, wrongs or acts is not admissible to prove the character of a person in order to show that he acted in conformity therewith. It may, however, be admissible where such evidence is probative of any other fact that is of consequence to the determination of the action, such as proof of motive, opportunity, intent, preparation, plan, knowledge, identity, modus operandi, or absence of mistake or accident.

See State v. Hester, 760 P.2d 27, 33-34 (Idaho 1988); People v. Walkey, 223 Cal. Rptr. 132, 137-39 (Ct. App. 1986); McCormick on Evidence § 206 (John W. Strong ed., 4th ed. 1992). May the defendant prove that he does not fit the incriminating profile? See State v. Cavallo, 443 A.2d 1020 (N.J. 1982); McCormick on Evidence § 206, at 636 (E. Cleary ed., 3d ed. 1984).

The evocative term "syndrome" usually is adopted by the proponents of psychology testimony. More recently, it has been embraced by those who question expert (and other) testimony that an adult has "recovered" memories of sexual abuse. See supra chapter 18. Thus, the False Memory Syndrome Foundation and the Johns Hopkins Medical Institutions sponsored a conference on "Memory and Reality: Reconciliation — Scientific, Clinical and Legal Issues of False Memory Syndrome," Dec. 9-11, 1994. The conference brochure proclaims that:

> False Memory Syndrome (FMS) is a condition in which a person's identity and relationships are centered around the memory of a traumatic expe-

rience which is objectively false but the person strongly believes it to be true. It has a devastating effect on the victim and typically produces a continuing dependency on the therapeutic program that created the syndrome. FMS proceeds to destroy the psychological well-being of the primary victim, the integrity of the family and . . . secondary victims falsely accused of vile acts of incest and abuse.

5. *Opinions on credibility.* As the preceding materials indicate, courts are loathe to admit expert testimony explicitly directed to "credibility." In State v. Lindsey, 720 P.2d 73 (Ariz. 1986), for instance, the Arizona Supreme Court reversed a conviction for incest because of what it deemed "direct opinion testimony on truthfulness" from the state's expert. The court remarked:

> Opinion evidence on who is telling the truth in cases such as this is nothing more than the expert's opinion on how the case should be decided. We believe that such testimony is inadmissible, both because it usurps the jury's traditional functions and roles and because, when given insight into the behavioral sciences, the jury needs nothing further from the expert. We do not invite battles of opposing experts testifying to opinions about the truthfulness of the prosecution witness as compared to that of the defense witnesses.

See also State v. Moran, 728 P.2d 248 (Ariz. 1986); Lindsey v. United States, 237 F.2d 893 (9th Cir. 1956); People v. Hughes, 453 N.E. 2d 484 (N.Y. 1983) ("when presented with scientific evidence purporting to guage the credibility of participants or witnesses to a criminal incident, we have established a very high level of reliability, tantamount to certainty, as a predicate for its admissibility"). On the value of the traditional aversion to expert testimony on credibility, compare Michael W. Mullane, The Truthsayer and the Court: Expert Testimony and Credibility, 43 Me. L. Rev. 53 (1991) (should be treated like other expert testimony), with Steven I. Friedland, On Common Sense and the Evaluation of Witness Credibility, 40 Case W. L. Rev. 165 (1989-90) (prohibition warranted except in narrowly defined circumstances).

In addition to this general aversion to expert assessments of truthfulness, the relatively intricate and confusing rules of evidence involving "character" and "character for credibility" affect the admissibility of expert assessments of credibility. For instance, whether or not an expert's conclusion of deception might be admissible to attack credibility, an opinion bolstering truthfulness would be inadmissible if the witness's character for credibility has not been attacked. See, e.g., State v. Kim, 645 P.2d 1330, 1339 n.14 (Haw. 1982), overruled on other grounds in State v. Batagan, 799 P.2d 48 (Haw. 1990); supra chapter 18.

Part VI

SCIENCE IN TOXIC TORT CASES

Chapter 21
Epidemiology and Toxicology

In re Joint Eastern & Southern District Asbestos Litigation
827 F. Supp. 1014 (S.D.N.Y. 1993)

SWEET, DISTRICT JUDGE

Following a jury verdict rendered on February 10, 1993, in favor of the plaintiff Arlene Maiorana, certain defendants and third-party defendants in this action have filed post-trial motions. The plaintiff alleged and the jury found that the asbestos-containing products of certain of the defendants were the proximate cause of the death of her husband, John Maiorana ("Maiorana").

After the verdict, defendant and second third-party plaintiff United States Mineral Product Company (USMP), the sole remaining direct defendant left in the trial, moved . . . for judgment notwithstanding the verdict or, more properly, for judgment as a matter of law. USMP also moved for a new trial or, in the alternative, for remittitur . . . . Third-party defendants Mario & DiBono Plastering Co. (Mario & DiBono), Castagna & Son, Inc. (Castagna), and Tishman Realty & Construction Co. of New York, Inc. (Tishman), have sought similar relief. . . .

The plaintiff filed her original complaint in this diversity action on July 28, 1987, as part of a case brought by sixteen plaintiffs on behalf of themselves and their deceased spouses, see In re Joint E. & S. Dist. Asbestos Litig., 758 F. Supp. 199 (SDNY 1991) (Asbestos Litig. I), rev'd, 964 F.2d 92 (2d Cir. 1992) (Asbestos Litig. II). Defendant and second third-party plaintiff USMP filed its second third-party complaint on December 14, 1990.

Certain defendants, including USMP, moved for summary judgment alleging that the only evidence which the plaintiff had set forth to prove that her husband's colon cancer was caused by his exposure to asbestos was epidemiological evidence, and because this evidence did not indicate that asbestos exposure created at least a two-fold increase in the risks of getting colon cancer and thus the Defendants' actions could not have been "more likely than not" the cause of his cancer, it was insufficient as a matter of law. The motion for summary judgment was granted on February 26, 1991.

The plaintiff appealed, and the Court of Appeals reversed the grant of summary judgment status on the grounds that the plaintiff had presented clinical evidence of causation in addition to the epidemiological studies: "Maiorana's own medical records and personal history were the clinical evidence upon which plaintiff's expert witnesses based their opinions that asbestos exposure was a significant factor in causing his colon cancer." Asbestos Litig. II, 964 F.2d at 96. The Court found that the plaintiff's experts could testify that Maiorana's exposure to asbestos was a "significant factor" and "a proximate cause, and a substantial factor" in the development of his colon cancer because:

> [t]hey based their conclusions on their review of Mr. Maiorana's medical records, occupational and medical history, their knowledge as experts either in occupational medicine or epidemiology and their review of epidemiological studies. They also appropriately based their conclusions on the lack of other factors that could have caused Mr. Maiorana's colon cancer. . . . Granting plaintiff all favorable inferences, these statements are the equivalent of stating that asbestos exposure more probably than not caused the colon cancer. Medical experts need not invoke technical legal phrases in order to convey their medical opinions.

Id. at 96-97.

The case was tried to a jury from January 20 to February 10, 1993. The jury was charged on strict liability and negligence of manufacturers and on the negligence of all third party defendants. The jury, after allocating percentages of fault among the defendants and certain non-parties via special verdict, returned a verdict in favor of the plaintiff in the total amount of $4,510,000. The jury found USMP 50% responsible for the plaintiffs' damages and three of the third-parties approximately equally negligent (both contractors were assessed to be 14% responsible; subcontractor Mario & DiBono was assessed to be 15% responsible). The jury absolved the Port Authority of any liability. . . .

USMP was the manufacturer of Cafco D, an asbestos-containing fireproof spray material used in the construction of both the WTC in Manhattan and Meadowbrook Hospital in Nassau County, New York. The Port Authority was the owner of the WTC. Tishman was the Port Authority's prime or general contractor at the WTC job site and the Port Authority's designated agent for dealing with the subcontractors and trade workers. Castagna was the general contractor for Meadowbrook Hospital.

Proof offered at trial established that both Castagna and Tishman had inspectors and workers on the site with direct control and authority over the various subcontractors and employees. Both Castagna and Tishman entered into contracts with the respective site owners which gave them certain authority and control over the job sites. These contracts were admitted into evidence at trial. One of these subcontractors was Mario & DiBono, the asbestos spray contractor for Meadowbrook and for interior work at the WTC.

Maiorana worked at the WTC in 1969 and 1970 and at Meadowbrook from September 1969 until sometime in 1970 as a sheet metal worker for Alpine, a small sheet metal company no longer in operation, and another subcontractor. The plaintiff's theory at trial was that the sheet metal workers, who worked alongside of and followed the work of the asbestos sprayers, were exposed to asbestos through contact with USMP's sprayed insulation, Cafco D. Maiorana was exposed to asbestos-containing dust which hung in the air and accumulated on the floor after a session of spraying.

Mario & DiBono began spraying Cafco D at the WTC in approximately August 1969. The Port Authority and Tishman banned the use of Cafco D at the WTC in April of 1970. USMP shipped Cafco D to Meadowbrook in the fall of 1969.

Maiorana was diagnosed as having colon cancer in January 1983, and he died from the disease six months later, on June 16, 1983. He was 40 years of age. . . .

I. The Standard for Judgement . . .

USMP and all the defendants allege that they are entitled to judgment as a matter of law. A motion for judgment as a matter of law should be denied unless, viewed in the light most favorable to the nonmoving party, "the evidence is such that, without weighing the credibility of the witnesses or otherwise considering the weight of the evidence, there can be but one conclusion as the verdict that reasonable men could have reached." Samuels v. Air Transport Local 504, 992 F.2d 12, 14 (2d Cir. 1993) . . .

II. Sufficiency of the Evidence

. . . At issue here is the sufficiency of the evidence that Maiorana's exposure to asbestos was the proximate cause of his colon cancer. That evidence was exclusively scientific in nature.

A recent decision by the Supreme Court in Daubert v. Merrell Dow Pharmaceuticals, Inc., 113 S.Ct. 2786 (1993), clarified the standards for admitting scientific evidence. While there is no question in this case that the testimony of both sides' experts — all of whom possess impressive credentials — is admissible, certain passages in *Daubert* speak to the sufficiency required of scientific evidence and the gatekeeping role of the trial judge with regard to misleading evidence. In other words, although *Daubert* focuses on the admissibility of the evidence, dicta in that opinion about the methods by which a trial court may determine the reliability of the evidence are instructive as well.

The recent decision in *Daubert* does not change the fundamental test of law, however. The evidence supplied by the plaintiff at trial must be sufficient as a matter of law to show that Maiorana's exposure to asbestos was a proximate cause of his colon cancer. To competently analyze the legal issues presented by this appeal, an understanding of the relevant scientific principles, albeit necessarily a rudimentary one drawn primarily from the relevant sources cited to by the parties, is essential. . . .

A. The Problem of Causation in Toxic and Carcinogenic Tort Actions

Courts employ no fewer than three distinct concepts of "cause": cause-in-fact, proximate cause, and causal linkage. Cause-in-fact is but-for causation: it is the particular necessary condition without which the event causing the injury would not have occurred, to wit, if event x *qua* cause-in-fact occurs, then event y will follow. Proximate cause is more important from the legal perspective because it is the cause whose proximity in time and space qualifies it as the legally significant cause that is sufficient to sustain a cause of action in tort. Causal linkage, in contrast, asserts a causal relationship between events x and y on the basis of statistical probability: if x occurs, there is probability p that event y will follow.

In the area of toxic and carcinogenic torts, the discussion of causation is substantially complicated by the importance of scientific hypotheses and theories in determining whether a causal relationship exists between person A being exposed to carcinogen c and subsequently developing disease d. The most straightforward concept of causation is that used to frame universal laws of the form: *ceteris paribus* for all occurrences of an event of type x, then an event of type y will necessarily follow.

Such universal causal relationships have been identified for certain "signature" diseases such as mesothelioma. The causal link between exposure to asbestos and mesothelioma has been demonstrated to such a high degree of probability, while at the same time few if any other possible causes have been identified, that if A is diagnosed as having mesothelioma and A was exposed to asbestos, A's exposure to asbestos is recognized to be the cause of A's mesothelioma.

Of course, in order to assert such a universal connection between events x and y, it is necessary to have a thorough understanding of the relevant physical mechanisms involved in the relationship. Obvious difficulties emerge when those mechanisms are complex and imprecisely understood. Simply subjecting A to clinical evaluation will not be sufficient because of the difficulty involved in excluding other possible causes and confounding factors that may be have caused or causally contributed to A's disease. In these cases, the scientist is compelled to frame hypotheses in terms of laws asserting a statistical probability that if x, then y, rather than a universal connection between the two events. Thus, in addition to the aforementioned legal concepts of cause, the court is inevitably confronted with the myriad uses of the concept by scientists.

B. Epidemiological Evidence

Epidemiology is a scientific discipline that by the very nature of its subject matter employs the concept of cause *qua* statistical probability. Useful hypotheses are framed, tested, refined, and used in identifying relations between one event, such as the exposure to carcinogenic substance c, and a subsequent event, such as the development of disease d. However, because the physiological, biological, and chemical mechanisms involved with c and d and the interaction between them are not sufficiently well-known for any single individual to frame a universal law regarding the causal relationship between c and d, the epidemiologist focuses on a group of persons or a "cohort" and assesses the statistical probability that a percentage of individuals in a given cohort will develop *d* after being exposed to *c*.

The Honorable Jack B. Weinstein has summarized the tasks and methods of the epidemiologist as follows:

> Epidemiological studies rely on "statistical methods to detect abnormally high incidences of disease in a study population and to associate these incidences with unusual exposures to suspect environmental factors." In their study of diseases in human populations, epidemiologists use data from surveys, death certificates, and medical and clinical observations.

In re "Agent Orange" Prod. Liab. Litig., 611 F. Supp. 1223, 1231 (EDNY 1985) (Agent Orange II).

The epidemiologist proceeds in two stages in analyzing the relationship between *c* and *d:* first, he determines whether a relationship . . . is biologically possible; and second, if he concludes that it is, he then determines whether this relationship is causal in nature by considering whether there is a statistically significant association between the cohort's exposure to c and the outbreak of *d* in the cohort. This association is determined by using a mathematical formula that produces a ratio for the relative risk of contracting the disease:

> The relative risk ratio is computed by dividing the observed number of cases of a particular disease for a particular time period (numerator data) by the expected number of cases of that disease for the same time period based on historical information not influenced by the event in question (denominator data).
>
> A relative risk of [1.0] is the expected rate of contracting a disease in a population not influenced by the event under investigation. A relative risk of [2.0] means that the disease occurs among the population not subject to the event under investigation. Phrased another way, *a relative risk of [2.0] means* that, on the average, there is a *fifty percent likelihood* that a particular case of the disease was caused by the event under investigation and a fifty percent likelihood that the disease was caused by chance alone. *A relative risk greater than [2.0] means that the disease more likely than not was caused by the event.*

Manko v. United States, 636 F. Supp. 1419, 1434 (W.D. Mo. 1986), aff'd in part and rev'd in part, 830 F.2d 831 (8th Cir. 1987).

Once a statistically significant percentage of a cohort is determined to have developed *d* following exposure to *c,* the epidemiologist can then evaluate the nature and scope of the causal link between *c* and *d.*

Nowhere is the imprecision confronting the epidemiologist clearer than that posed by the present state of scientific understanding of the causal relationships between environmental and occupational carcinogens and cancer.

The imprecision of estimating the impact of environmental and occupational carcinogens derives from the central uncertainty surrounding the nature of carcinogenesis. Like the study of toxicology in general, the lack of clear insights into the disease's molecular basis hampers the study of carcinogenicity. Cancer biologists have developed useful hypotheses or carcinogenicity, some of which are now guiding potentially useful research. Nonetheless, the statement by a group of experts convened by the International Agency for Research on Cancer . . . in 1980 remains true today: "the mechanisms by which chemicals induce cancer and the developmental stages from initial exposure to frank neoplasia are poorly understood."

Troyen A. Brennan, Causal Chains and Statistical Links: The Role of Scientific Uncertainty in Hazardous-Substance Litigation, 73 Cornell L. Rev. 469, 474-75 (1988).

Scientifically valid links, therefore, will not always demonstrate the connection between the causal event and the harmful effect to establish a legally cognizable proximate cause which is sufficient to sustain or succeed in a tort action. While an epidemiologist might be inclined to conclude that a causal relationship exists between c and d, despite the fact that the relative risk ratio is less than or equal to 2.0, the "more likely than not" test, which a plaintiff must satisfy to sustain a cause of action in tort, is not satisfied by epidemiological evidence alone unless the plaintiff establishes that the relative risk ratio or, in the case of epidemiological studies of asbestos, the standardized mortality ratio (SMR) between c and d is greater than 2.0. In other words, "at least a two-fold increase in incidence of the disease attributable to . . . exposure [to asbestos] is required to permit recovery if epidemiological studies alone are relied upon." In re "Agent Orange" Prod. Liab. Litig., 597 F. Supp. 740, 785 (EDNY 1984) (Agent Orange I).

C. Clinical and Experimental Evidence

A plaintiff need not rely exclusively on epidemiological studies in support of her causation proof. A plaintiff may rely on conclusions derived from experimental studies involving animals or discrete groups of persons, or from clinical evidence including the medical, personal, and family history of the individual suffering from the disease.

On the issue of clinical evidence, Judge Weinstein considered that courts were divided between "strong" and "weak" versions of the preponderance of the evidence of causation, Agent Orange II, 611 F. Supp. at 1260. Under the "strong" version, a plaintiff must offer both epidemiologic evidence that the probability of causation exceeds 50% in the exposed population and "particularistic" proof that the conduct complained of caused his individual harm. Judge Weinstein considered the law in New York to require "strong" evidence of causation . . . .

In the case at bar, the Court of Appeals noted that:

Maiorana's own medical records and personal history were the clinical evidence upon which plaintiff's expert witnesses based their opinions that asbestos exposure was a significant factor in causing his colon cancer. Plaintiff's experts used epidemiological studies as one basis for an expert opinion but did not rely solely on epidemiological evidence. Thus, plaintiff did not need to provide epidemiological evidence of a certain magnitude to defeat a summary judgment motion because she did not rely on epidemiological studies alone.

Asbestos Litig. II, 964 F.2d 92, 97 (2d Cir. 1992).

The Court of Appeals went on to conclude that it:

agreed with the observation that a "physician or other such qualified expert may view the epidemiological studies and factor out other known risk factors such as family history, diet ... or other factors which might enhance the remaining recognized risks, even though the risk study fell short of the 2.0 correlation." Grassis v. Johns-Manville Corp., 248 N.J. Super. 446, 591 A.2d 671, 675 (1991). Accordingly, an expert should be "permitted to testify respecting the bases for her causation opinion, including the epidemiological studies upon which she relied." Id., 591 A.2d at 676.

Asbestos Litig. II, 964 F.2d at 97.

However, *Grassis* has been interpreted by the New Jersey courts to require more rigorous scientific evidence than the opinion itself seems to indicate is necessary. In Dafler v. Raymark Indus., Inc., 259 N.J. Super. 17, 611 A.2d 136 (N.J. Sup. 1992), and Landrigan v. Celotex Corp., 127 N.J. 404, 605 A.2d 1079, 1086 (1992), both cases where the only clinical evidence that asbestos caused colon cancer was differential diagnosis (i.e., the ruling out of other known risk factors), the court found that the medical testimony about the particular plaintiff was not the compelling source of testimony about causation. In *Landrigan,* both witnesses reviewed specific evidence about the decedent's medical and occupational histories, and:

[b]oth witnesses also excluded certain known risk factors for colon cancer, such as excessive alcohol consumption, a high-fat diet, and a positive family history. From statistical population studies to the conclusion of causation in an individual, however, is a broad leap. . . . Nonetheless, proof of causation in toxic-tort cases depends largely on inferences derived from statistics about groups.

Landrigan, 127 N.J. at 422, 605 A.2d 1079. *Landrigan* held that since a toxic tort victim might be compelled to report epidemiological evidence to prove causation, an expert's testimony on such causation should be permitted provided the expert's

methodology was sound. Other courts in New Jersey since *Grassis* have concluded the proof of causation in toxic tort cases rests essentially on the epidemiological evidence.

These cases uphold *Grassis* in the sense that they do not create a strict
threshold for statistical evidence below which the case will not be considered, as
the federal courts did in most of the Bendectin cases. However, they do admit that
where the clinical evidence is merely an elimination of other possible known
sources of cancer, such evidence is less than compelling, and under those circumstances, the plaintiff may be forced to rely on epidemiological evidence in order
to establish causation.

It is also important to note that all three of the New Jersey cases concern
summary judgment or the admissibility of testimony; they do not rule out the
proposition that once the testimony is admitted, it may prove insufficient as a matter of law. Rather they support the proposition that epidemiological evidence
should be admitted at trial because the plaintiff may be compelled to rely upon it,
and they suggest that strictly clinical evidence would be insufficient for proof of
causation as a matter of law. The question of sufficiency after all the evidence has
been adduced is a different question from whether the evidence should be admitted or whether the action should be terminated through the mechanism of summary judgment.

D. The "More Likely Than Not" Test

Regardless of the kinds of evidence employed by a plaintiff in support of his
causation proof in a carcinogenic tort action, the plaintiff must satisfy requirement
of tort law that the purported cause was in fact *more likely than not* the actual
cause of the injury in question. As Judge Weinstein has noted,

> A government administrative agency may regulate or prohibit the use of
> toxic substances through rulemaking, despite a very low probability of any
> causal relationship. A court, in contrast, must observe the tort law require-
> ment that a plaintiff establish a probability of more than fifty percent that
> the defendant's action injured him.

Agent Orange I, 597 F. Supp. 740, 785.

Therefore, even though epidemiological evidence regarding the relationship
between exposure to c and the development of d may fall short of the 2.0 threshold of statistical significance, if this evidence is combined with clinical or experimental evidence which eliminates confounding factors and strengthens the connection between c and d specifically in the circumstances surrounding the plaintiff's case of d, then the plaintiff's causation proof may be sufficient to support a
jury's finding that it was more likely than not that the plaintiff's case of d was
cased by his exposure to c.

E. Battle of the Experts

The traditional view was that determining whether scientific evidence was viable was a matter for the jury, not for the court. As long as the expert testimony was admissible under Rules 702 and 703, Fed. R. Evid., and not more prejudicial than probative under Rule 403, causation was an issue of weighing the evidence that was left to the jury. . . .

The courts' fidelity to this traditional standard of deference has cracked in the face of huge cases and huge jury awards based on doubtful or nonexistent scientific evidence. Expert evidence in toxic tort cases has led courts to superimpose or replace the standard of deference with a threshold of causation designed to eliminate a perceived abuse of expert testimony in the context of certain alleged toxins. Toxic tort litigation over Bendectin (a drug marketed until 1983 for morning sickness) alleged to cause birth defects, and over Agent Orange (sprayed as a defoliant in Vietnam) demonstrate the changes in the law. . . .

The question has recently been considered by the Supreme Court in *Daubert,* whose holding requires the judge to make his own assessment of whether the methodology underlying the expert's opinion is fundamentally sound. Such a threshold evaluation of the expert's methodology, even though it still leaves the evaluation of the weight of the evidence to the jury, limits the "battle of the experts."

[The court describes various federal toxic tort cases in which trial or appellate courts demanded substantial epidemiological proof of causation.]

Against this background of the state of law and accepting as axiomatic that without more than credentials and a subjective opinion, an expert's testimony that "it is so" is not sufficient to sustain a jury's verdict, the epidemiological, clinical, and experimental studies testified to at trial by the plaintiff's experts must be carefully scrutinized to determine whether they are, in fact, sufficient. . . .

III. The Plaintiff's Causation Proof

A. The Sufficiency Criteria: Evaluating the Sufficiency of the Plaintiff's Epidemiological Evidence

As has been noted, if an epidemiological study reveals that the SMR between exposure to carcinogen c and the subsequent development of disease d in a cohort is greater than 2.0, that SMR is statistically significant and supports the conclusion that c and d are causally linked. This statistical conclusion also justifies the proposition that it is more likely than not that individual A's exposure to c is the cause of d in A. However, this is not the end of the analysis to determine whether the plaintiff's causation proof is sufficient to withstand the defendants' motions for judgment as a matter of law. There are several additional criteria that have to be taken into consideration in assessing the conclusions of an epidemiological study to determine the soundness of an allegedly statistically significant SMR.

In order to assess fully the accuracy of the conclusions offered in an epidemiological study regarding a purported causal relationship between exposure to *c* and the subsequent development of *d,* several factors must be considered. The SMR is only one of these factors, and it defines the strength of the possible association between exposure to *c* and the development of *d.* In addition to considering the SMR, the following five factors must be analyzed to assess accurately whether or not evidence has achieved the status of scientific knowledge (collectively, the Sufficiency Criteria): first, the consistency of the association between *c* and *d,* which raises the question, Is the SMR of a single epidemiological study addressing the relationship between *c* and *d* consistent with the SMRs derived in other epidemiological studies? second, the dose-response relationship between *c* and *d:* What is the epidemiological response in a cohort to estimated doses of *c*?; third, the results of experimental studies: Have experimental studies been conducted on animals, for example, and if so, were they positive?; fourth, the plausibility of there being a biological link between *c* and *d:* Given the biological and chemical mechanisms involved, what is the degree of probability that exposure to *c* can give rise to the subsequent development of *d*?; and fifth, the coherence between *c* and *d:* How many "confounding" or alternative factors or conditions can contribute to the development of *d* in A? And how difficult is it to exclude these confounding conditions thereby isolating A's exposure to *c* as the statistically significant and "more likely than not" cause of *d* in A?

While none of the Sufficiency Criteria is decisive by itself in determining the sufficiency of a plaintiff's epidemiological evidence in the context of a Rule 50(b) motion, sufficient epidemiological evidence will necessarily satisfy several of these criteria. More significantly, when epidemiological evidence fails to satisfy any of the Sufficiency Criteria, it cannot be relied on to support a jury verdict in the face of a motion for judgment as a matter of law.

B. The Epidemiological Evidence

When the Sufficiency Criteria are applied to the epidemiological evidence offered at trial by the plaintiff's experts, the plaintiff's causation proof only weakly satisfies the plausibility criterion and fails to satisfy any of the other Sufficiency Criteria. Therefore, the plaintiff's proof fails to support the jury's conclusion that Maiorana's exposure to asbestos was the proximate cause of his colon cancer, and the defendants' Rule 50(b) motions must be granted.

1. Strength and Consistency of Association

Of course, the stronger and more consistent an association, the more likely it represents a cause-and-effect relationship.

Weak associations often turn out to be spurious and explainable by some known, or as yet unknown, confounding variable. In order for an association to be spurious, the underlying factor that explains it must have a stronger relationship to the disease than the suspected causal factor. When the causal factor under consideration is strongly related to the disease, it is likely, although not certain, that the underlying variable with the necessarily even stronger relationship to the disease would be recognizable.

Strength of association is usually measured by the relative risk or the ratio of the disease rate in those with the factor to the rate in those without. The relative risk of lung cancer in cigarette smokers as compared to non-smokers is on the order of 10:1, whereas the relative risk of pancreatic cancer is about 2:1. The difference suggests that cigarette smoking is more likely to be a causal factor for lung cancer than for pancreatic cancer.

Landrigan, 127 N.J. at 416, 605 A.2d 1079.

Consistency is measured by comparing the association between a purported cause and effect identified in one study with the results of other studies and with other relevant scientific knowledge.

During the course of the trial, approximately 45 epidemiological studies and surveys of studies were discussed by the parties' experts, by Drs. Steven Markowitz, Carl Shy, and Kenneth Smith[20] for the plaintiff and by Dr. Edward Gaensler for USMC.

Markowitz testified that, although there is nothing pathologically in the colon cancer tumor cell itself which would identify it as being caused by asbestos, asbestos fibers have been found in the colon cancer tissues of some asbestos workers who developed that disease. Markowitz's opinion was based on the findings reported by Albert Ehrlich, who studied a cohort which included 44 asbestos workers who had developed colon cancer.[21] Of those 44 workers, Ehrlich found asbestos fibers in the cancerous tissue of 14 of them. However, this consideration was irrelevant because there was no finding in the pathology reports at issue here that there were asbestos fibers in Maiorana's tumorous tissues.[22]

In his direct testimony, Markowitz noted that between 20 and 30 epidemiological studies had been conducted that examined the relationship between expo-

---

[20] The plaintiff read the 1976 deposition testimony of Smith into the record. Smith's testimony focused on the general causal linkage between asbestos and cancer and the historical development of the understanding of the carcinogenic dangers of the substance. His own research and expertise was in the area of pulmonary disabilities caused by asbestos. Aside from supporting the general proposition that asbestos causes lung cancer, asbestosis, and mesothelioma, Smith's testimony offered no support for Plaintiff's specific causation contention that exposure to asbestos causes colon cancer.

[21] See A. Ehrlich et al., Asbestos Bodies in Carcinoma of Colon in an Insulation Worker With Asbestosis, 254 J. Am. Med. Ass'n 2932 (1985).

[22] Markowitz also testified that the pathology reports were devoid of any mention of asbestos fibers in Maiorana's lungs.

sure to asbestos and the development of lung and colon cancer. Markowitz focused on a 1985 study by Zoloth and Michaels in which they asserted that sheet metal workers exposed to asbestos faced an "approximately two-fold increase" in the risk of developing colon cancer.[23] This study was based on 385 deaths among members of a sheet workers union local. Markowitz acknowledged that this study was methodologically flawed but noted that to his knowledge "it's the only direct study of sheet metal workers and colon cancer."

In a follow-up study, however, Zoloth and Michaels found that, while exposure to asbestos appeared to be causally linked to significantly elevated proportional mortality ratios for all malignant neoplasms, as well as for cancers of the stomach, liver, lung, and lymphatic tissue, the ratio for colon cancer was statistically non-significant.[24]

Markowitz testified that when Maiorana underwent surgery, during which his colon was resected, two areas of polypoid mucosa were found. Although he acknowledged that polypoid mucosa is distinct from polyps, Markowitz discussed the relationship between polyps and the development of colon cancer, noting that polyps constitute a risk factor and were associated with a stage in the development of colon cancer.

In support of his analysis, Markowitz referred two studies involving humans, one by J.C. McDonald,[25] the other by Alfred Neugut.[26] Markowitz summarized Neugut's findings as follows:

> more people who had polyps had a[n] occupational history of working in a trade associated with exposure to asbestos than did the people without polyps, and calculated that there was an approximate four-fold increase in risk to get a polyp if there is an occupational history of exposure to asbestos.

In contrast to Markowitz's summary of Neugut's study in definitive terms, Neugut himself advances only tentative and limited conclusions from his cohort regarding the relationship between asbestos exposure and polyps:

> *To date, no one has examined the relationship between asbestos exposure and the occurrence of colorectal adenomatous polyps.*
>
> While the *sample sizes were relatively small* for both case groups, an elevated risk was observed for those with a history of significant asbestos

---

[23] Stephen Zoloth & David Michaels, Asbestos Disease in Sheet Metal Workers: The Results of a Proportional Mortality Analysis, 7 Am. J. Indus. Med. 315 (1985).

[24] See David Michaels & Stephen Zoloth, Asbestos Disease in Sheet Metal Workers: Proportional Mortality Update, 13 Am. J. Indus. Med. 731, 732 (1988).

[25] See J.C. McDonald et al., Dust Exposure and Mortality in Chrysotile Mining, 1910-75, 37 Brit. J. Indus. Med. 11 (1980).

[26] See Alfred I. Neugut et al., Association of Asbestos Exposure With Colorectal Adenomatous Polyps and Cancer, 83 J. Nat'l Cancer Inst. 1827 (1991).

exposure. *If true,* this elevation would suggest that asbestos acts as a carcinogen at a fairly early stage (prior to the development of adenomatous polyps) in the colon carcinogenesis pathway. . . .

Nonetheless, *one must regard these findings as preliminary.* The odds ratios were significant only at the 0.05 to 0.10 levels.

On cross-examination, Markowitz explained that he arrived at his conclusion from Neugut's analysis by "extrapolation," and the weakness of this extrapolation was evident in Markowitz's summary of his position in his direct testimony:

One risk factor is his occupational history of exposure to asbestos, a sheet metal worker. He also had these two areas of mucosal abnormality, polypoid mucosa, which may well present a risk factor. These may in turn be caused by asbestos. There's limited evidence of that. It's not exactly clear, but they may well be caused by asbestos.

In light of Neugut's qualifications regarding the causal relationship between asbestos and polyps, and in light of the fact that the condition of polypoid mucosa is even further removed in the tentatively asserted causal chain between asbestos exposure and colon cancer than are polyps, it is not surprising that Markowitz conceded on cross-examination that he could not state with reasonable medical certainty that the condition of polypoid mucosa generally, or Maiorana's polypoid mucosa in particular, was caused by asbestos exposure.[28]

Markowitz attempted to extrapolate from McDonald's findings in a similar manner. McDonald studied the rates of cancer in workers exposed to asbestos dust in the processes of mining and milling chrysotile asbestos and concluded that "the lung cancer risk was increased at 1.25 or 125, which is statistically significant. . . ." From the conclusion that asbestos causes lung cancer, Markowitz made the assumption that lung cancer could be used as a substitute for exposure to asbestos, and armed with that assumption, Markowitz asserted that it could be expected that the correlation between the incidence of lung cancer and colon cancer is statistically significant. The fatal flaws inherent to this assumption are discussed below in the analysis of the Sufficiency Criterion of the dose-response relationship. For the purposes of Sufficiency Criteria of strength and consistency of association it suffices to note that Markowitz conceded on cross-examination that McDonald's study does not support the conclusion that asbestos exposure causes polypoid mucosa.

In addition to the studies already mentioned, Markowitz based his conclusion that Maiorana's colon cancer was caused by his exposure to asbestos on a number of studies that showed an increase in the rate of colon cancer in cohorts exposed to asbestos. However, Markowitz acknowledged under cross-examination that the increases yielded in these studies were not statistically significant.

---

[28] Shy testified similarly that Neugut's conclusion regarding the association between asbestos and polyps "was of borderline significance."

Of the various studies discussed by the plaintiff's experts that included calculations of SMRs for colorectal cancer, only three yielded SMRs that were significantly high. In their study of 12,051 U.S. and Canadian insulation workers who
were first exposed to asbestos 20 or more years before they were diagnosed with
colorectal cancer, Selikoff, Hammond, and Seidman expected 34 occurrences of
the disease but actually observed 55 occurrences for an SMR of 1.62.[29] In their
subsequent study of amosite asbestos factory workers, Seidman and Selikoff,
joined this time by Gelb, studied 820 workers in a New Jersey asbestos factory.
See Herbert Seidman, et al., Mortality Experience of Amosite Asbestos Factory
Workers: Dose-Response Relationships 5 to 40 Years After Onset of Short-Term
Work Exposure, 10 Am. J. Indus. Med. 479 (1986). While 11.9 occurrences of colorectal cancer were expected in this cohort, 22 were observed, for an SMR of 1.85.
Finally, in their 1991 study of insulation workers in the United States and Canada,
Selikoff and Seidman evaluated their largest cohort, consisting of 17,800 workers,
and derived a statistically insignificant SMR of 1.37.[32]

A third study yielded a statistically significant SMR of 2.27 for colon cancer
appearing in workers at a nitric acid production plant where they were exposed to
varying levels of asbestos. See Bjorn Hilt et al., Asbestos Exposure, Smoking
Habits, and Cancer Incidence Among Production and Maintenance Workers in an
Electrochemical Plant, 8 Am. J. Indus. Med. 565, 571 (1985). 2.2 occurrences of
colon cancer were expected and 5 were observed. These five cases of colon cancer occurred 15, 27, 30, 31, and 35 years after the first exposure.

When taken together, the SMRs of these studies are statistically significant
and, at first glance, appear to support the plaintiff's contention that there is a
causal relationship between exposure to asbestos and colon cancer. However, to
assess accurately the strength of these studies, they must be considered within the
broader context defined by the other epidemiological studies in which SMRs for
colorectal cancer have been calculated. It is only by taking this next step of comparative analysis that one can determine the degree to which the plaintiff's assert-

---

[29] See Irving J. Selikoff, et al., Mortality Experience of Insulation Workers in the United States
and Canada, 1943-1976, 330 Annals N.Y. Acad. Sci. 91, 108 (1979). This SMR was significantly
lower from the 3.08 SMR for colorectal and stomach cancer Selikoff found in insulation workers in
a 1965 study he undertook with Hammond and Churg. See E.C. Hammond et al., Neoplasia Among
Insulation Workers in the United States With Special Reference to Intra-Abdominal Neoplasia, 132
Annals N.Y. Acad. Sci. 519, 521 (1965). The substantially lower SMRs for colorectal cancer in the
subsequent studies suggest that there was a disproportionate incidence of stomach cancer in the
cohort of 1522 workers.

[32] See Irving J. Selikoff & Herbert Seidman, Asbestos-Associated Deaths Among Insulation
Workers in the United States and Canada, 1967-1987, 643 Annals N.Y. Acad. Sci. 1, 8 (1991).
Selikoff and Seidman derive the SMRs in these studies from so-called "best evidence. "Best evi-
dence" refers to data taken from a number of sources other than death certificates to calculate SMRs.
Morgan et al. reject the use of "best evidence" by Selikoff and others on the ground that it introduces
an erroneous bias into the calculation of SMRs and results in their being unjustifiably inflated. See
Robert W. Morgan et al., Asbestos and Gastrointestinal Cancer: A Review of the Literature, 143 W.
J. Med. 60, 63-64 (1985).

ed causal linkage between exposure to asbestos and colon cancer satisfies the Sufficiency Criteria of strength and consistency of association and is supported by all relevant epidemiological studies.[36]

In support of the plaintiff's causation claim, eight studies reveal an apparent increased risk in contracting colorectal cancer from exposure from cancer with SMRs for colorectal cancer ranging from 1.14 to 1.47.[37] While an SMR of less than 1.50 is statistically insignificant, Markowitz asserted that these studies, when taken together, reveal a pattern of causation which is statistically significant. The fact that these studies consistently yielded colorectal cancer SMRs greater than 1.0 indicated, in Markowitz's opinion, that there is a causal link between exposure asbestos and colorectal cancer.

The plausibility and ultimately the sufficiency of the conclusion of the plaintiff's causation proof is undermined by two considerations: First, no matter how many studies yield a positive but statistically insignificant SMR for colorectal cancer, the results remain statistically insignificant. Just as adding a series of zeros together yields yet another zero as the product, adding a series of positive but statistically insignificant SMRs together does not produce a statistically significant pattern.

Second, 10 studies discussed by Markowitz and Gaensler yielded low colorectal cancer SMRs, suggesting the startling proposition that exposure to asbestos may actually decrease the risk of developing colorectal cancer.[38]

---

[36] Of course, the conclusions of Hilt's study regarding the SMR of colorectal cancer can be seriously questioned without undertaking the proposed comparative analysis simply by noting the limited cohort of 287, the smallest cohort of all of the studies discussed at trial. The corresponding power of the study is, as would be expected, a mere 0.08.

[37] See E.D. Acheson et al., Cancer in a Factory Using Amosite Asbestos, 13 Int'l J. Epidemiology 3 (1984) (colorectal cancer SMR 1.32); B.K. Armstrong et al., Mortality in Miners and Millers of Crocidolite in Western Australia, 45 Brit. J. Indus. Med. 5 (1988) (SMR 1.14); P.E. Enterline et al., Asbestos and Cancer: A Cohort Followed Up to Death, 44 Brit. J. Indus. Med. 396 (1987) (SMR 1.16); Thomas F. Mancuso & Elizabeth J. Coulter, Methodology in Industrial Health Studies, 6 Archives of Envtl. Health 210 (1963) (SMR 1.47); Riccaro Putoni et al., Mortality Among Shipyard Workers in Genoa, Italy, 330 Annals N.Y. Acad. Sci. 353 (1979) (SMR 1.39).

[38] See Johannes Clemmesen & S. Hjalgrim-Jensen, Cancer Incidence Among 5686 Asbestos-Cement Workers Followed From 1943 Through 1976, 5 Ecotoxicology & Envtl. Safety 15 (1980) (SMR 0.86); M.J. Gardner & C.A. Powell, Mortality of Asbestos Cement Workers Using Almost Exclusively Chrysotile Fibre, 36 J. Soc'y Occup. Med. 124 (1986) (SMR 0.71); J.T. Hodgson & R.D. Jones, Mortality of Asbestos Workers in England and Wales 1971-81, 43 Brit. J. Indus. Med. 158 (1986) (SMR 0.81); Janet M. Hughes, Mortality of Workers Employed in Two Asbestos Cement Manufacturing Plants, 44 Brit. J. Indus. Med. 161 (1987) (SMR 0.90); McDonald, supra note 25 (SMR 0.78); C.G. Ohlson & C. Hogstedt, Lung Cancer Among Asbestos Cement Workers. A Swedish Cohort Study and a Review, 42 Brit. J. Indus. Med. 397 (1985) (SMR 0.59); C.G. Ohlson, Mortality Among Asbestos-Exposed Workers in a Railroad Workshop, 10 Scand. J. Envtl. Health 283 (1984) (SMR 0.71); J. Peto et al., Relationship of Mortality to Measures of Environmental Asbestos Pollution in an Asbestos Textile Factory, 29 Annals Occup. Hygiene 305 (1985) (SMR 0.80); Vilhjalmur Rafnsson et al., Mortality and Cancer Incidence Among Marine Engineers and Machinists in Iceland, 14 Scand. J. Work Envtl. Health 197 (1988) (SMR 0.88); S. Tola, et al., Incidence of Cancer Among Welders, Platers, Machinists, and Pipe Fitters in Shipyards and Machine Shops, 45 Brit. J. Indus. Med. 209 (1988) (SMR 0.80).

However, because these low SMRs are just as statistically insignificant as the aforementioned high SMRs, the suggestion that asbestos exposure may be beneficial and decrease the risk of colorectal cancer is as unjustified as the plaintiff's contention that it increases that risk.

The remaining study, which analyzed cancer rates in workers who were exposed to asbestos in the process of manufacturing gas masks, was inconclusive with regard to the alleged causal linkage between asbestos exposure and colorectal cancer. No unexpected occurrences of colorectal cancer were observed in the cohort of 1327 women. See E.D. Acheson et al., Mortality of Two Groups of Women Who Manufactured Gas Masks From Chrysotile and Crocidolite Asbestos: A 40-Year Follow-Up, 39 Brit. J. Indus. Med. 344 (1982).

On the record before the jury at trial, the various epidemiological studies relied on in the plaintiff's causation proof establishes only the conclusions that the association between exposure to asbestos and developing colon cancer is, at best, weak, and that the consistency of this purported association across the studies is, at best, poor.[40] This is particularly true of the results generated by those studies which had the largest cohorts and therefore, are statistically the most powerful and compelling.[41]

This conclusion was supported not only by the testimony of the defendant's experts, but also by reviews of the epidemiological studies in question which were testified to at the trial and discussed by Markowitz and Shy. D.A. Edelman analyzed the results of studies involving 32 independent cohorts of asbestos workers and "found no consistent statistical association between exposure to asbestos and gastrointestinal cancer. . . ." D.A. Edelman, Exposure to Asbestos and the Risk of Gastrointestinal Cancer: A Reassessment, 45 Brit. J. Indus. Med. 75, 81 (1988). William Weiss concluded from his review of studies on 21 cohorts, in which he focused specifically on the possible causal relationship between asbestos and colorectal cancer, that those studies failed to satisfy the consistency criterion and had showed only little strength of association. See Weiss, supra note 18, at 881. Weiss' analysis yielded summary SMRs[44] of 0.90 among "inception" cohorts and 1.14 among "cross-sectional" cohorts,[45] neither of which differed in a statistically sig-

---

[40] Gaensler arrived at this conclusion and based it on his survey of epidemiological studies involving 19 cohorts.

[41] See Acheson, supra note 37 (cohort of 4,820; SMR 1.32); Armstrong, supra note 39 (6,505; 0.36); Clemmesen, supra note 38 (5,686; 0.86); Hodgson, supra note 38 (15,999; 0.61); Hughes, supra note 38 (6,171; 0.09); McDonald, supra note 25 (10,939; 0.99); Selikoff, supra note 29 (12,051; 1.59); Tola, supra note 38 (7,775; 0.80).

[44] In the summary SMR, risk estimates from various studies are combined and standardized in the following equation: Summary SMR = (Sum of Observed Deaths / Sum of Expected Deaths).

[45] Weiss divided the studies he considered into two categories according to the worker registration method employed by the study. The "inception" cohorts registered all workers whose exposure to asbestos began in stipulated periods, whereas the "cross-sectional" cohorts registered only those workers who were employed as of a particular date without regard for their previous exposure histories. See id. at 876.

nificant manner from 1.00. Similarly, a review of more than 45 cohort studies by Robert Morgan, Donna Foliart, and Otto Wong concluded that the summary SMR for colorectal cancer was 1.13, and that the SMR dropped to 1.03 once the correction was made of deleting "best evidence" data. And finally, Howard Frumkin and Jesse Berlin's review of studies involving 31 cohorts, concluded that the total summary SMR for colorectal cancer was only 1.11.[48]

These reviews, each of which was acknowledged by Markowitz and Shy, seriously undermine their shared claim regarding the probability that there is a causal linkage between asbestos and colorectal cancer. The plaintiff's causation proof simply does not satisfy the Sufficiency Criteria of strength and consistency of association between A's exposure to asbestos and the subsequent development of this kind of cancer in A. On cross-examination, Markowitz and Shy acknowledged that all of the reviews came to the same conclusion, namely, that there is no statistically significant increase in the rate of colorectal cancer as a result of exposure to asbestos.

Finally, neither Markowitz nor Shy disputed the findings of David Garabrant in his recent study of 746 confirmed cases of colon cancer, which focused specifically on the relationship between asbestos exposure and colon cancer. See David H. Garabrant et al., Asbestos and Colon Cancer: Lack of Association in Large Case-Control Study, 135 Am. J. Epidemiology 843 (1992). Garabrant concluded that, even when no attempt is made to correct for possible confounding factors which inevitably inflate the SMR, the association between asbestos and colon cancer is extremely weak and statistically insignificant 1.14.

The plaintiff's epidemiological evidence failed to satisfy the Sufficiency Criteria of strength and consistency of association and, as such, failed to contribute to the sufficiency of her proof on the issue of causation.

2. Dose-Response Relationship

The critical assumption in Markowitz's evaluation of the epidemiological literature, upon which his expert opinion regarding Maiorana's death was based, was

---

[48] See Howard Frumkin & Jesse Berlin, Asbestos Exposure and Gastrointestinal Malignancy Review and Meta-Analysis, 14 Am. J. Indus. Med. 79, 89 (1988). Frumkin and Berlin divided the cohorts into two categories according to whether the lung cancer SMR yielded by the particular study was greater or less than 2.0 in an attempt to use the rate of lung cancer as a surrogate for exposure to asbestos. Thus the 1.11 is the total summary SMR for both of these categories. The difficulties of categorizing cohorts in this manner are discussed below. Note that Frumkin and Berlin use the following summary SMR equation: Summary SMR = (Sum of Observed Deaths / Sum of Expected Deaths) x 100. However, to facilitate consistency in the following discussion of their survey and other surveys which employ this formula, the quotient of (Sum of Observed Deaths / Sum of Expected Deaths) is not multiplied by 100. The jury also heard testimony regarding the difficulties inherent to the survey approach to epidemiological literature and the difficulties unique to Frumkin and Berlin's meta-analysis. Each study evaluates the methodological and conceptual difficulties posed by the inevitable "mixing [of] apples and oranges." For a general discussion of the meta-analytical approach, see generally Frederic M. Wolf, Meta-Analysis: Quantitative Methods for Research Synthesis (1986).

that lung cancer rates can be used as a substitute measure for a cohort's exposure to asbestos, and Shy suggested that "[t]he dose-response relationship is the . . . most important criterion for establishing causality. . . ." However, the plaintiff's evidence presented at trial demonstrated that the dose-response relationship between asbestos and colorectal cancer is erratic at best. The practical problem of satisfying the Sufficiency Criterion of the dose-response relationship was succinctly stated by Gaensler:

> Nobody knows exactly anything about dose response because the times when all of these things happened were 20 and 30 and 40 and 50 years ago, when the measurements of dust were totally different, expressed in different terms, and when for the most part no measurements were made at all.[51]

This conclusion on the issue of a determining the dose-response relationship is consistent with those arrived at in the various surveys of the epidemiological literature with the exception of Frumkin and Berlin's meta-analysis of various epidemiological studies. Frumkin and Berlin attempted to examine the effect of dosage on the total cohort, and it was their meta-analysis that appeared to support the position of Markowitz and Shy.

One obvious problem with epidemiological studies generally is that there is virtually no data available regarding the doses of asbestos exposure in the studies. To surmount this difficulty, Frumkin and Berlin divided the studies they considered into two categories, namely, those with a lung cancer SMRs greater than 2.0 and those with lung cancer SMRs less than 2.0. They use the lung cancer SMR as a surrogate for dosage by treating cohorts with lung cancer SMRs less than 2.0 as having low asbestos exposure. According to their results, those cohorts having a statistically significant lung cancer SMR of greater than 2.0 have a summary colorectal cancer SMR of 1.61.

While this 1.61 SMR appears to approach the level of statistical significance and to support the conclusion that there is a dose-response relationship between asbestos and colorectal cancer, Frumkin and Berlin's methodology, assumptions, and conclusions have attracted serious criticism. Two criticisms are most damaging: first, this meta-analysis is based on the assumption that Markowitz failed to justify, namely, that the same mechanism underlies both lung and colorectal cancer; and second, "[i]t is highly likely that cohorts in which pleural mesothelioma is misdiagnosed as lung cancer will also have peritoneal mesothelioma misdiag-

---

[51] At his 1976 deposition Smith alluded to the difficulty of assessing the doses of asbestos workers are exposed to on the job. In response to the question: "do you believe that the insulation workers that you observed were exposed to substantially the same asbestos hazard as the persons involved in mining, milling and manufacturing process at Asbestos, Quebec?," Smith answered: "They were exposed to the same potential hazards, definitely. I can't say exactly the same exposure, because very often the manufacturer because of the size of his company can take better precautions for controlling of the dust than the small operator can in the field."

nosed as digestive cancer, creating a false correlation between digestive cancer and lung cancer."[54]

Frumkin and Berlin's methodology and conclusions appear to be arbitrary and flawed in light of the "seemingly improbable observation in their data that low levels of asbestos exposure appear to protect against all gastrointestinal cancer, especially stomach and colorectal"[55] and of the total colorectal SMR of all cohorts amounting to a statistically insignificant 1.11. Furthermore, as Shy acknowledged, this meta-analysis failed to account for the effect of smoking in the development of lung cancer. This is particularly significant because, as Shy testified, asbestos workers as a group have had a higher incidence of smoking than the general population.

Given the insurmountable difficulties in satisfying the Sufficiency Criterion of dose-response relationship, Edelman's conclusions are appropriate: There is "no consistent statistical association between exposure to asbestos and gastrointestinal cancer, a dose response relation was not apparent," and "[a]lthough the data from some studies suggest dose-response relations, they are most probably an artifact of the way in which accumulated dose was measured." Significantly, these conclusions are consistent with the plaintiff's causation proof presented at trial and reflect the plaintiff's failure to satisfy the Sufficiency Criterion of dose-response relationship.

3. Experimental Evidence

Although the failure to demonstrate pathological changes in animals after exposure to asbestos does not negate other evidence supporting the assertion of causal linkage, successful demonstrations of changes similar to those seen in humans would strengthen the claim for causation.

Markowitz testified that studies on the cancer-causing effects of asbestos in animals have been conducted through the government-sponsored National Toxicology program. He summarized these results as follows:

> Specifically, [adenomatous] polyps, which are the most common variety, and the one that are closest related to a risk of developing colon cancer, that the animals developed these polyps [at] a greater rate than the control group did, it was about a . . . five- or six-fold increase. . . .

---

[54] Robert W. Morgan, Letter to the Editor, Re: Meta-Analysis of Asbestos and Gastrointestinal Cancer, 19 Am. J. Indus. Med. 407, 407 (1991); accord Richard Doll & Julian Peto, Asbestos: Effects on Health of Exposure to Asbestos (1985). For further criticisms, see Weiss, supra note 18, at 881 (concluding that the hypothesis is that the association between lung cancer risk and the risk of cancers other than mesothelioma is caused by misdiagnosis of lung cancer and mesothelioma is more plausible than the assertion the asbestos is a systemic carcinogen).

[55] Morgan, supra note 54, at 407 (cohorts with lung cancer SMRs of less than 2.00 have a summary colorectal cancer SMR of 0.86).

Markowitz also referred to the work of Kelly Donham to support this thesis.

In fact, the experimental evidence, including Donham's research, fails to establish any causal relationship between exposure to asbestos and the development of cancer in animals. Most notably, rats that were orally fed asbestos showed no pathological changes that would satisfy the Sufficiency Criterion of positive experimental evidence.[60] Markowitz conceded this on cross-examination with regard to Donham's findings and with regard to vast bulk of the experimental data on the subject.

Markowitz acknowledged the results of Lyman Condie's survey of the experimental findings of 11 published studies. Lyman W. Condie, Review of Published Studies of Orally Administered Asbestos, 53 Envtl. Health Persp. 3 (1983). Condie concluded that:

> The bulk of the experimental evidence indicates that the long-term, high-level ingestion exposure to various types of asbestos fibers failed to produce any definite, reproducible, organ-specific carcinogenic effect. . . . These studies also cast some doubt on the hypothesis that peritoneal mesotheliomas and gastrointestinal cancers result from the ingestion of asbestos fibers cleared from the lungs following inhalation exposure.[62]

In response to Condie's review, Markowitz could identify only one study in support of his position, to wit, a 1985 technical report by McDonald which fails to establish a statistically significant relationship between exposure to asbestos and cancer in animals. Markowitz asserted that McDonald's study was more compelling because it was one of the more recent studies conducted. However, Markowitz also acknowledged that the 1989 study by Truhaut and Chouroulinkov concluded that ingestion of asbestos fibers at high doses had neither a toxic nor a carcinogenic effect in rats and did not affect animal survival.[63]

Thus, no support for the claim that asbestos and colorectal cancer are causally related is forthcoming from experimental evidence gathered from studies of

---

[60] See J.M.G. Davis et al., Penetration of Cells by Asbestos Fibers, 9 Envtl. Health Persp. 255 (1974); Kelly J. Donham et al., The Effects of Long-Term Ingestion of Asbestos on the Colon of F344 Rats, 45 Cancer 1073 (1980); Anderson C. Hilding et al., Biological Effects of Ingested Amosite Asbestos, Taconite Tailings, Diatomaceous Earth and Lake Superior Water in Rats, 36 Archives Envtl. Health 298 (1981); Ernest E. McConnell et al., Chronic Effects of Dietary Exposure to Amosite Asbestos and Tremolite in F344 Rats, 53 Envtl. Health Persp. 27 (1983); R. Truhaut & I. Chouroulinkov, Effect of Long-Term Ingestion of Asbestos Fibres in Rats, 90 Int'l Ass'n Research Cancer Sci. Pubs. 123 (1989).

[62] Id. at 8-9; see also Weiss, supra note 18, at 883 ("there is no support for the hypothesis of causality from animal experiments in which asbestos has been administered orally"); Edelman, supra note 42, at 81 (same).

[63] See Truhaut, supra note 60, at 123. In his cross-examination testimony, Shy did not dispute the shared conclusion arrived at by Donham, McConnell, Hilding, Truhaut, and Condie that no carcinogenic effects are observable in animals which have ingested high doses of asbestos fibers.

both animals and humans, and the plaintiff's attempt to establish such a claim failed to contribute to the sufficiency of the causation proof.[64]

4. Plausibility

While there is no doubt that asbestos causes cancer and that there is a possible causal linkage between exposure to asbestos and colorectal cancer, the present state of scientific knowledge as presented by the plaintiff at trial, as previously discussed, does not support the conclusion that this relationship is anything more than possible. Such a showing falls short of satisfying the Sufficiency Criterion of plausibility and fails to contribute to the sufficiency of the plaintiff's causation proof in the face of the motions for judgment as a matter of law.

5. Coherence

"Coherence requires that the hypothesis of causality fits with the known facts in the natural history and biological character of the disease." William Weiss, Asbestos and Colorectal Cancer, 99 Gastroenterology 876, 882 (1990). In the context of toxic and carcinogenic torts generally, the issue of coherence turns on the plaintiff's ability to eliminate alternative or confounding causes which may have been the actual cause of the disease in question.

The Sufficiency Criterion of coherence can be satisfied either by using epidemiological evidence to establish that there are no (or at least, very few) confounding factors or by using clinical evidence regarding the individual's specific medical and personal history to eliminate the possibility that one or more of the various confounding factors were more likely than not to have caused the disease. Of course, a plaintiff necessarily employs a combination of epidemiological and clinical evidence in establishing causation.[67]

---

[64]Although experimental data on humans is necessarily limited, the experimental evidence that has been gathered parallels the findings of the studies involving experiments with animals. Various epidemiological studies of populations drinking amphibole-contaminated water revealed no convincing increase in gastrointestinal cancer. See Hilding, supra note 60, at 300 (referring to three studies made of residents of Duluth, Minnesota who were exposed to asbestos through the city's water supply); see also Weiss, supra note 18, at 882-83 (discussing McDonald's conclusion that neither air nor water pollution with asbestos has been directly linked as a cause of either respiratory or gastrointestinal cancer).

[67] The New Jersey Supreme Court has discussed this necessity at length:

[E]pidemiology deals with the movement of different diseases within human populations. It does not address questions of specific causation in the individual case. While epidemiological information, taken together with other medical facts, may be useful to a physician in forming a particular diagnosis or in determining the etiology of an illness, court determinations as to such matters cannot be based on an expert opinion which rests on the application of statistical skills and studies alone. Landrigan, 127 N.J. at 412, 605 A.2d 1079.

Unlike the signature disease mesothelioma, colon cancer has various known confounding conditions. Thus epidemiological evidence alone is insufficient to establish the requisite causal relationship, and at trial, the plaintiff was forced to rely heavily on clinical evidence in her attempt to establish causation. As Markowitz testified, cancers are normally thought to be causally "multi factorial" in nature.

> [I]n general cancer as well as other chronic diseases are thought to have a number of causes, even within the same individual. For instance, a person who develops heart disease, say with a heart attack, frequently that person will have a problem with cholesterol, and a problem with high blood pressure and diabetes. These risk factors often run together.

From this overview of the problem of coherence for cancer generally, Markowitz asserted the existence of a specific causal link between asbestos and colon cancer in his suggestion that "[m]ost people who are exposed to any particular agent do not develop the cancer. So clearly those that do, the agent played a role." Id. However, the epidemiological evidence proffered by the plaintiff and discussed by Markowitz and Shy does not support this conclusion.

a. Epidemiological Evidence

On cross-examination, Markowitz acknowledged that asbestos is not considered to be a risk factor for colon cancer. Exposure to asbestos is not included on the various diagnostic lists of factors causing colon cancer published by important authorities in the medical field. Rather, a high-fat or low-fiber diet, inflammatory bowel disease, streptococcus bovis bacteremia, ureterosigmoidostomy, and hereditary syndromes such as polyposis coli and non-polyposis syndrome are recognized as significant confounding factors for colon cancer. See American Cancer Society, Cancer Facts & Figures — 1992 8 (1992); Harrison's Principles of Internal Medicine 1289 (Jean D. Wilson et al. eds., 12th ed. 1991).

Markowitz testified that Weiss' 1990 review of 21 cohorts led Weiss to conclude that there was no increase in colorectal cancer from exposure to asbestos. In rejecting the hypothesis that colorectal cancer is causally linked to exposure to asbestos, Weiss notes that there is simply no coherence between exposure and the disease:

> The descriptive epidemiology of colorectal cancer includes the observation that its incidence in the United States increased in men over the past four decades only in those aged 65 years and older when the incidence actually decreased among those aged less than 45 years. Overall mortality rates declined from 1950 to 1980. These facts are not consistent with the

marked increase in asbestos consumption in the United States from 1940 to 1970, given the long latency period for colorectal cancer, if it is postulated that asbestos made a substantial contribution to this type of cancer in the form of occupational exposure. . . .

Although there is a recent report of the presence of asbestos bodies and fibers in digested colon and mesentery samples from a case of asbestosis and adenocarcinoma of the colon, it establishes only site-specific evidence of exposure, not causation. Among insulators, the relative risk for gastrointestinal cancer . . . was 1.58. However, the relative risk was just as high 7.5 years after the onset of exposure to asbestos as it was later. . . . This pattern was quite different from the pattern in lung cancer relative to risk, which rose to a peak in the fourth decade after the onset of exposure and declined thereafter. The data for gastrointestinal cancer suggests an induction-latency period of less than 10 years with no increase after that, an idea which is biologically implausible for solid tumors and the known increase of colorectal cancer incidence with increasing age.

Weiss, supra, at 882-83.

The simple fact is that numerous confounding factors which, when considered in light of the long latency period for colon cancer, conceal the inner workings of the biological and chemical mechanism relevant to the development of colon cancer.

These facts present tremendous difficulties for every epidemiological study. Thus, as Edelman notes: "Although various factors associated with an increased risk of gastrointestinal cancer have been identified, none of the 32 studies made any adjustments to the risk estimates for any of these factors." Edelman, supra note 42, at 81. The result is that the colorectal SMRs in these and every other study are necessarily inflated by the inclusion of occurrences of cancer that are actually caused by these other factors. Therefore, if the appropriate corrections could be made in the SMRs, they would be even less statistically significant than they presently are in the studies relied upon by the plaintiff.

It is also particularly relevant in considering the Sufficiency Criterion of coherence that Nassau County, the New York county in which Maiorana resided, has had a cancer mortality rate substantially higher than that of the rest of the United States. This fact was confirmed by Shy, who testified on cross-examination regarding a study conducted by the Office of Cancer and Toxic Substance Research of the New Jersey Department of Environmental Protection which examined cancer mortality trends in the New York/New Jersey/Philadelphia region covering the years between 1950 and 1975.

Between 1970 and 1975 the cancer morality rate for cancer of the large intestine — the particular form of cancer Maiorana developed — was 18.1 per 100,000 persons, nationally. However, the rate for that same cancer during the same time period in Nassau County was 25.7 per 100,000. In other words, as Shy explained, the rate of cancer of the large intestine was, for some inexplicable reason, 33% higher in Nassau County than in the rest of the United States from 1970 to 1975.

Shy noted further that the mortality rates for cancer of the large intestine in Nassau County were higher than the national rates throughout the entire period of the study from 1950 to 1975.

This study raises a serious question about the various carcinogenic substances to which Maiorana and all the other residents of Nassau County have been exposed over the years and which constitute confounding factors in assessing the proximate cause of Maiorana's cancer of the large intestine.

Once again, the plaintiff has failed to satisfy a fundamental Sufficiency Criterion. The studies and surveys relied on in the plaintiffs causation proof simply do not justify the conclusion that just because a person who has been exposed to asbestos develops colon cancer, the asbestos "clearly . . . played a role" in the development of that cancer. The plaintiff's epidemiological evidence failed to satisfy the Sufficiency Criterion of coherence at trial, and the plaintiff cannot appeal to the alleged coherence of that evidence to support the claim that the causation proof was sufficient to withstand these motions for judgment as a matter of law.

b. Clinical Evidence: The Plaintiff Offers
Only a Differential Diagnosis

The plaintiff's clinical evidence in this case consisted of ruling out confounding causes of his disease. This constituted nothing more than a differential diagnosis. "The terms 'differential diagnosis' are used to describe a process whereby medical doctors experienced in diagnostic techniques provide testimony countering other possible causes (e.g., other than exposure to PCBs) of the injury at issue." Hines v. Consolidated Rail Corp., 926 F.2d 262, 270 n.6 (3rd Cir. 1991). This data includes the plaintiff's medical records and personal history and can be used to exclude such confounding causes as diet, physical activity, genetic tendencies and family history, obesity, and exposure to other toxins.

Here, the plaintiff's experts testified that Maiorana's exposure to asbestos caused his colon cancer based on a lack of confounding causes. In the face of the weak epidemiological evidence regarding the coherence of asbestos exposure and colon cancer, however, such clinical evidence presented by the plaintiff takes on critical importance, and must be examined by the Court to determine whether it constitutes a sufficient ground for the plaintiff's proof of causation. If the treating physician has no more evidence of causation than the epidemiologist re-analyzing the data, the mere fact that the expert was the decedent's treating physician by itself is not sufficient to sustain a jury verdict in favor of the plaintiff.

In addition to the testimony of Markowitz and Shy, the plaintiff called Doctor Nathan Rothman, a specialist in internal medicine who treated Maiorana. Rothman, an expert in pulmonary medicine and lung disease, undertook a differential diagnosis of Maiorana, but because he acknowledged that he was not an expert in asbestos-related diseases, was not familiar with either the epidemiological or experimental literature on the subject, did not know the latency period for colon cancer, and had never undertaken any research regarding colon cancer or diseases of the colon, he was not qualified to draw the conclusion from his differential diagnosis that asbestos exposure was the cause of Maiorana's colon cancer. Thus it was left to Shy and Markowitz to opine that because Maiorana was 40 years old at the time of his death, had no family history of cancer, suffered from no special disease or syndrome, and did not face an abnormal risk from his diet, his exposure to asbestos must have been the cause of his colon cancer. However, their opinions failed to contribute to the sufficiency of the plaintiff's causation proof.

Colon cancer is not rare. In 1992 alone, 111,000 new cases of colon cancer were diagnosed and 51,000 deaths from colon cancer were reported. See American Cancer Society, supra note 68, at 8. Shy acknowledged these statistics and noted that colon cancer is the second-leading cause of death from cancer in the country. In the face of those statistics, the question is whether Maiorana's case of colon cancer can be distinguished from other occurrences of the disease in such a way that it can be causally linked to his exposure to asbestos.

The plaintiff suggested that the fact that Maiorana was relatively young when he died from the disease is an important point at which such a distinction can be drawn. However, on cross-examination, Markowitz did not dispute either the American Cancer Society's findings that the risk of colorectal cancer begins to increase precisely at 40 years of age or the Society's suggestion that an individual have a digital rectal examination annually after the age of 40. Therefore, while it may be uncommon for a 40-year-old man to develop colon cancer, it is neither startling nor so uncommon that it constitutes a mesothelioma-like signature disease arising only when a person of that age is exposed to asbestos.

Furthermore, the plaintiff's causation proof had to address the issue of latency. The various epidemiological studies conduct by Selikoff and relied on by Markowitz and Shy revealed a latency period for colorectal cancer of more than 20 years from the first exposure to asbestos. In fact, in his 1979 study of a cohort of 12,051 insulation workers, Selikoff found that there were no occurrences of gastrointestinal cancer in persons whose first exposure to asbestos was less than 20 years earlier. See Selikoff, supra note 29, at 96.

In the case of Maiorana's colon cancer, only 13 years had elapsed from his first exposure to asbestos to the time he was diagnosed as having the disease. In light of this fact, the plaintiff asserted only that the latency findings of Selikoff and others were irrelevant because Maiorana was exposed to asbestos and he did have cancer. The only studies the plaintiff's experts referred to suggesting lower latency periods were those involving exposure to other forms of occupational carcinogens such as radiation from atomic explosions. Thus, while Maiorana's age at the time of his death raises legitimate questions about the probability of developing colon cancer and about the possible causes of colon cancer in a person his age, the likelihood that exposure to asbestos was the cause of his cancer is seriously diminished by the consistent findings of studies, otherwise relied on by the plaintiffs, regarding the latency periods for asbestos-related cancers.

The plaintiff's clinical evidence conclusively establish, at most, only that Maiorana had no family history of cancer, suffered from no special disease or syndrome, and did not face an abnormal risk from his diet. Given that the plaintiff's epidemiological evidence fails to satisfy any of the Sufficiency Criteria and the mechanisms by which chemicals induce cancer and the developmental stages from initial exposure to frank neoplasia are poorly understood, the plaintiff's clinical evidence, which amounts to nothing more than a superficial differential diagnosis, is insufficient to support either the claim that Maiorana's exposure to asbestos was causally linked to his colon cancer or the jury's verdict for the plaintiff.

C. The Plaintiff's Causation Proof Was Not Sufficient To Support The Jury's Verdict

Ultimately, the plaintiff's causation evidence supports the conclusion that, "[f]or colorectal cancer, at this time there is no discernible relationship to asbestos exposure." Morgan, supra note 32, at 65. "The evidence reviewed . . . indicates that the criteria for causality [between asbestos and colorectal cancer] are not met. The association is inconsistent, weak, nonspecific, and incoherent." Weiss, supra note 18, at 883. These conclusions are supported by the rather remarkable similarity in the numbers arrived at in the surveys of Gaensler and Weiss. Weiss' 1990 survey of 21 cohorts, which totalled 94,177 persons, had a summary colorectal cancer SMR of a statistically insignificant 0.97. Gaensler's 1992 survey of 19 cohorts covered 93,200 persons and yielded a summary colorectal cancer SMR of an equally statistically insignificant 1.05.

The plaintiff's experts acknowledged without refuting either the conclusions derived by the various epidemiologists used in Weiss and Gaensler's surveys or the conclusions of Weiss and Gaensler. In the face of this substantial and notably consistent body of scientific evidence, the opinions of Markowitz and Shy asserting a causal connection between asbestos and Maiorana's colon cancer were nothing more than sheer surmise and conjecture, masquerading behind the guise of sound science.

On the present Rule 50(b) motions, the sufficiency of the plaintiff's epidemiological evidence must be determined by analyzing that evidence on its face and without weighing the defendants' opposing evidence against it. However, even when it is considered under this standard, the plaintiff's epidemiological evidence fails to support the claim that exposure to asbestos causes colon cancer. The plaintiff's epidemiological evidence does not satisfy any of the various Sufficiency Criteria. The causal relationship is not established by the statistical analyses of the two events, exposure to asbestos and developing colon cancer, and as such, the epidemiological evidence falls far short of the requisite level of sufficiency to support the jury's verdict.

The plaintiff's causation proof failed to establish the existence of any asbestos fibers in Maiorana's cancerous tissues, as noted above. To adopt the plaintiff's causal theory without affirmative clinical evidence regarding the presence of asbestos in Maiorana's system would permit any person suffering from any form of cancer who had been exposed to asbestos at some time in the past to sustain a cause of action based on that exposure alone. . . .

Additionally, when the inadequate epidemiological evidence is considered together with the plaintiff's experimental and clinical evidence, the plaintiff's causation proof still fails to justify the jury's verdict. The testimony of the plaintiff's experts regarding various experimental studies evaluating the effects of asbestos on animals provided no support for the plaintiff's theory of causation, and the plaintiff's clinical evidence constituted nothing more than a superficial and insignificant differential diagnosis. Under the circumstances, this is but a scintilla of evidence which is too insufficient to allow the verdict to stand. It is appropriate to grant the defendants judgment as a matter of law.

Therefore, despite the length and detail of the testimony given by the plaintiff's expert witnesses and the self-assured manner in which they stated they conclusory opinions, "[t]here [was] such a complete absence of evidence supporting the verdict that the jury's finding could only have been the result of sheer surmise and conjecture . . . [that] reasonable and fair minded jurors could not arrive at a verdict against [the defendants]." Samuels, 992 F.2d at 14 (citations and internal quotation marks omitted). The defendants' Rule 50(b) motions are granted. . . .

NOTES

1. *General and specific causation.* Ultimately, a plaintiff in a "toxic tort" case must prove that exposure to an allegedly toxic substance — be it cigarette smoke, radiation, asbestos, extremely low frequency electromagnetic fields, or a host of chemicals encountered in the environment or workplace — caused the complained-of harm — be it cancer, birth defects, or anything else. Almost always, there are no medical tests to answer this question. Colon cancer triggered, in some sense, by agent *A,* is indistinguishable from colon cancer triggered by agent *B.* Therefore, three conditions may be required to justify an inference of causation: (a) general causation — the alleged toxin can cause the harm in human beings; (b) exposure to the allegedly toxic substance — the plaintiff was exposed to the toxin in quantities sufficient to cause the harm; and (c) lack of exposure to other possible causes — the plaintiff was not exposed to other factors that were, collectively, at least as likely to have caused the harm. When these conditions are satisfied, the inference of specific causation — harm to the plaintiff from the exposure to the toxin — seems justified.

2. *Importance of toxicological and epidemiological studies.* Proof of general causation is necessarily scientific, involving the specialties of toxicology and epidemiology. Each speciality has something to contribute. Toxicological experiments may show that an agent is harmful when administered in high dosages to cells or animals, but extrapolating these results to much lower dosages and to human beings is fraught with uncertainty. See, e.g., National Research Council Committee on Risk Assessment Technology, Issues in Risk Assessment (1993). Some courts have held that the uncertainties are so great as to make confirming epidemiological studies essential. See, e.g., cases cited, Michael D. Green, Expert Witnesses and Sufficiency of Evidence in Toxic Substance Litigation: The Legacy of *Agent Orange* and *Bendectin* Litigation, 86 Nw. L. Rev. 643 (1992); infra note 5. Very few toxicologists seem willing to report a "track record" that might indicate how often animal studies of putative carcinogens produce false alarms when extrapolated to human beings and that might be helpful in evaluating the admissibility under *Daubert* of an expert opinion based primarily on animal toxicology.

Whether or not a court deems epidemiological studies essential, they are always important to a scientific assessment. Recognizing as much, the Court of Appeals explained in DeLuca v. Merrell Dow Pharmaceuticals, 911 F. 2d 941, 954 (3d Cir. 1990): "[t]he reliability of expert testimony founded on reasoning from epidemiological data is generally a fit subject for judicial notice; epidemiology is a well-established branch of science and medicine, and epidemiological evidence has been accepted in numerous cases."

3. *Cohort and case control studies.* The most revealing epidemiologic studies usually are "cohort" or "case control" studies like those discussed in the *Joint Asbestos Litigation* case.* In a cohort study, a group of subjects is identified — for example, all workers in a sheet metal plant at a certain time. Typically, exposure is determined before the followup starts ("When did you start working at this plant?") and during followup (as the study goes on, workers' exposure to asbestos fibers is measured). Health impacts ("morbidity" or illness, and "mortality" or death) are measured during followup. If the endpoint of interest is death, mortality rates during followup can be determined (for instance, by examining death certificates). Typically, many endpoints will be considered — death from all causes, death from lung cancer, death from colon cancer, and so on. A classic example is the Doll and Peto study of smoking in British doctors. The subjects were all persons on a registry of British doctors at the time the study began. The exposure of interest was smoking, measured by questionnaire at the start of the study; as the study progressed, exposure was measured again, several times. Mortality was measured during the followup period. Death rates were related to exposure: Smokers died faster, from many causes (including lung cancer and heart disease); heavy smokers died faster than light smokers.

---

*The description in these notes of study design and statistical terminology draws heavily from unpublished materials prepared by David Freedman for Federal Judicial Center seminars in 1994 and 1995.

Certain statistics can be used to express just how much faster the exposed individuals (the smokers) die (from certain cancers). In a cohort study, there will be some number of deaths from the diseases of interest over a given time period. That is the "observed" number. The "expected" number of deaths is computed from some external reference group, such as a population matched to the cohort on sex, race and county of residence. The "expected" number of deaths is based on the theory that the exposure has no effect, and members of the cohort die (of the specified disease) at the same rate as members of the reference group.

The standardized mortality ratio (SMR) is the ratio of the observed number of deaths to the expected number of deaths. If the observed number is O, and the expected number is E, then SMR = O/E. An SMR can be computed for all-cause mortality, or for mortality from a specific disease (lung cancer, colon cancer, etc.). If the SMR for a disease is around 1.0, that suggests the exposure has little effect on that disease: members of the cohort are dying from it at the same rate as the reference group. If the SMR is large (e.g., five or ten), members of the cohort are dying at a much faster rate from the disease than members of the reference group, suggesting the exposure causes death; at least, there is a strong association between exposure and death. The SMR is often expressed as a percent: 1.0 is 100%, 5.6 is 560%, and so forth.

Sometimes, the "expected" number of deaths for the heavily exposed members of a cohort is computed from the mortality experience of the lightly-exposed (e.g., doctors who smoke versus non-smokers; workers at a sheet metal factory with jobs on the factory floor versus those doing clerical jobs). Then, O/E often is called the "relative risk," or "risk ratio," abbreviated RR. For Doll and Hill's cohort study of British doctors, there was a lung cancer RR of about 13 for the pack-a-day smokers versus the non-smokers, as of 1976. Today, this RR would be considerably higher. If it is granted that exposure has a noticeable effect on death rates, the "expected" number and the risk ratio become harder to interpret, because the theory underlying their computation has been rejected.

In a case-control study, a sample is chosen of people with the disease of interest — for instance, all patients with colon cancer in a certain hospital at a certain time. Another sample is chosen of "controls" — persons who do not have the disease of interest. Then the rates of exposure are compared in the two groups. In contrast to a cohort study, in which health impacts are measured during the follow-up period, the hallmark of a case-control study is that subjects are recruited on the basis of their health status.

Doll and Hill ran a case-control study of lung cancer (the disease) and smoking (the exposure). The cases consisted of all persons diagnosed with lung cancer in a certain group of hospitals over a certain time period; the controls consisted of all persons diagnosed with certain other diseases at the same hospitals in the same period. The lung cancer cases turned out to smoke at a much higher rate than the controls. The data are typically presented as a two-by-two table, showing exposure (Yes or No) for the cases and the controls. For Doll and Hill's hospital based case-control study of lung cancer and smoking, the data were as follows:

		Case	Control
	Yes	1350	1296
Smokes			
	No	7	61

The odds ratio is then $(1350/7) \div (1296/61) = 9$. Smoking is much more common among the lung cancer cases than among the controls (persons hospitalized for other diseases). This demonstrates a strong association between smoking and lung cancer, and the question becomes, is this association causal? Controls may be matched to the cases (e.g., by age, sex, area of residence and income group). Then, the data analysis is a little more complicated, because the matching has to be taken into account.

   4. *Clusters.* Disease "clusters" in certain locations or among the patients seen by particular physicians also are important in epidemiology. A physician who notices an unusual incidence of a rare disease among patients taking a new drug, for example, might report it as a "case series." These case reports may prompt more definitive studies that confirm (or fail to confirm) the suggested association. Reports of grossly deformed children born to mothers taking the drug Thalidomide suggested an association that was confirmed. In contrast, a large number of toxicological and epidemiological studies have failed, on balance, to confirm suspicions fueled by case reports. See Michael D. Green, Bendectin and Birth Defects: The Challenges of Mass Toxic Substances Litigation (1996).
   A geographic cluster is a concentration of cases that is higher than average. For instance, the discovery of a cancer cluster among people living near an electric substation on Meadow Street in Guilford, Connecticut, first prompted widespread concern over electromagnetic fields from substations and transmission lines. Between 1968 and 1988, four people who lived along a power line running north from the substation were diagnosed as having brain tumors. Bette Hileman, Health Effects of Electromagnetic Fields Remain Unresolved, Chemical & Engineering News, Nov. 8, 1993, at 15, 16. However, "clusters come up very often," and "99 out of 100 are coincidental." Paul O'Donnell, Fallout of an Invisible War, Newsweek, July 25, 1994, at 61 (quoting Allen Wilcox, chief of reproductive epidemiology, National Institute of Environmental Health Sciences). Indeed, some writers claim that only one carcinogen in the residential environment has ever been identified by clustering. This was arionite mineral, which contains asbestos, in a small town in Europe. Hileman, supra, at 16; Lori Miller Kase, Why Community Cancer Clusters are Often Ignored, Sci. Am., Sept. 1996, at 85.
   Why do so few clusters pan out? For one thing, the identification of the cluster may be problematic:

Among the reasons for which health officials may discount a community's suspicion of common cause is that local groups often lump together different types of cancers (which are unlikely to be triggered by the same carcinogen). These citizens tend to include cases that were diagnosed before the afflicted individuals moved into the neighborhood, or they conduct what epidemiologist Robert W. Miller of the National Cancer Institute calls epidemiologic gerrymandering: "They find the cases, draw boundaries around the cases, and say, 'Aha, we've found a cluster.'"

Kase, supra, at 86-87. For another, even true cancer clusters are expected to arise on statistical grounds in the absence of causation. Over time, a purely random process will produce some above-average (and some below-average) results. Consider the the pattern of heads and tails that might result from flipping a fair coin. The probability that a fair coin will produce ten heads when tossed ten times is $(1/2)^{10}$, or 1/1,024. Observing ten heads in the first ten tosses, therefore, would be surprising. But if a fair coin is tossed thousands of times, it is likely that at least one string of ten consecutive heads will appear. Finding a run of ten heads is then no evidence that the coin is weighted in favor of heads. Likewise, even if the chance of a cancer were the same in every community, some communities would experience above-average cancer rates for some types of cancers. Thus, it has been calculated that 17% of the 29,000 town or census tracts in the U.S. will have at least one of the 80 recognized types of cancers elevated in any given decade, producing 4,930 chance clusters. Id. at 86.

Therefore, epidemiologists do not rely even on well-defined clusters to *prove* that some factor associated with the clustering causes the disease, but merely to suggest more rigorous epidmeiological research. And this raises the following questions for the law: Should evidence of case reports and clusters be admissible at trial? Should findings of clusters, combined with a physician's opinion, be sufficient to support a finding of causation? Traditionally, they have been. See, e.g., Hopkins v. Dow Corning Corp., 33 F.3d 1116 (9th Cir. 1994), cert. denied, 115 S. Ct. 734 (1995); Jonathan Harr, A Civil Action (1995). But do *Daubert* or *Frye* demand more? Is it scientifically accepted or scientifically sound to reach a conclusion of causation with human experimentation or well-designed epidemiological investigations? Some members of the medical establishment would say that it is not:

[M]edical researchers did not systematically begin to collect evidence on breast implants until around the time of the FDA ban [1992], when several large studies were initiated. These were epidemiologic studies that sought to determine whether the diseases said to be caused by breast implants are more common in women with implants than in women without implants. Until this question is answered, it is impossible to say whether breast implants contribute to the diseases. Other types of studies, including animal studies, laboratory studies, and case reports, raise interesting questions and answer some, but they cannot answer this one.

Marcia Angell, Science on Trial: The Clash of Medical Evidence and the Law in the Breast Implant Case 27 (1996).

5. *Necessity of "significant" epidemiological evidence.* In a portion of the opinion not included above, the *Joint Asbestos* court described several cases that insisted on "statistically significant" epidemiological proof of general causation:

> In *Agent Orange II,* Judge Weinstein found the plaintiffs' evidence that the dioxin in Agent Orange caused their injuries insufficient as a matter of law because he found they needed epidemiological evidence to establish causal connections between dioxin and diseases in individual plaintiffs . . . .
>
> In *Brock I* [Brock v. Merrell Dow Pharmaceuticals, Inc., 874 F.2d 307 (5th Cir. 1989)], the Court of Appeals for the Fifth Circuit held:

>> [o]ne certainly might infer from the evidence in the case that Bendectin causes birth defects, and further that Bendectin caused Rachel Brock's limb reduction defect — in fact, the jury concluded that this very thing occurred. However, the court must determine whether this is a reasonable inference to be drawn from the evidence presented. 874 F.2d at 309. . . .

> The Brocks' major evidence was a reanalysis by their expert of a previously conducted study which had found no increase in risk of birth defects due to Bendectin. After the plaintiffs' expert admitted that the confidence interval in his reanalysis made it statistically insignificant, the court noted that the plaintiffs' expert had not published his results for peer criticism and review.

>> While we do not hold that this failure, in and of itself, renders his conclusions inadmissible, courts must nonetheless be especially skeptical of medical and other scientific evidence that has not been subject to thorough peer review. . . . We find, in this case, the lack of conclusive epidemiological proof to be fatal to the Brock's case. Id. at 313. . . .

> Upon rehearing, the court replaced its use of the phrase "conclusiveness of studies" with "statistically significant studies." Brock II [884 F.2d 166 (5th Cir. 1989)] . . .
>
> The *Brock* opinions were relied on by a district court granting judgment n.o.v. after a jury awarded $1,000,000 to a plaintiff who alleged the drug Accutane caused her seizures. See Thomas v. Hoffman-La Roche, Inc., 731 F. Supp. 224 (N.D. Miss. 1989), aff'd, 949 F.2d 806 (5th Cir. 1992). The trial court held that *Brock* required at least some "statistically significant epidemiological proof." 731 F. Supp. at 228. . . .

827 F. Supp. at 1033-34.

Should the existence of "statistically significant" proof be essential for a finding of causation? The question can be broken down into two inquiries: (a) Do scientists require such proof? (b) Should the law embrace the institutional skepticism of the scientific community before relying on scientific evidence or reaching conclusions about phenomena that scientists investigate? Consider the following remarks on the relationship between science and public policy:

> Environmental and occupational regulations are based on evidence gathered by researchers in laboratory and field. However, the process by which the regulations are established can be unsettling to those who have provided the evidence. As students, we were taught to withhold final judgment until incontrovertible proof was established. Yet, governmental regulations and standards must often be established in the absence of sufficient proof. They are often based on flawed or preliminary scientific studies.

Anne N. Hirshfield, Problems Beyond Pesticides, 272 Science 1444, 1445 (1996) (book review).

Is statistical significance tantamount to "incontrovertible proof"? Should the same standards of proof be used for tort law as for administrative regulation? If all available studies are *flawed or preliminary,* is it better to presume that a substance is toxic or that it is not? Should the need for statistical significance depend on whether the allegedly toxic substance has been extensively studied and consistently found not to be associated with the alleged harm, or whether epidemiological studies are just emerging and the message from the scientific community is that it is too early to tell? See, e.g., Richardson v. Richardson-Merrell, Inc., 857 F.2d 823, 831-32 (D.C. Cir. 1988), cert. denied, 493 U.S. 882 (1989) ("courts should be very reluctant to alter a jury's verdict when the causation issue is novel and stands at the frontier of current medical and epidemiological inquiry. . . . The case before us, however, is . . . at the other end of the spectrum . . . . [T]he drug has been extensively studied and a wealth of published epidemiological date has been amassed, none of which has concluded that the drug is teratogenic. Uniquely to this case, the law now has the benefit of twenty years of scientific study, and the published results must be given their just due."); Modern Scientific Evidence § 27-1.2 (David Faigman et al. eds., 1997).

6. *Meaning of "statistical significance" and "confidence intervals."* Tests of statistical significance and estimates known as confidence intervals are two related devices for describing the extent or likely effect of random error in empirical studies. Often, a 95% confidence interval will be quoted for a risk ratio. For instance, the 1986 American Cancer Society fifty-state cohort study of smoking estimated an RR for lung cancer (current smokers versus never-smokers, men aged 35 and over) of 22.4, with a 95% confidence interval of 17.8 to 28.1. This interval attempts to take into account statistical uncertainty in the RR, due to the fact that there are only a finite number of deaths. The computational procedure guarantees that (under certain stringent assumptions) there is a 95% probability for intervals to cover the true underlying RR.

When is an RR "statistically significant"? Suppose an RR exceeds 1.0. If the excess can be explained as the result of chance variation (in selection of subjects for the study), the finding would seem to have little consequence. An RR is said to be "statistically significant" when the departure from 1.0 is hard to explain by chance. Typically, the 0.05 level is used. If the true underlying RR is 1.0, there is only a chance of 0.05 of seeing a "statistically significant" RR in the data:

Prob{ statistically significant observed RR given true RR = 1} = .05.

Statistical significance can be found by inspecting the confidence interval. If the observed RR is so large that its 95% confidence interval is entirely above 1.0, the the observed RR is significant. Thus, the RR of 22.4 for lung cancer from smoking is statistically significant. The lower end of the 95% confidence interval is 17.8, which is well above the innocuous value of 1.0.

The meaning of statistical significance may be contrasted with the apparently more natural statement that

Prob{ true RR = 1 given statistically significant observed RR } = .05.

There is no way to know whether this statement is correct. The true RR is either 1.0, or it is something else. If it is 1.0, the probability of an observed RR being significant is 0.05 or less. The mathematics of statistical significance do not give a "probability" for the true RR.

To sum up, the confidence interval indicates some allowance for statistical uncertainty in an estimate. An RR is statistically significant if chance is not a good explanation for the departure from 1.0. If the RR is not statistically significant, or the confidence interval is unduly wide, epidemiologists would hesitate to draw causal inferences from the study.

With this understanding of "statistical significance," we ask again: Should statistical significance at the 0.05 level be required of epidemiologic evidence offered to prove causation? Why? The issue was much mooted in the many briefs filed in *Daubert v. Merrell Dow Pharmaceuticals,* supra chapter 7, but the Supreme Court never addressed the issue. See also DeLuca v. Merrell Dow Pharmaceuticals, 911 F. 2d 941, 955-56 (3d Cir. 1990) (remanding):

> The root issue it poses is what risk of what type of error the judicial system is willing to tolerate. This is not an easy issue to resolve and one possible resolution is a conclusion that the system should not tolerate any expert opinion rooted in statistical analysis where the results of the underlying studies are not significant at a .05 level. We believe strongly, however, that this issue should not be resolved in a case where the record contains virtually no relevant help from the parties or from qualified experts.

The literature evidences that there are legal scholars and epidemiologists who have given considerable thought to this and related issues . . . .

7. *Meta-analysis.* Even if statistical significance at the 0.05 level is deemed essential, can a series of studies, each of which fails to achieve significance, collectively amount to statistically significant proof? The *Joint Asbestos Litigation* court seems to think not:

> [N]o matter how many studies yield a positive but statistically insignificant SMR for colorectal cancer, the results remain statistically insignificant. Just as adding a series of zeros together yields yet another zero as the product, adding a series of positive but statistically insignificant SMRs together does not produce a statistically significant pattern.

827 F. Supp. at 1042. But suppose that a coin is tossed four times, and it comes up heads each time. The coin may or may not be fair (evenly balanced). The probability of these data for a fair coin is $(1/2)^4 = 1/16$. Because $1/16 > 0.05$, the data from this first study are not statistically significant evidence that the coin is unfair. Now the coin is flipped another four times. It comes up heads each time. This second batch of data is not statistically significant. We toss the coin another four times. . . . Is it true that "adding a series of positive but statistically insignificant [statistics] together [can] not produce a statistically significant pattern"?

In cases such as *Daubert* and *DeLuca,* plaintiffs' experts maintained that the many studies that individually failed to show statistically significant relative risks showed a statistically significant risk in the aggregate, or at least do not amount to proof that Bendectin is safe. See supra chapter 7.

One way to address this problem of combining information is by fitting all the statistical studies into a overarching statistical model — a "meta-analysis." See, e.g., K. Dickerson & J.A. Berlin, Meta-Analysis: State of the Science, 14 Epidemiologic Rev. 154 (1992); Jerome P. Kassirer, Clinical Trials and Meta-Analysis: What Do They Do for Us? 327 New Eng. J. Med. 273 (1992); Panel on Statistical Issues and Opportunities for Research in the Combination of Information, National Research Council, Combining Information: Statistical Issues and Opportunities for Research (1992). The enthusiasm for this approach varies. See, e.g., Charles Mann, Meta-Analysis in the Breech, 249 Science 470 (1990); C.L. Meinert, Meta-Analysis: Science or Religion?, Controlled 10 Clinical Trials 257S-263S (1989); Michael Oakes, Statistical Inference: A Commentary for the Social and Behavioral Sciences 157 (1986) ("a retrograde development"); Diana Petitti, Meta-Analysis, Decision Analysis, Cost-Effectiveness Analysis in Medicine: Methods for Quantitative Synthesis of Information (1994). On the admissibility of meta-analyses, see, e.g., In re Paoli Yard PCB Litigation, 916 F.2d 829 (3d Cir. 1990), *cert. denied sub nom.* General Elec. Co. v. Knight, 499 U.S. 961 (1991).

The *Joint Asbestos* opinion discussed one meta-analysis in its review of the dose-response relationship between asbestos and colon cancer. The court concluded that this meta-analysis failed to prove anything. 827 F. Supp. at 1044-45. What flaws did they court identify in the meta-analysis?

A potential problem with meta-analysis — and even with a single reported "significant" result — is that the research and publication process can favor the reporting of statistically significant results and the suppression of negative results. If many studies on the same question are performed and journals are disinclined to publish findings that are not "statistically significant," then a false impression of predominantly significant results will arise. Stuart J. Pocock, Michael D. Hughes & Robert J. Lee, Statistical Problems in the Reporting of Clinical Trials: A Survey of Three Medical Journals, 317 N. Eng. J. Med. 426 (1987). If many statistical models are formulated or many statistical tests are performed on the same data set, some "significant" comparisons can emerge even if the exposure has no effect. This "multiple-comparison" problem is common in epidemiology, where many studies are done and many endpoints are examined. Death from colon cancer, for instance, is one endpoint; death from lung cancer is another; reduced lung function, yet another; opacity of pleura on X-ray examination, yet another. See, e.g., James L. Mills, Data Torturing, 329 New Eng. J. Med. 1196 (1993).

8. *Confounding and bias.* The *Joint Asbestos Litigation* court referred to "such confounding causes [of colon cancer] as diet, physical activity, genetic tendencies and family history, obesity, and exposure to other toxins." 827 F. Supp. at 1048. Confounding is a ubiquitous concern in epidemiology. Despite the researchers' best efforts to create a "control" group that is comparable to the exposed group in all relevant respects, the groups may differ in some way that is correlated with the outcome under study. For example, if the factory workers who are more heavily exposed to asbestos fibers are also eating a poorer diet (high in fat, low in fruits and vegetables), even a statistically significant difference in colon cancers may not be due to the asbestos, but to diet. The *Joint Asbestos* court dismissed plaintiff's reliance on a meta-analysis of colon cancer studies, in part, because "this meta-analysis failed to account for the effect of smoking in the development of lung cancer" even though "asbestos workers as a group have a higher incidence of smoking than the general population." Id. at 1045.

From an epidemiological perspective, there are at least three explanations for an observed association (an elevated SMR): (i) chance, the association is an accidental feature of the data; (ii) confounding, the association between exposure and disease is due to some other factor (the confounder); (iii) causation. Generally, all three explanations are at work. In observational studies, of the kind routinely done by epidemiologists, some degree of confounding always should be expected. Thus, smokers do differ from non-smokers in ways that matter; however, the differences do not seem large enough to account for the whole difference in death rates from lung cancer or heart disease.

Confidence intervals and statistical significance address the first explanation by comparing the actual results with those expected under a statistical model. To the extent that the idealized model applies, one can conclude that statistically significant differences are unlikely if only chance is at work.

But these statistical tools offer no protection against confounding or bias. There are numerous sources of bias, including errors in estimated exposure and errors in recording of death certificates. The "healthy worker effect" should also be mentioned. Almost by definition, workers are healthier than average, and will therefore have lower death rates, biasing SMRs downward — at least when the expecteds are computed from the mortality experience of the general population.

The *Brock* court pointed out the problem of bias in epidemiological studies:

> For example, there would be a dependence between variables if women who took Bendectin during pregnancy were more or less likely to smoke than women who did not take Bendectin. Another source of error in epidemiological studies is selective recall — i.e., women who have children with birth defects may be more likely to remember taking Bendectin during pregnancy than those women with normal children.

Brock v. Merrell-Dow Pharmaceuticals, 874 F.2d 307, 311-12, *modified,* 884 F.2d 166 (5th Cir. 1989), *cert. denied,* 494 U.S. 1046 (1990). This selective recall produces errors in the estimated exposure, and it biases comparisons between samples from the two groups of women. Having recognized the potential problem, however, the court wrote that the confidence interval solved it:

> Fortunately, we do not have to resolve any of the above questions, since the studies presented to us incorporate the possibility of these factors by use of a confidence interval. The purpose of our mentioning these sources of error is to provide some background regarding the importance of confidence intervals.

Id. at 311-12. But how can confidence intervals account for bias? Consider the following analysis:

> Even if sampling error were nonexistent, which would be the case if one could interview every woman who had a child in the period that the drug was available, selective recall would produce a difference in the percentages of reported drug exposure between mothers of children with birth defects and those with normal children. In this hypothetical situation, the standard error [which determines the width of the confidence interval] would vanish; therefore, the standard error can disclose nothing about the impact of selective recall.

David H. Kaye & David H. Freedman, Reference Guide on Statistics, in Reference Manual on Scientific Evidence 330, 377-78 n.136 (1994).

9. *Necessity of a relative risk in excess of two.* The district court in the *Joint Asbestos Litigation* case originally granted summary judgment for defendants on the theory that there could be no recovery when the available epidemiological studies did not disclose a relative risk in excess of two. The court of appeals reversed, and the case went to the jury. In granting the defendant's motion for post-verdict relief, the district court observed that:

> While an epidemiologist might be inclined to conclude that a causal relationship exists . . . despite the fact that the relative risk ratio is less than or equal to 2.0, the "more likely than not" test, which a plaintiff must satisfy to sustain a cause of action in tort, is not satisfied by epidemiological evidence alone unless the plaintiff establishes that the relative risk ratio or, in the case of epidemiological studies of asbestos, the standardized mortality ratio (SMR) . . . is greater than 2.0. In other words, "at least a two-fold increase in incidence of the disease attributable to . . . exposure [to asbestos] is required to permit recovery if epidemiological studies alone are relied upon." In re "Agent Orange" Prod. Liab. Litig., 597 F. Supp. 740, 785 (EDNY 1984) (Agent Orange I).

827 F. Supp. at 1028. The court thinks that "a relative risk of [2.0] means that, on the average, there is a fifty percent likelihood that a particular case of the disease was caused by the event under investigation and a fifty percent likelihood that the disease was caused by chance alone. A relative risk greater than [2.0] means that the disease more likely than not was caused by the event." Id. at 1026. It notes that some courts have demanded a relative risk in excess of 2.0 as a prerequisite to a finding of liability, and it repeatedly characterizes relative risks that fall below 2.0 as failing to meet the standard of "statistical significance." Id. at 1029, 1036, 1041, 1044, 1045, 1050.

These dicta raise two issues: (a) the relationship between a relative risk of a given magnitude and statistical significance; and (b) the connection between a relative risk of 2.0 and the more-probable-than-not standard. As for the first, a relative risk that is less than 2.0 can be statistically significant, and a relative risk in excess of 2.0 need not be. Can you explain why there is no necessary connection between a statistically significant relative risk and a relative risk that exceeds 2.0?

As for the second issue, does the more-probable-than-not standard require the relative risk to exceed 2.0 when there is other evidence of causation? When there is not? When the individuals in the study have been exposed to varying amounts of the suspected toxin? For some cases apparently imposing a flat rule that the relative risk must exceed 2.0, see Daubert v. Merrell Dow Pharmaceuticals, Inc., 43 F. 3d 1311, 1321 (1994) (9th Cir. 1994) (on remand); DeLuca v. Merrell Dow Pharmaceuticals, Inc., 911 F. 2d 941, 958-59 (3d Cir. 1990), and cases cited. The idea was popularized in a law review article written by a lawyer and an epidemiologist. See Bert Black & David Lilienfeld, Epidemiological Proof In Toxic Tort Litigation, 52 Fordham L. Rev. 732, 769 (1984) ("In no case . . . can evidence suffice to establish a causal link if it does not include at least reasonable estimates of exposure levels and durations, and data that reasonably indicate a relative risk greater than 2."). This conclusion is challenged in, e.g., Stephen E. Fienberg et al., Understanding and Evaluating Statistical Evidence in Litigation, 36 Jurimetrics J. 159, 168 (1996).

10. *Limits of the epidemiologist's testimony.* Should an epidemiologist be permitted to give an opinion as to the cause of the plaintiff's condition? Or should the epidemiologist's role be confined to describing the risk factors and the knowledge about the effects of exposure? See Landrigan v. Celotex Corp., 605 A.2d 1079 (N.J. 1992); compare the cases in chapter 20 distinguishing between expert opinions on the veracity of specific witnesses or the accuracy of particular eyewitness identification and more general psychological testimony on the circumstances conducive to veracity or accuracy.

11. *Necessity of exposure data.* As indicated in note 1, an inference of causation requires proof of exposure to the alleged toxin. When an expert offers an opinion that rests on poorly documented dosage data, the opinion may be challenged under Federal and Uniform Rule of Evidence 703. Cf. Christophersen v. Allied-Signal Corp., 939 F.2d 1106 (5th Cir. 1991), cert. denied, 503 U.S. 912 (1992) (relying more on the lack of general acceptance of such reasoning).

12. *Value of "differential diagnoses."* The district court in the *Asbestos Litigation* case dismissed plaintiff's "clinical evidence" as a "superficial differential diagnosis." The phrase "differential diagnosis" ordinarily means: "the determination of which of two or more diseases with similar symptoms is the one from which the patient is suffering, by a systematic comparison and contrasting of the clinical findings." Stedman's Medical Dictionary 428 (25th ed. 1990). Thus, a physician examining a patient who complains of a sore throat may scrape some material from the throat for a laboratory test to determine whether the disease is bacterial or viral. The differential diagnosis here is important to the treatment, since an antibiotic will be useless if the infection is viral. Because a correct differential diagnosis may be crucial to the choice of a treatment, physicians are trained in the art of making these diagnoses.

The "differential diagnosis" in *Joint Asbestos Litigation* is quite different. It refers to determining which factor caused a disease when the determination of the cause does not affect the treatment and when clinical testing can give no clues as to the cause. Whether the diagnostician has any special expertise at discerning the cause is therefore open to question. In addition, the notion that eliminating certain risk factors enhances the probability that the alleged toxic substance caused the disease sounds plausible, but "rests on two unstated, and usually untested, assumptions":

First, such reasoning treats toxic exposure and the other risks as alternatives. In other words, it assumes that the disease was caused by the toxic exposure or by some other cause, such as the other identified risk factors. Second, it assumes that most causes of the disease in question are known; otherwise the elimination of other risk factors would not significantly increase the likelihood that the toxic exposure was the cause of the plaintiff's disease.

Susan R. Poulter, Science and Toxic Torts: Is There a Rational Solution to the Problem of Causation? 7 High Tech. L. Rev. 189, 233 (1993) (footnotes omitted). If these assumptions cannot be verified, should the toxic tort version of the "differential diagnosis" be admissible?

TABLE OF CASES

INDEX